Current Trends in Data Management Technology

Asuman Dogac
Middle East Technical University

M. Tamer Özsu
University of Alberta

Ozgur Ulusoy
Bilkent University

IDEA GROUP PUBLISHING
Hershey USA • London UK

Senior Editor:	Mehdi Khosrowpour
Managing Editor:	Jan Travers
Copy Editor:	John Syphrit
Typesetter:	Tamara Gillis
Cover Design:	Marjaneh Talebi
Printed at:	BookCrafters

Published in the United States of America by
    Idea Group Publishing
    1331 E. Chocolate Avenue
    Hershey PA 17033-1117
    Tel: 717-533-8845
    Fax: 717-533-8661
    E-mail: jtravers@idea-group.com
    Website: http://www.idea-group.com

and in the United Kingdom by
    Idea Group Publishing
    3 Henrietta Street
    Covent Garden
    London WC2E 8LU
    Tel: 171-240 0856
    Fax: 171-379 0609
    Website: http://www.eurospan.co.uk

Library of Congress Cataloging-in-Publication Data

Dogac, Asuman, 1951-
    Current trends in data management technology / Asuman Dogac, M. Tamer
Özsu, Ozgur Ulusoy.
    p. cm.
    Includes bibliographical references.
    ISBN 1-878289-57-8 (pbk.)
    1. Database management. I. Özsu, M. Tamer, 1951- . II. Ulusoy, Ozgur,
1964-- . III. Title.
QA76.9.D3D63 1999
05.74--dc21   98-55193
                                               CIP

British Cataloguing in Publication Data
A Cataloguing in Publication record for this book is available from the British Library.

Other IDEA GROUP Publishing Books

Receive the Idea Group Publishing catalog with descriptions of these books by calling, toll free 1/800-345-4332 or visit the IGP web site at: http://www.idea-group.com!

Excellent additions to your library!

Current Trends in Data Management Technology

Table of Contents

Preface

This book provides a collection of outstanding chapters from across many different areas of database systems and is primarily intended for researchers and practitioners from academia and industry working in this field. The chapters include theoretical and applied contributions to the field. The book covers traditional issues in databases, such as query processing and optimization, as well as emerging technologies like electronic commerce and workflow management.

Many of the chapters in this book are expanded versions of the best papers presented at the First International Workshop on Issues and Applications of Database Technology, which was held in Berlin in July 1998. The papers were selected based on the reviews for the workshop and then were improved substantially by the authors. In addition to these selected papers, the book also features invited chapters from the fields of workflow technology and electronic commerce.

The first chapter, by Peter Muth, Jeanine Weissenfels and Gerhard Weikum, provides a discussion of the state of the art in workflow research and technology with regard to its applicability to and benefits for electronic commerce. The next chapter, *Trading Workflows on Electronic Markets* by Andreas Geppert, Markus Kradolfer and Dimitrios Tombros, presents a framework for market-based interorganizational workflow management. In this framework, the tasks executed in a workflow are regarded as goods traded on an electronic market. In *An Electronic Marketplace Architecture* by Asuman Dogac, Ilker Durusoy, Sena Arpinar, Nesime Tatbul and Pinar Koksal, an architecture is described for a distributed marketplace whose scope can be the whole Web where electronic commerce is realized through buying agents representing the customers and selling agents representing the resources like electronic catalogs. Aphrodite Tsalgatidou describes a set of criteria for selecting appropriate tools to be used for business process transformation and automation among a diversity of tools offered by software vendors in her chapter, *Reengineering and Automation of Business Processes: Criteria for Selecting Supporting Tools.*

David Taniar and J. Wenny Rahayu (*A Taxonomy for Object-Oriented Queries*) present a comprehensive study on object-oriented queries considering all aspects of an object data model. Then Rahul Tikekar, Farshad Fotouhi and Don Ragan extend previous work on query optimization by considering a tertiary storage system complementing primary and secondary storage devices in their chapter, *Query Optimization in Tertiary Storage Based Systems Using a Generalized Storage Model.* Some relational join algorithms are optimized in a tertiary storage system setup.

The chapter by Ahmet Cosar (Alternative Plan Generation for *Multiple Query Optimization*) presents a heuristic algorithm for the problem of selecting an alternative plan from among a set of alternative execution plans for multiple queries. The algorithm minimizes the total cost of evaluating all of the queries. It also provides the evaluation results of two new methods proposed for generating alternative execution plans for a given query. Manegold and Waas present a new strategy to utilize parallel resources in a shared-everything environment for efficient query processing in their chapter, *Integrating I/O Processing and Transparent Parallelism: Toward Comprehensive Query Execution in Parallel Database Systems.*

In *Rule Inheritance and Overriding in Active Object-Oriented Databases,* Naumann Chaudhry, James Moyne, and Elke Rundensteiner present a formal model for rule inheritance and overriding in active object-oriented databases. The notion of syntactic compatibility is extended to active rules and enforced in the proposed formal model. Arne Koschel, Stella Gatziu, Gunter von Bultzingsloewen and Hans Fritschi apply unbundling to active database systems in their chapter, *Unbundling Active Database Systems.* This allows the use of active capabilities with any arbitrary database management system and in broader contexts like heterogeneous and distributed information systems. Mario Nascimento 's chapter presents an approach to yield efficient access to degenerate temporal relations; i.e., temporal relations where valid time behaves as transaction time. The chapter also includes the evaluation results of the proposed approach.

In *Three-Dimensional Spatial Match Representation and Retrieval for Iconic Image Databases,* Jae-Wood Chang and Yeon-Jung Kim provide new three-dimensional spatial match representation schemes to support context-based image retrieval in an efficient way. Wassili Kazakos, Ralf Kramer, Ralf Nokolai, Claudia Roler, Sigfus Bjarnason and Stefan Jensen's chapter, *WebCDS-A Java Based Catalogue System for European Environment Data,* presents a web-based catalogue system for European environmental data that takes the advantage of most recent Java technology at the server site. The last chapter, *Mining Library Catalogues: Best-Match Retrieval Based on exact-Match Interfaces* by J.E. Wolff and J. Kalinski presents an approach to maximize the number of highly relevant data records that are transferred in gathering information from distributed repositories, transferred in gathering information from distributed repositories, considering the restrictions of local warehouse resources and generated load.

We are pleased to have assembled these high-quality chapters for this book. We would like to thank all contributing authors; without their cooperation this book would not have been possible. We are also grateful to Jan Travers, managing editor of Idea Group Publishing, for her assistance in the preparation of this volume.

Asuman Dogac, Middle East Technical University, Turkey
M. Tamer Özsu, University of Alberta, Canada
Ozgur Ulusoy, Bilkent University, Turkey

CHAPTER 1

What Workflow Technology Can Do for Electronic Commerce

Peter Muth, Jeanine Weissenfels, and Gerhard Weikum
University of the Saarland, Germany

Electronic commerce (EC) is a rapidly growing research and development area of very high practical relevance. A major challenge in successfully designing EC applications is to identify existing building-block technologies and integrate them into a common application framework. We argue that workflow management technology should be a key building block for EC applications. Workflow technology aims to provide as much computer support as possible to the modeling, execution, supervision, and possibly reengineering of business processes. Hence, it is beneficial to model major parts of EC applications also as workflows. We identify properties and requirements of workflows specific to EC, and describe solutions which can already be provided by current workflow management technology. In addition, we point out necessary extensions to the state of the art of workflow management which require future research in several directions.

INTRODUCTION

Electronic commerce (EC) is a rapidly growing research and development area of very high practical relevance (Adam, Yesha, 1996; Sistla, Wolfson, Dao et al., 1996; CommerceNet, 1998). A major challenge in successfully designing EC applications is to identify existing building-block technologies and integrate them into a common application framework. *Workflow management* is one of these enabling technologies for EC. In fact, we argue in this paper that it should play a key role in providing a highly dependable infrastructure for EC.

As an example consider the following EC scenario. A customer wants to buy a new PC for her home. The whole process of buying the PC consist of three phases:

1. In a *pre-sales* phase, the customer collects information about PCs, about PC vendors and prices. This phase consists of mostly unstructured activities that the customer dynamically decides to perform. For example, in addition to the standard criteria such as technical parameters, price, shipping terms, etc., a customer may become inter-

ested in looking up specific benchmark results for certain models, or in checking out the system requirements of some fancy computer games. In the pre-sales phase, the customer frequently faces inaccurate or outdated information.

2. In the actual *sales phase*, the customer requests legally binding sales offers, makes a decision and places an order. The PC vendor ships the PC and sends the bill to the customer. Different protocols can be used for shipment and payment, e.g., paying before or after the PC is shipped, paying by credit card or cheque, etc. The customer and the vendor have to agree upon a well defined protocol for the sales phase. In contrast to the pre-sales phase, such protocols are highly structured and their execution needs to be highly dependable.

3. The *post-sales phase* consists of auxiliary activities, either related to the purchased product or to general relationships between the customer and the PC vendor. For example, the vendor is interested in advertisement of products to the customer, the customers' bank or credit card company is interested in building up or refining customer profiles. All these activities aim to prepare further purchases by the customer, e.g., a maintenance contract, software sales, hardware upgrades or, in case of the bank, a credit for a more powerful PC. The post-sales phase then turns into a new pre-sales phase. Unlike the initial pre-sales phase, the post-sales phase and the new pre-sales phase are more structured and more specific for the individual parties, so that the new sales phase should be established much more efficiently.

Workflow technology aims to provide as much computer support as possible to the modeling, execution, supervision, and possibly reengineering of business processes (Georgakopoulos, Hornick, Sheth, 1995; Jablonski, Bussler, 1996; Vossen, Becker, 1996; Alonso, Mohan, 1997; Cichocki, Helal, Rusinkiewicz et al., 1998). Such computer-supported processes are then referred to as workflows. It seems natural to consider EC as the glue between previously independently modeled business processes. Hence, it is beneficial to model major parts of EC applications also as workflows. Following this approach, we can identify several specific requirements that EC applications pose on workflow technology.

The probably most important requirement is *dependability*, which subsumes a reliable, fault tolerant, secure, and provably correct execution on a highly available platform. While these requirements are ubiquitous in mission-critical computer applications, there are a few key technologies that have achieved substantial progress towards these goals over the last three decades. In particular, database and transaction systems are the backbone of today's mission-critical commercial applications such as banking and insurance businesses, travel planning and booking, or financial trading (Gray, Reuter, 1993; Bernstein, Newcomer, 1997). The last decade has witnessed major efforts towards generalizing the functionality of transaction-based applications, and this has been one of the roots of today's workflow technology. Thus, an important objective and, to some extent, achievement of workflow technology is to reconcile rich specification languages for the control flow (and data flow) of complex, long-lived, often widely distributed, organizationally decentralized applications with the industrial-strength dependability features of transaction processing systems. To this end, workflow technology does itself make intensive use of database systems and transaction services (Reuter, Schneider, Schwenkreis, 1997; Leymann, 1996, Alonso, Guenthoer, Kamath et al., 1996; Muth, Wodtke, Weissenfels et al., 1998a; Jablonski, Bussler, 1996). Thus, we believe that workflow technology today provides the most mature and promising basis for becoming the backbone of EC applications.

A second overriding requirement of EC is the need for interoperability among largely autonomous, often heterogeneous subsystems. This can span a spectrum from widely established standard protocols between information servers all the way to "intelligent agents" that have capabilities for negotiation, sophisticated exception handling, etc. Again, we believe that the database and transaction technology has a fairly good success story in dealing with heterogeneity and interoperability issues (to the extent that some "semantic integration" issues are inherently hard). Thus, workflow technology inherits a number of these salient properties, and this is why it can integrate almost arbitrary application programs into a unifying execution framework. However, there are still major deficiencies in the interoperability between different workflow management systems. These need to be overcome to provide full-fledged support for enterprise-spanning applications including EC applications. Initial ideas along these lines do exist, but more research is needed. It should be noted, in any case, that the highly structured, rigorous yet dynamically adjustable nature of workflows make them an excellent candidate for addressing the interoperability problems, as opposed to say a general-purpose, arbitrarily complex, distributed programming language such as Java.

In this chapter, we discuss the state of the art in workflow research and technology with regard to its applicability to and benefits for EC. We identify necessary extensions to workflow management systems to support EC, and sketch the research issues towards these extensions. The chapter is organized as follows: the next section discusses properties and requirements of workflows in the EC context. Then, we discuss contributions of workflow technology to address these requirements. For the sake of concreteness, we will occasionally refer to our own prototype system, Mentor (Wodtke, Weikum, 1997; Muth, Wodtke, Weissenfels et al., 1998a; Muth, Wodtke, Weissenfels et al., 1998b), as an example for what state-of-the-art workflow management systems can do for EC. We go on to point out necessary extensions that go beyond the current generation of workflow management systems. Finally, we conclude the chapter and give an outlook on future research issues.

PROPERTIES AND REQUIREMENTS OF WORKFLOWS IN ELECTRONIC COMMERCE

Workflows that capture (major parts of) EC applications have specific properties. In the following, we denote such workflows as EC workflows for simplicity. In this section we discuss these specific properties of EC workflows and derive from them specific requirements on workflow management systems. The discussion is broken down into build-time issues that arise in the modeling and analysis of an EC workflow, and run-time issues that are relevant during the execution of EC workflows.

Build-time Issues

We can identify a number of specific properties of EC workflow specifications:

- The core part of EC workflows, which is typically centered around the payment scheme (i.e., the sales phase), is rather static. So there is no need for supporting dynamic modifications of running workflows. On the contrary, this core part can be viewed as a specific protocol that has been agreed upon by all EC partners at one point, and thus must not be changed further on. In fact, it is highly desirable that certain properties of the payment protocol can be verified in a formal manner. This is only feasible for static workflows.

- Both the pre- and post-sales phases of EC workflows should, however, allow for flexibility at run-time. So a workflow model for these phases is more likely to be a skeleton that is dynamically enriched by introducing additional activities along with their control and data flow, and also possibly skipping parts of the prespecified workflow skeleton. The need for such improvisation is particularly evident in the pre-sales phase that includes filtering ads, bargaining, etc.
- In all phases, EC workflows involve multiple parties. In the pre-sales phase, there are rather loose interactions between customers and merchant. In the sales and post-sales phase, customer and merchant and banks or credit card companies are more tightly coupled. The coupling is based on standard interfaces, enabling the establishment of the sales and post-sales phases without complex negotiations.
- The core part of EC workflows can be fully automated. So none of the underlying activities should require human intervention, other than simple typing of initial input parameters. In contrast to certain high-value workflows in banking (e.g., approval of company loans), for example, EC payment schemes rarely involve intellectual decision processes. Such automation is indeed an important factor in promoting EC as a mass opportunity.

From these properties we can directly derive the following requirements that EC workflows pose on the underlying workflow management systems:

- *Verifiability (Provable Correctness)*: For the core part of an EC workflow, guaranteeing the correctness of the specification is of utmost importance. This involves proving both safety and liveness properties, examples being "the customer's credit card number is not shown to anybody other than the merchant's bank" and "money is eventually credited on the merchant's bank account", respectively. So, unless such critical properties are formally verified, an error-prone specification bears the risk of exposing confidential information or even losing money. Superficially, it may seem that the required correctness guarantees can also be given intellectually by "carefully looking at the specification", but it often turns out that such distributed payment protocols can raise a fairly large number of different exceptions all of which need to be handled correctly as well. Once the effect of multiple of these exception handling methods can interfere with each other or with the "mainstream" of the workflow, it is often extremely hard to capture all the resulting effects intellectually. Thus, automatic verification methods or at least support tools are called for. These should be able to deal with the complete control flow specification, including all exception handling, and also the data flow specification.

Composability of Building Blocks: As we discussed above, the payment scheme itself, albeit constituting the core part, is only one phase of an entire EC workflow. Both the pre- and post-sales phases require much more flexibility, and may involve subworkflows that are provided and have been designed by different parties (e.g., the merchant, the credit card company, the bank, etc.). Thus EC workflows are inherently heterogeneous in that independently designed workflows have to be composed into more comprehensive higher-level processes. The specification method must support this kind of composability in an easy-to-manage manner.

- *Interoperability*: Interaction between different parties involved in an EC workflow is required in all phases. However, the type of interaction differs, which requires different interfaces for interoperability. The loose coupling of customer and merchants in the pre-sales phase can be supported by a web-like interface, posing little requirements on specifications. As the customer has to face incomplete and outdated information anyway, the focus is on a fast access to information with low overhead, not on dependability. In the sales phase, the picture changes completely. As correctness and dependability are of utmost importance here, it must be possible to specify the corresponding interoperability protocols.

Run-time Issues

As for the run-time issues of EC workflows, we can again highlight certain properties. These are not exclusively specific for EC workflows, but they are of absolutely crucial importance in the EC area and play less of a role in most other application areas of workflow technology.

- EC workflows in-the-large usually involve several autonomous parties and would therefore often run in a truly distributed manner on several, possibly heterogeneous workflow management systems.
- The actual EC workflow will be accompanied or surrounded by state-of-the-art security protocols for encryption, authentication, digital signatures, etc. Without confidentiality or even anonymity and, especially, the guaranteed value of "cybercash" currencies, EC applications cannot be successfully established.
- EC workflows will ideally become mass operations: millions of customers initiating billions of workflows every month or even week, with heavy load peaks in certain popular time periods.
- Frequent failures and unavailability of EC workflow servers would immediately weaken the market position of the merchant (or the EC provider that acts on behalf of one or more merchants) and eventually result in significant financial losses.

From these properties we can infer the following execution-related requirements that EC workflows pose on the underlying workflow management systems:

- *Scalability*: The mass-business characteristics of EC workflows requires a high-throughput execution engine. Thus, load distribution across multiple workflow servers is necessary to ensure this kind of scalability.
- *Dependability*: This subsumes a number of technical requirements: fault tolerance, reliability, availability, and also security. The execution environment for EC workflows must be fault tolerant in that transient failures of system components (e.g., workflow servers) do not lead to incorrect behavior of the workflow execution. Further, failures that hamper the progress of workflow executions should be very infrequent; that is, the overall execution should be highly reliable. This may already call for redundant components within the system, so that many failures can be completely masked. In addition, the few failures that cannot be completely masked should be repaired sufficiently fast, for example, by restarting system components based on logged data. The

net effect should then be very high availability of the EC services: customers are satisfactorily served without noticeable delays with extremely high probability (e.g., 99.99 percent). Finally, security measures such as encryption must be well coordinated with the other system components to ensure the desired overall dependability.

*   *Trackability*: Comprehensive traces of EC workflow instances must be available for documentation purposes and possibly also for data mining towards better marketing. This calls for an elaborate workflow history management component with powerful temporal querying. On the technical side, extremely reliable and long-lived archiving must be provided, too.

CONTRIBUTION OF WORKFLOW TECHNOLOGY

Workflow specifications serve as a basis for the largely automated execution of business processes. They are often derived from business process specifications by refining the business process specification into a more detailed and executable form. Automated and computer-assisted execution means that a *workflow management system (WfMS)* (Georgakopoulos, Hornick, Sheth, 1995; Jablonski, Bussler, 1996; Vossen, Becker, 1996) controls the processing of work steps, denoted as *activities*, within a workflow. Some activities may have a manual or intellectual part, to be performed by a human. But the workflow management system is in charge of determining the (partial) invocation order of these activities. In contrast to business process specifications, this requires a formal specification of control flow and data flow.

To a large extent, the requirements stated in Section 2 can already be addressed by current workflow technology. In the following, we discuss contributions of workflow technology in detail.

Build-Time Issues

The use of workflow management systems in different application areas has led to different approaches for specifying workflows. There exists a wide range of languages including script-based, net-based, rule-based, and logic-based languages. They differ widely in their expressiveness, formal foundations, and ease of use. Beyond the "pure" approaches that fit into the given categories, hybrid methods have also been proposed. Because of its designated role as an industry standard, the Workflow Process Definition Language (WPDL) of the Workflow Management Coalition is especially notable among these hybrid methods (Workflow Management Coalition, 1998). The Workflow Management Coalition, an industry consortium, aims at a unified terminology and a standardization of interfaces between key components of workflow management systems.

Provable Correctness

For specifying the sales phase of EC workflows, a high-level specification language with mathematically rigorous semantics is required. Its semantics must be sufficiently expressive for the complex protocols executed during the sales phase. Control flow as well as data flow must be captured in order to model all aspects which are relevant for the correctness of the EC workflow. On the other hand, the specification language should be simple enough to support automatic *verification* of workflow properties by means of verification tools.

The formalism of *state charts* and *activity charts* (Harel, 1987a; Harel, 1987b; Harel,

1988; Harel et al., 1990; Harel, Gery, 1997) meets these demands. In the Mentor project, we have explored its use for workflows (Wodtke, Weikum, 1997; Muth, Wodtke, Weissenfels et al., 1998a; Muth, Wodtke, Weissenfels et al., 1998b), and it seems that state and activity charts are gradually finding wider use and acceptance. They have been adopted for the behavioral dimension of the UML industry standard (Unified Modeling Language, 1997). State and activity charts comprise two dual views of a specification. *Activities* reflect the functional decomposition of a system and denote the "active" components of a specification; they correspond directly to the activities of a workflow. An *activity chart* specifies the data flow between activities, in the form of a directed graph with data items as arc annotations. *State charts* capture the behavior of a system by specifying the control flow between activities. A state chart is essentially a finite state machine with a distinguished initial state and transitions driven by Event-Condition-Action rules (ECA rules).

In the Mentor project, we have investigated the feasibility of verifying certain properties for workflows specified as state and activity charts. A prerequisite for the verification is the modeling of these properties in a formal language. For this purpose, variants of temporal logic are well established (Emerson, 1990; Manna, Pnueli, 1992). Temporal logic extends predicate logic by temporal operators. With these operators, invariants (both safety and liveness properties) can be modelled, such as: 'If p was true in the past, q will be true at some point in the future'. A temporal logic with an expressive power suitable for properties of workflows (according to our experience) is CTL (*Computation Tree Logic*) (Emerson, Srinivasan, 1988).

Once the critical workflow properties are formally stated, they can be verified against the formal specification of the workflow. Two different approaches are possible here. The first approach is using theorem provers, which automatically verify that a given specification has the desired properties. However, in many cases this approach is computationally infeasible. As a less powerful, but much more efficient approach, model checking can be used. In essence, *model checking* verifies whether a given finite state automaton (the workflow specification) is a model of a given temporal logic formula (Clarke, Emerson, Sistla, 1986). The most efficient variant of model checking is known as symbolic model checking (McMillan, 1993). Symbolic model checking is based on a compact, symbolic representation of a finite state automaton in terms of an *ordered binary decision diagram (OBDD)*. Because state charts are closely related to finite state automatons, model checking can be applied to state charts. Tools for symbolic model checking already exist (at least as research prototypes) and are used mainly in hardware design and for reactive embedded systems. In the Mentor project we have used a tool for symbolic model checking described in (Helbig, Kelb, 1994). Although the resource requirements were high, we found symbolic model checking to be suitable even for the interactive verification of workflow specifications of non-trivial size.

Composability of Building Blocks and Exception Handling
As EC workflows involve multiple parties with already existing business processes, the specification language has to provide means for combining existing workflows into higher-level specifications that provide more comprehensive EC support. Starting with a skeleton workflow, e.g., only specifying the existence of the sequence of pre-sales, sales, and post-sales phase, workflow composition can be used to dynamically refine the workflow, even during execution. The mechanism of nested states, i.e., substituting states by entire state charts provides this composability for state and activity charts. The semantics is that

upon entering the higher-level state, the initial state of the embedded lower-level state chart is automatically entered, and upon leaving the higher-level state all embedded lower-level states are left.

In addition to the composability of workflow specifications, EC workflows need a flexible exception handling. Exception handling code should not be sprinkled throughout the specification. Otherwise, the specification can easily become unmanageable. In state and activity charts, orthogonal components provide a convenient means for incorporating exception handling in an easy and clear (i.e., truly orthogonal) manner. Orthogonal components denote the parallel execution of two state charts that are embedded in the same higher-level state (where the entire state chart can be viewed as a single top-level state). Both components enter their initial states simultaneously, and the transitions in the two components proceed in parallel, subject to the preconditions for a transition to fire. Using this concept, an execution handling for a "watchdog" component would simply stay in its initial state until a certain condition becomes true or a certain event is raised.

Run-time Issues

The run-time requirements for EC workflows stated previously are quite similar to those for current business workflows in large enterprises. Workflow management systems supporting such workflows or even workflows that span several enterprises also have to face scalability, dependability and trackability problems.

Scalability

At the merchant's and at the bank's or credit card company's site, a large number of EC subworkflows have to be executed concurrently. This is usually not the case at the customer's sites, as a customer will typically be involved only in the purchase of a small number of items at a time. However, this does not mean that the issue of scalability is limited to the merchant and the bank or credit card company. In fact, the need for scalability may arise in three different forms:

1. *Upward scalability* is needed mostly from a throughput perspective, that is, to cope with larger numbers of workflow instances simultaneously while still guaranteeing acceptable response times. This is the kind of scalability required for the merchant and the bank or credit card company. Upward scalability is usually achieved by using distributed, multi-server workflow management systems (Sheth, Kochut, 1998; Dogac, Gokkoca, Arpinar et al., 1998; Muth, Wodtke, Weissenfels et al., 1998a, Alonso, Guenthoer, Kamath, 1996; Alonso, Mohan, 1997).

2. *Downward scalability* is desirable towards the lower end of performance demands in environments with scarce resources, the goal being a light-weight workflow management system with a small footprint (e.g., low disk space for the installation, low runtime memory demand, little need for manual system administration, etc.) (Barbara, Mehrotra, Rusinkiewicz, 1996; Sheth, Kochut, 1998; Vossen, Weske, 1998; Weissenfels, Muth, Weikum, 1998). As a customer is typically involved only in a limited number of EC workflows at a time, and rarely uses advanced functionality like analyzing the history of a workflow, light-weight and tailorable workflow management systems are the systems of choice at the customer's site.

3. *Sideward (or horizontal) scalability* aims at a high degree of interoperability with other workflow management systems. This is of crucial importance for EC workflows.

In all phases, EC workflows involve multiple parties, which will typically use different workflow management systems. The Workflow Management Coalition (WfMC) (Workflow Management Coalition, 1998) has proposed a standard interoperability interface for workflow management systems. However, this interface is currently in a proposal stage. It remains open how suitable it is for EC workflows.

Dependability

The sales phase of EC workflows requires a highly dependable execution platform. This subsumes the following issues:

1. *Fault tolerance*: In a fault tolerant execution, system failures do not harm the correctness of workflow execution. When a failure occurs, the system is rolled back to the most recent consistent state. Workflow execution can then be resumed from this state. In database systems, fault tolerance is achieved by atomic transactions (Gray, Reuter, 1993). Workflows are typically more complex, consist of more activities and are of longer duration than database transactions. Workflows are usually executed as sequences of short transactions (Reuter, Schneider, Schwenkreis, 1997; Muth, Wodtke, Weissenfels et al, 1998a). In case of distributed workflows, distributed transactions are required. Middleware services like TP monitors (Primatesta, 1994; Gray, Reuter 1993) or OTS transaction services (OMG, 1995) are used for controlling the execution of distributed transactions, also in case multiple different database systems are involved. Reliable message queues provide the "glue" between transactions implementing the steps of a workflow (Primatesta, 1994; Gray, Reuter, 1993; Muth, Wodtke, Weissenfels et al. 1998a). Their usage guarantees that after a transaction has successfully finished, the next transaction is eventually started.

2. *Reliability:* In reliable systems, failures must be infrequent. Obviously, this requires well designed and rigorously tested software, running on reliable hardware platforms. Workflow management systems rely on database management systems as one of their core components, which have proven to be among the most reliable software products. In addition, redundancy can be used to increase reliablity. For example, a failed server process can be dynamically replaced by a "standby" process that has access to the underlying persistent data (i.e., a database and/or a log file) which may again be replicated if necessary. This way, even less reliable components can be used in a system with high reliability demands.

3. *Availability*: Highly available systems ensure that users find the system operational with very high probability. This can be achieved by ensuring that complete system failures are sufficiently infrequent and by providing very fast recovery and restart after such failures. In addition to very low system downtimes, a workflow should almost never be delayed in a user-noticeable manner. Redundant workflow servers are again an appropriate means to increase availability. For less demanding workflows, for example in the pre-sales phase of EC workflows, simpler modes with lower or no redundancy should be supported to improve the cost/performance ratio of the overall system. Such a configurable approach has been studied in the Exotica project (Kamath, Alonso, Guenthoer et al., 1996) as an extension to IBM's Flowmark (IBM, 1994).

4. *Security*: EC workflows probably have the highest demands on security among all classes of workflow applications. Up to now, this issue has only received limited attention in the workflow community. Hiding confidential workflow data from unau-

thorized third parties can be achieved by using encryption protocols. In addition, specific secure payment and negotiation protocols have to be implemented (Asokan, Janson, Steiner et al., 1998), for example, as a special high-security class of workflows.

Trackability

In all environments where non-trivial amounts of money are handled, trackability is a major requirement. The need for archiving the history of workflows is already considered a major requirement in many workflow management systems, because the history can also be used to improve the underlying business process model, e.g. by determining workflow steps that frequently miss their deadlines, involve more resources as expected, etc. (Agrawal, Gunopulos, Leymann, 1998; Sheth, Kochut, 1998; Dogac, Gokkoca, Arpinar, 1998; Muth, Wodtke, Weissenfels et al., 1998a; IBM, 1994). Improving the overall workflow is typically based on aggregated, statistical data, whereas tracking EC workflows requires detailed data on a per instance basis. Workflow management systems can provide the necessary archiving service for this purpose as well.

RESEARCH DEMANDS ON WORKFLOW TECHNOLOGY

The previous sections have shown that using workflow technology in EC applications is promising and already solves many of the encountered problems. However, substantial further research is needed to solve problems that are not yet addressed by workflow technology and arise in the new application environment of EC.

Dynamics

The need for dynamic adaptation of workflows has already been recognized independently of EC. For example, in medical applications, the treatment of patients can usually not be determined in advance. Instead, the corresponding workflow has to be constantly adapted to new diagnostic results. The current generation of workflow management systems still provides only primitive support for such dynamics. Systems supporting modifications of control flow and data flow at runtime are often weak in other respects such as administration, correctness of execution, reliability, scalability, and security.

Interoperability

EC workflows involve multiple, autonomous parties. Thus, interoperability is crucial. A specific kind of interoperability has already been addressed by most workflow management systems, as they have to provide access to arbitrarily heterogeneous applications. This is achieved through the wrapper/mediator paradigm, that is, encapsulating the actual application, surrounding it with a standard-compliant interface, and invoking applications through a broker service (the mediator in this case). Usually, appropriate middleware such as CORBA or DCOM is employed. Only little work has been done, however, on the interoperability between different workflow management systems. In this regard, EC workflows have higher demands than most other workflow applications, since EC involves multiple, autonomous parties by definition.

The most promising approach to address the interoperability between different workflow management systems seems to be again a wrapper/mediator architecture, where each system is encapsulated and enriched by a common language for process definition, state introspection, and manipulation. Once such a common language were established, different systems could communicate in a straightforward manner, possibly again through some "broker" or "mediator" services. More research is needed along these lines.

Security

Security issues have to be addressed jointly with the security research community. The challenge is to integrate security protocols into workflow management systems in a seamless yet easily maintainable manner. This is not a straightforward task, as multiple components of workflow management systems such as communication managers and history managers are involved. Modifying these components accordingly may conflict with existing solutions for scalability and availability. In addition, different levels of security have to be supported in order to execute, for example, information gathering workflows in the pre-sales phase as inexpensively as possible. If different security levels are used in different phases of an EC workflow, we have to make sure that the security of the critical workflow parts is not compromised by parts executed at low security levels or by transition problems between security levels.

CONCLUSIONS AND OPEN ISSUES

Electronic commerce (EC) can be regarded as a specific kind of business process involving several enterprises. As workflow management systems have been developed to implement such business processes, EC can largely benefit from current workflow technology. In particular, the core of electronic commerce, sales and money-handling transactions, can be modeled as special kinds of workflows. We have identified the main requirements that EC poses on workflow management systems. Pre-sales and post-sales phases of EC workflows require highly flexible, light-weight workflow management, whereas the core sales phase including money transfer has to be executed in a highly fault tolerant, reliable, and secure manner on a highly available system. Future research is particularly needed on the following topics:

- **Flexibility**: What kinds of dynamic modifications of control flow and data flow must be supported in workflow management systems suitable for EC? How can such dynamics be efficiently implemented? How can we ensure, in the presence of such dynamics, that the specification of an EC workflow correctly models the corresponding business process? This is especially crucial if money is transferred by the EC workflow.
- **Interoperability**: EC workflows typically involve several participants, usually running different workflow management systems. How can we make these systems interoperable without violating the above requirements?
- **Security**: How can we make EC workflows safe with respect to unauthorized observations and modifications?
- **"Lawyer's interface"**: Transactions in electronic commerce will always be subject to lawsuits. How can a comprehensive and legally binding documentation of EC workflows be implemented?

REFERENCES

Adam, N., Yesha, Y. (1996). Electronic Commerce and Digital Libraries: Towards a Digital Agora, *ACM Computing Surveys*. 28(4).

Agrawal, R., Gunopulos, D., Leymann, F. (1998). Mining Process Models from Workflow Logs. *International Conference on Extending Database Technology*.

Alonso, G., Guenthoer, R., Kamath, M., Agrawal, D., El Abbadi, A., Mohan, C. (1996). Exotica/FMDC: A Workflow Management System for Mobile and Disconnected Clients. *Distributed and Parallel Databases*. 4(3).

Alonso, G., Mohan, C. (1997). WFMS: The Next Generation of Distributed Processing Tools. In: (*Jajodia, Kerschberg*, 1997).

Asokan, N., Janson, P., Steiner, M., Waidner, M. (1998). Electronic Payment Systems, to appear in *IEEE Computer*.

Barbara, D., Mehrotra, S., Rusinkiewicz, R. (1996). INCAs: Managing Dynamic Workflows in Distributed Environments. *Journal of Database Management, Special Issue on Multidatabases*. 7(1).

Bernstein, P.A., Newcomer, E. (1997). *Principles of Transaction Processing*. Morgan Kaufmann Publishers.

Clarke, E.M., Emerson, E.A., Sistla, A.P. (1986). Automatic Verification of Finite State Concurrent Systems Using Temporal Logic Specifications; A Practical Approach. *ACM Transactions on Programming Languages and Systems*. 8(2).

Cichocki, A., Helal, A., Rusinkiewicz, M., Woelk, D. (1998). *Workflow and Process Automation: Concepts and Technology*, Kluwer.

CommerceNet (1998). http://www.commerce.net.

Dogac, A., Gokkoca, E., Arpinar, S. et al. (1998). Design and Implementation of a Distributed Workflow Management System. In: (*Dogac, Kalinichenko, Ozsu*, 1998).

Dogac, A., Kalinichenko, L., Ozsu, M.T., Sheth, A. (Eds.) (1998). *Advances in Workflow Management Systems and Interoperability*, NATO Advanced Study Institute, Springer-Verlag.

Emerson, E.A. (1990). Temporal and Modal Logic. In: J. van Leeuwen (Ed.), *Handbook of Theoretical Computer Science*. Elsevier.

Emerson, E.A., Srinivasan, J. (1988). Branching Temporal Logic. In: J. W. de Bakker, W.-P. de Roever, G. Rozenberg (Eds.), *Lecture Notes in Computer Science 354*. Springer-Verlag.

Georgakopoulos, D., Hornick, M., Sheth, A. (1995). An Overview of Workflow Management: From Process Modeling to Workflow Automation Infrastructure. *Distributed and Parallel Databases*. 3(2).

Gray, J., Reuter, A. (1993). *Transaction Processing: Concepts and Techniques*. Morgan Kaufmann.Harel, D. (1987a). State Charts: A Visual Formalism for Complex Systems. *Science of Computer Programming*. 8.

Harel, D. (1987b). On the Formal Semantics of State Charts. *Symposium on Logics in Computer Science*. Ithaca, New York.

Harel, D. (1988). On Visual Formalisms. *Communications of the ACM*. 31(5).

Harel, D. et al. (1990). STATEMATE: A Working Environment for the Development of Complex Reactive Systems. *IEEE Transactions on Software Engineering*. 16(4).

Harel, D., Gery, E. (1997). Executable Object Modeling with Statecharts, *IEEE Computer*, 30(7).

Helbig, J., Kelb, P. (1994). An OBDD-Representation of state charts. *Proc. European Design and Test Conference*.

IBM Corp. (1994). *FlowMark Rel. 1, Programming Guide and Modelling Guide*.

Jablonski, S., Bussler, C. (1996). *Workflow Management, Modeling Concepts, Architecture, and Implementation*. International Thomson Computer Press.

Jajodia, S., Kerschberg, L. (Eds.) (1997). *Advanced Transaction Models and Architectures*. Kluwer.

Kamath, M., Alonso, G., Guenthoer, R., Mohan, C. (1996). Providing High Availability in Very Large Workflow Management Systems, *International Conference on Extending Database Technology*.

Leymann, F. (1996). Transaction Concepts for Workflow Management Systems. In: (*Vossen, Becker,* 1996) (in German).

Manna, Z., Pnueli, A. (1992). *The Temporal Logic of Reactive and Concurrent Systems - Specification*, Springer-Verlag.

McMillan, K. L. (1993). *Symbolic Model Checking*, Kluwer.

Muth, P., Wodtke, D., Weissenfels, J., Kotz Dittrich, A., Weikum, G. (1998a). From Centralized Workflow Specification to Distributed Workflow Execution, *Journal of Intelligent Information Systems - Special Issue on Workflow Managament*, 10(2).

Muth, P., Wodtke, D., Weissenfels, J., Weikum, G., Kotz Dittrich, A. (1998b). Enterprise-wide Workflow Management based on State and Activity Charts, In: (*Dogac, Kalinichenko, Ozsu,* 1998).

OMG (1995). CORBAservices: *Common Object Services Specification. Technical Report*, Object Management Group.

Primatesta, F. (1994). TUXEDO, *An Open Approach to OLTP*, Prentice Hall.

Reuter, A., Schneider, K., Schwenkreis, F. (1997). ConTracts Revisited, In: (*Jajodia, Kerschberg*, 1997).

Sheth, A., Kochut, K.J. (1998). Workflow Applications to Research Agenda: Scalable and Dynamic Work Coordination and Collaboration Systems. In: (*Dogac, Kalinichenko, Ozsu*, 1998).

Sistla, P., Wolfson, O., Dao, S., Narayanan, K., Raj, R. (1996). An Architecture for Consumer-Oriented On-line Database Services. *Proceedings RIDE-NDS*.

Unified Modeling Language (UML) (1997). Version 1.1. *http://www.rational.com/uml/documentation.html*.

Vossen, G., Becker, J. (Eds.) (1996). *Business Process Modelling and Workflow Managment, Models, Methods, and Tools*. International Thomson Publishing.

Vossen, G., Weske, M. (1998). The WASA Approach to Workflow Management for Scientific Applications. In (*Dogac, Kalinichenko, Ozsu*, 1998).

Weissenfels, J., Muth, P., Weikum, G. (1998). Flexible Worklist Management in a Light-Weight Workflow Management System. *Procceedings of the EDBT Workshop on Workflow Management*.

Wodtke, D., Weikum, G. (1997). A Formal Foundation for Distributed Workflow Execution Based on State Charts, *Proceedings of the International Conference on Database Theory*, Springer LNCS 1186.

Workflow Management Coalition (1998). *http://www.aiai.ed.ac.uk/WfMC/*.

CHAPTER 2

Trading Workflows on Electronic Markets

Andreas Geppert, IBM Almaden Research Center, USA
Markus Kradolfer, University of Zurich, Switzerland
Dimitrios Tombros, University of Zurich, Switzerland

This chapter presents market-based interorganizational workflow management, a novel approach to workflow specification and execution which regards tasks executed in a workflow as goods traded on an electronic market. Workflow federations are built out of individual workflow systems, which in turn define a set of workflow types. Workflow systems can export workflow types to the federation, and they can also import workflow types offered by other parties as subworkflows of complex workflows. At execution time, the federation acts as a marketplace in which executions of (exported) workflow types are traded. For that matter, a bidding protocol is used, in which each eligible provider specifies under which terms it can provide the workflow execution. The bids are evaluated with respect to price, execution time, and quality of service. The winner of a specific bidding process is requested to execute the workflow, and earns the amount specified in the corresponding bid. In addition, information about expected cost and execution time is considered for subworkflow specifications, and is used at runtime for bid evaluation.

INTRODUCTION AND MOTIVATION

Workflow management (Georgakopoulos et al, 1995; Jablonski & Bussler, 1996) has recently found great attention in the information systems field, as it allows to capture knowledge about business processes, to define workflows in a formal language/framework, and to enact workflows according to their specification. Hereby, a *workflow specification* defines workflow types and their structure (e.g., atomic activities/steps), processing entities responsible/capable of executing these activities, and further constraints such as execution or temporal dependencies. *Workflow management systems* (WFMS) are the software systems that support the specification and the execution of workflows.

Often, enterprises need to cooperate in the context of at least some business processes. The large number of vendors active in the WFMS market inevitably leads to a heterogeneous system landscape. Even within the same organization, it is often the case that different WFMS have been installed; the problem is only intensified when different organizations have to cooperate. In order to achieve workflow system cooperation, the various heterogeneous WFMS must be integrated into a federated inter-enterprise system. Nevertheless, in the current state of the art, this kind of interoperability is not yet possible to achieve (Alonso et al, 1996, Tombros & Geppert, 1997).

The problem of achieving WFMS interoperability is similar to that of the integration of heterogeneous database systems into a database federation (Sheth & Larson, 1990), since both aim at integrating heterogeneous local/component systems into one global system. Just like component database systems in a federation can have different data models, the component WFMS can have different (conceptual) workflow models, and it is generally not feasible to assume a single model that applies to all component systems. Similar to database federations, a WFMS-federation might require the maintenance of autonomy among participating WFMS. For instance, the execution of workflows can be required to remain under full control of the component WFMS, and requestors might not have the possibility to monitor or even influence such executions. Likewise, component WFMS might be willing to publish the interfaces of workflows they offer globally, but would hide the detailed workflow specification from other WFMS.

As soon as inter-organizational workflow management is possible, questions pertaining to electronic markets become crucial. In particular, if one of the parties in the federation requires a (sub)workflow execution from another one, the latter will not be willing to provide its services for free. Similarly, in order to save costs an organization may consider to "outsource" a subworkflow to someone else, i.e., to acquire a workflow execution from another party instead of performing it in-house. Ultimately, the real-world business is characterized by the presence of multiple competing providers, and the assessment of offers as well as the selection of cheapest/best providers has to be supported.

In consequence, inter-organizational workflow management requires an economic perspective that allows quantification of costs of workflow execution (so that decisions like "make or buy" are facilitated). The selection of optimal providers in case of multiple eligible ones must also be possible based on economic criteria (such as cost, time, and quality). Hence, it is a basic requirement for inter-organizational workflow management to apply the principles of (electronic) markets to it. This is accomplished by enhancing a workflow system federation with electronic market mechanisms, where workflows offered by the parties are the traded goods.

In this chapter, we present a framework for inter-organizational workflow management which is based on the principle of *agoric open systems* (Miller & Drexler, 1988) or, synonymously, *computational ecologies* (Hubermann, 1988). In such systems, (software) components are regarded to act as buyers or sellers of computational resources, such as processor time or memory in a market. We show that these principles can be beneficially applied to inter-organizational workflow management. Concretely, workflows that a federation party provides are treated as resources that must be paid for. At execution time, an open market mechanism based on bidding is used to assign workflows to specific federation components. Each eligible party capable of providing the subworkflow can bid for it by naming a price, an expected response time, and the quality level. Depending on the accumulated time and cost of the execution of the workflow until bid time, that is depending on whether cost or time is critical, an appropriate provider can then be chosen.

The contributions of this chapter, thus, are the following:

- it facilitates inter-organizational workflow management;
- it considers cost, time, and quality characteristics of workflows in their specifications;
- it allows the application of market mechanisms to (inter-organizational) workflow management; and
- it optimizes workflow execution in such a way that quality standards are met and execution cost and time are balanced for the entire workflow execution.

The remainder of this paper is organized as follows: in the next section, we introduce necessary terminology and give an overview about our approach towards market-based inter-organizational workflow management. In the three subsequent sections, we investigate market-based workflow management on three different levels: workflow specification, the software architecture of workflow federations, and workflow execution. We then survey related work, and conclude the paper.

TERMINOLOGY AND OVERVIEW

In this section, we first introduce the relevant terminology, and then give an overview of our approach towards inter-organizational and market-based workflow management.

A workflow management system consists of a buildtime and a runtime component. The buildtime component supports the definition of *workflow types* in some language or notation, for example, a script language, Petri nets, or statecharts. The notation/language is henceforth referred to as *workflow model*. For a workflow type, we assume that it defines an *interface*, consisting of a unique name and sets of typed formal input and output parameters, and a *body* which specifies in terms of the workflow model the internal structure of the workflow, that is, subworkflows/activities, task assignment rules, involved processing entities, etc. The runtime component of the WFMS supports the enactment of workflow instances as prescribed by the corresponding workflow type. A *workflow system* (WS) consists of a WFMS and a set of workflow types. The latter is called the *workflow schema* of the workflow system.

Before we give an overview of our approach towards market-based inter-organizational workflow management, we present a running example (see Fig. 1). The company Innova SA specifies a workflow for evaluating new product concepts. Initially, the marketing department develops a new product concept (activity newConcept). Subsequently a concept evaluation must be performed (conceptTest). Parallel to the concept evaluation, a marketing plan is developed in which price, distribution, and positioning of the new product are determined (marketPlanning). After successful concept testing and completion of the marketing plan, an extensive market survey is performed (marketSurvey). As soon as the survey is completed, its results are evaluated and following the profit/cost estimation (profit/costEstimate) the go-ahead decision is taken by the marketing management of Innova SA (decide). We note that conceptTest and marketSurvey are themselves complex processes, which are outsourced according to current business practice.

Workflow System Federations

A *federated WS* (or *federation*, for short) consists of a set of individual, possibly het-

Figure 1: The Product Concept Evaluation (PCE) workflow type

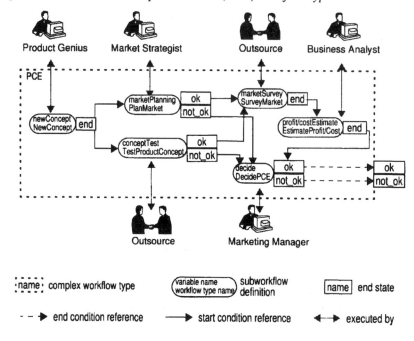

erogeneous yet interoperable workflow systems. The underlying individual WFMS may be heterogeneous with respect to the workflow models they use, workflow enactment techniques, underlying data stores, etc.

A workflow system whose schema contains a workflow type, that is, the workflow system *owns* that type, can export it to the federation by publishing its interface. Exported workflow types are managed by a *workflow market broker* (WMB). This component maintains the *repository* of the federation, whereby for each exported type, information about its interface, its owner(s), other workflow systems using the type, and further information is maintained. Using a workflow type from the repository actually means that a workflow system different from the owner imports the interface. Imported workflow types can be instantiated just as any other workflow types that are defined by the importer itself.

In order to abstract from API-based point-to-point connections in federations, special intermediary components are introduced. On the client-side (i.e., where a global workflow executes), the federation is represented by a software component as processing entity that offers imported workflows in the form of services. On the server side (i.e., the remote component workflow systems where subworkflows of a global workflow can be executed), specific clients mediate between the rest of the federation and the local WFMS.

In our example, assume that the marketSurvey step is outsourced. To that end, a workflow system federation must be established that comprises at least Innova's workflow system and that of one or more providers of the marketSurvey workflow. These providers export this workflow type (to the federation), and some time later upon specification of the PCE-workflow type, it can be imported into the Innova workflow system.

Market-based Workflow Management

In this section, we give an overview of market-based workflow management and identify assumptions that have to hold in order to make the market mechanism work. Note that we investigate market-mechanisms for inter-organizational workflows; for the intra-enterprise case which is restricted to the trading of atomic activities, see Geppert et al. (1998a, 1998c).

The principle of market-based workflow management is to establish a market in which tasks and subworkflows executed in a workflow are traded goods. Thus, workflow systems act as consumers by buying services from other workflow systems (the sellers). Each service offered by a seller is characterized by the time period the workflow system needs to execute it, by a price the seller charges, and by a domain-specific notion of quality the seller can guarantee. Prices are specified in units of some electronic currency. Quality of service (QoS) is domain-specific, i.e., depends on the service (workflow type) in question. For each workflow type, a set of quality criteria can be defined, where in turn each criterion is expressed as a discrete, totally ordered set of quality levels.

The market mechanism helps to optimize each single workflow execution in such a way that total execution time and overall aggregated costs are balanced and remain within predefined limits, while simultaneously the requirements to QoS of each workflow step are met. This objective is achieved by using a bidding protocol for task assignment, and by taking the required quality levels as well as expenditures and execution time of the workflow into account when selecting the best bidder for a concrete step to be executed.

Market-based workflow management affects all levels of workflow management. On the specification level, information about expected cost/time of step executions as well as quality attributes of each step must be defined. This information is later on used to determine the optimal bid. At the federation architecture level, workflow systems must be able to participate in a market; they thus must be enabled to bid for workflow executions (i.e., compute the time and cost at which they can provide services with particular quality attributes). At the workflow execution level, the execution engines must facilitate market-based workflow management by keeping track of actual execution times and expenditures of workflows, and the federation broker must be able to trade workflow executions.

In order to put market-based workflow management to work, several underlying assumptions have to be met. Assume that within a workflow type WFT, a step S will be (or can be) executed. Thus, for the specification of WFT, the following information about S is required:

(1) the expected execution time of S;
(2) the expected execution cost of S; and
(3) the QoS-criteria of S as well as the quality level for each such criterion WFT minimally expects from S.

This information is needed in order to determine at runtime whether expenditures and/or execution time lie within the predefined limits. Information about quality levels is needed in order to ensure that the entire execution of workflows meets quality standards.

For workflow systems, we assume that:

(4) for at least several workflow types, there are multiple workflow systems capable of executing them, and

(5) workflow systems do not agree on prices for workflow executions.

Assumption (4) ensures that no monopoly exists. In fact, this assumption is expected to be met in inter-organizational workflow management, where multiple workflow systems compete. Assumption (5) implies that workflow systems decide on prices independently of each other. This assumption is also basic in free markets, since its violation implies the existence of cartels.

In our example, consider again the outsourced marketSurvey (sub)workflow type. In the PCE workflow type definition, the expected execution time (say, 30 time units), the expected execution cost (say, 350 currency units), and the required levels of quality (e.g., random sample) should be specified.

SPECIFYING WORKFLOWS

In this chapter the specification of inter-organizational workflows as well as of information necessary to enable the trading of workflows is addressed.

Specifying Inter-Organizational Workflows

A workflow wf is called *inter-organizational* if at least one of its subworkflows is executed by a component workflow system different from the workflow system wf is enacted by. Simply stated, an inter-organizational workflow can be specified by a workflow system using workflow types provided by other workflow systems. In order to enable the specification of inter-organizational workflows by a workflow system, the following three prerequisites have to be met:

(1) it must be possible for a workflow system to find out which workflow types are offered by other workflow systems,
(2) the workflow types offered by a certain workflow system can be represented in another workflow system, and
(3) software components must be representable as processing entities, and task assignment rules must be specifiable (note that this functionality is fairly standard).

The first prerequisite is addressed by the workflow market broker, which runs at a well-known location in the federation. This broker offers trading functionality (Object Management Group, 1997a), i.e., it allows to exporters to advertise offered workflow types. Clients (i.e., importers) can query the broker in order to retrieve information about workflow types offered in the federation. In addition to the trading functions, the broker also supports proper brokering functionality (see below). The broker maintains a repository, in which it stores information about the workflow types exported by federation components. This repository contains the following information for each exported workflow type:

- its name,
- a set of typed formal input parameters,
- a set of typed formal output parameters,
- a set of workflow systems that implement and export this workflow type,
- a set of workflow systems that import the workflow type,
- a documentation, explaining what a workflow type does, without providing implementation details,

- further market-related information (see below).

In order to meet the second prerequisite, a workflow system must be able to import workflow types from the repository such that they can be instantiated by the workflow system as any other workflow type defined by the workflow system itself. Such imported workflow types are declared as automated, atomic activities. "Atomic" means that the activity has no internal structure, or at least its structure is not known to the WFMS. "Automated" means that the activity can be executed by a software system without interaction with humans.

Note that the fact that such an activity represents an imported workflow is not obvious from the specification. In order to render this information visible in the specification, uses of imported workflow types could be labeled with an additional keyword (e.g., "external workflow"). This would however require an extension of the workflow specification language or model. Since this is not desirable in most cases, we do not consider this alternative further. In order to at least implicitly identify workflows as imported, appropriate naming conventions can be used.

The information about which resource can execute a workflow task is specified by *task assignment rules*. In our case, this executing resource is another component workflow system, so that an importing workflow system has to invoke the remote WFMS. In order to abstract from the technical details such as calling API-functions, converting parameters, and communicating with remote WFMS, importing workflow systems define a processing entity that—from their perspective—is able to execute these activities (i.e., external workflows). Thus, when a workflow type WT is imported by a workflow system, a representation as a (server) processing entity of the workflow federation supporting WT has to be created (cf. the third requirement). The representation of this PE solely depends on the WFMS used by the importing workflow system, so that it needs to be implemented only once. Upon importing additional workflow types, the corresponding processing entity can be extended automatically to also offer the new types as activities.

In our example, we assume that there are two market research companies Exel Market Co. and Good Surveys Ltd. currently specializing in product concept testing. Both export a workflow type named TestProductConcept. They also compete in performing market surveys by exporting a workflow type SurveyMarket. Table 1 shows the information about the workflow types TestProductConcept and SurveyMarket that is contained in the reposi-

Table 1: Repository information about exported workflow types

WFType	Test Product Concept	Survey Market
In-Parameters	consumer: string, concept: Document	consumer: string, concept: Document
Out-Parameters	testResults: Document	SurveyResults: Document
Exporter/Provider	Exel Market Co. Good Surveys Ltd.	Exel Market Co. Good Surveys Ltd.
Imposter/User	Innova SA	Innova SA
Quality Criteria	testType: {sketch, mock-up}	sample: {random, non-random} interview: {personal, mail, telephone}

tory.

Note that in our approach only workflow type interfaces are exported and imported. Thus, in contrast to other proposals (Ben-Shaul & Kaiser, 1995, Ben-Shaul and Kaiser, 1998; Casati et al, 1996; Object Management Group, 1997c; Workflow Management Coalition, 1996) the body of a workflow is not visible to importers. In practice, workflow specifications define how an enterprise conducts its business, and an optimized, efficient workflow specification will represent a competitive advantage for an enterprise. Hence, workflow specification internals represent a strategic asset that enterprises would not like to exhibit to other companies, especially not to competitors.

Specifying Information Relevant for Trading Workflows

In order to trade workflows in a workflow federation, data relevant for the trading process must be known. Minimally, providers must be able to determine the cost, time, and quality level at which they are able to provide each of their workflow types. This information is required so that a workflow system can participate in a market. Furthermore, these data can also be used on the client side to optimize workflow executions according to a multi-criterion, namely cost, time, and quality. This optimization requires information about expected values and tries to adjust (say) cost at the expense of time whenever costs of a workflow have been overdrawn up to a certain point in time.

Different quality attributes are associated with each of these workflow types. For example, TestProductConcept can be performed based on a physical mock-up or on sketches of the product, while the sample for the market survey can be random or non-random.

Information about cost and time can be calibrated in the course of workflow system operation (see below). The remaining question to be addressed thus is how to choose initial values.

For a potential seller S, i.e., a server, assume that it exports a workflow WF to the federation, and that this workflow is going to be traded in the federation. For S it must therefore be specified how the execution time and cost of WF by S can be determined. This is generally possible in several ways. First, it is reasonable to assume that S has already executed WF numerous times. S thus can analyze its workflow log and determine the required data based on previous executions of WF. Second, the results of an activity based accounting can be used to determine these values. Finally, process modeling tools can be used to simulate executions of WF and thereby compute the required information. These three variants can also be used in combination, thereby validating the results of each of them.

For a potential buyer (i.e., a client) execution cost and time are important to know so that it can determine at runtime whether the budget of a workflow is likely to be overdrawn or deadlines cannot be met. Thus, if a workflow system C is likely to buy the execution of a workflow WF on the market, it has to determine the expected cost and execution time of WF. For this, again several variants exist. First, it might be that C actually is going to outsource WF, i.e., it has implemented and executed WF itself, and thus can analyze its execution log. The data gained from the log then serves as an upper limit, since outsourcing generally makes sense only if the outsourced WF is cheaper and faster than the one executed in-house. Second, C can conduct an own activity based accounting or simulation. Finally, execution time and cost can be determined by asking the broker that keeps track of workflow sales on the market.

In addition to the information described in the previous section, the repository contains for each exported workflow type a description of the quality criteria that exist for the workflow type (see Table 1).

Figure 2 represents the example ProductConceptEvaluation (PCE) workflow type defined within the workflow system of Innova SA using the TRAMs workflow specification approach (Kradolfer & Geppert, 1997). In TRAMs, the basic modeling construct is the workflow type that is either an *actitvity type*, representing a basic work step or a *complex workflow type* defining a set of subworkflows and data and control flows among these subworkflows. A workflow type defines a unique name and a set of typed input parameters that represent the data consumed by the workflow. Each workflow runs through the execution states Initiated and Executing and finally ends in one of several possible end states, each of which represents a different outcome of the workflow. Thus, activity types as well as complex workflow types define one or more end states with a set of typed output parameters representing the data produced by the workflow. A complex workflow type additionally comprises one or more subworkflow definitions, where a subworkflow definition defines a variable name and references a workflow type. Control flow can be specified by defining guards on the state transitions of workflows. For a subworkflow definition, an optional start condition (a guard on the transition leading from state Initiated to state Executing) can be defined. A complex workflow type defines an end condition for each of its end states specifying when the end state can be reached.

In Figure 2, solid resp. dashed black arrows indicate which references to other subworkflow definitions the start conditions of subworkflow definitions resp. the end condition of the complex workflow type include. Data flows (not shown in Figure 2) are defined by associating pairs of workflow parameters such that one member of each pair is the data source and the other one the data sink. As a first step in the creation of PCE, the

Figure 2: The Product Concept Evaluation (PCE) workflow type

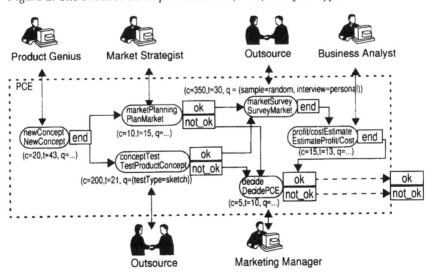

| c | expected costs | t | expected execution time | q | required quality of service |

types of the subworkflows conceptTest and MarketSurvey to be outsourced have to be imported from the repository. Next, estimates of the execution cost, execution time, and required quality of service for the subworkflows are specified. In this case, the estimates for subworkflows to be outsourced (marketSurvey and conceptTest) are derived by querying the market broker. The estimates for the rest of the subworkflows are defined based on internal information available by Innova SA, such as prior executions, simulations, and activity based costing.

THE SOFTWARE ARCHITECTURE OF WORKFLOW FEDERATIONS

In order for workflow systems to interoperate in a federation, mediation components are necessary that form the "glue" between them. The mediation is provided by two types of software components: *customers* and *providers* (see Figure 3). Customer-components allow a workflow system in the federation to request the execution of subworkflows defined in another workflow system of the federation, i.e., each such component represents a subworkflow supplier in the client workflow system. Provider components allow other workflow systems in the federation to request the execution of workflows defined in the provider's workflow system.

The client workflow system defines task assignment rules specifying that the customer-component is involved whenever one of the imported workflows has to be executed. The customer interacts with the provider which is essentially a client application of the provider workflow system. A prerequisite for the WFMS of the provider workflow systems is that the client-API allows the automatic initiation of workflows; as soon as the workflow is terminated, the provider (WFMS-client) receives results and passes them back to the customer component which in turn forwards results to the WFMS that originally requested the subworkflow.

The two types of mediating components are plugged into each of the component workflow systems that should participate in the federation and use a common model of messages and parameters. The introduction of customers and providers means that the former do not need to know the concrete interface of the WFMS offering workflows—they simply have to know the service interface of the providers. Similarly, providers do not need to know interfaces/formats of their clients' WFMS, but only need to use the API

Figure 3: Architecture of a market-based workflow federation

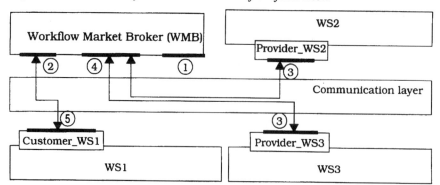

of their local WFMS. In this way, customer and provider components have to be written once for each type of WFMS.

The concrete choice how to represent and implement customers and providers as well as the concrete communication software is of minor concern—provided that they all run on all platforms involved in the federation. For instance, an ORB (Object Management Group, 1997b) may be used for communication; in this case it is quite natural to use the OMG object model for representation and transmission of parameters. The component WFMS is then represented as an application object, providers implement skeletons, and customers implement stubs (in CORBA terminology).

In market-based workflow management, the interesting question is which workflow provider to choose in case there are multiple eligible ones. Depending on its provider, the requested quality parameters, or even the moment in time at which a workflow is requested, it may have different cost and response times. It may even be the case that a workflow type with specific qualitative attributes is provided only by a subset of the exporters of this type. Workflow trading in the workflow federation is achieved by introducing an intermediary between customer and provider components—the *workflow market broker (WMB)*. The selection of providers is performed by the WMB during the actual workflow execution through an appropriate bidding protocol. The WMB acts as a trusted third party from the perspective of the subworkflow client and server systems (see Figure 3)[1].

The WMB offers a set of services to the workflow federation with which potential clients of workflows traded in the workflow market can "buy" the offered workflows. The provider bidding and subsequent selection is performed by the WMB. These services are grouped into two kinds of interfaces, a buildtime interface (circle 1 in Figure 3), the runtime customer/WMB interface (circles 2 and 5 in Figure 3), and the runtime provider/WMB interface (circles 3 and 4 in Figure 3).These interfaces define the following functionality:

- provide an export interface to the potential workflow providers and buildtime information to workflow federation parties about the actual workflow market (interface 1);
- accept a request from a customer for a workflow type with specific price, duration, and quality requirements (interface 2); this initiates a bidding process (interface 3);
- accept and evaluate bids from potential workflow providers (interface 4); and
- accept workflow execution replies (interface 4) from providers in order to forward them to customers (interface 5).

The WMB must have enough information from the workflow customer and the workflow providers to be able to evaluate these bids.

The bidding protocol proceeds as follows (see Figure 4): the client workflow system posts a request to the service market by communicating its requirements to the market broker through the customer component. The market broker reacts by selecting potential supplier workflow systems from the federation and communicating them the posted workflow requirements through their provider components. The bids are subsequently collected by the service market broker—within a time limit known to the providers—who then chooses the winning bidder and notifies all bidders of the selection result. The winner then starts the execution of the requested workflow. Figure 4 shows the messages generated during the protocol execution by the participating components. The efficiency of this protocol depends on the communication delays between workflow systems and the length of the bidding interval.

Figure 4: The bidding protocol

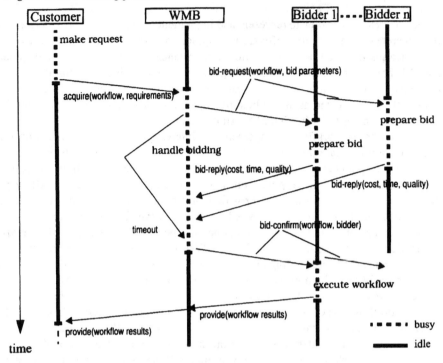

The implementation of customers and providers is specific to each workflow management system. We illustrate the implementation of the approach based on the Broker/Services Model (B/SM) (Tombros et al, 1996; Tombros et al, 1997) which describes the software architecture of workflow systems. In this model, the components—called brokers—are reactive processing entities that offer services to their peers. Brokers encapsulate heterogeneous applications that participate in workflows. The connectors are services described by their signature consisting of a name, input parameters, replies, and optionally exceptions. Services are implemented by *event-condition-action rules* (ECA rules) (ACT-Net Consortium, 1996); brokers interact with each other by generating events which trigger the ECA rules. Brokers define a persistent state and a set of state operations to describe the wrapping of external applications. Responsibility rules are defined for events; they can refer to event parameters, broker states, etc. and filter the set of brokers that react to occurrences of an event.

Services in B/S systems are requested by clients that raise a *service request event* with actual event parameters corresponding to the request parameters defined for this service. The server broker of a particular service is determined by special responsibility and task assignment functions. It executes the requested service and generates an appropriate *service reply event*. Exceptions are raised in case of abnormal service termination. Subworkflows that are executed by component WFMS in a federation are defined as normal services with the following signature:

- the service name is the exported workflow type name;

- the service input parameters correspond to the formal input parameters of the exported workflow type;
- a reply corresponding to completed external subworkflow execution with formal parameters as defined for the return type of the exported workflow; and
- an exception corresponding to abnormal termination of the remote workflow.

The representation of customers and/or providers is straightforward. Customers are represented as brokers which provide the respective subworkflow services, i.e. react to a request event for the subworkflow and use the WMB interface to acquire the service from other workflow systems in the federation. Providers are also represented as brokers which generate request events in their workflow system and react to the reply event by providing the workflow results through the WMB interface to their customer. The access to the respective WMB interfaces is part of the state operations of these brokers.

MARKET-BASED EXECUTION OF INTER-ORGANIZATIONAL WORKFLOWS

In this section, we address market-based workflow execution in federated workflow systems. Provided that workflows have been specified and federations modeled as described above, external workflow execution is seamlessly possible in the usual workflow execution cycle:

(1) the local WFMS determines that a subworkflow should be executed; how this fact is determined depends on the enactment paradigm applied by the WFMS;
(2) it performs task assignment (and in the case of external workflows discovers that the customer component is responsible);
(3) it commands this component with the subworkflow execution;
(4) the customer forwards the request to the workflow market broker; and
(5) the market broker sends the request to an eligible provider.

At some point in time, the market broker will receive a reply and forward it to the original customer, which in turn will forward it to its local workflow system. The local workflow system does not need to be aware of the fact that the reply represents the result of an external workflow and make any special provisions.

Consider the example shown in Figure 5. At one workflow system (WS-INN, which runs under control of our own WFMS EVE (Geppert & Tombros, 1998; Geppert et al, 1998b) a workflow of type SurveyMarket is executing. Assume that the ConceptTest subworkflow is to be outsourced to an external provider. As soon as this subworkflow is scheduled, the customer-component (Customer-INN) is notified about the request. This component forwards the request to the market broker, which in turn determines Excel Market Co. as an eligible provider. It then informs the corresponding specialized provider-component (Provider-Exel), which triggers the execution of the ConceptTest workflow in its workflow system (that, say, runs under control of the WFMS ProFlow[2]). Upon completion, the provider component collects the workflow results and sends them to the market broker, which in turn forwards them to the original requestor (Customer-INN).

In order to implement market-based workflow execution, the procedure just described needs to be extended, i.e., the eligible broker is chosen based on economic criteria. The

Figure 5: Global workflow execution in the SurveyMarket example

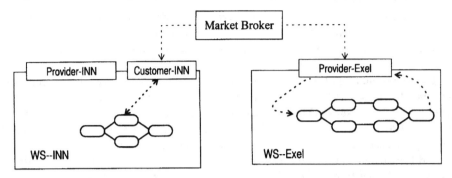

aim is to trade activity executions in such a way that the "optimal" bidder is assigned the workflow execution. This is accomplished by the procedure described below.

Cost and Time Computation in Market-based Workflow Management

In order to find the optimal bid with respect to the current workflow execution state, information about the current (aggregated) execution cost and duration of the requesting workflow instance have to be taken into account, and thus have to be consecutively computed at runtime. The following measures are required for each executing workflow instance wf and step SWF within wf:

- C_{real}(wf, SWF) are the actual aggregated costs spent in wf until SWF's scheduling;
- $C_{planned}$(wf, SWF) are the aggregated costs planned for wf until SWF's scheduling;
- T_{real}(wf, SWF) is the actual execution time of wf until SWF is scheduled; and
- $T_{planned}$(wf, SWF) is the expected execution time of wf until SWF is scheduled .

Execution Cost and Time Computation in EVE

The computation of the four aforementioned measures is best done by each WFMS and thus requires extensions to the WFMS. We show how these computations are performed by the workflow engine *EVE*. EVE (Event Engine) implements event-driven workflow execution, that is, every happening relevant for workflow execution is expressed as a (possibly composite) event. EVE's major purpose is to support B/SM brokers by providing event management, storage, and notification functionality. The principle by which brokers use EVE to execute workflows is the following (Figure 6): broker ECA-rules are translated to rules stored and executed in EVE. Whenever a broker generates a primitive event, it notifies its local EVE-server about the occurrence. Supported primitive events are

- request events, denoting that an activity or subworkflow has to be executed;
- reply events, indicating that a subworkflow or activity has been terminated; and
- exception events, expressing the occurrence of an abnormal situation.

Whenever a primitive event has been signalled, EVE performs composite event detection and determines brokers that should be notified for such primitive and potentially detected composite event occurrences which may have resulted from this event. All these

Figure 6: The workflow execution process in EVE

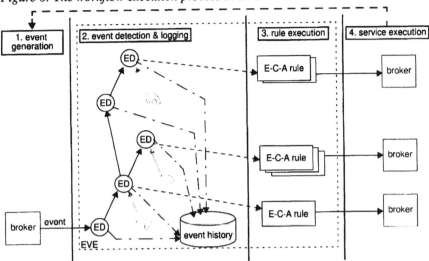

brokers are then appropriately informed and react as defined by their ECA-rules (whereby these reactions can in turn generate new events, and so forth).

Computation of aggregated execution time

In this model of event-driven workflow execution, aggregated execution time is computed as follows. Whenever a step (an activity or a subworkflow) is terminated, the planned execution time as specified for the step is added to the planned execution time given in the request event. The same computation is made for effective execution time. Both new measures are stored in the attributes of the reply event and are thus visible in other events that contain the reply event or refer to it. In case of composite events (which, e.g., represent "join"-nodes of parallel branches), the appropriate measures have to be taken from the longest of the parallel branches, i.e., in this case, the time measures are determined by the largest planned/effective execution time (this is obtained as the maximum of the measures as stored in the component events' attributes).

Computation of aggregated cost

The cost measures are also computed successively at runtime. As soon as an atomic activity a is terminated, the actual cost is computed as $C_{real}(wf, a)$ plus the execution cost of a. Similarly, the planned costs is the sum of $C_{planned}(wf, a)$ and the planned execution cost of a. These rules also apply to local subworkflows (i.e., those that have been executed in the same workflow system as wf). Once a local subworkflow has been terminated, its actual/expected costs are added to those of the parent workflow. In case of an external subworkflow, the expected cost is obtained from the specification of wf, and the actual cost is determined by the market. Upon termination of such a subworkflow, both measures are added to those of the superworkflow

Example

Assume a PCE-workflow wf is executing. The newConcept activity has been executed within 40 time units at a price of 25 currency units. In the next step, both the activity marketPlanning and the subworkflow conceptTest are executed. marketPlanning terminates first (after 22 time units, at costs of 12 currency units), followed by conceptTest (after 32 time units, at costs of 180). The subsequent step to be executed is marketSurvey. Based on this execution, we obtain the cost and time measures as shown in Table 3.

Assessing the current workflow execution state

The four measures are used to determine whether and to which extent the workflow execution has exceeded time and or cost limits, i.e., they are used to compute the amount of time saved or overdrawn, and the amount of money saved or overdrawn. Based on these computations, further assignments can then stress cost or time. This is, when execution time up to a certain point has been minimized at the expense of an overdrawn cost limit, then in the subsequent steps assignment would weight costs more than time.

The *cost overrun ratio* of wf directly before the scheduling of a is defined as:
$$COR(wf, a) = C_{real}(wf, a) / C_{planned}(wf, a)$$
and the *time overrun ratio* is defined as
$$TOR(wf, a) = T_{real}(wf, a) / T_{planned}(wf, a).$$

For activities which have no predecessors COR and TOR have the default value 1. Based on the values in Table 2, we obtain the overrun rations shown in Table 3.

A Protocol for Market-based Workflow Execution

Assume that within a complex workflow wf a subworkflow SWF is to be outsourced to some other party of a federation, and that the assignment should be based on bids. This is accomplished in that the requesting WS sends a request to the market broker. This request (see step (4) above) carries the following information:

- the workflow type name,
- the input parameters,
- minimally required quality levels,
- a maximal price,
- a maximal execution time,
- cost overrun ratio COR(wf, SWF),
- time overrun ratio TOR(wf, SWF).

All parameters except the first two are optional. Upon reception of such a request, the market broker tries to find the optimal provider in the federation by executing the bidding process:

Table 2: Aggregated cost and time for a sample workflow execution

Step	$T_{Planned}$	T_{Real}	$C_{Planned}$	C_{Real}
newConcept	-	-	-	
marketPlanning	43	40	20	25
conceptTest	43	40	20	25
marketSurvey	64	72	230	217

(1) Determine the set of eligible WS based on the information stored in the repository.
(2) Send the bid request for the workflow to each of them.
(3) Collect bids for a certain (pre-defined) period of time. Each bid is specified by a triple B= (P, T, Q), where P is the price (specified in currency units) at which the bidder is willing to execute the workflow. T is the time (in time units) the PE will need to execute the workflow. Q is a set of quality level specifications.
(4) Evaluate bids, i.e., select the "optimal" bid. The PE who has sent the optimal bid is called the "winner".
(5) Notify the winner (and all other bidders).

In the first step, only those WS are considered that can provide for the minimally required quality levels. In case a maximal price (execution time) has been specified, then in step (4) only those bids are considered that stay below the given limit. Furthermore, bid evaluation is based on information about the cost and time overrun ratios. If these (or one of them) has not been specified by the requestor, then the market broker assumes a default value of 1. In this case, it determines the best bid without taking the workflow execution state of the requestor into account. The n bids (P_i, T_i, Q_i) are evaluated according to the following formula:

winning bid = min $\{ P_i^{COR(wf,SWF)} * T_i^{TOR(wf,SWF)} \}$

COR and TOR are used in the exponents in order to weight cost and/or time. If cost (time) has been overrun, then the difference in price (time) attributes from multiple bids will be increased (while we refrain from choosing the bid with the minimal price/time regardless of the other component). Thus, even if (say) cost has been overrun, then we still might choose a bid with a non-minimal price, provided that its specified time is by far the smallest one.

In case the market broker cannot determine any eligible workflow system (because none can provide for the required quality, or can stay below specified time and cost limits), then the market broker informs the requestor that (and why) no provider could be found.

In our example, we assume that two bids were collected by the WMB for the marketSurvey subworkflow satisfying the minimal quality requirements:

Bid 1: (c = 400, t=25, q = (sample = random, interview = personal))
Bid 2: (c = 330, t=30, q = (sample = random, interview = personal))

The winning bid is calculated as min(Bid 1: $400^{0.94}$ x $25^{1.11}$ = 9'946, Bid 2: $330^{0.94}$ x $30^{1.11}$ = 10'162) which is Bid 1. Note that for each single bidding process, it is determined whether either cost or time are more critical for the workflow in question. This means that costs are stressed whenever actual costs have exceeded expected costs, and execution time stayed within the limit, or alternatively—as in our example—duration is stressed when time is the critical factor. The fact that for a workflow cost or time are weighted more can

Table 3: COR and TOR values for a sample workflow

Step	Time Overrun Ratio	Cost Overrun Ratio
newConcept	1	1
marketPlanning	0.93	1.25
conceptTest	0.93	1.25
marketSurvey	1.11	0.94

change arbitrarily often within its execution. Table 4 contains the expected COR and TOR values before profit/costEstimate and depending on the bid chosen. The bid selection formula aims at minimizing the sum of the deviations of TOR and COR from the ideal value of 1.

Calibration of Cost Limits, Deadlines, and Bids

Like any other market, a workflow federation will be calibrated in various respects (e.g., prices paid and offered, number of players on the market). In particular, requestors will calibrate their demand and the related information, providers will calibrate their bids, and the market itself will be calibrated in that new providers enter the market or old ones vanish from it.

Calibration on Requestors' Side

For a workflow type it might happen that for many of its instances, deadlines and/or cost limits cannot be met. The reaction of the market broker in case either one of them is exceeded is to optimize accordingly. This is the reason to include the cost and time overrun ratios in requests sent to the broker. If, however, both of them have been exceeded repeatedly within a workflow execution, the corresponding WS can suspend it and inform the workflow administrator. He/she can then decide to resume or abort the workflow execution.

The reason for exceeding cost limits and deadlines can be that the handled case is much more complex than the average case for which the workflow is designed. However, the reason can also be that budgets/deadlines for steps have been calculated too sharply. This kind of inappropriateness should then be remedied by adjusting the corresponding cost limits and/or execution time of the responsible steps. Alternatively, if for example deadlines cannot be extended for some reason, then a possible remedy would be to increase the cost limit for the problematic steps. Finally, if quality criteria cannot be guaranteed at the cost and time limit, then a possible calibration action can be to change required quality to a lower level (which then can be provided such that cost and time limits are met).

In order to calibrate cost and time limits, the workflow administrator needs information about problematic steps, i.e., those that repeatedly exceed expected costs and deadlines. In order to provide this information, the functionality of post-mortem analysis (Geppert & Tombros, 1997) must be extended. Then, post-mortem analysis also answers queries such as "how often did step executions overdraw their budget and deadline within executions of a certain workflow type".

Calibration by Providers

The workflow systems that act as providers also might need to calibrate their actions. Their aim naturally is to maximize income. To that end, they need to specify bids in such a way that they still make benefit but also win the bidding process. If a WS repeatedly loses the bidding process for requests of a workflow type, it thus needs to adapt its future

Table 4: Overrun ratios values for a sample workflow execution

Step	TOR(Bid 1)	COR(Bid 1)	TOR(Bid 2)	COR(Bid 2)
profit/costEstimate	1.03	1.06	1.09	0.94

bids for this workflow type. This kind of calibration is naturally done in three not mutually exclusive ways:

- lowering the price for the workflow executions,
- decreasing execution time,
- increasing quality levels.

These actions can also imply a workflow redesign and implementation (e.g., in order to attain shorter execution times).

Since benefit maximization is the ultimate goal of a WS, it might also adjust bids whenever it has *won* bidding processes repeatedly. In this case, it can rise prices or increase execution times (in order to decrease own costs).

In order to realize the necessity of bid adjustment, the WS again needs information from the log, in this case about past won and lost bids. How bid adjustment is undertaken depends on whether the bids are determined by humans or generated by software components. For instance, reactive components in B/SM can implement adjustment of bids in ECA-rules.

RELATED WORK

In this section, we survey related work in the areas of market-based inter-organizational workflow management. Both areas are still maturing, and we are not aware of any other work that combines both market mechanisms and inter-organizational workflow management in the sense of this chapter.

Inter-organizational Workflow Management

The Workflow Management Coalition (WfMC) has devoted one of its interfaces to workflow interoperability (Workflow Management Coalition, 1996). This interface allows the exchange of workflow type definitions; as already mentioned, we do not consider this feature as viable in inter-enterprise workflow management. Interface 4 defines 8 "levels of interoperability", where actually the first one represents the absence of interoperability, and the highest one—the same standard user interface for all WFMS—might never be achieved interoperability (Workflow Management Coalition, 1996). Several WFMS currently comply to level 4, which is characterized by a limited common API subset. It is questionable whether compliance to higher levels is realistic, because these levels assume a complete standardized API (level 5, product-specific extensions are excluded), a shared process modeling language (level 6), and standardized client/server communication (level 7, including transmission of definitions, and workflow transactions).

The workflow facility under definition of the OMG also addresses workflow interoperability. In this case, component systems can interoperate via the CORBA middleware. Nevertheless, this requires that the underlying WFMS complies to the workflow facility standard, and in order to be able to invoke a subprocess at another component of a federation, the WFMS has to be modified. In the Workflow Management Facility (Object Management Group, 1997c) it is also possible to retrieve workflow type definitions from other federation components, which in our belief is not viable in federations involving competing parties.

It has also been argued that the OMG-facility requires a complex technological infrastructure to be installed at each site of the federation; and apparently the WfMC-efforts are assessed as progressing too slowly. In consequence, several WFMS-vendors together with further companies have recently announced the Simple Workflow Access Protocol, SWAP (Svenson, 1998), which uses HTTP to enable WFMS-interoperation. SWAP defines a protocol for web-based remote workflow execution, but does not address issues such as maintaining information about exported/imported workflow types.

Interoperability has been investigated in the Oz-project. Ben-Shaul & Kaiser (1995) address the question of how to establish interoperability between different process-centered software engineering environments (PCSE). The various component systems can have different process models (i.e., workflow types), while heterogeneity of execution engines and process modeling formalisms is not addressed there. In another paper (Ben-Shaul & Kaiser, 1998), the same authors address architectural issues in federating PCSE. This paper addresses mainly homogeneous federations (i.e., those where the component systems are instantiations of the same PCSE), while the heterogeneous case in which components are instances of heterogeneous PCSE is only briefly sketched. In both works, components can coordinate their processes and thus share information on their process models. This is certainly necessary in design applications such as software engineering, while it is not feasible in the general workflow applications we consider.

Sheth et al. (1996) discuss workflow execution in heterogeneous environments. However, they focus on the access to heterogeneous resources, such as databases, using a variety of infrastructure technologies (such as ORBs and the Web). They use a single WFMS (METEOR$_2$) and therefore do not consider workflow system federations in the sense of this chapter.

Some prototypes and commercial products such as FlowMark (Leymann & Altenhuber, 1994) allow to call executable programs or scripts from within a workflow execution. In this way, external subworkflows can be executed. In contrast to our approach based on a global repository and mediation components, this solution implies a more complex, low-level and hard-wired implementation of interoperability, which must be implemented manually and is less well maintainable.

Casati et al. (1996) also address workflow interoperability. They assume a global conceptual workflow model for the federation, and also a homogeneous enactment engine. Information between component engines can be exchanged via the underlying database. Their main focus is on the synchronization of active workflows.

Market-based Workflow Management

Current WFMS allow to specify deadlines, some even allow the adjustment of deadlines. However, we are not aware of any WFMS that allows to specify information about costs and execution times and to use this information together with the knowledge about the current workflow state for task assignment.

Panagos & Rabinovich (1997) address (only) execution times and try to minimize costs occurring due to workflow escalations (note, however, that the notion of "cost" there does not bear any budget or financial meaning as in our model). Similar to our model, during task assignment in FlowMark (Leymann & Altenhuber, 1994), requests are sent to all eligible participants. In contrast to our model, task assignment is then not based on bids of PE, but the task is assigned to that participant whose affirmative reply is received first.

Market-based mechanisms have been used for the assignment of resources and scheduling of tasks. The work reported in (Drexler & Miller, 1988; Miller & Drexler, 1988; Waldspurger et al, 1992) describes how resources such as processor slices or memory can be assigned using market-based techniques. There, processes (or their users) are clients bidding for the usage of a resource, and machines (or their owners) sell these resources at some price. Thus, these approaches typically consider one "seller" and multiple buyers who bid for the resource or a service. In contrast, our model is characterized by the presence of one buyer (at a certain point in time), but several potential providers. Therefore, the techniques proposed for agoric open systems cannot be directly applied to our case.

A market-based approach has also been proposed for query processing and optimization in Mariposa (Stonebraker et al, 1996), a distributed database management system. In Mariposa, there is also one buyer (a query) and several providers which can answer (parts of) the query. Each query has a budget, and the query optimizer then tries to answer the query as fast as possible while staying within the budget limits. The major difference between Mariposa's approach and our model is that budget and time limits are known and considered only for a single step (i.e., a query), while in workflow management the problem is apparently to optimize the utilization of both, time and cost in such a way that the past execution time exceeded and expenditures can be taken into account (so that both limits are more likely to be met for the entire workflow).

The CORBAservices (Object Management Group, 1997a) specify a trader service, which however does not cover bidding or billing. Recent research in electronic markets has also focussed on trading of services in distributed object systems (e.g., Merz et al, 1996).

CONCLUSION

This chapter introduced a novel approach towards market-based inter-organizational workflow management. The workflow market is formed by a federation of workflow systems, in which the federation parties demand and offer the execution of workflows. Workflow trading is implemented by a market broker, which in its repository maintains information about workflow types traded in the federation. We have also shown how workflow specifications have to be extended by deadlines, budgets, and quality requirements (for subworkflows). We have discussed workflow execution, which based on a bidding protocol facilitates inter-organizational workflow enactment in a market-based way. Finally, we have shown how to optimize workflow executions by taking into account the current execution state of requestors (aggregated execution time and cost).

Thus, the contribution of this work is that it allows to consider workflows from a market perspective, and that it leverages the concept of electronic markets to inter-organizational workflow management. This approach is feasible for workflow federations in which many parties participate and tasks to be executed are complex and/or intellectually demanding (it would be less meaningful for workflows consisting of only small routine jobs).

We are convinced that the integration of market mechanisms and inter-organizational workflow management is of paramount importance for computerized business-to-business operations, because otherwise the economic perspective of involved enterprises cannot be adequately reflected on the workflow management level.

Some aspects have been out of the scope of this chapter. For instance, we assume that the market broker is a trusted third party mediating between workflow buyers and sellers, and providing guarantees to either side (the provider will be paid for delivering its service, and the seller will receive the service he is paying for). Another aspect beyond the scope of this chapter is relationship management in this kind of business-to-business operation, i.e., how potential market actors become aware of the market and how they can enter it. Since these questions are not specific to workflow management, we simply assume that current techniques developed in the respective research areas apply to our case, too.

For the integration of (component) workflow systems into the federation, we have so far assumed that the exporting parties agree on workflow type interfaces, and that these interfaces together with documentations and further definitions (such as quality criteria) provides enough information for clients to find out whether a specific workflow type is useful for them. These two assumptions will be loosened in our future work. For the integration/export step, we will investigate how semantic heterogeneity of workflow types can be resolved (e.g., heterogeneous interfaces of workflow types with the same purpose, homonyms/synonyms of workflow types). Note that this is also a crucial step in schema integration for federated database systems (Sheth & Larson, 1996). With respect to the degree of information about workflow types maintained by the repository, we will investigate how workflow types can be described in such a way that clients can unambigiously decide whether the workflow type is what they are looking for, while information confidential and valuable for the provider is not exposed.

ENDNOTES

[1] Note that in the non-market-based case of inter-organizational workflow management, a workflow trader is needed only for managing import/export-relationships at buildtime, while the mediation components can directly communicate with each other at runtime.

[2] ProFlow is a WFMS we are using. ProFlow is a registered trademark of OpenInfo (http://www.openinfo.ch/).

REFERENCES

The ACT-NET Consortium (1996). The Active Database Management System Manifesto: A Rulebase of ADBMS Features. *ACM SIGMOD Record* 25(3).

G. Alonso et al. (1996). Functionality and Limitations of Current Workflow Management Systems. *IEEE Expert.*

I.Z. Ben-Shaul & G.E. Kaiser (1995). *An Interoperability Model for Process-Centered Software Engineering Environments and its Implementation in Oz.* Technical Report CUCS-034-95, Columbia University Department of Computer Science.

I.Z. Ben-Shaul & G.E. Kaiser (1998). Federating Process-Centered Environments: the Oz Experience. *Automated Software Engineering* 5(1).

F. Casati et al. (1996). Semantic WorkFlow Interoperability. *Proc. 5th Intl. Conf. on Extending Database Technology*, Avignon, France.

K.E. Drexler & M.S. Miller (1988). *Incentive Engineering for Computational Resource Management.* In (Hubermann, 1988).

D. Georgakopoulos et al. (1995). An Overview of Workflow Management: From Process Modeling to Workflow Automation Infrastructure. *Distributed and Parallel Databases* 3(2).

A. Geppert & D. Tombros (1997). Logging and Post-Mortem Analysis of Workflow Executions based on Event Histories. *Proc. 3rd Intl. Workshop on Rules in Database Systems (RIDS)*, Skoevde, Sweden.

A. Geppert & D. Tombros (1998). EvE, an Event Engine for Workflow Enactment in Distributed Environments. *Proc. IFIP Int'l Conf. on Distributed Systems Platforms and Open Distributed Processing (Middleware '98)*, The Lake District, England.

A. Geppert et al. (1998a). Market-based Workflow Management. *Proc. Int'l IFIP Working Conf. on Trends in Distributed Systems for Electronic Commerce*, Hamburg, Germany.

A. Geppert et al. (1998b). Defining the Semantics of Reactive Components in Event-Driven Workflow Execution with Event Histories. *Information Systems* 23(4).

A. Geppert et al. (1998c). Market-Based Workflow Management To appear in *Int'l Journal on Cooperative Information Systems* 7(4).

B.A. Huberman, editor (1988). *The Ecology of Computation*. Studies in Computer Science and Artificial Intelligence, North-Holland, Amsterdam.

S. Jablonski & C. Bussler (1996). *Workflow Management. Modeling Concepts, Architecture, and Implementation*. International Thomson Computer Press, London.

M. Kradolfer & A. Geppert (1997). *Modeling Concepts for Workflow Specification. Technical Report*, Department of Computer Science, University of Zurich.

F. Leymann & W. Altenhuber (1994). Managing Business Processes as an Information Resource. *IBM Systems Journal* 33(2).

M. Merz et al. (1996). Agents, Services, and Markets: How do they integrate? *Proc. IFIP/ IEEE Int'l Conf. on Distributed Platforms*, Dresden, Germany.

M.S. Miller & K.E. Drexler. Markets and Computation: Agoric Open Systems. In (Huberman, 1988).

Object Management Group (1997a). *CORBAservices: Common Object Services Specification*. (http://www.omg.org/corba/sectran1.htm).

Object Management Group (1997b). *The Common Object Request Broker: Architecture and Specification*. Revision 2.

Object Management Group (1997c). *Workflow Management Facility*. BODTF-RFP 2 Submission.

E. Panagos & M. Rabinovich (1997). Reducing Escalation-Related Costs in WFMSs. *NATO Advanced Study Institute (ASI) on Workflow Management Systems and Interoperability*, Istanbul. Turkey.

A.P. Sheth & J.A. Larson (1990). Federated Database Systems for Managing Distributed, Heterogeneous and Autonomous Databases. *ACM Computing Surveys* 22(3).

A. Sheth et al. (1996). Supporting State-wide Immunization Tracking using Multi-Paradigm Workflow Technology. *Proc. 22nd Int'l Conf. on Very Large Data Bases*, Bombay, India.

M. Stonebraker et al. (1996). Mariposa: A Wide-area Distributed Database System. *VLDB Journal* 5(1).

K. Svenson (1998). Simple Workflow Access Protocol (SWAP). Draft Document, Internet Engineering Task Force (http://www.ics.uci.edu/~ietfswap/SWAP9807.html).

D. Tombros et al. (1996). Brokers and Services: Constructs for the Implementation of Process-Oriented Environments. In B. Freitag, C.B. Jones, C. Lengauer, H.-J. Schek (eds). *Object-Orientation with Parallelism and Persistence*. Kluwer Academic Publishers.

D. Tombros et al. (1997). *The Broker/Services Model for the Design of Cooperative Process Oriented Environments*. Technical Report 97.06, Department of Computer Science, University of Zurich.

D. Tombros & A. Geppert (1997). *Managing Heterogeneity in Commercially Available Workflow Management Systems: A Critical Evaluation.* SWORDIES Project Report No. 5, Department of Computer Science, University of Zurich.

C.A. Waldspurger et al. (1992). Spawn: A Distributed Computational Economy. *IEEE Trans. on Software Engineering* 18(2).

Workflow Management Coalition (1996). *Interface 4 - Interoperability - Abstract Specification.* WFMC-TC-1012 (http://www.aiai.ed.ac.uk/project/wfmc/).

CHAPTER 3

An Electronic Marketplace Architecture

Asuman Dogac, Ilker Durusoy, Sena Arpinar,
Nesime Tatbul, Pinar Koksal
Middle East Technical University, Turkey

In this chapter, we describe a scenario for a distributed marketplace whose scope can be the whole Web where resource discovery agents find out about resources that may want to join the marketplace and electronic commerce is realized through buying agents representing the customers and the selling agents representing the resources like electronic catalogs. The marketplace contains an Intelligent Directory Service (IDS) which makes it possible for agents to find out about each other and also contains references to the related Document Type Definitions (DTDs).

We propose a possible architecture to support this scenario which is based on the emerging technologies and standards. In this architecture, the resources expose their metadata using Resource Description Framework (RDF) to be accessed by the resource discovery agents and their content through Extensible Markup Language (XML) to be accessed by the selling agents by using Document Object Model (DOM).

The IDS contains the template workflows for buying and selling agents, a trader mechanism, Resource Discovery Agents, Document Type Definitions (DTDs) and a dictionary of synonyms to be used by the buying agents to help the customer to specify the item s/he wishes to purchase. The agents and IDS communicate through KQML messages. The modifications necessary to the proposed architecture considering only the available technology are also discussed.

INTRODUCTION

Electronic commerce is a generic term that encompasses numerous information technologies and services used to implement business practices ranging from customer service to inter-corporation coordination. One of the most common instances of electronic commerce is the exchange of goods and services over the Internet. However, the electronic commerce services that are established so far are still far from being mature. There is no real integration of the available underlying technologies, and the provided services lack many important but also more challenging features.

One such feature is the automation of a marketplace on the Web through agents. For such a marketplace, there is a need for a facility which enables the semantic interoperability of resources on the Web so that buyers are able to reach the sellers that can meet their needs and vice versa. In this respect, the currently emerging standards like XML, RDF and DTDs are very promising. Furthermore, after the resources are discovered, the process of interaction between buyers and sellers (resources), that is commerce, should be automated. In other words, a virtual marketplace on the Web should be created which not only makes buyers and sellers meet but also helps the exchange of goods between them through negotiations.

With these considerations in mind, we envision a scenario for an electronic marketplace on the Web. The distribution infrastructure of the marketplace is Web. The marketplace contains buying and selling agents as well as Intelligent Directory Service (IDS). The IDS contains the template workflows for buying and selling agents, a trader mechanism, Resource Discovery Agents, Document Type Definitions (DTDs) and a dictionary of synonyms to be used by the buying agents to help the customer to specify the item s/he wishes to purchase. The trader mechanism lets agents find out about each other.

In this scenario, resource discovery agents of IDS working in the background discover resources. If a resource is willing to join the marketplace, the IDS sends a selling agent workflow template to the seller's site. The resource creates a selling agent by automatically customizing the template by using the information obtained from the resource through a user friendly graphical interface. The resulting agent is registered with the trader. However if the resource already has a selling agent, that one is registered. The trader makes the related buying agents already in the marketplace aware of this newly created selling agent.

When a customer wants to buy a service or an item from the marketplace, s/he provides the item name to the IDS. IDS first checks the related DTDs with the item name specified by the buyer. However, the buyer may not know the right term (used in DTD) to use for the item, therefore an intelligent dictionary of synonyms is used for this purpose. For example, consider a computer shop using a computer DTD in describing its service. If a customer wants to buy a CPU and uses the term "Processor" and if "CPU" is the term used in DTD, then dictionary of synonyms is used to match the word "Processor" with "CPU". Then IDS sends the names and types of the properties as well as a buying agent template and the list of related selling agents to the buyer's site. Obtaining the names and types of properties from DTDs is necessary since the buyer may not know in advance all the properties of the item. The proposed XML namespace facility can also be used together with DTD to associate DTD's and the documents.

The buying agent workflow template presents the user a form containing the values or ranges for the properties of the item along with the criteria that the customer wishes to be optimized in the negotiation phase and the required parameters. The buying agent is automatically created by customizing the workflow template using this information. The buying agent negotiates with the related selling agents to realize the transaction. A comparative analysis of the available alternatives can also be presented to the customer by the buying agent if the customer wishes so.

The chapter describes an architecture for the proposed scenario, called METU-EMar, and is organized as follows: First we summarize the technologies that can be used as build-

ing blocks in the implemention. Then, we describe the overall architecture of the marketplace, followed by a section that details agent architecture, including implementation of
agents as workflow templates are given. Subsequently, we present the feasibility and the
advantages of the proposed system, and an alternative communication infrastructure to KQML
namely CORBA is discussed. Finally the conclusions are given.

RELATED TECHNOLOGIES

In this section we briefly summarize the advanced technologies and emerging standards which constitute the building blocks of the proposed architecture. In this respect,
agent technology, Knowledge Query and Manipulation Language (KQML), Extensible
Markup Language (XML), Document Type Definition (DTD), Resource Description Framework (RDF) and Document Object Model (DOM) are covered.

Agent Technology

Agents are programs that perform specific tasks on behalf of their users. Agents are
distinguished from other types of software because they are independent entities capable
of completing complex assignments without intervention, rather than as tools that must be
manipulated by a user.

The fundamental properties of software agents are as follows [Woolridge, 1995]:

- **Autonomy:** Agents operate without the direct intervention of humans or others, and
  have some kind of control over their actions and internal state.
- **Social ability:** Agents interact with other agents (and possibly with humans) via some
  kind of agent communication language.
- **Reactivity:** Agents perceive their environment, (which may be the physical world, a
  user via a graphical user interface, a collection of other agents, the Internet, or perhaps
  all of these combined), and respond in a timely fashion to changes that occur in it.
- **Pro-activeness:** Agents do not simply act in response to their environment, they are
  able to exhibit goal-directed behaviour by taking the initiative.

Agents can be made more intelligent with the following additional properties:

- **Rationality:** Agents select actions that follow from knowledge and goals.
- **Adaptivity:** Agents are able to modify knowledge and behaviour based on experi-
  ence.
- **Collaboration:** Agents can plan and execute multi-agent problem solving.

An earlier example of a software agent for electronic commerce is ShopBot (Shopping Robot) [Doorenbos, 1997] which is a domain-independent comparison-shopping agent.
Given the home pages of several online stores, ShopBot automatically learns how to shop
at these vendors. Learning process involves extracting product descriptions from home
pages. This is not an easy problem because home pages may vary in format and also contain other information like advertisements and links to other sites. After learning, ShopBot
is able to visit over a dozen of software vendors, extract product information, and summarize the results for the user. Preliminary results show that ShopBot enables users to both
find superior prices and substantially reduce Web shopping time. ShopBot relies on a com-

bination of heuristic search, pattern matching, and inductive learning techniques.

Yet ShopBot has several limitations. It works only on home pages that have a searchable index. It expects product descriptions to start on a fresh line. Furthermore, ShopBot heavily relies on HTML. If a vendor provides information exclusively by embedding graphics or using Java, ShopBot will be unable to handle that vendor. More importantly ShopBot shopper's performance is linear in the number of vendors it accesses which is not acceptable given the number of resources on the Web.

The Michigan Internet AuctionBot [AuctionBot, 1998] is an experimental auction server developed and operating at the University of Michigan Artificial Intelligence Laboratory. The purpose of the server is to allow anybody on the Internet to run an auction over the net. The AuctionBot provides facilities for examining ongoing auctions (which are accessible through catalog information or through keyword search), starting a new auction, biding in an existing auction and inspecting account activities. The AuctionBot provides only an information service. Registered buyers and sellers give their bids to AuctionBot which determines a resulting allocation as entailed by a well-defined set of auction rules, and notifies the participants.

The AuctionBot simulates the auction process on a central site where the buyers and sellers meet. In other words the marketplace for the AuctionBot is a web site where buyers and sellers are registered. The sellers and buyers first access to the AuctionBot's web site through a web browser and log in to the system, then they can monitor the auctions and bid for auctions in this site.

There is extensive work on the mobile agents which have ability to transfer themselves between the systems that provide an agent server of some kind on a network. This ability lets a mobile agent move to a system that contains an object with which the agent wants to interact, then take the advantage of being in the same host or on the network as the object.

IBM's aglets [IBMAglets, 1998] are an example of a mobile agent technology. Aglet requires a host java application, an "aglet host" to be running on the destination computer. Before the aglet is transferred between the hosts, its current state is saved by using object serialization (which is available in JDK 1.1) to export the state of aglet (image of heap) to stream of bytes. When the aglet is transferred to a new aglet host, aglet host installs a security manager to enforce restrictions on the activities of untrusted aglets. Host uploads aglets through class loaders that know how to retrieve the class files and the state of an aglet from the remote aglet host. The state of the aglet is reconstructed from the stream of bytes and the aglet continues execution where it left of in the new host.

Object Management Group is currently working on the specification of an agent framework to support agent mobility and management, named Mobile Agent Facility (MAF) [MAF, 1998] which is built on top of CORBA, thus providing the integration of traditional client/server paradigm and mobile agent technology. This work will help to ensure that different agent systems are able to work together by using standard MAFAgentSystem and MAFFinder interfaces. There are Mobile Agent Environments already developed in accordance with the MAF standards [Grasshoper, 1998].

One of the earliest examples of an electronic marketplace is Kasbah [Chavez, 1996] where users create autonomous agents that buy and sell goods on their behalf in the marketplace. Kasbah's selling agents are pro-active, they contact interested parties (namely, buying agents) and negotiate with them to find the best deal. A selling agent is autonomous in that, once released into the marketplace, it negotiates and makes decisions on its own, without requiring user intervention. Marketplace's job is to facilitate interaction between the agents by letting buying and selling agents know each other and by ensuring that they speak a common language and use a common terminology to describe the goods.

Another work that can be mentioned in this framework is OFFER which is CORBA based electronic broker, described in [Bichler, 1998]. The business model consists of suppliers, customers and electronic brokers (e-broker). Suppliers and e-brokers offer services which can be accessed over the Internet and which are procured by customers. The interfaces of these services are described in OMG's Interface Definition Language (IDL). Therefore, there is a need in establishing an interface standard on which all suppliers of a certain product category agree.

Suppliers offer an electronic catalog (e-catalog) to the customer; suppliers can also register with the e-broker. The e-broker can either maintain its own database of registered e-catalogs or it can use services of an Object Trader implemented through Trading Object Services of OMG. Hence, a customer can search for a service either directly in the catalog of a supplier or can use the e-broker to search in all the e-catalogs of all the suppliers which are registered with this broker. An IDL interface is specified for the e-catalogs and for the e-broker which they should conform. The electronic broker described supports search in underlying catalogs and it provides a centralized marketplace with the possibility to use an auction mechanism to buy or sell goods.

Knowledge Query and Manipulation Language (KQML)

One of the requirements for software agents to interact and interoperate effectively is a common communication language (*social ability property*). KQML [Finin, 1995] is an agent communication language and a protocol developed by the Knowledge Sharing Effort (KSE) Consortium. It has been developed both as a message format and a message-handling protocol to support run-time knowledge sharing among agents which may have different content languages. It is a communication language which expresses communicative acts and it is different from the content language which expresses facts about the domain. The aim of KQML is to support computer programs in identifying, connecting with and exchanging information with other programs.

KQML language consists of three main layers: the content layer, the message layer, and the communication layer. The content layer contains the actual content of the message in the program's own representation language. This layer enables KQML to carry any message written in any representation language. The communication layer encodes a set of lower level communication parameters to the message like the identity of the sender and recipient and a unique identifier associated with the communication. The message layer is the core of KQML and determines the kinds of interactions one can have with a KQML-speaking agent. It identifies the protocol to be used to deliver the message and supplies a performative which the sender attaches to the content (such as that it is an assertion, a query, a command, or any set of known performatives). The performatives comprise a substrate on which to develop higher-level models of inter-agent interaction such as contract nets and negotiation.

In the following KQML example message John asks score-server about her score.
```
(ask-one:
:sender john
:receiver score-server
```

```
:content (SCORE JOHN ?score)
:reply-with c-score
:language LPROLOG)
```

In this message the KQML performative is ask-one, the content is (score john ?score), the receiver of the message is a server identified as score-server and the query is written in LPROLOG language. The value of the :content keyword is the content level, the values of :reply-with, :sender, :receiver keywords form the communication layer and the performative name (ask-one) with the :language form the message layer. In due time, score-server might send John the following message:

```
(tell
:sender score-server
:content (SCORE John 74 )
: receiver john
:in-reply-to c-score
:language LPROLOG)
```

The set of performatives defined by KSE is extensible. A group of agents may agree on to use additional performatives if they agree on their interpretation and the protocol associated with each.

The message layer also includes optional features which describe the content language, the ontology, and some type of description of the content. These features make it possible for KQML implementations to analyze, route and properly deliver messages even though their content is inaccessible.

Following are the main advantages of KQML as an agent communication language:
- KQML messages are declarative, simple, readable and extensible,
- Since KQML has a layered structure and since KQML messages are unaware of the content of the message they carry, KQML can easily be integrated with other system components,
- KQML imposes no restrictions about the transport protocol and the content language.

In addition to these, KQML has the potential to enhance the capabilities and functionality of large-scale integration and interoperability efforts in communication and information technology such as OMG's CORBA, as well as in application areas like electronic commerce [Finin, 1995].

Extensible Markup Language (XML) and Document Type Definitions (DTDs)

World Wide Web Consortium's (W3C) Extensible Markup Language (XML) [XML, 1998] defines a simple subset of SGML (the Standard Generalized Markup Language). Unlike HTML, which defines a fixed set of tags, XML allows the definition of customized markup languages with application specific tags [Manola, 1998]. That is, XML provides support for the representation of data in terms of attribute/value pairs with user defined tags.

XML differs from HTML in three major respects [Bosak, 1998]:
1. Information providers can define new tag and attribute names at will.
2. Document structures can be nested to any level of complexity.

3. Any XML document can contain an optional description of its grammar for use by applications that need to perform structural validation.

Document Type Definitions (DTD) which are defined for user groups provide a formal definition of documents for that group, that is, they define what names can be used for elements, where they may occur and how they all fit together in an XML file.

The XML working group is currently developing a facility [XMLNames, 1998] that will allow tag names to have a prefix which make them unique and prevent name clashes when developing documents that mix elements from different schemas. XML namespace proposal provides a way to define relationship between the use of particular element name in a document and the standard vocabulary (DTD) from which the name is taken.

As an example, the following XML file (staff.xml) can be used to represent the staff report for a university. The related DTD states that faculties have a NAME attribute and contain department elements. Departments have a NAME attribute and contain a STAFF and a STUD elements. STAFF shows the number of full-time and part-time staff, while STUD gives the number of graduate and undergraduate students.

Staff.xml :

```
<?XML VERSION="1.0" ?>
<!DOCTYPE STAFFREPORT "staff.dtd">
<STAFFREPORT>
<FACULTY NAME="ENG">
<DEPARTMENT NAME="CS">
<STAFF FT="30" PT="10"/>
<STUD G="60" U="300"/>
</DEPARTMENT>
<DEPARTMENT NAME="EE">
<STAFF FT="55" PT="10"/>
<STUD G="70" U="600"/>
</DEPARTMENT>
</FACULTY>
</STAFFREPORT>
```

Staff.dtd

```
<!ELEMENT FACULTY (DEPARTMENT)+>
<!ATTLIST FACULTY NAME CDATA #REQUIRED">
<!ELEMENT DEPARTMENT (STAFF, STUD)>
<!ATTLIST DEPARTMENT NAME CDATA #REQUIRED">
<!ELEMENT STAFF EMPTY>
<!ATTLIST STAFF NAME FT CDATA #REQUIRED">
<!ATTLIST STAFF NAME PT CDATA #REQUIRED">
<!ELEMENT STUD EMPTY>
<!ATTLIST STUD NAME GS CDATA #REQUIRED">
<!ATTLIST STUD NAME US CDATA #REQUIRED">
```

Resource Description Framework (RDF)

As ShopBot's limitations given earlier clearly demonstrated, there is a need for machine understandable information on the Web. An emerging solution to letting automated agents surf the Web is to provide a mechanism which allows a more precise description of the resources that are available on the Web [Lassila, 1998a]. The Resource Description Framework (RDF) [RDF, 1998] by the World Wide Web Consortium (W3C) is a standard for metadata that provides interoperability between applications that exchange machine-understandable information on the Web.

RDF defines both a data model for representing RDF metadata, and an XML-based syntax for expressing and transporting metadata. RDF is a model for representing named properties and their values. These properties serve both to represent attributes of resources and to represent relationship between resources. The RDF data model is syntax independent way of representing RDF expressions and in [RDF, 1998], three representations of the model are given, that is, representation as 3-tuples, as a graph and in XML.

In 3-tuple representation, a property is a three tuple consisting of the resource being described, a property name or type, and a value. A collection of property triples describing the same resource is called an *assertion*. In graph representation, the resources being described and the values describing them are nodes in a directed graph, with the edges being labelled by the property names. An RDF statement can itself be the target node of an arc (i.e., the value of some property) or the source node of an arc (i.e., it can have properties) [Manola, 1998a].

It is clear that RDF will provide the much needed information for the agent technologies working on the Web. RDF can be used not only by the agents for describing their capabilities and negotiating the terminologies used in communication, but also for describing the other resources on the Web.

Document Object Model (DOM)

W3C's Document Object Model (DOM) [DOM, 1998] defines an object-oriented API for HTML and XML documents which a Web client can present to programs that need to process the documents [Manola, 1998b]. DOM represents a document as a hierarchy of objects with proper inheritance relationship among them, called nodes, which are derived (by parsing) from a source representation of a document (HTML or XML). In other words, the DOM object classes represent generic components of a document, and hence define a document object meta model. The major DOM classes are: Node, Document, Element, Attribute, Text, Processing Instruction, and Comment. The representation of a Web page in terms of objects makes it easy to associate code with the various sub-components of the page. For example, Document object has a "documentType" method which returns DTD for XML documents (and "null" for HTML and XML documents without DTDs) and a "getElementsByTagName" method which produces an enumerator that iterates over all Element nodes within the document whose "tagName" matches the input name provided. Thus DOM provides a general means for applications to access and traverse documents written in HTML and XML without having themselves to perform complex parsing.

METU-EMAR ARCHITECTURE

A possible architecture realizing the scenario given initially that uses the technology summarized earlier is described in the following (Figure 1):

The electronic commerce in the marketplace is realized in five phases. Resource Discovery Agents finds out resources on the Web and the selling agents are created in Phase

Figure 1: The Architecture of the METU-Emar

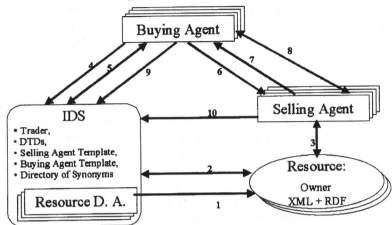

Phase I: 1. RDA find out about Resources and informs owners about METU-EMar.
           2. Resource loads SA template, then configures SA and registers with the trader.
           3. SA accesses Resource through DOM.
Phase II: 4. Buyer contacts with IDS, and gives the name of the item.
           5. Buyer loads BA template, item properties and a list of SAs, then creates and registers BA with the trader.
Phase III: 6. BA asks related SAs about the required item and requests proposals.
           7. SAs respond with their proposals if they sell the required item (Alternatively send negative response).
Phase IV: 8. Parties perform negotiation.
Phase V: 9. BA informs IDS about the completion of the process. IDS removes it from the trader.
           10. SA informs IDS if it is no longer selling the item. IDS remove it from the trader.

I. In Phase II, a buying agent is created for the customer that operates in the marketplace in order to make a purchase. In Phase III, the buying agents contact with the all possible selling agents to determine the ones that can provide the item with required properties. Phase IV contains the negotiation between buying and selling agents. Finally, the result of the transaction is reported to the IDS to make proper updates like deleting the agent that leaves the marketplace from the trader.

PHASE I:

The resource discovery agents working in the background find out about the resources providing products and services. We expect resources to expose their semantics by using the Resource Description Framework (RDF) [Lassila, 1998b] and the Extensible Markup Language (XML) [XML, 1998]. RDF defines both a data model for representing RDF metadata, and an XML-based syntax for expressing and transporting the metadata. Since resources use RDF to expose their metadata, the resource discovery agents do not need intelligence in extracting information from the resources. However, they do have other properties of agents like being autonomous, reactive and proactive.

Resource Discovery Agents contact the owner of the resource by using the means (possibly an e-mail address) available on the resource. If the resource wants to join the marketplace, the owner of the resource accesses to the marketplace's web site through a web browser and marketplace provides it with a template workflow of a selling agent.

Then the owner of the resource (user) configures the workflow agent template by filling the form generated by the template. The form contains information automaticaly extracted from the resource (items or services provided, their prices) and request information from the user (owner of the resource) about the negotiation policy and the desired user interaction characteristics like how and when the user wants to be informed about the progress of the negotiation. On completion of the form, the selling agent is automatically created and registered with the trader of the IDS. If the resource already has a selling agent, this one is registered.

PHASE II:

When a customer wants to make a purchase on the marketplace, s/he connects to the marketplace's web site through a web browser and specifies a service or a product s/he wishes to purchase from the marketplace. The IDS that contains references to the DTDs, accesses to the related Document Type Definitions (DTDs) to obtain names and types of properties of the product. DTDs which are defined for customer groups provide a formal definition of documents for that group, that is, DTDs define what names can be used for elements, where they may occur and how they all fit together in an XML file as described earlier. In our case, all the merchants use the same definition in their DTDs for the item accessed by the selling agent. Therefore, there is no need for a translation among terminologies (which is necessary when XML files have different DTDs and different customers define their own ways of using attribute/value pairs to represent the same information).

Different names can be provided for the same product by the customers, in other words, the customers may not know the standard terms used in DTDs. Therefore, a dictionary of synonyms is necessary in the IDS. This dictionary of synonyms may be implemented to contain some intelligence in the sense that whenever an item or service is not found in the dictionary, the customer may be asked to provide synonyms and these terms can be added to the dictionary for later use.

Then IDS sends a buying agent workflow template, the names and types of the properties of the item and a list of related selling agents to the buyer's site. The customer (user) using the standard forms that is presented to him specifies the desired property values of the item, and the negotiation strategy. Using this information the buying agent is automatically created and registered with the trader.

In filling out the form, the buyer defines all the required properties of the item. Some of those properties may be open to negotiation while the others may not be negotiable. If the property is determined as non-negotiable the selling agents are not allowed to give a proposal that may have a different value than the required one.

PHASE III:

A buying agent contacts all the related selling agents using the list provided by the IDS in Phase II and asks them if they can provide the item with the desired properties and conditions. For example the buying agent which wants to buy a "second hand domestic car" has the list of all the selling agents that sell cars. But only some of them may have the car with desired properties ("second hand" and "domestic").

All the sellers respond to the request of the buyer with the list of proposals for matching items that they sell or send a negative response if their items do not meet the required properties. The proposals contain all the negotiable properties that the sellers offer including the price.

Using the responses from the selling agents and considering the hints and restrictions given by the user, buying agent determines the buying strategy. For example, if a selling agent with a bargaining facility is already giving a lower price than a selling agent without a negotiation facility, the second is eliminated. Such a strategy is also possible for the selling agents. In other words, the buying and selling agents are playing a game where each is trying to satisfy its goals. The buying agents are on the customers' side and the selling agents are on the resources' side.

PHASE IV:

The buying agents go in a direct negotiation with selling agents by sending and receiving proposals. In this respect, RDF is used in encoding resources and query capabilities and KQML [Labrou, 1997] is used to communicate RDF among agents.

The buying and selling agents in the marketplace act autonomously, that is, once released in the marketplace, they negotiate and make decisions on their own, without requiring customer intervention. They are proactive in contacting the other interested agents and reactive to the changes in the marketplace like arrival of new agents.

The resources should provide semantic information about their content to the selling agent. In this respect, the resources should be defined in XML. DOM is used by the selling agents in processing XML pages to obtain specific product data, like the price of the product. The selling agents should be authorized to invoke certain applications at the resource to obtain the bargaining strategy and its parameters which implies that the resources should provide this information through a standard interface.

The negotiation strategies as described in [Chavez, 1996] can be used in the negotiation phase. Several parameters can be specified, like the desired date to sell (buy) the item, desired price, lowest (highest) acceptable price and a decay function if the agent wants to decrease (increase) the price over its given time frame. However, there is a need for more solid bargaining algorithms [Bichler, 1998].

PHASE V:

This phase starts after the successful completion of a negotiation. When the negotiation is complete, the buying agent informs the IDS that it is done. Then the IDS removes the buying agent from the trader. Also in completion of the negotiation, all the items of the selling agent may be sold. In this case the selling agent informs IDS about it and IDS updates the trader.

Initial Configuration of an Agent

The user (buyer or seller) configures the agent template by filling in the form provided by the template. The form includes the questions about Property Parameters, Price Function and User Interaction Characteristics in the negotiation.

Property parameters are used to evaluate a proposal. To be able to compare the received proposals, it is necessary to evaluate a proposal to a numeric value. For this purpose, negotiable properties are assigned with two parameters. First, each property has a user defined weight (over 100) which reflects the comparative importance of the property among other negotiable properties. Second, for the properties whose values lie within a desired range, a function is evaluated that returns a real number between 0 and 1. By multiplying the weight and the result of the function, the value of the property is obtained. By summing up all the property values, the value of the proposal is obtained.

As an example, assume that a user wants to buy a "domestic second hand automobile" and defines the property "year" as negotiable. First, he is asked the weight of the year

Figure 2: The Price Function for Buying Agent

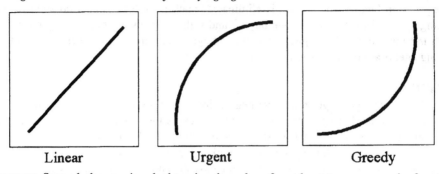

| Linear | Urgent | Greedy |

property. Second, the user is asked to give the values for at least two years and a function type (linear or exponential). Then using a curve fitting algorithm, the function is obtained for the year. For example, user may give 0.8 for the year 1998, 0.4 for the year 1994, and may define function type as linear. In this case, the function becomes (0.1*x - 199), x denoting the year, and the year 1996's value becomes 0.6 (The important point in the function is that: it allways returns a value between 0 and 1)

Price Function is used by the agent to define the buying or selling prices during negotiations. It represents the rate at which agents reduces (selling agent) or increases (buyer agent) the price. As it is in Kasbah [Chavez, 1996] three types of function can be selected (Figure 2).

The User Interaction Characteristics defines how and when the user is to be informed or his interaction is required in negotiation. User selects either e-mail or message-box as a means for being informed. The possible alternatives for informing the user include:

- inform (and wait) at every step,
- inform (and wait) at the last step,
- inform (and wait) when price exceeds a certain value,
- inform (and wait) when time exceeds a certain value.

AGENT ARCHITECTURE

There are three types of agents in the system namely Resource Discovery Agents, Buying and Selling Agents. The resource discovery agents work in the background and find out about resources that may want to join the marketplace. The buying and selling agents, on the other hand perform automated negotiation based on a strategy hinted by the user. The architecture of the resource discovery agents is simpler compared to the buying and selling agents.

Resource Discovery Agents

The resource discovery agents of the IDS are as the name implies responsible for finding the XML resources on the whole Web. This functionality is achieved by searching all the web sites and following the links to find related resources. Since the resources that are acceptable to the marketplace present the metadata about themselves in RDF, the job of resource discovery agents is not complex.

Once resource discovery agents obtain an XML page, the RDF description is accessed and metadata available in the RDF is processed in order to understand the content of the

ing mechanism, finding out about the pieces of a process instance and exerting control on them becomes very inefficient.

Our solution to this problem is as follows: We handle the run time modifications within the scope of a block which nicely fits with the requirements of agents. We exert central control over the activities in the block with a block scheduler which determines the execution sequence of activities within its scope. Yet the sheduling of the blocks within a workflow are distributed.

Hence having central schedulers for blocks facilitates run time modifications on the blocks, and having blocks scheduled in a distributed manner increases the failure resiliency and performance of the system.

Components of Agents

The buying and selling agents in our architecture contain some standard modules as indicated in Figure 3, which are:

1. Communication Manager,
2. Internal Knowledge Repository,
3. External Knowledge Repository, and
4. User GUI.

In our model, agents communicate with each other and with IDS directly by sending and receiving KQML messages. The Communication Manager is responsible for receiving and sending these messages in a convenient and secure way. It contains low level information related to communication and security and provides abstraction to the other modules. It is the communication manager that

- obtains the network addresses of the counter parties from IDS and stores them locally to prevent communication overhead and maps agent ids to the network addresses,
- performs message format conversion that gets KQML messages from the other agents and converts them to internal structure,
- ensures security (if requested) by authentication, and encryption and decryption of the messages. In this respect, the trader can give a pair of keys (public and private) to the agents when they are initially created to be used in the negotiation phase. When the agents are informed about the counter agents they are provided with the public keys of these agents which they can use to encrypt messages to be sent to them and to perform authentication.

It should be noted that when the communication manager is implemented as a separate component, the interagent communication method can be easily modified to CORBA or e-mail by modifiying this component.

The Internal Knowledge Repository stores and provides information about the internal structure of the agent itself. This information contains

- the product information including names, range, desired values and weights for properties and
- strategy information that is used in determining the negotiation strategy, which includes deadlines, price determination function and preferences of the user

Both selling and buying agents keep the state information to be used in determining the negotiation strategy. The External Knowledge Repository stores and provides information about the counterpart agents. This information includes:

- the counterpart agent information such as id, location etc.,
- history of the negotiation for each agent which is exploited in determining negotiation strategy and
- current state for each negotiated item, that is current bid and their evaluated value.

User interaction is critical for the success of the agents. The user GUI is responsible for the interaction between the agent and the user. This interaction involves:

- initial configuration of the workflow,
- monitoring of the progress by the user and
- direct intervention of the user to the negotiation strategy determination activity.

An Alternative: Mobile Agents

An alternative to realize agents is to use mobile agent paradigm. It is obvious that mobile agents can make certain applications easier to develop, or improve reliability and efficiency when used in the proper content. For example in applications that depend on collaboration among a large number of people who are not colocated, people can be represented by mobile agents, gathering in one central location to do their collaboration and then returning home to display details. Another area in which mobile agents may be useful is in processing large amounts of data over low-reliability networks where mobile agents are transferred to the locations that data resides to perform processing and are returned to home to present results [Kinnery, 1998].

In spite of the stated advantages of the mobile agents, they have some drawbacks. Firstly, in order for them to visit a site, the site must run a special agent server software, hence it is not possible to move agents to every site. Secondly, security is a very important issue to consider: when a mobile agent which contains private information moves to another host, one should be certain that its information will not be broken. In our scenario we prefer to use stationary agents rather than mobile agents for the following reasons:

1. Our agents do not perform large amount data processing. Therefore, it is not critical to take advantage of locality during the operations.
2. The selling and buying agents are created by using templates on the sites of buyer or seller. It may not be possible or desirable to load and run the mobile agent host systems on these sites.
3. The buying agents may contain private information such as credit card number, and the owners may not want it to be transferred to another system over the network.
4. The buying and selling agents may require (depending on the desires of the owner) owner interaction which makes it desirable to run the agents on the site of the owners so that they can easily communicate and be monitored through a GUI.

FEASIBILITY

The technological requirement of the architecture proposed is the semantic interoperability of the Web resources. The building blocks for this, although have already been defined or are being defined mostly as standards, are at their infancy. For example, work is underway to define XML-based data exchange formats in both the chemical and the health care communities. A number of industry groups defined SGML DTDs for their documents (e.g. the US Defense Department, which requires much of its documentation to be submitted according to SGML DTDs) [Manola, 1998]. A large US project aims to define specific property names for specific elements in computer industry that can possibly be implemented through XML DTDs [Danish, 1998].

The architecture we describe requires the DTDs for the user groups to be available. Note that since RDF assertions use properties defined in the schemas, the use of RDF also depends on the availability of standard schemas. Until the standard DTDs and RDF schemas become available there is a need for the following modifications in METU-EMar architecture in realizing the proposed scenario:

1. The resource discovery agents utilize machine understandable information (RDF) and therefore can not be implemented easily when the standard vocabulary used by RDF is not available. In this case, resource discovery agents should either be more intelligent or include heuristic techniques to understand the content of the resources.

2. When XML files have different DTDs (i.e., different users define their own ways of using attribute/value pairs to represent the same information), there is a need for a mechanism to identify associations among the terminologies of the XML files. This can be achieved through a translation mechanism between terminologies. This translation is also needed in the negotiation phase among the buying and the selling agents.

Also as stated previously, more solid bargaining algorithms must be developed [Bichler, 1998] to better exploit the scheme described.

ADVANTAGES

It is clear that in a marketplace as large as the one provided by the Web, the service provided by the proposed architecture is invaluable. It will not only help to locate better opportunities for both the buyers and the sellers but it will also save a lot of their time in negotiations. In other words, the proposed marketplace aims to find the best conditions for its clients and help to overcome the limitations of direct communications between customers and suppliers. The marketplace enables the customers to reach various suppliers whose existence they are unaware of and hence it would be impossible for them to reach otherwise. Symmetrically, the marketplace also gives the suppliers the chance to contact to a much wider range of customers.

AN ALTERNATIVE APPROACH TO KQML: CORBA

CORBA together with the Web can also be used as the distribution infrastructure. In this case, all the agents in the system and IDS can be implemented as CORBA objects. Using CORBA as the infrastructure provides the opportunity to use OMG's Trading Object Service as a trader of IDS.

CORBA as Distribution Infrastructure

Web itself and the distributed object platforms like CORBA or Active X/DCOM provide a distribution infrastructure. It is possible to use the Web (HTTP, HTML and Java) in conjunction with an object-oriented "communication bus" following Common Object Request Broker Architecture's (CORBA) Object Request Brokers (CORBA 2.0 and IIOP). Indeed, these sets of technologies constitute the basis of some of the major electronic commerce platforms like Netscape ONE (Open Network Environment), Oracle's NCA (Network Computing Architecture), IBM's CommercePoint and Sun and JavaSoft's Java Electronic Commerce Framework [Tanenbaum, 1997].

Using CORBA 2.0 and IIOP with Web rather than using Web alone provides the following advantages [Orfali, 1997]:

1. In Web, method invocation is realized through HTTP and Common Gateway Interface (CGI) protocol. When this HTTP/CGI layer is replaced by CORBA, since CORBA allows clients to directly invoke methods on a server, a lot of overhead is avoided. Furthermore, any IDL defined method on the server can be invoked and typed parameters can be passed instead of just strings.
2. With CGI, a new instance of a program must be started every time an applet invokes a method on the server. With CORBA, the same server object receives successive calls from the client and preserves the state between these invocations.
3. HTTP/CGI is a stateless protocol, that is, CGI does not maintain information from one form to the next. Therefore, hidden fields within a form are used to maintain state on the client side. CORBA maintains the state between client invocations avoiding this overhead, too.
4. CGI creates a bottleneck because it has no way to distribute the incoming requests across multiple processes and processors. CORBA ORBs on the other hand can create as many server objects as necessary. These server objects can run on multiple servers to provide load balancing for incoming client requests.
5. With CORBA, Java clients and applets can invoke a wide variety of IDL defined operations on the server. In contrast, HTTP clients are restricted to a limited set of operations.
6. CORBA provides a rich set of distributed object services that augment Java, including trader, transactions, security, naming and persistence.

It should be noted that, like HTTP, CORBA's IIOP uses Internet as the backbone. This means that both IIOP and HTTP can run on the same networks.

As a summary, CORBA in conjunction with Web seems to be a very promising infrastructure for electronic commerce applications.

Trading Object Service (TOS) as Trader

The OMG Trading Object Service [OMG, 1996] facilitates the offering and the discovery of instances of services of particular types. A trader is an object that supports the Trading Object Service in a distributed environment. It can be viewed as an object through which other objects can advertise their capabilities and match their needs against advertised capabilities. Advertising a capability or offering a service is called "export". Matching against needs or discovering services is called "import". Export and import facilitate dynamic discovery of, and late binding to, services.

To export, an object gives the trader a description of a service together with the location of an interface at which that service is available. To import, an object asks the trader for a service having certain characteristics. The trader checks against the service descriptions it holds and responds the importer with the location of the selected service's interface. The importer is then able to interact with the service.

Due to the sheer number of service offers that will be available worldwide, and the differing requirements that users of a trading service will have, it is inevitable that a trading service will be split up and that the service offers will be partitioned. Traders in different partitions interact with each other to answer the needs of a client.

Comparison of KQML with CORBA in Communication

CORBA provides the following basic advantages to our architecture:

- CORBA provides simpler communication mechanism among the agents and the IDS compared to KQML which introduces a lot of communication overhead. When the agents and the IDS are defined as CORBA objects, the communication among them can be handled using predefined CORBA interfaces rather than the KQML messages. When communication among the objects is required the objects (agents or IDS) invoke each other's predefined methods using IIOP and passing the parameters instead of sending KQML messages.
- Using CORBA as the infrastructure provides the opportunity to use OMG's Trading Object Service as a trader of IDS. The selling agents of the resources as well as the buying agents can be registered to the related trader objects through the "Register" interface of this service and the buying agents find out about the selling agents through the "Lookup" interface and vice versa. Trading Object Service is distributed in the sense that several traders can be linked through the "Link" interface and can be searched depending on the prespecified policies.

Using CORBA as the infrastructure, on the other hand, requires an ORB at every site of the marketplace which may restrict the scope of the marketplace. Also it may be necessary to provide an ORB specific worklow template.

CONCLUSIONS

The Internet is revolutionizing commerce. However, closed markets that cannot use each other's services, incompatible applications and frameworks that can not interoperate or build upon each other are hampering the progress of electronic commerce [Tanenbaum, 1997].

The need for semantic interoperability of the resources on the Web resulted in a series of standardization efforts from the World Wide Web Consortium. In this paper, we present an electronic marketplace architecture that exploits these standards as well as some other emerging technologies like workflow agents. We also present a workflow agent architecture to meet the demands of buying and selling agents in the marketplace presented.

REFERENCES

AuctionBot (1998) AuctionBot, http://auction.eecs.umich.edu.

Bichler, M., Beam, C., Segev, A (1998). "Offer: A Broker-centered Object Framework for Electronic Requisitioning", in *Proc. of Intl. IFIP Working Conference: Trends in Electronic Commerce,* Hamburg, Germany, June 1998.

Bosak, J. (1998). "XML, Java, and the Future of the Web", http://sunsite.unc.edu/pub/ sun-info/standards/xml/why /xmlapps.html.

Chavez, A.& Maes, P. (1996). "Kasbah: An Agent Marketplace for Buying and Selling

Goods", in *Proc. of the First Intl. Conference on the Practical Application of Intelligent Agents and Multi-Agent Technology*, London, UK, April 1996, http://agents.www.media.mit.edu:80/groups /agents/Publications/kasbah-paam96.ps.

Danish, S.(1998). Personal Communication.

Dogac, A., Gokkoca, E., Arpinar, S., Koksal, P., Cingil, I., Arpinar, B., Tatbul, N., Karagoz, P., Halici, U., Altinel, M.(1998a). *Design and Implementation of a Distributed Workflow Management System: METUFlow,* in (Dogac, 1998b).

Dogac, A., Kalinichenko, L., Ozsu, T., Sheth, A., (Edtrs.) (1998b). *Advances in Workflow Management Systems and Interoperability,* Springer-Verlag.

Document Object Model (DOM) (1998). http://www.w3.org/DOM/.

Doorenbos, R. B., Etzioni, O., Weld, D. S. (1997). "A Scalable Comparison-Shopping Agent for the World Wide Web", *ACM Agents '97 Conference*, 1997.

Extensible Markup Language (XML) (1998). http://www.w3.org/XML/.

Finin, T., Labrou, Y., Mayfield, J.(1995). "KQML as an agent communication language", in Jeffery M. Bradshaw, editor, Software Agents, MIT Press, 1995.

Grasshoper (1998). http://www.ikv.de/products/grasshoper/ architecture.html.

IBMAglets (1998). http://www.trl.ibm.com/aglets/

Kinnery, J. & D. Zimmerman (1997). "A hands-on look at java mobile agents " *IEEE Internet Computing*, August..

Koksal, P., Arpinar, S.& Dogac, A., (1998)."Workflow History Management", *ACM Sigmod Record,* Vol. 27, No. 1, March.

Labrou, Y. & Finin, T.. (1997)."A Proposal for a new KQML Specification", Report TR-97-03, Computer Science and Electrical Engineering Department, University of Maryland Baltimore County. Available on-line as http://www.cs.umbc.edu/jklabrou/publications/tr9703.ps.

Lassila, O. (1998a). "RDF Metadata and Agent Architectures", http://www.objs.com/ workshops/ws9801/papers/paper056.html.

Lassila, O. & Swick, R. R. (1998b)."Resource Description Framework (RDF) Model and Syntax", Working Draft, World Wide Web Consortium. Available on-line as http://www.w3.org/TR/WD-rdf-syntax/.

Mobile Agent Facility (1998). http://www.genmagic.com./agents/MAF.

Manola, F. (1998a)."Towards a Web Object Model", http://www.objs.com/OSA/wom.htm.

Manola, F.,(1998b)."Towards a Richer Web Object Model", *ACM Sigmod Record*, 27(1).

Muth, P., Weissenfels, J. & Weikum, G. (1998)."What Workflow Technology Can Do for Electronic Commerce", in *Current Trends in Data Management Technology*, Dogac, A., Khosrowpour, M., Ozsu, T., Ulusoy, O., (Edtrs.), Idea Group Publishing, 1999.

Orfali, R. & Harkey, D.(1997). *The Essential Client/Server Programming with JAVA and CORBA*, John Wiley.

OMG's Trading Object Service (1996). OMG Document orbos/96-05-06, Version 1.0.0, May 10, 1996.

Tanenbaum, J. M.(1997)."Eco System: An Internet Commerce Architecture", *IEEE Computer,* 30(5), May.

Resource Description Framework (RDF) (1998). http://www.w3.org/Metadata/RDF.

Woolridge, M., & Jennings, N (1995)."Intelligent Agents- Theory and Practice", *Knowledge Engineering Journal,* June 1995.

XMLNames (1998). http://www.w3.org/TR/1998/NOTE-xml-names-0119.

some core business process information, like activities, resources, control information, flow of data and organizational structure, which has to be modeled at both modeling levels. Information like execution time and cost of each activity, activity waiting time, cost of people, laws governing the organization etc. is information captured in the model at the re-engineering level. Information like information technology required, details about the working environment and any other information necessary for the implementation of the business process is captured in the workflow model at the automation level, see figure 1. More about business process modeling may be found in (Tsalgatidou & Junginger, 1995)

Popular tools supporting the modeling, re-engineering and automation of a business process are *Business Process Modeling Tools (BPMT)* and *Workflow Management Systems (WFMS)*. More specifically:

- *BPMT* aim at the development of business process models for management, documentation or re-engineering purposes. They focus on capturing and modeling details that are essential for business process analysis and simulation, like for example, time, cost, resources, etc., the results of which can then be used for business process re-engineering and subsequent automation (examples of BPMT are the ARIS Toolset (IDS-Scheer, 1997), the Workflow-BPR (Holosofx, 1997), the Workflow Analyzer (Metasoftware, 1997) or the Process Wise (ICL & Fujitsu, 1997) to name a few).
- *WFMS* aim at the development and subsequent automation of workflow models and thus, they differ in the level of detail their scope is located and their focus of attention: whilst BPMT focus on higher-level chunks of business operations and their re-engineering, the WFMS aim mainly at transferring the process models (usually developed previously by BMPT) in real-world settings. In order to accomplish that, they may interoperate with databases, LANs, document handling and imaging systems, legacy applications, etc. (examples of WFMS are the FlowMark (IBM, 1997), Visual Workflow

Figure 1: Business Process Modeling for Re-engineering and Automation Purposes

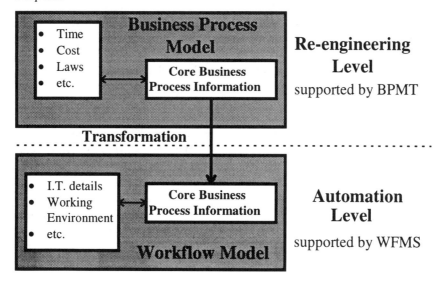

(FileNet, 1997), InConcert (InConcert, 1997) etc.)

Therefore, it seems that an organization, in order to successfully support the whole business process lifecycle (from modeling of a process to its automation), needs to use appropriate BPMT and WFMS tools. A very important issue that arises here is the integration between BPMT and WFMS so that business process models developed by a BPMT can be then transformed in workflow models and utilized by a WFMS. We call this issue vertical interoperability which is one of the main criteria for selecting appropriate tools. This, along with other criteria, which are based on the above intended functionality of BPMT and WFMS and can assist in the selection of appropriate commercial tools, are presented in the following section.

Criteria for Selecting BPMT and WFMS

The criteria are classified into the following categories: *user interface, modeling, analysis and validation, technical and process automation aspects.* They are presented as follows: in each category, the requirements concerning both categories of tools are presented first; these are then followed by a description of requirements specific for BPMT or WFMS, if any. The first three sets of criteria concern both categories of tools and mainly BPMTs while the automation aspects mainly concern WFMS.

User Interface Aspects

Requirements on user interface aspects can be classified into two categories: user interface requirements related to users and user interface requirements related to machines.

• *User Interface Requirements related to users*

These concern mainly the provision of a highly interactive and graphical user interface (GUI), which, in the current state of the art is more or less a truism. However, the provision of a GUI does not imply that all aspects of the process analysis and design can be carried out graphically. It is usually the case that a broad solution can be graphically designed, while the details must be filled in using some kind of high level programming language scripts. Therefore, an additional requirement for *entire GUI definition* is set here. Support for efficient *GUI navigation* in the process models produced is also required. This support must be in accordance with the conceptual modeling mechanisms provided by the tool. *End user customization* facilities should also be provided.

• *Machine Related User Interface Requirements*

Portability and *Adaptability* of the user interfaces are key issues here. Given the fact that the hardware infrastructure of business environments consists of diverse hardware architectures and operating systems and that a large number of employees is likely to access business computing resources from different access points, e.g. desktop PCs, portable PCs, etc., the user interface should be portable across these diverse access points. This should affect neither the functionality of the interface itself nor its user friendliness. Portable languages such as Sun's Java Programming Language combined with CGI techniques enable the fulfillment of this criterion. Furthermore, given the ongoing increase of interest for intranet related technologies, it is highly unlikely that BPMT and WFMS will escape the need to adapt to business intranets. As intranets promote the interoperability of diverse software platforms and since an increasing number of intranet applications provide a Web accessible gateway, it is a natural consequence that the user interface of the tools this chapter is dealing with, should be adaptable to the changing intranet environment. The possibility of dynamically downloading user interfaces from central interface repositories should not be excluded as an option.

Modeling Aspects

- *Modeling Philosophy.* The modeling philosophy employed by a tool is often advertised as the major feature of a BPMT. Actually, the model provided is the single most important founding principle of a BPMT since all analysis and subsequent benefits provided by a tool are based on the model expressiveness and its properties. For example, if a process is not accurately modeled in a BPMT, no analysis facilities can serve any useful purpose. Additionally, a BPMT without sufficient modeling depth can be counter-productive, since conclusions will be reached based on incomplete or inaccurate information. The Conversation for Action Model (Winograd & Flores, 1987) used in the Action Workflow (Medina-Mora et al, 1992), Petri Nets (Tsalgatidou et al, 1996) or some form of data flow diagrams (DeMarco, 1979) enriched with control information, are popular approaches. Assuming that BPMTs are used to model business processes and that BPMT and WFMS interoperate, the role of WFMS in workflow modeling is limited, since either the entire workflow model or a significant part of it is usually performed at the BMPT.

- *Conceptual modeling mechanisms.* Business process and workflow modeling results in the construction of conceptual models of a given part of reality. Hence, requirements on conceptual modeling tools apply to BPMT & WFMS as well, the most prevalent of which being: abstraction mechanisms (classification, aggregation, generalization/ specialization) and structuring mechanisms (for example, a model may be structured in terms of the processes investigated, the stakeholders involved, etc.).

- *Flexible and explicit time modeling.* Despite long and intense efforts, time has proved especially difficult to be effectively modeled; the repeated attempts of the database community bear witness to this. BPMT & WFMS could not be an exception; thus, a fitting representation of time, along with constraints, precedences and antecedences is invariably needed in business process and workflow modeling.

- *Model annotations.* No modeling formalism can capture all relevant details and pertinent facts. Process models often need to be annotated with extra-model information such as designer comments and rationale, analysis and validation statements, etc.

- *Organizational structure modeling.* The modeling of human resources in a business process as simple agents may not be enough for conveying all relevant information. A more rigorous modeling of the organizational structure is in need, encompassing entities such as departments, actors, roles and so forth. The resulting organization models must be suitable for integration with the process models per se, so that, actor participation in specific activities, actor permissions on specific resources, along with more general security specifications, could be specified accordingly.

- *Resource modeling.* Resources can be modeled simply as input and/or outputs of process steps. A more economic and comprehensive approach is to create a model of the resources in use, for example creating a document type ontology, placing documents in a hierarchy, etc.

- *Representation of control, data and materials*. Representation of data flow as well as materials and control flow among process steps is essential.
- *Flow type*. Most existing BPMT & WFMS are built around a sequential process paradigm (sequential flow), that is, process steps are modeled as following each other in a well-ordered succession. This usually fails to capture the dynamics of a real business environment. Although no final propositions have been made, some rule-based formalisms (rule-based flow) do offer a plausible alternative.

Analysis and Validation

- *Business process and workflow models should be formal, or amenable to formal analysis, for static analysis and validation*. Static analysis and validation of a model refer to the study of the derived models using specific algorithms and analysis approaches (not simulation). Such analysis and validation should be able to derive results on process metrics, identification of constraints and resource cost evaluation, among others. This entails some kind of mathematical formalism along which the relevant models are structured. Absence of such a foundation does not render static analysis and validation infeasible; they are, however, more difficult to use and more dependent on ad hoc approaches. Analytical tools used by BPMT usually include: case analysis, weighted average analysis, critical path analysis, throughput analysis, resource utilization, value chain analysis and activity based costing.
- *Executable business process and workflow models for dynamic analysis and validation*. Dynamic validation refers to the study of the derived models by way of their dynamic behavior. Simulation of the model specification is the main approach used for dynamic validation. By varying rates of input a BPMT can simulate activities and assess performance issues, such as bottlenecks in a process. Procedures can then be developed based on these simulations to successfully plan for and manage uncontrollable variations of input. What-if analysis and if-what analysis of changes in business process and workflow models should also be provided. Most WFMS provide workflow process animation tools but depend on external BPMT for simulation and analysis. Therefore, the sophistication of analysis and simulation provided by BPMT as well as the degree of integration and interoperability between BPMT and WFMS have a direct impact on the ability to validate and evaluate workflow process models.

Technical Aspects

- *Vertical Interoperability*. As discussed in the second section, one of the major objectives of BPMT, apart from assisting the re-engineering process, is to provide for implementation and automation of business processes through integration with WFMS. For example, consider a situation where the business process model used by a BPMT is different than the workflow process model utilized by a WFMS. In such a case, their integration involves filtering business process model objects, validating the resulting workflow process model and placing it in the representation used by the WFMS engine. Therefore, BPMT must export and possibly translate their process definitions to WFMS or share process models and definitions with WFMS. More detailed discussion on this may be found in (Georgakopoulos & Tsalgatidou, 1998).
- *Horizontal Interoperability*. At the business process modeling level, this refers to the ability of the product to handle models created by other BPMT. At the workflow level,

this refers to the interoperability between various WFMS and between WFMS and various heterogeneous systems participating in the workflow process. Connectivity to database systems used in the organisation as well as to mainframes is also required here. Furthermore, interoperability at the workflow level requires additional technology and standards that exploit and extend current industry solutions for interoperability, such as those developed by the Object Management Group and the World Wide Web Consortium.

- *Object-Oriented Toolset.* The usefulness of object orientation in process modeling rests in its potential for developing intuitive and economical conceptual models of the real world. An object-oriented toolset should provide the ability to model processes, resources and organization structure in an object-oriented framework, thus reducing redundancy and enhancing re-use of model components.

- *Process Models Repository.* All business process modeling tools offer some kind of repository for storing and retrieving the constructed models. The functionality offered by such repositories may vary considerably, ranging from simple storage schemes to full database management systems. In the case of an object-oriented toolset, an underlying object-oriented database can improve the tool's capabilities and consolidate smoothly conceptual models and physical storage. Actually, the repository is a critical component in such systems and often distinguishes between a system that can be used in business production and one that simply cannot. Important issues here are concurrency control, recovery and advanced transactions. Therefore, it seems that there must be a database management system as part of the WFMS, even if this increases the cost of the system.

- *Integration with other tools.* Communication software (like, for example, mail systems) becomes an indispensable component of corporate-wide networking. Smooth integration between workflow and communication tools should therefore be demanded. This has actually been followed in cases where companies sell workflow products to be embedded in a larger communication system, thus viewing flow of work as a special kind of communication-coordination among agents. Interoperability with other similar product families (e.g. document management systems, text retrieval or imaging systems, editing tools, fax, or payment packages if we are talking about electronic commerce applications, etc.), is required, too.

- *API Support.* Although graphical specifications of workflow are user friendly and usually effective, the need for fine tuning or a more detailed specification than the one carried out graphically frequently arises. APIs can also be used to introduce specialized user interfaces or tools to meet specific application requirements. Furthermore, APIs can promote integration of favorable functionally equivalent components. For example, if the WFMS cooperates with a word processor, this should not be necessarily provided as part of the WFMS, but, instead, provide APIs for integrating the word processor the customer prefers. Workflow vendors provide APIs to accommodate such needs. Such APIs can be judged in terms of comprehensiveness, ease of use, libraries provided, etc.

- *Concurrency Control, Recovery and Advanced Transactions.* WFMS should support concurrency control and recovery. These are well understood issues in database and transaction processing products, but current approaches followed by WFMS (e.g. check-in/check-out, pass-by-reference/pass-by-value, etc.) are primitive when compared to the concurrency support provided by database management systems.

- *Robustness and Availability.* Continuous availability of WFMS is crucial especially for critical systems. WFMS should be resilient to failures and provide mechanisms for backup and efficient recovery. According to (Alonso et al, 1997), the lack of robustness and the very limited availability constitute one of the major limitations of existing WFMS, which lack the redundancy and flexibility necessary to replace failed components without having to interrupt the function of the system. Therefore, special attention should be paid on this aspect when selecting a WFMS.

- *High Volume Processing, Performance and Scalability.* High volume processing is a key requirement for WFMS. Many business processes require handling of a large number of workflow instances. Performance of a WFMS should be independent of the workload in the sense that many workflow instances could be created and processed when needed, without penalties to system performance. The use of more powerful computers may not necessarily yield corresponding improvements in WFMS throughput. Therefore, scalability of the workflow engine (server) and worklist handler to deal with load balancing is an important requirement.

- *General Requirements.* Both BPMT and WFMS share some requirements in common with most industrial-strength software products, such as availability in specific platforms usually encountered in business environments. UNIX, Windows NT, OS/2 or AIX are among the most popular server platforms, while Windows95 is the platform usually encountered to clients. Compliance to industry standards (e.g. (WfMC, 1997), CORBA (Object Management Group, 1997) etc.), version update and customer support, ready case studies and product maturity is also required.

Process Automation Requirements

These requirements concern mainly WFMS used for the automation of business processes and are the following:

- *Work-in-Process Tracking.* All objects of a workflow must be monitored by the system so that the process status is visible to management whenever required.

- *Automatic Resource Allocation.* This refers to an intelligent balancing of work among different employees, depending on particular persons' or groups' work load and responsibilities. This may, for example, involve task monitoring and "pushing" tasks to employees as well as identification of inactive human resources.

- *Manual Resource Allocation.* It is clear that automatic resource allocation cannot be a surrogate for human control; the complexity of an organizational setting, along with the exigencies of a competitive business environment often require human intervention. Such intervention may take the following forms: "pull applications" (employees may choose their next piece of work from a pool of tasks) to be completed, negotiation of work among people in the organization (including the exchange of allocated work chunks, the splitting and/or sharing of work among related agents, etc.) and assignment of specific tasks to specific employees (usually carried out by the management).

- *Security.* Permissions must be potentially granted for initiating workflow processes, viewing status reports, re-routing a document, end-user customization, etc.

- *Statistics.* Already hinted at above, comprehensive statistical measures and status reports are indispensable for giving a clear and succinct picture of workflow execution. Such statistics and execution data should be possible to be fed back to BPMT and facilitate process evaluation and improvement.

- *Information Routing.* At least two kinds of information routing can be discerned: static routing which involves information transfer from one person to the next according to a predefined schedule (and cannot be altered at will while in operation) and dynamic routing which attempts to bring feedback concepts and responsiveness to information flow; techniques (like rule-based routing related to specific events) may be used to describe not a mere sequential list of actions, but situations along with the system responses.

- *Parallel Processing.* A prerequisite for modern multi-user systems, parallel processing allows work to be routed to multiple queues or in-baskets for simultaneous processing by distinct agents; priority and version control is essential, as well as handling of multi-user access problems, also encountered in the database community.

- *Document Rendezvous.* The term refers to the automatic matching of new incoming documents with existing documents, pertaining to them, already in the workflow; the resulting set of documents is then clipped together before being routed to the next action step.

- *Setting and Handling of Deadlines.* This can refer to setting and handling deadlines for task completion (task deadline), or for the termination of a specific activity carried out by a specific employee (employee deadline).

- *Tracing and Reporting.* Generation of reports with data about the business process from different perspectives (e.g. from enterprise perspective, resource flow perspective or from an activity perspective including scheduling and costing information) are very useful for analysis of the business process at hand and for re-engineering purposes. Such reports can also be used for business process documentation, management presentations, user training or ISO 9000 certification and should be provided by BPMTs. Furthermore, workflow monitoring facilities should be provided by WFMS, in order to give information about workflow execution and illustrate which activities are currently active, by whom they are performed, priorities, deadlines, duration and dependencies. Such data are very useful as they can be fed back to BPMT and facilitate process evaluation and improvement. Reporting involving OLAP (On-Line Analytical Processing) tools, in case they are integrated with the WFMS, is also critical, as it helps managers to make critical decisions based on the comprehensive facts of their business.

CONCLUSIONS

Successful business process re-engineering and automation in an organization is dependent on the selection of appropriate supporting software tools. This chapter attempted to give a description of the intended functionality of supporting tools and subsequently provide a set of criteria to help the interested engineer to select appropriate BPMT and WFMS among the diversity of tools offered by software vendors. It has to be mentioned that we could not have aimed, nor have achieved, a perfect or complete set of requirements. The result can be therefore judged in terms of pragmatics; that is, its utility to the users, purchasers and researchers in the area. Being the outcome of our own involvement in the field, we believe that the experience gained will be of help to others.

ACKNOWLEDGMENT—The author would like to thank Panos Louridas, currently a Ph.D. candidate at UMIST, Manchester, UK, for his contribution in this work.

REFERENCES

Alonso, G, Agrawal, D., El Abbadi & Mohan, C. (1997). Functionality and Limitations of *Current Workflow Management Systems*, Technical Report, http://www.inf.ethz.ch/personal/alonso/workflow_list.html.

Davenport, T.H. & Short, J.E. (1990). The New Industrial Engineering: Information Technology and Business Process Redesign. *Sloan Management Review*, Summer 1990, pp. 11-27.

DeMarco, T. (1979). *Structured Analysis & System Specification*. Englewood Cliffs, London: Prentice Hall.

Dogac, A., Kalinichenko, L., Oszu, T. & Sheth, A. (Eds.). (1998). *Workflow Management Systems and Interoperability*, NATO ASI Series F, Springer-Verlag.

Enix (1997). *Behaviour Modelling Techniques for Organisational Design*. http://www.enix.co.uk/behmod.htm.

FileNet (1997). http://www.filenet.com.

Georgakopoulos, D., Hornick, M., Sheth, A. (1995). An Overview of Workflow Management: From Process Modeling to Workflow Automation Infrastructure. *Distributed and Parallel Databases,* vol. 3, pp. 119-153.

Georgakopoulos, D. & Tsalgatidou, A. (1998). *Technology and Tools for Comprehensive Business Process Lifecycle Management*. In (Dogac et al, 1998).

Hammer, M. (1990). Re-engineering Work: Don't Automate, Obliterate. *Harvard Business Review*, July-August 1990, pp. 104-112.

Holosofx (1997). http://www.holosofx.com.

IBM (1997). http://www.software.ibm.com.

ICL & Fujitsu, (1997). http://www.process.icl.net.co.uk

IDS-Scheer, (1997). http://www.ids-scheer.de.

InConcert, (1997). http://www.inconcertsw.com.

Jacobson, I., Ericsson, M, Jacobson, A., (1995). *The Object Advantage: Business Process Re-engineering with Object Technology*. ACM Press.

Medina-Mora, R., Winograd, T., Flores, R. & Flores F. (1992). The Action Workflow Approach to Workflow Management Technology. *Proceedings of CSCW 92*, Nov. 1992, pp. 281-288.

Metasoftware (1997). http://www.metasoftware.com.

Object Management Group (1997). http://www.omg.com.

Schlueter, C. & Shaw, M. 1997. A Strategic Framework for Developing Electronic Commerce, *IEEE Internet Computing,* 1 (6), pp. 20-28.

Tsalgatidou, A. & Junginger, S. (1995). Modeling in the Re-engineering Process. ACM SIGOIS Bulletin, 16 (1), pp. 17-24.

Tsalgatidou, A., Louridas, P., Fesakis, G. & Schizas, T. (1996). Multilevel Petri Nets for Modeling and Simulating Organizational Dynamic Behaviour, *Simulation & Gaming,* Special Issue on Simulation of Information Systems, 27 (4), pp. 484-506.

WfMC (1997). http://www.aiai.ed.ac.uk/WfMC/index.htm.

Winograd, T. & Flores, F. (1987). *Understanding Computers and Cognition: A New Foundation for Design,* Addison-Wesley.

CHAPTER 5

A Taxonomy
for Object-Oriented Queries

David Taniar, RMIT University, Australia
J. Wenny Rahayu, La Trobe University, Australia

A comprehensive study of object-oriented queries gives not only an understanding of full capability of object query language, but also a direction for query processing and optimization. Why another taxonomy? The answer is that none of the existing object-oriented query taxonomy covers all aspects of object data model, which includes not only classes/objects and association (complex objects), but also inheritance and collection types. In this chapter, we present a comprehensive study on object-oriented queries. Our taxonomy for object-oriented queries basically consists of basic and complex queries. Basic queries include single-class queries, inheritance queries, path expression queries, and explicit join queries. Complex queries (i.e. cyclic queries, semi-cyclic queries, and acyclic-complex queries) are formed by a composition of basic query components.

INTRODUCTION

Query is an important part of any Database Management Systems (*DBMS*) (Bertino et al., 1992). Due to this importance, most Object-Oriented Database Systems (*OODB*) provide a querying capability through a query language. A standard body for object databases, *ODMG*, has formulated a standard query language for OODB, called Object Query Language (*OQL*). OQL is based on an object data model, which includes classes/objects, inheritance, association relationships, and collection types. Most existing object query model focuses on different part of object model. Some models exploits classes, methods, and path expressions, whilst others may concentrate on join and other aspects of objects. It is the aim of this chapter to present a comprehensive study of object-oriented queries. Our query model is based on not only classes/objects and path expressions (association relationships), but also inheritance and collection types.

Querying is an activity of retrieval and manipulation of a database. The manipulation operations basically include insertion, update, and delete. These operations normally focus on single entities (tables in relational databases or classes in object-oriented databases). On the other hand, retrieval operations are much more complex as they may involve multiple entities. This retrieval process is often used in conjunction with update, delete, and insert. Our query taxonomy concentrates on the retrieval process only. The study of retrieval processes is very much influenced by query optimization. It is a fact that there may be many access plans for a particular retrieval process. Therefore, the study of retrieval process often becomes the foundation of query optimization.

THE REFERENCE OBJECT MODEL

The object model adopted by most *Object-Oriented Database* (OODB) systems includes the concepts of *class and object, inheritance*, and *complex object* (Cattell, 1994; Kim, 1990, Bertino and Martino, 1993). The following sections introduce each of these concepts briefly.

Classes and Objects

It is important to distinguish between classes and objects. A *class* is a description of a set of objects, whilst *objects* are instances of a class (Coad and Yourdon, 1991; Meyer, 1988). In other words, A class defines a set of possible objects. A class has two aspects: *type* (attributes and applicable methods) and *container* of objects of same type.

An *object* is a data abstraction defined by a unique object identifier (*OID*), valued attributes (instance variables) which give a state to the object, and methods (operations) which access the state of the object (Coad and Yourdon, 1991; Meyer, 1988). Objects of the same class have common operations as well as uniform behaviour.

An *OID* is an invariant property of an object, which distinguishes it logically and physically from all other objects. An OID is therefore unique. Two objects can be equal without being identical (Masunaga, 1990). The state of an object is actually a set of values of its attributes. Methods are specified as operations, which are defined in the class that describe the object. The specified methods are the only operations that can be carried out on the attributes in the object. The client of the object cannot change the state (attributes) except by method invocation. Thus, an object encapsulates both state and operations.

Consider the following as an example of class and object. *Proceedings* is a class, and it consists of a list of attributes, such as *title, venue, dates*, etc; and a list of methods, such as *acceptance_rate*, etc. Objects of class Proceedings include *VLDB'98, ICDE'98, OOPSLA'98*, etc (assume that these are OIDs that uniquely identify each object).

Inheritance

Inheritance is one of the most important concepts in object-oriented technology, as it provides a mechanism for reusing some parts of an existing system (Meyer, 1988). Inheritance is a relation between classes that allows for the definition and implementation of one class to be based on other existing classes. Inheritance can be of type *extension* or *restriction* (Meyer, 1988). An extension inheritance is where a sub-class has all properties (i.e., attributes and methods) of the super-class and may have additional properties as well. In other words, a sub-class is more specialized than the super-class. In contrast, a restriction inheritance is where a sub-class inherits *some* properties of a super-class. This can be done by selecting the properties of the super-class to be inherited by its sub-class. In either type, some methods of a super-class may be redefined in a sub-class to have a different implementation.

If several classes have considerable commonality, it can be forced out in an *abstract* class (Coad and Yourdon, 1991). An abstract class is a class without any instances. The differences are provided in several sub-classes of the abstract class. An abstract class provides only partial implementation of a class or no implementation at all. The union of instances of its sub-classes gives a total representation of the abstract class.

A sub-class may inherit from more than one super-class; this is known as *multiple inheritance* (Meyer, 1988). Multiple inheritance sometimes causes method/attribute-naming conflicts. Method conflicts can be solved by either *renaming* or *restricting* one of the conflicted methods.

Inheritance raises the issue of polymorphism (Meyer, 1988). In general, polymorphism refers to the ability of an object to take more than one form. This means that an object declared to be of a class is able to become attached to an object of any descendant class. This kind of object is said to be polymorphic. For example, suppose class *Research_Paper* inherits from class *Journal_Paper*. Subsequently, objects of class *Research_Paper* are also objects of class *Journal_Paper*.

Complex Objects and Collections

Objects are said to be complex objects when they are built from complex data structures. The *domain* of an attribute/method can be of *simple* or *complex* data types. Simple data types are atomic types which include integer, real, string, etc; whereas, complex data types may include *structures*, *objects*, and *collections*. These complex data types give an object an ability to include other objects to form a complex object.

Some structure types are built into the system, eg, *Date(dd,mm,yy)*, *Money($, cents)*, etc. The ability to construct new structures manifests the concept of encapsulation in an object-oriented paradigm.

A complex data type may be built by nesting class-domain attributes. This is possible by having the domain of attribute of another class. These attributes are often known as relationship attributes (Cattell, 1994). A relationship between two classes *C1* and *C2* is established if one of the attributes of *C1* has *C2* as its domain. If the reverse is applied, the association is called an *inverse relation* (Cattell, 1994). For example, an association between class *Book* and class *Publisher* occurs when attribute *publisher* of class *Book* has class *Publisher* as the domain. An inverse relationship occurs when an attribute *book* of class *Publisher* has a domain of a set of *Book*.

Another complex data type is a collection data type. This is another unique feature in OODB; that is attributes of a class can be of a collection type. Collection types are introduced by ODMG (Cattell, 1994). The following sections briefly explain collection types and collection operations.

Collection Types

The main characteristic of a collection type is that an attribute value contains a collection of objects that may be structured, such as a list or an array, or unstructured, such as a set or a bag (Rahayu et al., 1995). The proposed object database standard, *ODMG*, also includes the definitions as well as the operations to manipulate these collection types in an OODB environment (Cattell, 1994). The collection types considered here are *sets*, *lists*, *arrays*, and *bags*.

Sets are basically unordered collections that do not allow duplicates. Each object that belongs to a set is unique. *Lists* are ordered collections that allow duplicates. The order of the elements in a list is based on the insertion order or the semantic of the elements. *Arrays* are one-dimensional arrays with variable length, and allow duplicates. The main difference between a list and an array is in the method used to store the pointers that assign the next element in the list/array. Because this difference is mainly from the implementation point of view, lists and arrays will have the same treatment in this chapter. A *bag* is similar to a set except for allowing duplicate values to exist. Thus, it is an unordered collection that allows duplicates. For example, an attribute *author* of class *Book* has a collection of *Person* as its domain. Because the order of persons in the attribute *author* is significant, the collection must be of type *list*. In other words, the type of the attribute *author* is *list of Person*. This example shows that the domain can be a collection, not only a single value or a single object.

Collection Operations

Collection operations include construction, conversion, binary operations, extraction, and Boolean expressions. Collections can be constructed by calling a constructor of each collection type accompanied by the elements of the collection. If the collection is a list or an array, the order of the elements in the construction determines the actual order of the elements in the collection. It is also allowed to create an empty collection by inserting a *nil* value as its only element. The following are some examples of collection constructions.

set (1, 2, 3)	creates a set of three elements: 1, 2, 3.
set (nil)	creates an empty set.
list (1, 2, 2, 3)	creates a list of four elements.
array (3, 4, 2, 1, 1)	creates an array of five elements.
bag (1, 1, 2, 3, 3)	creates a bag of five elements.

Collection types also provide a mechanism for conversion. Basically, there are three forms of conversion: converting from one form of collection to another, extracting an element of a collection, and flattening nested collections into one-level collections. The type conversion hierarchy is *List, Bag*, then *Set*. Conversion from a list to a bag is to loosen up the semantic ordering, whereas further conversion from a bag to a set is to remove duplicates. In other words, the conversion hierarchy represents the strictness level of collection types. Converting a set into a bag does not add or change any semantic. It is sometimes carried out merely for programming convenience.

Collection extraction can be done only if the collection contains one element only; otherwise an exception will be raised. As the elements of a collection can be those of other collections, flattening them into a collection is sometimes required. The following are some examples of collection conversion operations.

listtoset (list(1, 2, 3, 2))

element (list(1))

flatten (list (set (1,2,3), set (3,4,5,6))

The list_to_set example converts the list into a set containing 1, 2, and 3. The element operation above returns an atomic value of 1. And the flatten operation gives a set of 1, 2, 3, 4, 5, and 6.

Most collection operations are *binary* operations. The operations take two collections as the operand and produce another collection as a result. Basic sets/bags operations include *union, except*, and *intersect*. These are common collection operations widely known in set theory (Norris, 1985), which are then well adopted by object-orientation. To illustrate these operations, the following examples are given.

set (4,5,3,6) *union* set (7,5) = set (4,5,3,6,7)

set (4,5,3,6) *except* set (7,5) = set (4,3,6)

set (4,5,3,6) *intersect* set (7,5) = set (5)

Since sets do not allow duplicate values to exist, duplicate removal is incorporated in the *union* operator.

Operations on lists/arrays are usually to extract elements based on a specific index or a range of indexes. Some examples are as follows.

list (5,4,5,3) [1] = 4

list (5,4,5,3) [0:2] = (5,4,5)

When the index (indicated by a square bracket) is a single value, like the first example above, the list operation returns the element pointed by the index. The index numbering starts from zero. Therefore, the first list operation above retrieves the second element of the list. On the other hand, if the index forms a range (indicated by a colon between two indices, as in the second list example above), the list operation retrieves a range of elements specified by the index range. In the second list operation above, it retrieves a sub-collection of the list, which is ranging from the first to the third elements.

Collection expressions are to include standard boolean expressions, such as *universal quantifiers* (for all), *existential quantifiers* (exists), and *memberships* (in). The results of invoking these expressions are boolean values. Therefore, these expressions can be used as join predicates. The following shows some examples of collection expressions.

for all x in Conference: x.AcceptanceRate < 0.5

exists x in Paper: x.Author.Country = "Australia"

"PhD" in Qualification

The for all example above returns true if *all* the objects in the Conference collection have an acceptance rate below 50%. In contrast, the exists operation above returns true if *at least* one paper is written by someone who had worked in Australia. Finally, the in operation returns true if PhD is an *element* in the qualification collection.

A HIERARCHY OF OBJECT-ORIENTED QUERY

Based on their schemas, object-oriented query (OOQ) can be classified into two major categories: *Basic queries* and *Complex queries*. Basic queries mainly consist of *Single-Class* queries, *Inheritance* queries, *Path Expression* queries, and *Explicit Join* queries. These basic query types are the basic building block for more general and complex queries. *Complex queries*, made up of basic query components, can be classified into *Cyclic* queries, *Semi-Cyclic* queries, and *Acyclic-complex* queries. The relationship between these types of query is shown in Figure 1. The classification forms an "is_a" hierarchy. For example, all features of single-class queries are applicable to inheritance, path expression and explicit join queries; and further complex queries may use the features of the basic queries.

Queries are normally expressed in a non-procedural language, e.g., SQL. An object-oriented version of SQL, i.e., OQL (Cattell, 1994), is becoming a standard query language for object-oriented queries. An initial step of query processing is parsing and transforming the query written in a query language into its internal representation. A graphical notation is often used to show the internal representation of a query. The graphical notation for an object model is composed of two basic symbols: *nodes* and *arcs*. Nodes represent classes

Figure 1: Object-Oriented Query Classification

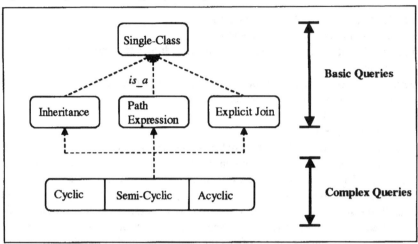

(abstract classes are represented as dotted nodes), whereas arcs represent relationships. Inheritance relationships are shown by dotted directed arcs from a sub-class to a super-class, and composition relationships are denoted by directed arcs. If an inverse relationship exists in the composition, the direction of the arc is bi-directional. Nodes may have labels. The label inside a node is a class name; a few important attributes may be shown underneath or beside the node. The label of an arc represents a relationship name between the two nodes. This relationship is actually the attribute name, which holds the relationship between the two classes. In the case where a collection type is used, a notation of { }, [], <> are used to represent sets, lists/arrays, and bags, respectively. The () notation is used to represent a structure.

Database schemas are represented as a complete relationship of classes. This network of classes shows all necessary information about classes, attributes, methods, inheritance, and relationships. As a running example, a simplified version of "Research Reference Library" is used. Figure 2 shows this database schema.

A query schema can be viewed as a sub-graph of a database schema. Additionally, a query schema contains some other information, such as σ(selection), π(projection), $\exists$(existential quantifier), $\forall$ (universal quantifier), etc.

BASIC QUERIES

Object-oriented queries are queries that exploit the basic concepts of object data model (i.e., classes, inheritance, and complex objects). Object-oriented queries can be classified into *single-class* queries, *inheritance* queries, *path expression* queries, and *explicit join* queries. These queries are explained in the following sections.

Single-Class Queries

As the name suggests, *single-class queries* involve single-classes only. The properties of single-class queries are similar to those of relational queries. They may contain selection, projection, and aggregate operations on single-classes. The only difference is that in

Figure 2: Database Schema

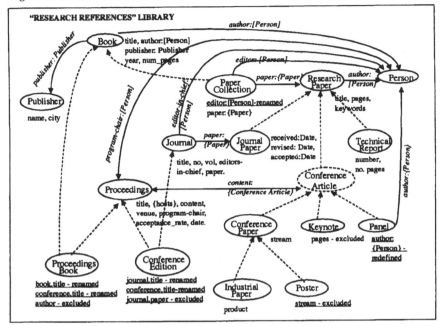

OOQ, methods may be included. Methods returning a value are said to be materialized, and hence acts like attributes. The only difference is that methods are capable of taking some input parameters (e.g., scalar, object) (Bertino et al., 1992). From a query point of view, however, methods are the same as attributes, since query predicates concentrate only on a comparison involving the value of an attribute or the return value of a method and, possibly, a constant. Like attributes, methods may also appear in the projection. A general format of single-class queries is as follows.

Select <projection list>
From <var **in** Class>
Where <selection predicates>

The var in the From clause is a variable pointing to the Class. Consequently, the selection predicates must indicate the use of var. To extract a particular attribute or method of the class, a dot notation is normally used. Furthermore, if the attribute/method is inside a structure, an additional dot notation must be used to indicate the depth of the level where the attribute/method is located. Consider the following query as an example: "Retrieve the title of proceedings of 1996 conference held in Melbourne or Sydney. Display the acceptance rate if known". The OQL is written as follows:

Select **x**.title, **x**.acceptance_rate
From   **x** in Proceedings
Where (**x**.venue.city = "Melbourne" **OR** **x**.venue.city = "Sydney")
    AND **x**.dates.start.year = 1996

The OQL shows that title and acceptance_rate are attributes/methods in the class Proceedings. The selection predicates show a number of conditions involving attributes inside a structure. In this case it is assumed that city is an attribute in the venue structure.

Since a class is normally connected to other classes (especially in an inheritance hierarchy), a single-class query usually appears in the form of an inheritance query.

Inheritance Queries

Inheritance queries are queries on an inheritance hierarchy. They can be categorized into two types: *super-class* queries and *sub-class* queries. The classification is based on the *target class*. A target class is the class on which the query focuses. A super-class query is defined as a query evaluating super-class objects, whereas a sub-class query is defined as a query evaluating sub-class objects. Since all sub-class objects are also super-class objects, a super-class query must also evaluate all of its sub-classes. The general format for inheritance queries is similar to that of single-class queries. The only minor difference is that the variable var may be dynamically bound to a super/sub-class. If the binding is downward, it means that var is originally from a super-class, and hence it is a super-class query. The opposite refers to a sub-class query. The binding process may appear in both projection and selection. The binding process in OQL is basically a casting operation, which can be performed by explicitly showing the class name where the variable var is now bound. For example, if x is originally from class Research_Paper, with ((Technical_Report) x), variable x is now bound to the Technical_Report.

An example of a super-class query is as follows: "Retrieve the title of research papers (excluding any technical reports) in the area of 'Object-Oriented'". The OQL for this query is as follows.

Select x.title
From   x in Research_Paper
Where NOT (**(Technical_Report)** x) AND
       "Object-Oriented" in x.keywords

It is convenient to show inheritance queries using a graphical notation. The bold printed node denotes the target node, and hence determines the type of inheritance query (i.e. super-class query or sub-class query). The graphical notation for the above super-class query is displayed in Figure 3. The target class of the above query is Research_Paper and the scope is to include sub-classes Journal_Paper, Conference_Article, and Technical_Report. This query scope expansion is a result of a type checking for class Technical_Report.

An example of a sub-class query is as follows: "Retrieve the title of technical reports released in 1996". The OQL looks like the following:

Select ((**Research_Paper**) x).title
From   x in Technical_Report
Where x.number Like "96%"

The corresponding query graph is displayed in Figure 4. The Technical_Report node is the target class, and the scope of the query is expanded to the super-class Research_Paper by projecting an attribute title declared in Research_Paper. The binding in this case is promoted from a sub-class to a super-class. Since a sub-class inherits all attributes/methods of its super-class, and moreover, all sub-class objects are all super-class objects, the binding process is not necessarily done explicitly. Therefore, casting from a sub-class to a super-class is optional. The above query can then be simplified to Select x.title instead of Select ((Research_Paper) x).title.

By using a type check operator, the distinction between sub-class and super-class queries becomes blurred, because a conversion from a sub-class query to a super-class

Figure 3: Super-class query

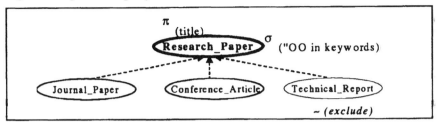

query, and vice-versa, is possible. For example, the above sub-class query can be transformed into a super-class query by shifting the focus of the target class. The query graph is shown in Figure 5 and the OQL become as follows.

Select x.title
From   x in Research_Paper
Where ((**Technical_Report**) x).number Like "96%"

Due to the nature of dynamic binding, casting is necessary only when a variable is initially bound to a super-class but at run-time is bound to a more specialized class. Therefore, the casting notation must be used in super-class queries. In contrast, upward binding is not critical as mentioned above. Subsequently, casting in sub-class queries is optional.

Path Expression Queries

Path expression queries are queries involving multiple classes along the class-domain hierarchies (Banerjee at al., 1988; Kim, 1989). Class-domain hierarchy is where the domain of an attribute is another class. As a result, a chain of classes is formed. Path expression queries normally involve *selection operations* along the path hierarchy. A general form of path expression queries expressed in Object Query Language (OQL) (Cattell, 1994) is as follows.

Select <projection list>
From <var1 **in** Class,
        var2 **in** var1.attr1,
        var3 **in** var2.attr2,
        ...>
Where <selection predicates>

The projection list is a list of attributes of classes along the path expression, which are

Figure 4: Sub-class query

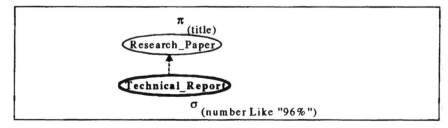

Figure 5: Super-class query

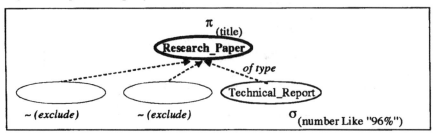

to be projected out. The path is explicitly shown in the From clause. The query starts from the class referred by var1. The path grows as attribute attr1, which has a domain of the next class, is pointed by var2, and so on. In this case, we assume that attribute attr1 of the first class, attribute attr2 of the second class, etc, are attributes of a class domain. Furthermore, these attributes can be of type collection. For example, the domain of attr1 of the first class is a set of objects of the second class, and the domain of attr2 of the second class is a list of objects of the third class, etc. This gives a complex implication to the selection predicates. Hence, it is essential to define collection selection predicates. Based on these predicates, path expression queries can be classified.

Collection Selection Predicates

Collection selection predicates are Boolean expressions that form selection conditions. Collection selection predicates can be categorized into three main parts: *"at-least-one"*, *"for-all"* and *"at-least-some"*. These predicates are shown in Table 1. The symbols S, L and B are set, list and bag, respectively, whilst a and b are atomic values.

1. The *membership* predicate is to evaluate whether an element is a member of a collection. The element a can also be a collection. If it is the case, collection S must be a collection of collections.
    The *existential quantifier* predicate is similar to the membership predicate. It checks whether there is *at least* one member (element) within a collection that satisfies a certain condition specified by an atomic value. This form is also similar to the universal quantifier, but with less restriction, as it requires only one member of the collection to satisfy the condition.
2. The *universal quantifier* predicate type is a comparison between a collection and an atomic value. This predicate is to check whether *all* members (elements) within one collection satisfy a certain condition specified by the atomic value. In the case where the atomic value is an OID, a universal quantifier refers to *all* members in a collection being identical objects.
3. Collection (multi-valued) attributes are often mistakenly considered merely as set-valued attributes. As the matter of fact, set is just one type of collections. The basic features of collection types can be said that some collections can have redundant elements (e.g. bags), whereas others may enforce the order of their elements within one collection (e.g. lists/bags). As a result, selection predicates may incorporate these two features, particularly to check for *duplication* and for *element order*.
    The duplicate checking predicate involves two steps: intersect the element and the collection, and count the number of elements in the intersection result. If it is more

Table 1. Collection Selection Predicates

	Name	Collection Selection Predicates	Description
1	at-least-one	a in S exist a in S : <condition on a>	Membership Existential quantifier
2	for-all	for all a in S : <condition on a>	Universal quantifier
3	at-least-some	count (B intersect bag(a)) > 1 list(a,b) in pairs (L)	Duplicate Succeeded

than one, the element is duplicated in the collection. The predicate looks like this: count(attr1 intersect bag(item)) > 1. Notice that attr1 is of type *bag*. If it is a *list*, it must then be converted to a *bag*.

The selection predicate may also check for an item to be immediately *succeeded* by another item. This predicate can be done by making the two elements a list and by checking whether this list is a sublist of a bigger list. The succeeded predicate is only interested in the sublists formed by two subsequent elements. Assume that the pairs expression is available, in which it returns all possible pairs of a given list. For example:

pairs (list(1, 2, 3)) = list(list(1,2), list(2,3))

The succeeded predicate can be constructed by employing a pairs operator and an in operator. The result of the pairs operator is then evaluated to determine whether it contains a list of the two subsequent elements. The join predicate may look like the following: list(element1, element2) in pairs (attr1).

Based on the type of the selection predicates, path expression queries can be categorized into *"at-least-one"* path expression, *"for-all"* path expression, and *"at-least-some"* path expression. The *"at-least-one"* path expression has been the most common forms of path expression queries in OODB, and provides the least restriction to the selection predicates. On the other hand, the *"for-all"* path expression contains the most restrictive predicates. Although, the *"at-least-some"* path expression is somewhere between the two extremes, the *"at-least-some"* path expression characteristics closely resemble the *"for-all"* path expression and hence, in query processing, the *"at-least-some"* path expression is often treated the same as *"for-all"* path expression.

"at-least-one" Path Expressions

The *"at-least-one"* path expression queries are path expression queries involving the *"at-least-one"* collection selection predicate. The most common form of this type of path expression query employs the membership predicate. An example of such query is to retrieve list of publications of "Kim". This query checks whether there is at least one author in each research paper named "Kim". The query written in OQL is as follows.

Select x
From x in Research_Paper, y in x.author
Where "Kim" in y.surname

Variable y is a collection of authors for each research paper x. Each author within a collection pointed by the variable y is a person object having name, address, etc. The selection predicate (printed in bold) checks whether literal "Kim" is a member of a collection of author's names.

"for-all" Path Expressions

The *"for-all"* path expressions contain the *universal quantifier ("for-all")* selection, predicates. These predicates require *all* objects within the collection to satisfy the selection predicate.

An example of a *"for-all"* path expression query is to retrieve papers written by authors having the same surname "Kim". Since each paper may have one or more authors, this query checks whether all of the authors within each paper satisfy the selection predicate. In other words, each of the authors within the same paper has the same characteristic pointed out by the selection predicate, in this case having the same surname. The query written in OQL is as follows.

Select x
From x in Research_Paper, y in x.author
Where **for all y in x.author : y.surname = "Kim"**

The From clause of the above query shows that variable y is a list of authors for a particular research paper x. The selection predicate checks whether all ys of a research paper x has surname="Kim".

"at-least-some" Path Expressions

As some collection types allow duplicate values to exist, it is essential to provide selection predicates to ascertain that *some* of the elements satisfy a certain condition. The *"at-least-some"* path expression queries contain the selection predicates, which check for the *some*ness of a collection. This includes checks for duplicates and order of elements.

In some cases, it is necessary to check whether a collection contains certain elements. If the collection is a set, this predicate is merely a *conjunctive* predicate, in a form of (element*1* in collection) AND (element2 in collection) AND ..... (element*n* in collection). However, if the collection is a list, it is sometimes necessary to evaluate the order of the elements as well. A typical example is to check whether one element is immediately succeeded by another element in a collection.

In other cases, it is necessary to check whether an element is repeated within a collection. The collection, in this case, must be either a list/array, or a bag, since only lists, arrays, and bags allow duplicate elements to exist. However, if the element is an object, this requirement is no longer valid. The duplication can be not only at an object level, but also at a part object level (an attribute level). Consider the following query as an example: "Retrieve papers such that there is more than one author named 'Kim'". A research paper is written by a list of authors. Each author is a person object, which is formed by a number of attributes, such as name, address, etc. The above query checks whether the number of authors within one research paper having a surname "Kim" is more than one. The author objects within one research paper are not repeated. However, the characteristics of authors within one research paper may be identical, in this case the surname. The query can be expressed in OQL as follows.

Select x
From x in Research_Paper, y in x.author
Where **count(y.surname intersect bag("Kim")) > 1**

As in the previous two queries above (i.e. *at-least-one* and *for-all*), it is clear that variable y is a collection of authors for each research paper x. The selection predicate checks whether the intersection of all surnames of the author for a particular research paper and a bag having one element (i.e. literal "Kim") has more than one element. This selection predicate resembles a duplicate predicate. Notice that bag("Kim") expression is actually a construction, in which a bag is constructed and it contains one element; that is the literal "Kim".

Explicit Join Queries

Explicit joins are basically making a connection between two or more classes that do not have any explicit connection prior to the join (Mishra and Eich, 1992). Explicit join queries are similar to relational join queries but with differences such as the join can be on common objects and collections, not only on simple values. Since join based on simple values or types is very much similar to relational join queries, in this paper we focus on join queries based on collection attributes. This type of queries is called "collection join" queries. The general form for join queries (collection or simple join) is as follows.

Select <projection list>

From <class list>

Where <join predicates> **And** <optional selection predicates>

The projection list and the class list in the Select and From clauses, respectively, are similar in format with relational join queries. The main difference is shown in the join predicate clause, in which collection join predicates are expressed. Although some collection operators are Boolean expressions (i.e., forall, exist, in) which may be used as join predicates, most join predicates are in a form of (collection operator collection), in which the operator is a relational operator (i.e., =, !=, >, <, >=, <=). These operators are overloaded operators. That means that, for example, the equality operator (=) can be applied to not only simple types, but also collection types. A problem faced by collection join queries is that basic collection operations are binary operations, not Boolean operations. Consequently, most join predicates must apply both basic binary collection operations and standard relational operators. For example, if the join predicate is to check whether there is an overlap between *editor-in-chief* and *program-chair* of a pair of Journal and Proceedings, the predicate may look like this:

(Journal.editor-in-chief **intersect** Proceedings.program-chair) != set(*nil*)

Processing this join predicate can be done by intersecting the two sets that will produce another set, and then by comparing it with an empty set. This is certainly not efficient, as an intermediate set has to be created before the *not equality* comparison is performed. Nevertheless, most collection predicates involve these two steps. Different types of join predicates involving collection expressions and Boolean operators must first be identified. A classification of collection join queries will then be based upon these join predicates.

Collection Join Predicates

Join predicates are Boolean expressions, which form join conditions (Mishra and Eich, 1992). In this section, join predicates involving collections are identified. Three collection predicate types, which combine binary collection expressions and comparison operators, are defined. They are shown in Table 2. *S1* and *S2* are of type set, *L1* and *L2* are of type list, and *a* and *b* are atomic values.

1. The simplest form of join predicate is using an *equality operator* (i.e. the = operator) in the form of (attribute = attribute). The main difference between this predicate type and the common equi-join is that the two operands in this predicate are collections, not simple atomic values.

2. An *intersect* join predicate is to check whether there is an overlap between two collection attributes. The predicate is normally in the form of (attr1 intersect attr2) != set(nil). The attributes attr1 and attr2 are of collection types. This predicate intersects the two collection attributes and checks whether or not the intersection result is empty. If the result is not an empty set, it means that the two collections are overlapped. The opposite refers to the two collections being totally distinct.

3. The third category of join predicates checks for a *sublist* or a *proper sublist*. They differ only when both collections are identical, as the proper sublist will return a false. The sublist predicate is very complex in its original form. Suppose a *sublist* expression is available where it builds all possible sublists of a given list. For example,

sublist (list(1, 2, 3)) = list(list(1), list(2), list(3), list(1,2), list(1,3) list(2,3), list(1,2,3))

By combining an *in* operator with the *sublist* operator, a predicate to check for a sublist can be constructed. The sublist join predicate may look like the following: (attr2 in sublist(attr1)), where attr1 and attr2 are of type list. To implement a proper sublist predicate, it must further check that the two lists are not identical.

Another join predicate is a *subset* predicate. The difference between the sublist and the subset predicates is that the subset predicate does not take the order of the elements into account. The subset predicate can be written by applying an intersection between the two sets and comparing the intersection result with the smaller set. The join predicate may look like the following: (attr1 intersect attr2) = attr1. In this case the attributes attr1 and attr2 are of type set. If one or both of them are of type bag, they must be converted to sets. The proper subset is similar to the proper sublist, where an additional non-equality comparison between the two collections must be carried out.

The characteristics of collection join predicates, to some extent, are similar to collection selection predicates. The *collection-equi* join predicate is similar to the *"for-all"* selection predicate. Both require all elements of both operands to be equal. The *intersection* join predicate is similar to the *"at-least-one"* selection predicate, as they both require only one instance of the evaluation to be true. And finally, the *sub-collection* join predicate is similar to the *"at-least-some"* selection predicate since both deal with a collection being a sub-collection of the other.

Join predicate defines the attributes and the operations involved in join queries. From this point of view, object-oriented join queries can be classified into three categories, namely: *Collection-Equi*, *Collection-Intersect*, and *Sub-Collection Join* queries.

Collection-Equi Join Queries

Collection-equi join queries contain join predicates in a form of standard comparison using a relational operator, particularly the equality operator (i.e. the = operator). The operands of these queries are attributes of any collection types. A typical collection-equi join query is to compare two collections for a full equality. Suppose the attribute *editor-in-chief* of class *Journal* and the attribute *program-chair* of class *Proceedings* are of type

Table 2. Collection Join Predicates

	Name	Collection Join Predicate	Description
1	*Equality*	$S1 = S2$	Collection Equality
		$L1[0:2]=L2$	Partial List Equality
2	*Intersection*	$(S1$ intersect $S2)$!= set(nil)	Overlap
3	*Sub-Collection*	$L2$ in sublist($L1$),	Sublist
		$L2$ in sublist($L1$) and $L2$!= $L1$	Proper Sublist
		$(S1$ intersect $S2) = S1$,	Subset
		$(S1$ intersect $S2) = S1$ and $S1$!= $S2$	Proper Subset

arrays of *Person*. To retrieve conferences chaired by *all* editor-in-chief of a journal, the join predicate becomes (editor-in-chief = program-chair). Only pairs having an exact match between the join attributes will be retrieved. The query expressed in OQL can be written as follows:

Select A, B

From A in Journal, B in Proceedings

Where **A.editor-in-chief = B.program-chair**

Notice that the join predicate is printed in bold. This join predicate is a collection equality predicate; that is the first category of the join collection predicates.

As a running example, consider the sample data shown in Figure 6. Suppose class *A* and class *B* are *Journal* and *Proceedings*, respectively. Both classes contain a few objects, shown by their OIDs (e.g., objects *a* to *i* are Journal objects and objects *p* to *w* are Proceedings objects). The join attributes are *editor-in-chief* of Journal and *program-chair* of Proceedings; and are of type collection of *Person*. The OID of each person in these attributes are shown in the brackets. For example *a(250,75)* denotes a Journal object with OID *a* and the editors of this journal are Persons with OIDs *250* and *75*.

The query results using the sample data shown in Figure 6 depends on the collection type adopted by the join attributes. If the attributes are of type *array*, the query results are a concatenation between object *i* of class *Journal* and object *w* of class Proceedings, since both have the exact match not only on the OIDs of all elements, but also in that order. However, if the join attributes are of type *set*, the query results also include objects: *b* and *p*.

Relational operators, like the = operator, are overloaded functions. This feature is not new to object-oriented join queries, because long before OODB exists, relational operators in relational joins have shown this capability. For example, it is permitted to compare an integer with a real number. One of the operand is automatically converted to the type of the other operand (in this case, *integer* to *real*). Casting a collection, however, must be done explicitly in the join predicate. Using the previous example, if *editor-in-chief* is a *list* and *program-chair* is a *set*, the equality predicate becomes (listtoset(editor-in-chief) = program-chair), where the editor-in-chief is converted from a list to a set (Cattell, 1994).

Collection-Intersect Join Queries

Collection-Intersect Join queries contain *intersection* join predicates on collections. The join predicate checks for an overlap between the two collections. A collection-intersect join query from the previous example is to check if there is at least one of the editor-

Figure 6: Sample data

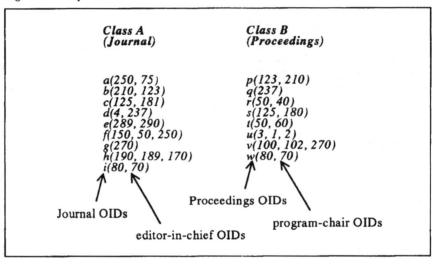

in-chiefs of a journal who has become a program-chair at conference proceedings. The OQL for the above query is as follows.

Select A, B

From A in Journal, B in Proceedings

Where (A.editor-in-chief intersect B.program-chair) != set(nil)

Notice that the join predicate is in a form of (attr1 intersect attr2) != set(nil). Seven pairs of Journal-Proceedings objects are formed as a result of the above query. They are: *b-p, c-s, d-q, f-r, f-t, g-v,* and *i-w.*

Sub-Collection Join Queries

Sub-collection join queries are queries in which the join predicates involve two collection attributes from two different classes. The predicates check for whether one attribute is a sub-collection of the other attribute. The sub-collection predicates can be in a form of *subset, sublist, proper subset,* or *proper sublist.* The difference between *proper* and *non-proper* is that the proper predicates require both join operands to be properly sub-collection. That means that if both operands are the same, they do not satisfy the predicate. The difference between subset and sublist is originated from the basic different between sets and lists. In other words, subset predicates are applied to sets/bags, whereas sublists are applied to lists/arrays.

An example of a sub-collection join is to retrieve pairs of Journal and Proceedings, where the program-chairs of a conference are a *subset* of the editors-in-chief of a journal. The query expressed in OQL can be written as follows:

Select A, B

From A in Journal, B in Proceedings

Where (A.editor-in-chief intersect B.program-chair) = B.program-chair

If the join predicate is a *proper subset,* the where clause of the above query must be ANDed with **A.editor-in-chief != B.program-chair.** This is necessary to enforce that both operands are not identical.

Using the previous sample data, there are three pairs of objects produced by the query, namely: *b-p*, *d-q*, and *i-w*. The first and the last pairs are produced because both collections within each pair are the same, whereas the second pair is because the collection in *q* is a subset of that of *d*. If a *proper subset* predicate is required, instead, a further process is needed to eliminate the pairs in which both collections are identical. In this case, the final query result will be just *d-q*.

COMPLEX QUERIES

By combining each basic component of basic queries (i.e., inheritance, path expression, and explicit join), complex queries can be classified into *Cyclic* queries, *Semi-Cyclic* queries, and *Acyclic* queries.

Cyclic Queries

Cyclic queries (Kim, 1989) feature a *complete walk* property (Norris, 1985), where it is possible to traverse all nodes starting from a given node and ending at the same node. This feature is actually a combination of a path expression and an explicit join. If we view a path traversal as a linear path line, the explicit join operation joins the two ends resulting a cycle. Each node in the cyclic query graph may involve inheritance hierarchies. A cycle can also be completed within a class. Some single-class cyclic is recursive; that is, the loop will not stop until certain conditions are satisfied. Because cyclic queries are originated from the graph theory, cyclic queries can be viewed more easily through a query graphical notation. A general cyclic query format in a graphical notation is shown in Figure 7.

A general format for cyclic queries written in OQL is as follows:
Select <projection list>
From <var$_1$ in Class$_1$,
     var$_2$ in var$_1$.attr$_1$,
     ...,
     var$_n$ in var$_{n-1}$.attr$_{n-1}$>
Where <var$_1$ in var$_n$>

The From clause denotes the path expression starting from Class$_1$ to Class$_n$, whereas the Where clause shows the joining process of both ends of the path expression. The join operation actually checks whether at least one object at the end of the path traversal is the same as the starting object of the path traversal.

Consider the following query as an example: "Retrieve all authors who presented papers at conferences they chaired". The OQL is expressed as follows.

Select x
From   x in Person,
       y in x.program-chair,
       z in y.content,
       w in z.author
Where x in w

The query graph corresponding with the above cyclic query is shown in Figure 8. The query graph clearly shows a cycle from Proceedings, to Conference_Article, and Person, and back to Proceedings. The Conference_Article node also involves an inheritance hierarchy. This implies that at run-time the contents of a proceedings will be bound to class

Figure 7: Cyclic query

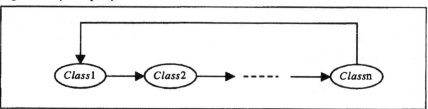

Conference_Paper. Since some of the attributes of the Conference_Paper are declared in the Research_Paper, the path expression continues from Research_Paper to Person. The join operation is carried out by the Proceedings where the authors of the papers have chaired, and the Proceedings where the path traversal initially starts.

It must be noted that some *cyclic graphs* are not necessarily *cyclic queries*. This is because the joining nodes do not represent joining operations. Since the joining operation is missing from the queries, the queries are actually path expression queries. For clarification, consider the following example: "Retrieve authors who presented papers in the ACM SIGMOD conference and have chaired a conference". The query graph may mistakenly look like Figure 9.

If the path traversal starts from node Proceedings, the starting node Proceedings can be different from the ending node Proceedings, since the query does not require the person to chair the same conference where the paper was published. The query requires that this person has chaired any conference. In other word, the node Proceedings, served as a starting point for path traversal, is not necessarily the same as the node Proceedings pointed by the node Person. Consequently, the query graph is actually a linear path starting from Proceedings and ending at a different Proceedings. The correct query graph for this query is shown in Figure 10.

The OQL for this query is written as follows.

Select z
From   x in Proceedings,
       y in x.content,
       z in y.author,
       w in z.program-chair
Where x.title = "ACM SIGMOD" AND w != set(nil)

From the OQL it is clear that it does not conform to the general format of cyclic queries, in which the Where clause does not contain any join operation. Therefore, the query is not a cyclic query, but a linear path expression query.

Semi-Cyclic Queries

Semi-cyclic queries are similar to cyclic queries, with an exception that it will be possible to perform a complete walk only by ignoring the direction of the path. This property is widely known as *semi-walk* (Norris, 1985). There are actually two categories of semi-cyclic queries: *double join semi-cyclic* and *single join semi-cyclic* (see Figure 11). Since the first type is actually an explicit join query with 2 join predicates, only the second type is considered as semi-cyclic queries.

Figure 8: An example of cyclic query

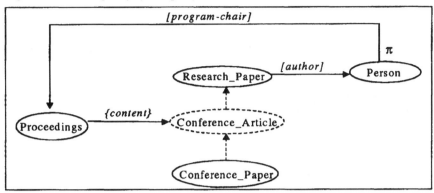

Figure 9: Non-cyclic query

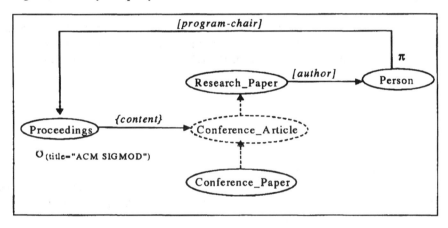

A general format for semi-cyclic queries written in OQL is as follows:
Select <projection list>
From <var_1 in Class$_1$>,
    <var_{11} in var_1.attr$_1$,
      var_{12} in var_{11}.attr$_{11}$,
      ...,
      var_{1n} in var_{1n-1}.attr $_{1n-1}$>,
    <var_{21} in var_1.attr$_1$,
      var_{22} in var_{21}.attr$_{21}$,
      ...,
      var_{2n} in var_{2n-1}.attr $_{2n-1}$>
Where <**join predicate involving var$_{1n}$ in var$_{2n}$**>

The From clause indicates that there are two path traversal starting from the same node; that is node Class$_1$. Apart from the same starting node, the two path traversals are distinct. The first traversal goes to Class$_{1n}$, whereas the second one goes to Class$_{2n}$. The

Figure 10: Linear Path Expression Query

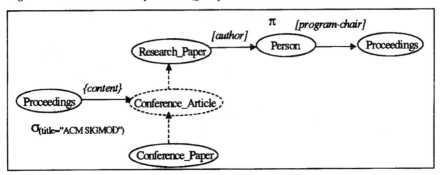

Where clause shows the join operation between the end of the two paths; that is a join between $Class_{1n}$ and $Class_{2n}$. By starting the traversal from the same node, by branching to a different direction, and by ending the same node through a join operation, a semi-cyclic walk is established. Therefore, the query is a semi-cyclic query.

An example of a semi-cyclic query is to retrieve authors who presented papers and participated in panels at the same conferences. Normally these persons are regarded as top persons in the area of the topic of the panel. The OQL for this query is as follows:

    Select w
    From   x in Proceedings,
           y in x.panel,
           z in x.paper,
           w in y.author,
           v in z.author
    Where (w intersect v) != set(nil)

The From clause forms two sets of path expressions starting from node Proceedings. One path goes to Person (or author), and so does the second path. The Where clause joins the two Person (or author) nodes with an intersect join predicate. To better view the semi-cyclic feature of this query, look at the query graph corresponding to this query in Figure 12.

From the query graph in Figure 12, it is clear that there are two different path travers-

Figure 11: Semi-cyclic queries

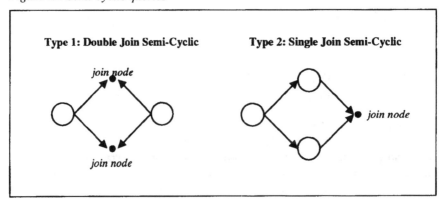

als, both starting from the same node; that is node Proceedings. The first path follows the top line, where it goes to the Conference_Article and Panel, and ends in node Person. The second path follows the bottom line, where it passes the Conference_Article and Research_Paper, and ends at the same node as that of the first traversal. This ending node represents a join operation of the two path traversals. The query graph exhibits a semi-walk property, since it is not possible to form a cycle. If the path direction is ignored, a cyclic graph can be formed. Based on the semi-walk property, the query graph is said to be a semi-cyclic query graph.

If bi-directional paths are available, a semi-cyclic query can be transformed into a join query with double join predicates. Furthermore, a cyclic query can be transformed into a semi-cyclic query or a join query with double predicates. The decision to perform this transformation must be made at the optimization stage. Consider the example shown in Figure 13.

Acyclic Complex Queries

Acyclic complex queries are basically joining two or more distinct path expressions through an explicit join. The difference between acyclic-complex and semi-cyclic is that in semi-cyclic the starting point is from the same node. In acyclic-complex, each of the paths is starting from a different node. A generic query graph for acyclic-complex query is presented in Figure 14. To avoid confusion with single path expression queries which also form acyclic graphs, acyclic queries of multiple path expressions are often called "*Acyclic Complex*" queries. It becomes obvious that acyclic path expression queries have one root, whereas acyclic complex queries have multiple roots, each root represents a path expression.

A general format for acyclic complex queries written in OQL is as follows:
Select <projection list>
From <**var**$_1$ **in Class**$_1$,
    var$_{11}$ in var$_1$.attr$_1$,
    ...,

Figure 12: Semi-Cyclic Query

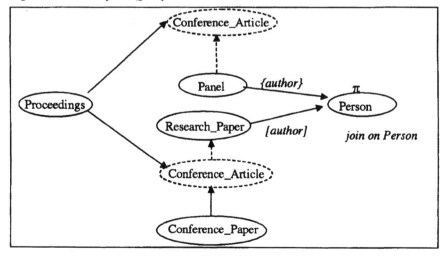

$$\text{var}_{1n} \text{ in var}_{1n-1}.\text{attr}_{1n-1}>,$$

<var₂ in Class₂,

$$\text{var}_{21} \text{ in var}_2.\text{attr}_2,$$

...,

$$\text{var}_{2n} \text{ in var}_{2n-1}.\text{attr}_{1n-1}>,$$

...

<varₘ in Classₘ,

$$\text{var}_{m1} \text{ in var}_m.\text{attr}_m,$$

...,

$$\text{var}_{mn} \text{ in var}_{mn-1}.\text{attr}_{mn-1}>$$

Where **<join predicate involving var₁ₙ, var₂ₙ,..., varₘₙ>**

The From clause indicates that a number of distinct path expressions each of which starts from $Class_1$, $Class_2$, ..., $Class_m$. These paths end at $Class_{1n}$, $Class_{2n}$, ..., $Class_{mn}$. Although the length of each path expression can be of single or multiple classes, at least one of the paths is a real path expression involving multiple classes. Otherwise, acyclic complex queries will be identical to *k-way* explicit join if all of the paths are single classes. The Where clause shows the join operation between the end of all of the paths; that is a join between $Class_{1n}$, $Class_{2n}$, ..., $Class_{mn}$.

An example of acyclic complex query is as follows: "Retrieve the title of conference papers in the area of object-orientation presented at high quality conferences (i.e., acceptance rate below 50%) and written by someone who worked in a city having hosted an Object-Oriented conference in 1996. Papers written by 'Smith' are excluded". The OQL is shown as follows.

Select x.title

From   x in Conference_Paper,

    y in x.author,

    z in x.proceedings,

Figure 13: Cyclic to Semi-cyclic

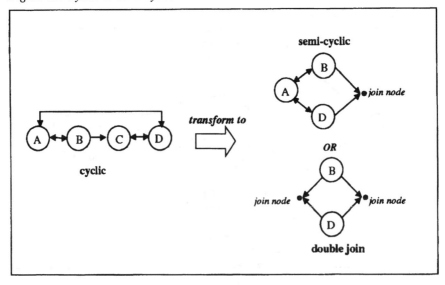

Figure 14: Acrylic Complex Query

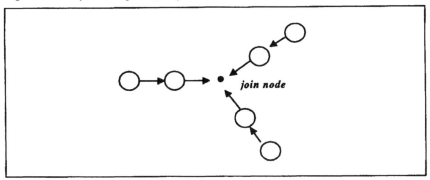

q in Proceedings
Where x.title = "%Object-Oriented%" and
      y.name != "Smith" and
      z.acceptance_rate < 0.5 and
      q.name = "Object-oriented conference" and
      q.year = 1996 and
      y.affiliation.city = q.hosts.city

The query graph of the above query (see Figure 15) contains two distinct paths. One path involves classes Conference_Paper, Person, and Proceedings; whereas the other path involves one node only (node Proceedings). The two paths meet through a join operation between the city of the affiliation of the person (the first path) and the city of the conference (the second path).

Comparison with other work

Most of existing object-oriented query models concentrate on path expressions through attribute-class hierarchy, as this kind of hierarchy provides an exciting feature in which query evaluation can be carried out by pointer navigation. Some of this work also introduces join queries into the model. Table 3 gives a summary of related work and a comparison with our query taxonomy.

Banerjee and Kim

The paper by Banerjee, Kim, and Kim (1988) has been recognized as a pioneer of a model for object-oriented queries, which was based on ORION. It focused on various query models on nested attributes, also known as path expressions. They did not include join queries, because join was considered to be more relational than object-oriented.

Kim (1989) extended the query model and introduced join queries. The join queries are similar to those in relational databases that involve simple attributes in the join predicate. Since a class may inherit from/to other classes, the join attributes may be of identical domain, or of super/sub-class type. Kim (1990) elaborated join queries by specifying four different join predicates, namely; *scalar-scalar*, *set-set*, *scalar-set*, and *set-scalar*. The first two join predicates employ relational operators, while the rests cover subset checking.

Kifer, Kim and Sagiv (1992) extended Kim's work (1989) by incorporating complex operations on path expressions (i.e. existential and universal quantifiers), and methods

Figure 15: Acrylic-complex query

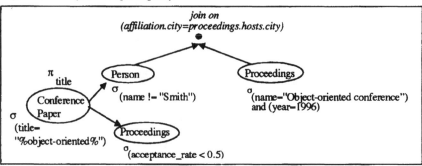

into their query model.

Cluet and Delobel

The query model presented in Cluet, et al. (1990) was influenced by O2. Mainly it covered path expression queries. The paper by Cluet and Delobel (1992), an extension of their previous work, introduced join queries based on simple attributes. The role of join operations was also enhanced as backward traversal of path expression queries, which was implemented in a semi-join. Cluet and Delobel (1994) further clarified the importance of the join-selection-projection operation in their optimization method. The shifting from pure path traversals to more elegant join operations was considered important as optimization can be achieved through high performance join algorithms. Join operation is still regarded as the basic building block in their query model.

Bertino

Bertino et al. (1992) presented an exhaustive study on object-oriented query languages. Queries involving inheritance and polymorphism were initially reported in this paper. They also identified two different types of join predicates, namely; *identity equality* and *value equality* predicates. The former is joining on object domain, while the latter is a traditional join on simple attributes. The query model did not put too much attention to set-valued or collection attributes, and hence, collection join queries were not reported explicitly. Join queries, described in Bertino and Martino (1993), were influenced by Kim (1990), where only scalar-scalar and set-set join predicates were concerned. This reflects their perception of an unimportant role for explicit join queries. Their recursive queries are similar to Kim's cyclic queries.

Cattell

Like Bertino et al. (1992), Cattell (1991) defined two types of join queries: *value join* and *object join*. Collection types were not considered to be object-oriented until they were included in the Object Database Standard ODMG (Cattell, 1994). Although to some degree ODMG has attempted to formalize object-oriented queries, collection join queries have not explicitly been defined. Collection join queries, however, can be extracted from binary collection expressions.

Although ODMG (Cattell, 1994) extensively discusses path expressions, it does not

Table 3. Comparison

Query Type	Banerjee & Kim	Cluet & Delobel	Bertino et al.	Cattell	Chan	Alhajj & Arkun	Ours
Simple predicate	√	√	√	√	√	√	√
Method predicate	√	√	√	√	√	√	√
Super-class	partial		√	partial	√	partial	√
Sub-class	partial		√	partial	√	partial	√
"at-least-one" PE	√	√	√	√	√	√	√
"for-all" PE	√		√	√	√	√	√
"at-least-some" PE	partial				partial		√
Simple Join	√	√	√	√	partial	√	√
Collection Join	partial		partial	partial			√
Cyclic	√		√		√		√
Semi-cyclic							√
Acyclic-complex	√		√	√	√	√	√

explicitly describe the *"at-least-some"* path expressions which can be indirectly derived from collection expressions and operations. Inheritance queries are also not explicitly mentioned, even though the casting operation is used to illustrate polymorphism.

Chan

The query model by Chan was extensively based on sets (Chan, 1994). Chan and Trinder (1994) expressed object-oriented queries in term of object comprehension. This query notation was claimed to be complete, even though it did not include join queries explicitly in the model. Join queries can be expressed as multiple generators, but join queries on collections were not considered at all. Chan et.al. (1995), one of the most recent work in object-oriented queries, defined an evaluation framework for object-oriented queries. The evaluation did not address join queries, reflecting that there was no intention to explore the richness of join operation in object-orientation. Although Chan (1994) presented a study on sets thoroughly (eg., quantifiers and set manipulation), collection-based joins were not of importance.

Alhajj and Arkun

Alhajj and Arkun (1992) focused on object algebra. Cross product was identified as one of the operations in the object algebra. Alhajj and Arkun (1993) later added a join operation to the model, but the join queries covered simple value joins and simple set joins only, in which two sets are compared for an equality.

DISCUSSION

All query models support simple predicates. Some of them also support method predicates. Our query model supports both simple and method predicates. In a query involving methods in the selection predicate, methods returning a value are regarded the same as simple attributes.

Inheritance queries are not explicitly included in most existing query models. The main reason is that when a sub-class inherits from a super-class, the inherited attributes are assumed to completely belong to the sub-class. Hence, inheritance queries are regarded the same as single-class queries, regardless the position of the class in the inheritance hierarchy.

Most query models support path expression queries, particularly the existential type ("*at-least-one*") of path expression queries. Only a few of them mentioned the universal type ("*for-all*") of path expression queries. Our model includes both types of path expression in the taxonomy. In addition, we also include the "*at-least-some*" predicates in the taxonomy.

Most query models have included the join operation as a basic operation. However, most join queries are based on simple value join and simple set join, and none of them really incorporate collection types. The impact of sets/collections in the object model becomes stronger, as ODMG includes them in the object database standard. Some work follows this standard, but not significantly, especially in collection join.

Cyclic queries were initially introduced by Kim (1989). They are similar to recursive queries reported in Bertino et al. (1992) and Chan (1994). Our model extends cyclic queries to include semi-cyclic queries.

CONCLUSIONS

In this chapter, *object-oriented queries* are formulated and classified. A query classification is essential, especially to exploit the full capacity of object-oriented queries. The classification is also essential for query optimization purposes in which it now becomes clear the types of object-oriented queries to be optimized. Consequently, the domain of query optimization is determined by the scope of object-oriented queries.

Object-oriented queries are queries exploiting object-oriented concepts, particularly classes/objects, inheritance, and complex objects. Based on these concepts, basic object-oriented queries can be classified into single-class queries, inheritance queries, path expression queries, and explicit join queries. Single-class queries are queries on single-classes, inheritance queries are queries on inheritance hierarchies, path expression queries are queries on complex objects, and explicit join queries are queries used to connect unrelated classes based on some common properties. By extending these basic query types, complex queries are developed. Complex queries can be classified into cyclic, semi-cyclic, and acyclic complex queries.

Query predicates based on collection types have also been formulated. These predicates serve as a basis for selection predicates and collection join predicates. The latter has been a salient feature of object-oriented query which highlights the difference between join queries in rational databases (based on simple attributes) and those in OODB (can be based on collections as well).

REFERENCES

Alhajj, R. and Arkun, M.E.(1993)."A Query Model for Object-Oriented Databases", *Proceedings of the Ninth International Conference on Data Engineering*, pp. 163- 172, Vienna, April.

Alhajj, R. and Arkun, M.E.(1992)."Queries in Object-Oriented Database Systems", *Proceedings of the First International Conference on Information and Knowledge Management CIKM*, 36-52, November.

Banerjee, J., Kim, W. and Kim, K-C.(1988)."Queries in Object-Oriented Databases", *Pro-

ceedings of the Fourth International Conference on Data Engineering, 31-38, February.

Bertino, E. and Martino, L (1993). *Object-Oriented Database Systems: Concepts and Architectures*, Addison-Wesley,.

Bertino, E., et al.(1992)."Object-Oriented Query Languages: The Notion and The Issues", *IEEE Transactions on Knowledge and Data Engineering*, 4(3), 223-237.

Cattell, R.G.G. (ed.) (1994). *The Object Database Standard: ODMG-93*, Release 1.1, Morgan Kaufmann.

Cattell, R.G.G.(1991). *Object Data Management: Object-Oriented and Extended Relational Database Systems*, Addison-Wesley.

Chan, D.K.C, Trinder, P.W. and Welland, R.C.(1995)."Evaluating Object-Oriented Query Languages", *Computer Journal*, 38(2), February.

Chan, D.K.C. and Trinder, P.W.(1994)."Object Comprehensions: A Query Notation for Object-Oriented Databases," *Proceedings of the British National Conference on Databases BNCOD 12*, 55-72, July.

Chan, D.K.C.)1994). *Object-Oriented Query Language Design and Processing*, PhD Thesis, University of Glasgow, September.

Cluet, S. and Delobel, C.(1992)."A General Framework for the Optimization of Object-Oriented Queries," *Proceedings of the ACM SIGMOD Conference*, 383-392.

Cluet, S. and Delobel, C.(1994)."Towards a Unification of Rewrite-Based Optimization Techniques for Object-Oriented Queries", *Query Processing for Advanced Database Systems*, J.C.Freytag, et al. (eds.), Morgan Kaufmann, 245-272.

Cluet, S., et al.(1990). "Reloop, an Algebra Based Query Language for an Object-Oriented Database System", *Deductive and Object-Oriented Databases DOOD Conference*, W.Kim, et al. (eds.), Elsevier Science Publishers, 313-332.

Coad, P. and Yourdon, E.(1991).*Object-Oriented Analysis*, second edition, Prentice Hall.

Kifer, M., Kim, W. and Sagiv, Y.(1992). "Querying Object-Oriented Databases", *Proceedings of the ACM SIGMOD Conference*, 393-402.

Kim, W. (1989)."A Model of Queries for Object-Oriented Databases", *Proceedings of the Fifteenth International Conference on Very Large Data Bases VLDB*, 423-432, Amsterdam.

Kim, W.(1990). *Introduction to Object-Oriented Databases*, The MIT Press.

Masunaga, Y (1990)."Object Identity, Equality and Relational Concept", *Deductive and Object-Oriented Databases*, W. Kim et al., (eds.), 185-202.

Meyer, B.(1988). *Object-Oriented Software Construction*, Prentice-Hall.

Mishra, P. and Eich, M.H.(1992). "Join Processing in Relational Databases", *ACM Computing Surveys*, 24(1), 63-113, March.

Norris, F.R.(1985). *Discrete Structures: An Introduction to Mathematics for Computer Science*, Prentice Hall.

Rahayu, W., Chang, E. and Dillon, T.S.(1995)."A Methodology for the Design of Relational Databases from Object-Oriented Conceptual Models Incorporating Collection Types", *Proceedings of the 18th International Conference on Technology of Object-Oriented Languages and Systems TOOLS Pacific*, Melbourne, 13-23.

Taniar, D. and Rahayu, W.(1996). "Object-Oriented Collection Join Queries", *Proceedings of the 21*[st] *Technology of Object-Oriented Languages and Systems TOOLS Pacific 21*, 115-125, Melbourne,.

Taniar, D., and Rahayu, J.W. (1998)."A Hierarchical Approach to Object-Oriented Query Classification", *Proceedings of the International Workshop on Issues and Applications of Database Technology IADT'98*, Berlin.

Taniar, D., and Rahayu, J.W. (1998)."Complex Object-Oriented Queries: A Graph-Based Approach", *Proceedings of the ISCA 13th International Conference on Computers and Their Applications CATA'98*, Hawaii, March.

CHAPTER 6

Query Optimization in Tertiary Storage Based Systems Using a Generalized Storage Model

Rahul V. Tikekar, University of California-Irvine, USA
Farshad Fotouhi, Wayne State University, USA
Don Ragan, Wayne State University, USA

Most of the research in the area of database query optimization has dealt with data that is either in main memory or on disk. Lately there has been growing interest in making tertiary memory a part of an information system. Query optimization algorithms proposed in the past may need to be modified in order to be efficient under tertiary storage based systems. The work done in the past in this area deals with a fixed tertiary storage setup. In this paper, we use a model for a generic storage system and generic data placement techniques. Such a model provides us a tool to modify the storage system and observe the effect of queries under different configurations. We will use the model in one aspect of query optimization. We will measure the cost of, and optimize, two relational join algorithms in a tertiary storage system setup: the nested loop algorithm and the hybrid hash algorithm. Our work is more general than the previous work in database query optimization in that, when the information system is reduced to that consisting of only primary and secondary storage devices, the results will will be consistent with those already proposed by others. Our work extends the modeling and query optimization methods to include other forms of storage.

INTRODUCTION

The amount of data being managed by DBMSs today is considerably larger than that which was managed just a few years ago and this trend will continue as organizations continue to produce large amounts of data (Winter, 1994; Carey et al., 1993). Also, with the advent of image and multimedia databases, the amount of data that needs to be managed becomes tremendous (Salem, 1992). Hence organizations will need to look at alternative methods to satisfy their growing storage requirements. One solution to this problem is hierarchical storage management (HSM)(Wallace, 1994; Stonebraker, 1991; Hall, 1996).

In such a system, a variety of secondary and tertiary storage devices are used to hold and manage data.

One class of applications that would benefit from such a system is hypermedia-based applications. Such applications will be rich in media such as images and video. Such applications can be designed in such a way that storage intensive data can be stored on low cost devices that offer more storage capacity. Since such devices will now be a part of the system, the application need not worry about the best way to store and retrieve data since this will be taken care of the by the HSM system. We take a specific example from the medical community. Hospitals today are moving toward a film-less system where patient data is stored digitally and can be accessed easily by physicians and researchers. Currently, data belonging only to the current patients is stored on disk; inactive and old patient data is archived offline. Retrieving archived data is difficult since one has to manually determine which data is stored where. For example, a researcher studying the effects of a particular treatment may need to refer to current and past cases. As another example, a physician treating a patient with an uncommon disease may want to see all data relating to previous patients with that disease. If applications are designed with the HSM system in mind, they will provide a seamless interface to all data regardless of where it is stored.

This paper looks at one aspect of query optimization in HSM systems: the relational join. This is an important and costly operation. Current data placement techniques regard tertiary storage as an archiving system and data that is too voluminous or old to be stored on secondary disk storage is moved to tertiary storage. Because tertiary storage is regarded as being external to the system, when data from tertiary storage is required, the device containing that data is loaded and that data is transferred to disk storage in units of files from where it is processed in a normal manner. While this might be an acceptable temporary solution, for a long term solution, we would like the tertiary storage to be considered as being part of the system and not external to the it. This gives us the advantage of creating applications that are not constrained by disk storage limitations. Also we believe that this will be the trend in the years to follow (Carey et al., 1993).

With a wide variety of secondary and tertiary storage devices available, each with varying characteristics, it will be difficult for users to decide on the best set of devices for their applications. Also, query optimization in such systems will now have to take the new devices and their characteristics into consideration. Current query optimizing strategies are geared toward data that resides entirely in main memory or entirely on hard disk. These query processing techniques may not work just as well for data that is now on secondary as well as tertiary storage (Sarawagi and Stonebraker, 1994).

Need for a Model

The work done with regard to query optimization in tertiary storage based systems deals with a fixed device setup and hence cannot be used in generic query optimization techniques (Sarawagi, 1995; Chen et al., 1993). The need to be able to model a generic storage system can be justified by the following questions that will arise when dealing with a tertiary storage based system.

Query processing cost related issues
1. How much time is spent in doing I/O for a given database operation and for a given storage setup? How much role do other parameters (e.g., data transfer rate, number of

platter switches, etc.) play in the execution of the query?

2. If the device setup is altered, how would the algorithm implementing a database operation be affected? For example, instead of having all data come into the main memory, if we were to first move all data into disk before processing it?

3. If a new device with better features (e.g., faster seek time, faster data transfer rate, lesser cost, etc.) is added to the system, would the performance of the database algorithm (in terms of I/O) improve? Or, how would one have to modify the algorithm implementing the database operation, in order to make the best use of this new device?

Query optimization and data placement related issues

1. How would the performance of the algorithm implementing a database operation be affected if the data were to be arranged differently? I.e., what is the cost of the operation given different placement techniques?

2. Given a query optimization technique and an acceptable I/O related cost, how can one place the data on the system so as to meet the given cost?

3. Can one partition a relation so that only the key attributes are on one device and the rest of the attributes are scattered on the other devices (vertical partitioning) and achieve an improvement in the database operation's performance?

4. If one were to increase/decrease the size of the unit of transfer, would there be any impact on the performance on the database operation? (One might do that to take into account the device characteristics.)

5. Which of the set of query processing schedules will result in the least overall I/O time? A query processing schedule is an ordered list of database operations. The order of the operations can be optimized so that the resultant I/O time is the lowest possible. Sarawagi (1995) has proposed heuristics that improve the I/O time in a system.

6. How much effect does the size of the relations have on the performance of the database operation?

System optimization related issues

1. Given an available budget and the storage needs of an organization, what is the best set of devices and their setup for the money that matches the given needs?

2. Given a storage system and a reliability criterion, how reliable is the system?

3. What type of queries are asked most often? Which relations are accessed most often? Answers to such questions can help us adaptively place fragments on the system so as to decrease the response time of queries.

The model used in this chapter will help the users of data warehouse systems in planning and analyzing their storage systems by being able to answer questions like those posed above.

RELATED WORK

Related work can be classified into two broad areas: those that deal with tertiary storage based systems and those that deal with query optimization techniques.

The only other work that we are aware of that deals with managing a hierarchy of storage devices, is by Stonebraker (Stonebraker, 1991; Olson, 1992; Sarawagi and Stonebraker, 1994) on the POSTGRES DBMS. It is suggested that a three level hierarchy consisting of main memory, disk memory and archival memory be used a model for such work (Stonebraker, 1991). In POSTGRES, archival storage is also managed by the DBMS and data can reside on any level of the hierarchy. In effect the DBMS then has to manage three separate, yet related, databases. One is the main memory database, another the disk memory database and the third the archive database. For given data, the store or device where it resides is termed its home device. Data in each of the three databases will be in the format or representation most appropriate for that database. When data is moved between levels, it will need to be converted to the representation of the level to which it is moved. Operators are provided for moving the data between different levels.

Other works dealing with tertiary devices are with respect to archival or file based mass storage systems (Cabrera at al., 1995; Chen et al., 1995; Ford and Myllymaki, 1995; Stephenson et al., 1993). Such systems deal with very large, possibly multi-dimensional, datasets that need to be archived. Thus the archival system is not a part of the main system but is considered to be external to it. When data that is on the archival system is required, it is brought to the disk in units of files. The archival data is almost always stored on tapes (Carey et al., 1993).

Chen et al. (1993) address the problem of placing a set of read-only multimedia objects on a jukebox. The objective is to reduce the seek time and the number of platter switches.

Chen et al. (1995) look at the problem of storing and retrieving multi dimensional data on tertiary storage. In the proposed scheme, multi-dimensional data is partitioned into datasets based on query access patterns. Here the tertiary device considered is the tape and the unit of transfer is a file.

Sarawagi and Stonebraker (1994) and Sarawagi (1995) have looked at query optimization issues relating to tertiary memory devices. A three level hierarchy of main memory connected to secondary memory connected to tertiary memory is used. All data is brought into a cache on the disk to be processed. The problems of single relation selection and two-way joins are considered. Relations are broken into units called fragments; each fragment is assumed to be stored on a storage unit (called a platter) in a contiguous manner. Multimedia data is treated as blobs; blobs are stored separately as individual fragments. When a relation involving a blob is selected, the relation minus the blob is brought in first, the blobs are then scheduled to be brought in next. The following issues are considered while optimizing and scheduling queries: avoiding random I/Os, intelligent query scheduling to reduce platter switching and unconventional caching. However this approach uses a fixed system setup and does not help in answering questions such as the time taken to complete a join, the effect of different placement and fetching techniques on a join, the effect of different scheduling techniques on database operations, the effect of varying the size of the unit of data transfer on an operation, etc.

Seeger et al. (1993) look at the problem of reading a set of pages stored contiguously on disk storage so as to reduce the input time as far as possible. Fotouhi and Pramanik (1989) look at the problem of determining an optimal sequence of pages to be fetched from secondary memory such that the least possible main memory buffer is required for a join. DeWitt et al. (1984) compare the performance of join algorithms and index structures in the presence of a large main memory. Blakeley and Martin (1990) evaluate three methods used for the join operation: join index, materialized view and the hybrid hash join. Pramanik and Fotouhi (1988) evaluate the use of partial relation schemes in relational joins.

A GENERALIZED STORAGE MODEL

A detailed description of a generalized storage model for tertiary based systems is given in Tikekar et al., (1997). In this section we will summarize the important details of the model. The storage system is viewed as being divided into a number of levels. At each level sit a number of devices.

A storage model, S, is a 4-tuple,

$$S = (L, \quad D, \quad G, \quad F) \quad \text{where}$$

$L = \{L_0, L_1, \dots, L_k\}$ are the one or more levels in the system. The level L_0 is the designated level of the main memory.

$D = \{D_1, D_2, \dots, D_n\}$ are the n devices in the system. This will be further expanded later.

$G = \{gp_1, gp_2, \dots, gp_m\}$ are the global parameters that are of importance while specifying the system. (Examples of global parameters are total storage, free storage, date of last compressions, etc.)

F $is\text{-}subset\text{-}of$ (L X L) defines the protocol of data transfer in the storage system.

The protocol of data transfer applies to the ways in which data moves in and out of the system. We look at four specific models to get data out of the system: the one-step flood, incremental-flood, two-step flood and hybrid flood models. We also look at two specific models to get data into the system: broadcast and trickle-down models.

In the incremental flood model data moves to level L_0 in an incremental manner such that each level L_i moves the data to level L_{i-1}. In the one-step flood model, retrieval is achieved by each level moving its data directly into the main memory cache. In the two-step flood model all devices send data to the hard disk (in a one-step manner) from where it is made available to the main memory cache as proposed in Stonebraker (1991) and Sarawagi (1995). In the hybrid flood model part of the system follows the incremental-flood model and part of the system follows the one-step model. In the trickle-down model the data "trickles down" from level L_i (or device D_i) to level L_{i+1} (or device D_{i+1}). In the broadcast model an allocator process at Level L_0 can place data at any level (or device).

We now elaborate on the Devices in the storage system. We define a device as a 3-tuple.

$$D_i = (L_m, P, F) \quad \text{where}$$

L_m $is\text{-}element\text{-}of$ L states the level, m, this device will sit at.

$P = \{p_1, p_2, \dots, p_n\}$ are the associated device parameters like capacity, data transfer time, number of platters, number of read heads, average seek time, average platter switch time, etc.

$F = \{f_1, f_2, \dots, f_k\}$ the set of functions that this device is capable of performing. Most devices today are capable of performing just two functions: read and write.

Finally, we elaborate on a model for the allocation of relations on a storage system defined above. We assume that there are m relations in the system and that each relation is characterized by k parameters like number of attributes, primary key, size of relation in MB, number of tuples, the distribution of data in the tuples, number of fragments, etc. We further assume that each relation is divided into one or more fragments (Sarawagi, 1995). Then, a data placement allocation is a tuple,

$$DP = (R, PL) \quad \text{where}$$

$R = (R_i, RP_i)$ where R_i is the relation i and $RP_i = <p_j: j=1, \dots, k>$ defines the k characteristics of relation Ri.

PL = $(R_{i,j}, D_l)$ defines fragment j of relation R_i (denoted by $R_{i,j}$) is placed on device D_l.

The model can be used as shown in figure 1. The input provided to the model will be the devices and their arrangement, the dataflow model, the relations and their placement, the join algorithm, etc. The system is then provided with the goals that we are interested in, for example, the total I/O cost of the join algorithm. The output produced by the system will be result that we are interested in. For example, the total cost of the join, the optimal placement strategy, etc.

USING THE GENERALIZED MODEL

In this section we will use the model to build a tertiary device based hierarchical storage system and measure the cost of two join algorithms under various data placement schemes. We will then modify the algorithms to reduce their cost. First we describe the implementation of the model.

Implementation of the Model

The object oriented paradigm is used to implement the model. The model takes shape as a complex object (container class) called *StorageModel* at the top level that contains the classes *Relation* and *Level*. In addition, there are methods to place fragments, fetch fragments, compute joins, etc. This class can be regarded as a base class from which other classes can be derived (e.g., OneStepFloodModel, IncrementalFloodModel, etc.). The class *Relation* is used to implement a relation and has attributes like name, size, number of tuples, distribution, etc. and operations to read, set and compute the various attributes. The class *Level* is used to implement the storage hierarchy as a set of levels. It is also a complex object that serves as the container for the class *Device*. It implements operations to add and delete devices at a level, to initialize devices and to place and retrieve fragments on and from devices at that level. Finally, the object *Device* implements devices. We implement a device as consisting of a set of platters. Each platter has room for a certain number of fragments depending on the size of each fragment.

Table 1 lists the devices and their characteristics that we used to build a hierarchical storage system. Table 2 lists the values used to implement the relations and fragments sizes used. As can be seen from the tables, we used three tertiary devices as part of the storage system. The arrangement of devices at each level is described in table 3. As can be seen, there are five levels in the system with one device assigned to each level. The relations were then placed on various levels as described in the next section.

Figure 1: Use a Generalized Storage Model

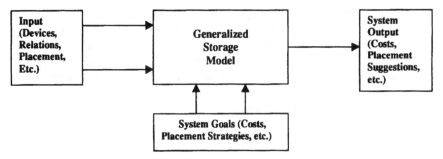

Join Algorithms

We used two popular join algorithms: the nested loop algorithm and the hybrid hash algorithm. Below we describe both.

Nested Loop Join

This algorithm also called the nested block join implements the join by defining an outer and an inner relation (Mishra and Eich 1992). For every fragment of the outer relation, the entire inner relation is read and a join is performed.

Hybrid Hash Join

This algorithm uses a partition approach to join two relations. The two relations are scanned and partitioned using a hash function. All except the first partitions of both relations are flushed to disk. Then the corresponding partitions of both relations are read and tested for the join condition. This algorithm has also been well described in Mishra and Eich (1992).

Modified Nested Loop Algorithm

Now we describe a modification of the nested loop algorithm (Algorithm MNL). The modification can potentially yield better results in terms of reducing the number of I/O operations.

Algorithm MNL

This algorithm modifies the nested loop algorithm to join two relations R and S with FR and FS fragments respectively. R is the outer relation and S is the inner relation. First R is read and a look up table (LUT) is constructed that has the format (join attribute, number

Table 1   Devices used in simulations

Device	Platters	DTR (MB/s)	Seek Time (s)	Switch Time (s)
RAM (0.5 GB)	-	-	-	-
Disk (50 GB)	-	15	0.02	-
Optical Jukebox(50GB)	12	0.8	-	8
CD-ROM Jukebox (80 GB)	20	0.6	-	25
Tape Library (2000 GB)	400	0.47	36	170

Table 2   Relation and Fragment Characteristics

Number of Relations	Relation Size	Fragment Size
2000	15-50 MB	3-5 MB

Table 3   Devices used at each level

Levels	L_0	L_1	L_2	L_3	L_4
Devices	RAM	Disk	Optical Jukebox	CD-ROM Jukebox	Tape Library

of occurrences). This table contains the values for the join attribute(s) and the number of occurrences of that value in the relation. The join then proceeds by reading a fragment of R and a fragment of S. When the tuples of R and S are compared to test the join condition, it is determined from the LUT if a tuple of S will be needed again. If so, it is saved. If not, it is discarded. If the number of saved tuples exceeds a fragment, it is flushed to the disk. When all of S is read, a new fragment of R is brought in. S now consists of the newly created fragments. This process is repeated until all of the fragments of R are read. This modification requires more processing but compared with the cost of reading from tertiary devices, it can be small.

```
Read all of R and create LUT as described
start = 1; end = FS
For i = 1 to FR
begin
     Get fragment i of R
     For j = start to end
     begin
          Get fragment j of S
          Do join and save necessary tuples
          If saved tuples form a new fragment of S
          begin
               Flush new fragment to disk
               FS = FS + 1
          end
     end
end
start = end + 1; end = FS
```

Modified Hybrid Hash Algorithm

We now describe a modification to the hybrid hash algorithm (Algorithm MHH1) that can potentially reduce the number of I/O operations. This modification combines various partitions of the relations into fragments and writes fragments to disk. Thus we can save on the number of I/O operations if the size of each partition is less than the fragment size.

Algorithm MHH1

This algorithm modifies the hybrid hash algorithm to join relations R and S with FR and Fs fragments respectively. The modification relies on the assumption that the size of each partition is less than the size of a fragment.

```
Get all of R
Divide R into n partitions
Combine the partitions into k (k < n) fragments
Flush all except the first fragment to disk
Repeat all the above steps for S
For i = 2 to k
begin
     Get fragment I of R and S
```

Extract partitions from the fragments
Join the corresponding partitions of R and S
end

Cost Measurements

We now elaborate on the costs that we will measure for the various join algorithms described. We assume our storage model is represented by

$$S = (L, D, G, F)$$

where $L = \{L_0, L_1, L_2, L_3, L_4\}$
D is the set of devices described in Table 1
G = {total storage, percent used} and,
F = {Broadcast, One-step flood}

We use five given placement strategies P_1, P_2, P_3, P_4, P_5 as described in Table 4. The table shows the percentage of each relation that is stored at each level. Placement P1 is the case where all of the data is on hard disk. The relations R_1 and R_2 are randomly chosen. The cost that we observed was the total IO time for each algorithm while performing the relational join. For more cost measurements, please refer to the work by Tikekar (1997).

Figures 2 and 3 show the results of the performance of the algorithms for two of the five placement schemes used. The x-axis depicts the total I/O time for each of the algorithms. The y-axis is relevant to algorithms MNL, MHH1 and MHH2. It denotes the amount of S that is needed to be saved (this is described as a percentage). As can be inferred, regardless of the distribution of S, the modified version performs better as long as less than 90% of it contains repeating values of the join attribute(s).

Limited Disk Space

We now use the model in another situation where the space available on the disk is limited. Hence there is little room to store temporary relations (like partitions in the hybrid hash method). In such a case, the algorithms requiring space to store temporary relations will need to be modified in order that their performance will not be affected significantly. We propose a modification to the hybrid hash algorithm to handle this condition.

Modified Hybrid Hash Join 2

We propose a further modification to the hybrid hash join algorithm. In this modification (Algorithm MHH2), we use the notion of partial relation schemes (Pramanik and Fotouhi, 1988) to reduce the size of the partitions by saving only the join attribute(s) of the relations involved.

Algorithm MHH2

This algorithm modifies the hybrid hash algorithm to join relations R and S with FR and FS fragments respectively. In this modification, when the relations are partitioned using the hash function, only the join attribute(s) are stored in the partition instead of the entire tuple. This will reduce the size of the partition considerably provided the size of the join attribute(s) is smaller than the size of a tuple. When the corresponding partitions are read in to be joined, the algorithm uses a two step approach. In the first step, the tuples of the relations that satisfying the join criterion are identified. In the second step the actual fragments containing those tuples are read in. The algorithm will work best when the

Table 4   Percentage allocations at each level for all placement strategies

Placement Strategy	L_1	L_2	L_3	L_4
P_1	100	-	-	-
P_2	75	15	5	5
P_3	50	20	20	10
P_4	25	35	25	15
P_5	10	20	35	45

Figure 2   IO Times for Placement P1

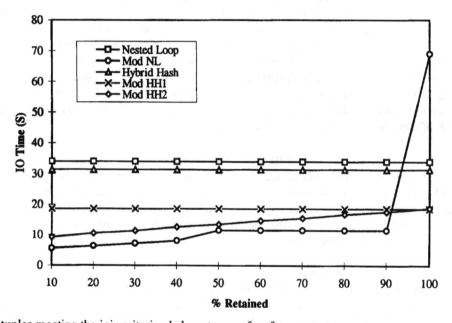

tuples meeting the join criterion belong to very few fragments.

Get all of R.

Partition R into n partitions based on a given hash function. Store only the join attribute(s) and fragment id in each partition.

Compact the partitions into k (k < n) hash-fragments.

Flush all except the first hash-fragment to disk. (If no room on disk, put them on the next available device.)

Do the same with S. (For simplicity assume that there are now equal number of hash-fragments, k, of R

and S after partitioning and compacting.)

For i = 1 to k

begin

Figure 3   IO Times for Placement P5

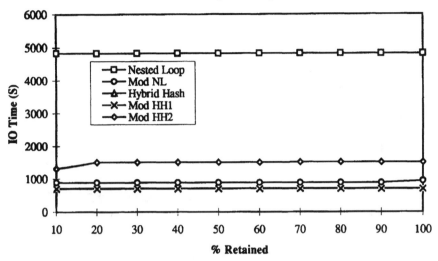

IO Time
Placement P5, One-step Flood Model

Get hash-fragment i of R and S.
Extract partitions from the hash-fragments.
Join the corresponding partitions of R and S and determine the actual
fragments that contain the tuples.
Make a list of the m fragments needed.
end
For j = 1 to m
begin
    Get fragments j of R and S and output the result tuples.
end

Figures 4 and 5 show the results of the performance of the algorithms for the same
two of the five placement schemes used. The x-axis depicts the total I/O time for each of
the algorithms. The y-axis applies to algorithms MNL, MHH1 and MHH2. It holds the
same meaning for algorithm MNL as before. In the case of algorithm MHH2, it also
denotes the size of the join attribute as a percentage of the entire tuple.

Intelligent Devices

In the discussion so far, it was assumed that the devices used could perform only
two operations: read and write. Consider the case of an imaging application in a hospi-
tal. The application involves a machine like a CT scanner. Such a machine has the ability
to capture images and store them locally. When required, specific images can be transferred to any desired location. In the model described, the CT scanner would occupy a
separate level on the storage hierarchy and demonstrates the power of the model: ability
to regard a device as being capable of performing a variety of operations (not just read
and write).

We will call devices capable of performing other operations in addition to read and

Figure 4   IO Time with Limited Disk and Placement P1

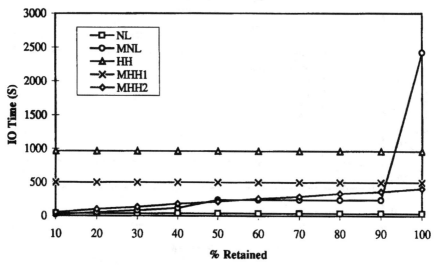

Figure 5   IO Time with Limited Disk for Placement P5

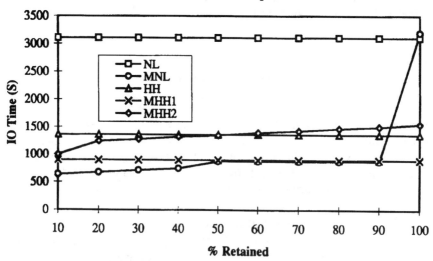

write as being intelligent. Having an intelligent device can help in improving the performance of join algorithms as will be demonstrated shortly. Incorporating such a capacity in the model is a simple matter of adding the necessary functions to F in the definition of a device. We will test the result of adding intelligence to devices by studying the nested loop algorithm. The enhanced algorithm will be described next.

Intelligent Nested Loop Algorithm

For this we assume that each device has the ability to return not only an entire tuple from a relation but only certain attributes from the tuple. Thus, for each intelligent device the set of functions would be

$$F = \{Read, Write, f_1\}$$

where f_1 is the function that make the device intelligent. In our case, we define f_1 as a function that accepts a fragment of a relation and performs a projection operation to yield the join attributes and the restrictions. The algorithm (Algorithm INL) is described next.

Algorithm INL

This algorithm uses the nested loop algorithm to join two relations R (the outer relation) and S (the inner relation) with FR and FS fragments, JR and JS as their join attributes and RR and RS as join restrictions. The join will be performed in a setup where the devices have intelligence as described above. When a request for a fragment is sent to a device, the device sends only the join attributes and the restrictions instead of the entire tuple. The intelligence of the device will help in improving the performance of the algorithm provided that the size of the join attributes and the restriction is less than the size of the tuple.

```
For i = 1 to FR
begin
        Get fragment i of R by executing function f1 on the device containing
        that fragment
        For j = 1 to FS
        begin
                Get fragment j of S by executing function f1 on the device
                containing that fargment
                Join fragments i and j
        end
end
```

Figure 6 shows the performance of the intelligent nested loop algorithm. The x-axis represents the percentage of the tuple size that forms the join attributes and restrictions. As can be expected this version performs better than the conventional one.

Details of Simulation Runs

In this section we discuss the details of the simulation runs that were carried out to test the different algorithms.

1. The fragment size was set between 3 and 5 MB.
2. 2000 relations were generated with varying random sizes between 15 and 50 MB.
3. The relations were then split into fragments and placed according to the placement strategies P_1 through P_5.
4. Of these 2000 relations, two relations to be joined were selected at random.
5. The various algorithms were then run, each run preceded by resetting the system and removing any temporary fragments that may have been created by the other algorithms.
6. Algorithm MNL was run in the following manner. This algorithm requires a LUT to

Figure 6   IO Time with Device Intelligence for the Nested Loop Algorithm

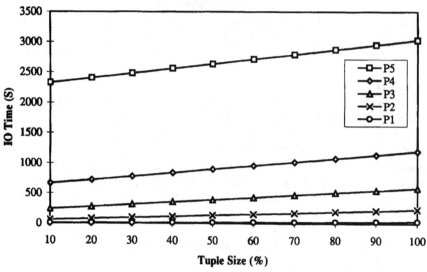

determine the number of tuples to save. The LUT was assumed to fit in main memory. This algorithm was run ten times, each time saving a percentage of the fragment of the inner relation, starting with 10% and going up to 100% of the fragment of inner relation. When the saved fraction, exceeded a fragment size, it was saved back to the disk.

7. The algorithm MHH2 was run in the following manner. This algorithm retains only the part of the tuple (that corresponds to the join attribute) during the partitioning phase. This algorithm was run ten times, each time saving a percentage of the tuple size starting with 10% and going up to 100% of the tuple size. This algorithm then reads the partitions and determines the tuples that have met the join criterion. Those tuples will then need to be brought in from both relations to prepare the final result. In the best case, all those tuples will belong to one fragment of each relation. In the worst case, the tuples will be dispersed among all of the fragments of each relation. We took the average case where the tuples are dispersed among half the fragments of each relation. Those fragments were then read in.

8. The I/O time measured is the sum of the seek-time, platter-switch time and the data transfer time for the device involved. The total I/O time for the algorithm is the sum of the individual I/O times involved.

9. The performance of the join algorithms was measured for the one-step flood, two-step flood and incremental-flood models. For lack of space, not all graphs have been shown.

10. The intelligent nested loop algorithm was run 10 times each time varying the size of the join attribute(s) and the restriction. This was done by varying the size of the join attribute(s) and the restriction from 10% to 100% of the tuple size. This process was repeated for all five placement startegies.

CONCLUSIONS AND FUTURE WORK

With the growing demand of applications for storage, it will become necessary for users to look at making tertiary storage a part of the system. Once that happens, users will need a tool to study the effect of various database operations under different device and data placement settings. In this paper, we proposed a generic storage and data placement model. This model can be used as a tool to measure the performance of data operations under any system settings. We demonstrated one use for the model by using it as a tool to measure the cost of two join algorithms namely, the nested loop and hybrid hash algorithms, in a tertiary storage based system. We used different data placement methods. We then modified the nested loop algorithm with a view to reducing the I/O time. We also used the model look at situations when the available disk space is limited hence prohibiting its use to store temporary relations. We modified the hybrid hash algorithm to take care of this situation. Both the modifications did better than their conventional methods. Currently we are using the model with other forms of data like images and applications like medical image databases where tertiary devices are of great significance. We are also investigating the use of the model with a learning tool to look at adaptive placement techniques as an advisor on the best set of devices given a set of requirements.

REFERENCES

Blakeley, J. and N. Martin, 1990, Join Index, Materialized View, and Hybrid-Hash Join: A Performance Analysis," *Proceedings IEEE 6th Conference on Data Engineering*, pp.256-263.

L-F. Cabrera, L-F et al., 1995, "ADSM: A Multi-Platform, Scalable, Backup and Archive Mass Storage System," *IBM Research Report* RJ 9936 (87895).

Carey, M.J., L.M. Haas and M. Livny, 1993, "Tapes Hold Data Too: Challenges on Tertiary Storage," *SIGMOD Record*, Vol.22, No.2.

Chen, L.T. et al., 1995, "Efficient Organization and Access of Multi-Dimensional Datasets on Tertiary Storage Systems," *Information Systems Journal*, Spring.

Chen, Y-T, et al., 1993, "Data Placement for Large Read-Only Interactive Multimedia Information Systems on Multi-Disk Environment," *Proceedings of SPIE*, Vol. 1908, pp.133-141.

DeWitt, D.J. et al., 1984, "Implementation Techniques for Main Memory Database Systems," *ACM*.

Ford, D.A. and J. Myllymaki, 1995, "A Log-Structured Organization for Tertiary Storage," *IBM Research Report* RJ 9941 (87900), Feb.

Fotouhi, F. and S. Pramanik, 1989, "Optimal Secondary Storage Access Sequence for Performing Relational Join," *IEEE Transactions on Knowledge and Data Engineering*, Vol.1, No.3, pp.318-328.

Hall, E., 1996, "Managing Mass-Storage Monsters," *Network Computing*, Vol.7, No.16,.

Mishra, P. and M.H. Eich, 1992, "Join Processing in Relational Databases," *ACM Computing Surveys*, Vol.24, No.1, pp.63-113.

Olson, M.A., 1992, "Extending the POSTGRES Database System to Manage Tertiary Storage," Master's Thesis, University of California at Berkeley.

Pramanik, S. and F. Fotouhi, 1988, "Optimizing the Cost of Relational Queries Using Partial-Relation Schemes," *Information Systems*, Vol.13, No.1, pp.71-79.

Salem, K., 1992, "MR-CDF: Managing Multi-Resolution Scientific Data," *Proceedings of the Goddard Conference on Mass Storage Systems and Technologies,* pp.101-111.

Sarawagi, S. and M. Stonebraker, 1994, "Single Query Optimization for Tertiary Memory," Technical Report, University of California at Berkeley.

Sarawagi, S., 1995, "Single Query Optimization for Tertiary Memory," *Proceedings of VLDB,* Zurich..

Seeger, B. et al., 1993, "Reading a Set of Disk Pages," *Proceedings of VLDB*, Dublin, pp.592-603.

Stephenson, T. et al., 1993, "Mass Storage Systems for Image Management and Distribution," *Proceedings of Twelfth IEEE Symposium on Mass Storage Systems,* pp.233-240, Apr.

Stonebraker, M., 1991, "Managing Persistent Objects in a Multi-level Store," *Proceedings of SIGMOD* 91, pp.2-11.

Tikekar, R. et al., 1997, "A Generalized Storage Model for Tertiary Storage Based Systems," *Proceedings of International Database Engineering and Applications Symposium* (IDEAS), Montreal, pp.161-170, Aug.

Tikekar, R, 1997, "Query Optimization in Tertiary Storage Based Systems Using a Generalized Storage Model," Ph.D. dissertation, Wayne State University.

Wallace, S., 1994, "Managing Mass Storage," *Byte,* pp.79-89, Mar.

Winter, R., 1994, "The Future of Very Large Database," *Database Programming and Design,* Vol.7, No.12, pp.27-31.

CHAPTER 7

Alternative Plan Generation for Multiple Query Optimization

Ahmet Cosar
Middle East Technical University, Turkey

The Multiple Query Optimization (MQO) tries to determine a maximal amount of shared tasks between a set of input queries so that a single global execution plan can be generated in such a way that these shared tasks are performed only once and the total cost of evaluating all of the queries is reduced.

This chapter presents a heuristic, h_c, such that the problem of selecting an alternative plan for each query, from among a set of given alternative plans, is solved in a much shorter time. Combinatorial algorithms such as iterative improvement and simulated annealing are also experimentally evaluated for cases that there is not sufficient time for finding an optimal solution to MQO.

We also investigate the problem of generating alternative plans for a given query and experimentally evaluate two methods that we propose.

INTRODUCTION

The work in the area of multiple query optimization (MQO) has mostly focused on recognizing the common operations or generating an optimal execution plan assuming that these common operations have already been figured out. There has not been any much effort in generating query execution plans which will allow more sharing between queries. We believe such an approach is important both because of increased sharing between queries and also for reducing the amount of work to be done in the alternative plan generation (APG) phase.

We develop algorithms for finding common operations between queries such that these operations can be performed only once and their results can be used by other queries thus reducing the overall execution cost of queries. The problem of determining common tasks between queries has been proven NP-Hard[Rosenkrantz, 1980], [Jarke, 1984] and is a significant task, the cost of which has been so far ignored in calculating the benefits from MQO. Our work helps to determine how much total work is necessary to obtain the benefits of multiple query processing and thus enables the users and database administraters to make a decision on whether MQO would benefit their applications.

In order to increase the amount of shared common tasks the APG phase may have to change join orders and delay selections and projections (unlike the optimal case of performing selections and projections as early as possible, for single query optimizers) so that more sharing is possible between query execution plans. For this purpose we propose a set of query transformation operations to generate equivalent alternative plans. We propose two different alternative plan generation algorithms, one requiring $O(N^2)$ and the other requiring $O(N^N)$ work where N is the number of queries to be used for multiple query optimization. We experimentally evaluate both methods and show that the $O(N^2)$ method generates as good plans as the $O(N^N)$ method, without much loss in benefits obtained from MQO while the amount of processing required by the $O(N^2)$ method is much less than the $O(N^N)$ method.

The step after generating a set of alternative plans for each query is to employ a multiple query optimizer for generating a global execution plan which will find the results for each query involved in the multiple query optimization. We have worked on this problem as well and developed new heuristics to improve the performance of previous MQO algorithms.

Finding the optimal solution to the problem of determining a global execution plan from a set of alternative plans, where there is one or more alternative plans for each query, has been studied in depth and reported in Grant (1980) using depth first search (DFS), in Sellis (1986) using A*, and in Park (1988) using dynamic programming (DP). The A* heuristic has been improved and combinatorial optimization methods such as Simulated Annealing (SA) and Successive Augmentation have been introduced in Cosar (1991). The query ordering heuristics in Sellis (1986) have also been enhanced by "dynamic query ordering" heuristic and its performance has been shown to be substantially better in Cosar (1993). The combinatorial methods used in Cosar (1991) have also shown to be quite promising and are good alternatives for cases where there might be only a limited amount of time for multiple query optimization.

BACKGROUND ON MQO PROBLEM

The multiple query optimization (MQO) problem is defined as consisting of a given set of queries and a set of alternative execution plans (and a plan is a set of tasks) for each query, from which a single plan is selected for each query in such a way that the sum of the execution costs of all the tasks in the selected plans is minimal amongst all such sets. It can be formulated formally as follows (Sellis, 1988; Sellis, 1990).

Let $Q_1,...,Q_n$ be n queries to be optimized together.

Query Q_i has a set of n_i alternative plans for its evaluation, namely $P_{i,1}$, $P_{i,2}$,..., $P_{i,ni}$

Plan $P_{i,j}$ is a set of tasks $t_{i,j,k}$.

A task $t_{i,j,k}$ has an associated cost of $cost(t_{i,j,k})$.

A solution, S, to the MQO problem is a set of plans

$P_S = \{P_{1,s1}, P_{2,s2},...,P_{n,sn}\}$.

Let $T_S = U_{(Pi,si \in Ps)} \{t_{i,j,k}, t_{i,j,k} \in P_{i,si}\}$ be the set of tasks in the solution S.

Now, $cost(S) = \Sigma_{(t \in TS)} cost(t)$ is the cost of the solution.

An optimal solution S^* is such that $cost(S^*)$ is minimal.

Example 1, below, shows a sample MQO problem with two queries and five plans. Query Q_1 has plans $P_{1,1}$ and $P_{1,2}$ while query Q_2 has plans $P_{2,1}$, $P_{2,2}$, and $P_{2,3}$. Table 1 gives the costs of the tasks used in this example.

Example 1: Let the plans for Q1 and Q2 have the following task sets:

$P_{1,1}=\{t_1,t_2,t_3\}$; $P_{1,2}=\{t_4,t_5\}$
$P_{2,1}=\{t_1,t_6,t_7\}$; $P_{2,2}=\{t_2,t_8,t_9\}$; $P_{2,3}=\{t_5,t_{10}\}$

There are six alternatives:

$S(P_{1,1}, P_{2,1})=cost(t_1)+cost(t_2)+cost(t_3)+cost(t_6)+cost(t_7)=90$
$S(P_{1,1}, P_{2,2})=cost(t_1)+cost(t_2)+cost(t_3)+cost(t_8)+cost(t_9)=90$
$S(P_{1,1}, P_{2,3})=cost(t_1)+cost(t_2)+cost(t_3)+cost(t_5)+cost(t_{10})=125$
$S(P_{1,2}, P_{2,1})=cost(t_1)+cost(t_4)+cost(t_5)+cost(t_6)+cost(t_7)=110$
$S(P_{1,2}, P_{2,2})=cost(t_2)+cost(t_4)+cost(t_5)+cost(t_8)+cost(t_9)=100$
$S(P_{1,2}, P_{2,3})=cost(t_4)+cost(t_5)+cost(t_{10})=85$

The minimum cost execution plans for queries Q_1 and Q_2 are $P_{1,2}$ and $P_{2,2}$, with costs 55 and 45, respectively. For MQO, however, the plan set which gives the minimum total execution cost of both plans is $\{P_{1,2},P_{2,3}\}$.

OPTIMAL SOLUTIONS TO THE MQO PROBLEM

AI Search Approach

The problem formulation defined above has been used to apply the A* (Sellis, 1990) and branch and bound (Grant, 1982) optimization methods to the MQO problem. Pruning has also been used for eliminating unpromising paths and is a major source of reduction in search time. The performance of the algorithm given in Sellis (1990) was the best attained until this work, therefore it has been used for comparing the performance of our heuristics.

Any improvement in the performance of the A* algorithm is dependent on (1) the heuristic function used for directing the search and estimating the lower bound on the cost of a given path, and (2) a good initial upper bound. With tighter upper and lower bounds, it will be possible to prune a large number of nodes, leading to improved performance. In Sellis (1990), several ordering heuristics have been used to achieve these goals. However, one disadvantage of these heuristics is that the order is determined once at the beginning of the optimization and remains constant during the search.

Heuristic Function h_s used in Sellis (1990)

Table 1: The tasks and their costs for Example 1.

Task Cost Table

	T1	T2	T3	T4	T5	T6	T7	T8	T9	T10
Cost	40	30	5	35	20	10	5	5	10	30

Assume that the state after selecting plans for queries Q1,...,Qk is $S_k=<P_{1,j1},...P_{k,jk},NULL,NULL,...,NULL>$.
Let $Cost_{est}(t_i)=cost(t_i)/n_i$.
Also, $cost_{est}(P_{i,j})=\Sigma_{t_i \in P_{i,j}} cost_{est}(t_i)$.

Here n_i is the number of queries, among all the queries, with a plan containing t_i.
Now, $h_s=cost_{est}(S_k)=\Sigma_{1<i\leq k} cost_{est}(P_{i,ji}) + \Sigma_{k<l\leq n} min(cost_{est}(P_{i,1}),...,cost_{est}(P_{i,ni}))$.

Heuristic Function h_c used in Cosar (1991)

Assume that the state after selecting plans for queries Q1,...,Qk is again Sk.
Let Tsel = $U(1<I\leq k) Pi,jk$ be the set of tasks of the selected plans.
Let $Cost_{est}(Q_i)=min\{\Sigma_{t_i \in P_{i,j}} cost_{est}(t_i)\}$.
Also, $cost_{est}(t_i)=0$, if $t_i \hat{I}$ tsel, and $cost_{est}(t_i)=cost(t_i)/m_i$, if $t_i \notin t_{sel}$.

Here m_i is the number of queries, among those not assigned a plan yet, with a plan containing t_i.
Now, $h_c=cost_{est}(S_k)=\Sigma_{tx \in tsel} cost(t_x) + \Sigma_{k<i\leq n} cost_{est}(Q_i)$.

Since the number of queries sharing a task cannot be more than m_i, the estimated cost contribution of a task is guaranteed to be smaller than its real cost. Moreover, if a task is already in one of the plans selected so far, its real cost is used in estimating the overall cost. This is a major improvement over h_s, which always uses estimated costs no matter which plans have already been selected.

Lemma 1: h_c is at least as informed as h_s.

Proof: Follows from above argument that m_i is always less than or equal to n_i.

Theorem 1: An A* algorithm for the multiple query optimization problem using h_c will expand no more states than one using h_s.

Proof: Follows from Lemma 1 and properties of A*, details are available in Cosar (1993).

The Query Ordering Heuristics

An important factor effecting the performance of A* search algorithm is the order in which the search space is traversed. This is done by ordering the queries so that plans are assigned to queries in a specific order. For h_s, six ordering heuristics were defined and investigated by Sellis (1988). These are:

- Order 1: The original order given by query index.
- Order 2: Increasing number of plans.
- Order 3: Decreasing average query cost.
- Order 4: Decreasing average estimated query cost.
- Order 5: Decreasing average query cost per plan.
- Order 6: Decreasing average estimated query cost per plan.

Each query ordering heuristic was extensively analyzed and experimentally evaluated by Sellis (1988) and the reported results show that Order3 is usually the best heuristic. We have defined a so called *dynamic query ordering* heuristic and compared its performance with Order3 heuristic.

Experimental Comparison of h_s and h_c

In order to evaluate the performance of the proposed heuristic, we randomly generated experimental query sets. The parameters that were used in generating these queries are given below:

- The number of queries: ranges from 5 to 15.
- The number of plans per query: Each query is randomly assigned between 3 to 5 alternative plans.
- The number of tasks per plan: Each plan is randomly assigned a number of tasks. The tasks are chosen from a randomly generated fixed set of tasks. By increasing this number the probability of having more shared tasks also increases since the tasks are selected from a fixed set.

Figure 1 gives the results of experiments on these randomly generated query sets and shows that hc performs substantially better than hs. For example, for 15 queries h_s expands 593,997 states while h_c expands only 691 states.

Since the calculation of hc cost estimation function requires more cpu time we also give in Figure 2 the execution times of MQO for h_s and h_c in order to compare the actual times both heuristics require to search the above states.

Figure 1: Comparison of h_s and h_c in terms of number of expanded states

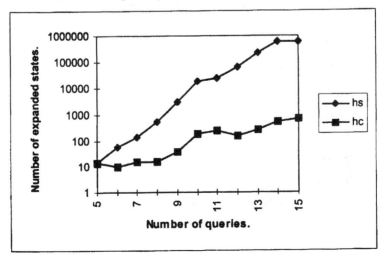

Figure 2: Comparison of h_s and h_c in terms of execution time.

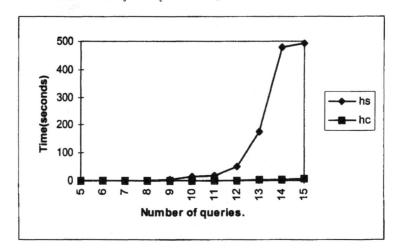

DYNAMIC QUERY ORDERING

From the results of Sellis (1988) it is seen that the query ordering heuristics greatly affects the number of expanded states. However, the fact that these ordering heuristics are static and are calculated only at the beginning of the search causes their benefits to diminish as the search progresses, while more information becomes available about the estimated cost of a partial global execution plan. We define a dynamic ordering heuristic which calculated during search by analyzing a given partial global plan. For this purpose, all alternative plans of queries which are not assigned a plan in the current global plan are checked to determine the plan with maximum sharing with the tasks already in the global plan. The amount of sharing is calculated by the formula (**original_cost – shared_cost**), but the ratio (**original_cost / shared_cost**) also performs quite well.

Figure 3: Comparison of static and dynamic query ordering.

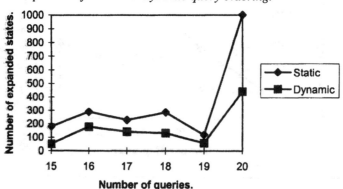

Experimental Comparison of Static and Dynamic Query Ordering Heuristics

In order to evaluate the performance of our dynamic query ordering heuristic, we again randomly generated query sets as described before and ran the A* algorithm using the Order3 of Sellis (1988) and our new dynamic ordering. The experimental results show that dynamic ordering heuristics will allow us to achieve about 50% more reduction in the number of expanded states. These results are given in Figure 3.

COMBINATORIAL OPTIMIZATION METHODS FOR MQO PROBLEM

Even though the A* algorithm is optimal in terms of the number of expanded states, the search becomes prohibitively expensive in terms of the amount of memory required to store the open states to be explored. It is also possible that only a limited amount of time could be reserved for MQO and a global plan is required and useful even if it is not necessarily an optimal plan. In order to address these concerns several probabilistic search algorithms such as Simulated Annealing and Iterative Improvement can be used. Simulated Annealing has already been proposed for single query optimization and experimentally evaluated by Ioannidis (1990). Here a two step method is proposed. The first step uses Iterative Improvement to obtain a good global plan and in the second step Simulated Annealing is used to improve this plan. The fact that the performance of Simulated Annealing greatly depends on selected parameters such as determining the *temperature, cooling ratio*, and the number of iterations at each temperature level makes its use difficult, but experiments show that reasonably good global execution plans are obtained by Simulated Annealing for query sizes 5 to 20 which are optimal or very close to optimal. However, for large query sets, of say 100 queries, we have no way of knowing how close the randomly found global plan is to an optimal solution.

Figure 4: Simulated Annealing plan costs with increasing number of iterations.

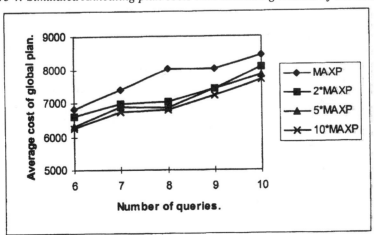

Simulated Annealing

The experimental results on Simulated Annealing were reported in [Cosar, 1996] and show that more work is needed to determine ways of finding more effective parameters to make best use of Simulated Annealing. The Figure 4 gives a comparison of the qualities of plans found by using Simulated Annealing with optimal plans, for 6 to 20 queries. The results for Simulated Annealing are averages taken over 100 random experiments for varying numbers of iterations(L), where L is changed from the total number of plans(MAXP) in MQO to 2*MAXP, 5*MAXP, and 10*MAXP.

The Figure 5 compares the average quality of plans obtained by Simulated Annealing to optimal plans. These results show that the plans are close to optimal, but nevertheless most of the time they are not optimal and the standard deviations reported in [Cosar, 1996] are about 10%. Therefore, more work needs to be done to make Simulated Annealing a

Figure 5: Comparison of Simulated Annealing plan costs with optimal costs.

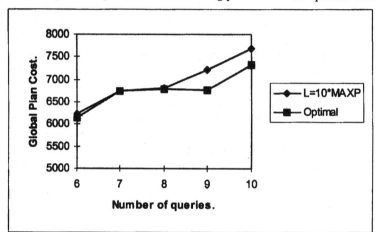

Figure 6: Comparison of Simulated Annealing and Iterative Improvement.

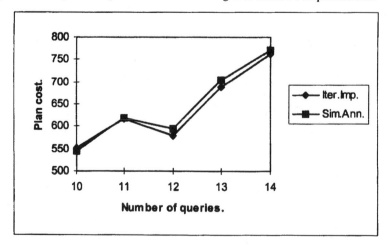

reliable alternative optimization method for MQO.

Iterative Improvement

Another combinatorial optimization method which is know to have good performance for single query optimization is Iterative Improvement (Swami, 1989). In order to experimentally evaluate the Iterative Improvement method the same experiments were run using both Simulated Annealing and Iterative Improvement, the average plan costs are reported in Figure 6 and show that they have similar performance.

Successive Augmentation

The Successive Augmentation heuristic is a method which has been shown to perform quite good for single query optimization. This method has been adapted to MQO problem and experimentally evaluated. In fact this methods was finally chosen for calculating an initial upper bound for A* algorithm as it has been shown to obtain global plans which are quite close to optimal. The combinatorial algorithms are given below and the experimental results are reported in Figure 7.

Successive Augmentation Algorithm.
```
S= <> // Empty initial solution
For(k=1;k≤N;k++) {
    P_{i,j}= Determine_Plan_With_Most_Sharing(S);
    S[i] = P_{i,j};
}
Simulated Annealing Algorithm.

LB = Initial_Lower_Bound(<>); // while no plans are chosen
S= Random_initial_solution();
Temp= Shared_Cost(S) – LB;
L= Total_Number_of_Plans;
R = exp(1.0/N*log(1.0/Temp); // N is 10 by default
While(Temp>0){
For(I=1;I≤L;I++) {
Old_Cost = Shared_Cost(S);
P_{x,y}= Select_Random_Plan();
New_Cost = Shared_Cost( S union P_{x,y});
Delta = New_Cost – Old_Cost;
If(Delta<0) {
Assign_Plan_to_Query(P_{x,y},Q_x);
LB= New_Cost;
}
else {
if((1-Delta/temp) < Random(1.0))
Assign_Plan_to_Query(P_{x,y},Q_x);
}

P_{i,j}= Determine_Plan_With_Most_Sharing(S);
```

```
    S[i] = P_{i,j};
    }
Temp = Temp *R;
}
Iterative Improvement Algorithm
LB = Initial_Lower_Bound(<>); // while no plans are chosen
S= Random_initial_solution();
For(maxgain=1;maxgain>0;) {
    Maxgain=0;
    For(I=1;I≤No_of_Queries;I++) {
            For(j=1;j≤Q[I].No_of_Plans;j++) {
                    Gain = old_cost – Shared_Cost(S union P_{i,j});
                    If(gain>maxgain) {
                            Maxgain = gain;
                            Selected_Plan_{x,y} = P_{i,j};
                    }
            }
    }
    If(maxgain>0) Assign_Plan_to_Query(Q_x,Selected_Plan_{x,y});
}
```

ALTERNATIVE PLAN GENERATION

In order to obtain the benefits of MQO a multiple query optimizer must first of all identify the common tasks between the queries. This work has decided to use the relational algebra as the model for representing queries and the common task identification is done by finding common relational algebra operators on the same operands. Since a query is relational algebra is represented as a tree a set of transformation operations have been defined such that when these operations are applied to a relational algebra tree the resulting modified tree will yield the same results as the original one. These transformation

Figure 7: The plan quality for Successive Augmentation.

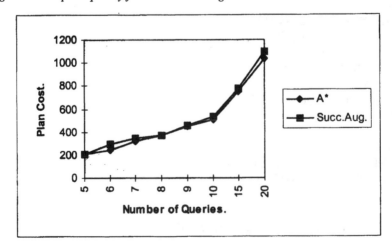

Figure 8: The commutativity transformation.

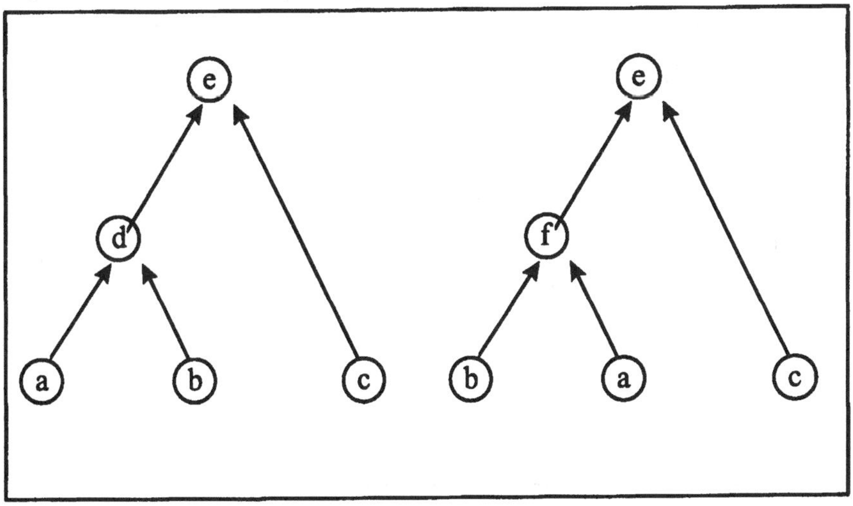

operations are given next.

Commutativity Transformation

This is the simplest transformation operation and swaps the two children of a join operation. The order of join operands are used to decide some join algorithm dependent parameters, such as the inner and outer relations for nested-loop join, or the relation to use for constructing the hash-table for hash-join.

Associativity Transformation

The join operation (we limit our work to natural joins) is associative and therefore join operations could be easily transformed to allow more sharing of join results, as long as the join conditions are compatible and this will be the case most of the time for joins over foreign and primary keys. Since join operations are, usually, very costly our alternative alternative plan generator tries to discover as many shared joins as possible and see if the the total execution cost is reduced.

Selection Fragmentation Transformation

Since different queries would usually be interested in only a subset of the tuples of relation (or join result), the queries will differ in the *selection criteria* they specify. In order to share the operations when such selection criteria exist, we need to identify a common subset of these selection criteria and transform the RA trees accordingly so that the common task identification process can generate more (and larger) common tasks. Please note that this is equivalent to delaying part of selection operations on input relations, while in single query optimization the selection operations are always performed as early as possible. Therefore, the cost of delaying a selection operation, both in terms of the number of tuples to be processed and also in terms of the higher I/O cost, needs to be outweighed by the gain from sharing tasks.

Figure 9: The associativity transformation.

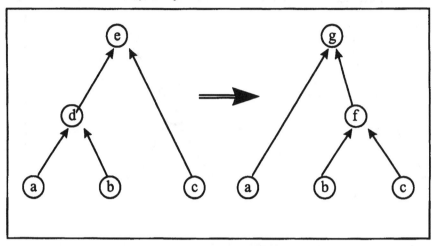

Figure 10: The selection fragmentation transformation.

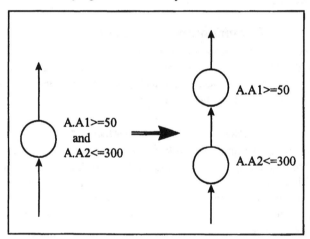

Projection Fragmentation Transformation

This operation is similar to *selection fragmentation* but it applies to the list of attributes. In single query optimization, attributes not needed in subsequent query processing are eliminated from relations and intermediate results as early as possible. While this is always optimal for single query optimization, in case of multiple query optimization early elimination of some attributes may prevent the sharing of intermediate results with other queries for which those eliminated attributes are significant, such as a selection condition or a join operation with another relation. Therefore, we introduce the *projection fragmentation* transformation in order to allow more sharing between queries.

Figure 11: The projection fragmentation transformation.

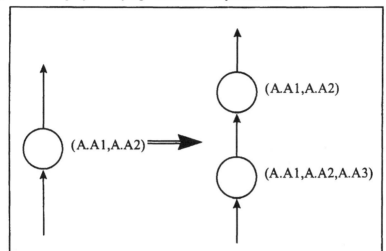

Figure 12: The selection propagation transformation.

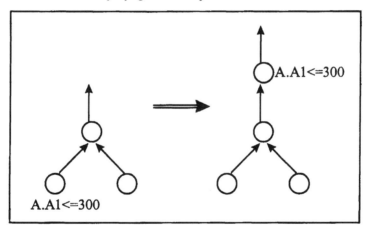

Selection and Projection Propagation Transformation

This transformation is used to delay selection and projection operations so that the intermediate results of operations can have more sharing with other queries. This will result in increasing the cost of a query but the benefits from sharing the intermediate results might offset this cost.

Task Sharing Determination Algorithm

In order to determine shared tasks in a MQO problem each query execution plan is transformed by considering the other query execution plans which share two or more relations with it.

Figure 13: The join sharing transformation algorithm.

```
    q: the root node of RA tree
                rl: list of relations to be shared
                moveup(): propagates an operation one level up in the RA
tree.
    sn= find_split_node(q,rl);
    While(sn !=NULL) {
        dn= find_disjoint_node(sn,rl);
        While(dn_is_child_of_sn(dn,sn)) {
                Moveup(dn);
                sn=find_split_node(q,rl);
        }
    }
```

Definition: A *relation list* of a node in a RA tree is the union of the relation lists of its children. For leaf nodes (which are all read operations) the relation list is the relation I is reading.

Definition: A *split node* n (which is a join node) with respect to a relation list rl such that *nl* and *nr* are left and right children of *n*, and relation_list(n)=rl and relation_list(nl) is a proper subset of rl.

Definition: A *disjoint node d* is the node of a RA tree such that for a given relation list *rl*, relation_list(d) ∩ rl must be null.

Figure 14: Alternative plan generation steps.

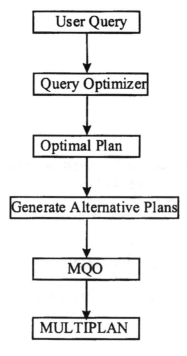

ALTERNATIVE PLAN GENERATION (APG)

In this work we decided to search for common tasks right after query execution plans for individual queries are found. In this way the queries in RA form can be modified using the commutativity and associativity properties for select-project-join operations and thus larger common tasks can be identified, resulting in more MQO savings. The process is summarized in Figure 14.

Pairwise Transformation Heuristic

This heuristic tries to determine shared tasks between every single query execution plan with plans for other queries on a pairwise basis and generates two alternative plans, one for each plan in the pair. With this heuristic each query can be potentially given N-1 alternative query execution plans if there are N queries. The time complexity of this heuristic is $O(N^2)$ and the resulting MQO problem will have a search space of $O(N^N)$ which shows the difficulty of the problem.

Complete Transformation Heuristic

In this heuristic each query execution plan is matched in turn with every other query execution plan (except the alternative plans of the same query). Each newly generated alternative plan will be included in the next iteration of the algorithm, thus all possible combinations of alternative plans will be searched. The time complexity of this algorithm is $O(NP^2)$ where NP is the total number of plans for all queries (in the worst case $NP \leq (N+1)!$).

Comparison of Pairwise and Complete Transformation Heuristics

In order to determine if the extra work done by the complete transformation heuristic would be worthwhile in terms of the improvements in the amoun of sharing achieved MQO, experiments were performed on both heuristics and their performances on the given set of queries were compared. For this purpose random MQO problems were generated by varying the number of queries from five to twenty. Then, the A* algorithm was used to determine an optimal global execution plan. The execution times of APG and MQO optimization were also recorded and are included for comparison in Table 2. These results show that it is possible to obtain additional benefits in terms of the achieved optimal plan but this needs to be weighed with the additional execution time for alternative plan genera-

Table 2: Benefits obtained from Alternative Plan Generation.

# of Qs	Non-Shared Cost(ms)	Shared Cost(ms)	APG+MQO(sec)
5	41773	36353	32.09+0.04
10	66147	43046	34.29+0.09
15	83448	43302	44.32+0.15
20	102273	44518	49.72+0.37

Table 3: Comparison of APG times and plan quality.

# of Qs	APG(sec)+MQO(sec)/Shared Cost(ms)			
	Pairwise		Complete	
5	1.18+0.07	10861	1.18+0.06	10861
6	1.43+0.09	15842	1.47+0.08	15842
7	3.08+0.22	15918	3.45+0.22	15918
8	3.44+0.29	15957	4.01+0.27	15957
9	4.45+0.47	16447	5.65+0.77	16433
10	5.00+0.43	16447	6.71+0.56	16433
20	25.11+108.7	35663	54.79+75.74	35663

tion. While the additional time required for small MQO problems of size five to ten queries is small, as the number of queries increases the increase in alternative plan generation time becomes more significant and almost doubles for twenty queries. However, an interesting observation is that in one instance (for twenty queries) the time for MQO itself was significantly reduced due to additional alternative plans.

The comparison of complete and pairwise heuristics in Table 3 show that no significant improvement was achieved in the quality of global query execution plans by using the complete transformation heuristic. The APG time more than doubles for twenty queries and no improvement was achieved in global query execution plan. For smaller query sets, still there is almost no improvement and for 9 queries an improvement of 14ms comes at the expense of 1200ms in APG time and 300ms in MQO time.

CONCLUSIONS AND FUTURE WORK

Our results on h_c and related dynamic query ordering heuristics show that it is feasible to employ MQO techniques in order to reduce the cost of query execution in a database. Optimal algorithms could be used for cases where upto 15 queries need to be executed together. For larger problems randomized algorithms such as iterative improvement, simulated annealing, and successive augmentation could be used.

The alternative plan generation was also shown to be feasible and the benefits from MQO could easily cover the cost of APG and MQO. It is possible to further reduce the APG time by filtering unpromising alternative plans. We believe MQO will help to answer the increasing demands both in the number of queries and also the number of users by grouping users' queries together and finding a global execution plan to calculate the results for all of them using MQO methods.

REFERENCES

Chakravarthy, U.S. & Minker, J. (1982).Processing multiple queries in database systems. In *Database Engineering* 5.3, pages 38-44.

Chakravarthy, S.(1990). "Divide and Conquer: A Basis for Augmenting a Conventional Query Optimizer with Multiple Query Processing Capabilities", in *IEEE Conf. On*

Data Engineering, pp.482-490.

Cosar, A., Srivastava, J. & Shekhar, S.(1991). "On the multiple pattern multiple object (mpmo) match problem", in *Intl. Conf. On Management of Data.*

Cosar, A., Lim, E-P., & Srivastava, J.(1993). "Multiple Query Optimization with Depth-First Branch-and-Bound and Dynamic Query Ordering", in *Journal of Database Management,* 1994, vol.6,no.1,pp.14-19.

Cosar, A. (1996). "Design and Experimental Analysis of a Multiple Query Optimizer". PhD Thesis, Dept. of CS, University of Minnesota, February 1996.

Grant, J. & Minker, J. (1980). "On optimizing the evaluation of a set of expressions". Technical Report, TR-916, College Park, MD, July.

Grant, J. & Minker, J.(1982). "On optimizing the evaluation of a set of expressions", in *Int. J. Comput. Inform. Sci.,* March.

Ioannidis, Y.E. & Kang, Y.C.(1990). "Randomized algorithms for optimizing large join queries" in *Proc. of the ACM-SIGMOD Intl. Conf. On the Management of Data*, pp. 312-321.

Jarke, M.(1984). "Common Subexpression Isolation in Multiple Query Optimization". Query Processing in Database Systems. W. Kim, D. Reiner, D. Batory, Eds., Springer Verlag, New York.

Park, J.& Segev, A.(1988). "Using common subexpressions to optimize multiple queries", in *Proc. of the Intl. Conf. On Data Engineering*, pp 311-319, 1988.

Rosenkrantz, D.J. & Kunt, H.E. (1980)."Processing Conjuntive Predicates and Queries", in *Proc. of VLDB Conf.*

Sellis, T. (1986)."Global query optimization" in P*roc. of the ACM-SIGMOD Intl. Conf. On the Management of Data.*

Sellis, T. (1988). "Multiple Query Optimization", in *ACM Transactions on Database Systems,* 13(1), pp. 23-52.

Sellis, T. & Ghosh, S.(1990). "On the multiple-query optimization problem", in *IEEE Trans. On Knowledge and Data Engineering,* pp. 262-266, 1990.

Swami, A.N.(1989). "Optimization of Large Join Queries". PhD Thesis, Dept. of CS, Stanford University, June 1989.

CHAPTER 8

Integrating I/O Processing and Transparent Parallelism — Toward Comprehensive Query Execution in Parallel Database Systems

Stefan Manegold and Florian Waas
Centrum voor Wiskunde en Informatica, The Netherlands

Query processing in parallel database systems stands or falls by efficient resource usage including CPU scheduling, I/O processing and memory allocation. Up to now, most research has focused on load balancing issues concerning several resources of the same kind only, i.e. balancing either CPU load or I/O load exclusively. In this chapter we present floating probe, a novel strategy to utilize parallel resources in a shared-everything environment efficiently. The key idea of floating probe is dynamic load balancing of CPU and I/O resources by overlapping I/O-bound build phase and CPU-bound probe phase of pipeline segments. The extent of interleaving is only limited by data dependencies. Simulation results show, that floating probe achieves considerably shorter execution times with less memory demands than conventional pipelining strategies.

INTRODUCTION

Parallel query processing is the key to the performance improvements demanded by modern database applications. Pipelining parallelism is of particular interest since it is easier to control and less resource consuming than independent parallelism yet offering a huge potential of parallelism. Moreover, for linear query trees, pipelining is the only possibility to exploit inter-operator parallelism (Hasan and Motwani, 1994).

The two major aspects of pipeline processing that need to be considered carefully are the processor scheduling—the actual parallelization—and the I/O processing to support the scheduling.

So far, much work has been devoted to different processor scheduling strategies.

Figure 1: Pipelining segment

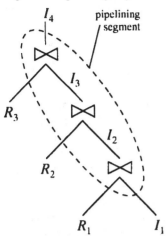

Schneider and DeWitt study pipelining techniques on right-deep trees of hash join operators, proposing two distinct phases of processing (Schneider and DeWitt, 1990): Firstly, during the *build phase*, the inner relations of the joins are read from disk and hash tables are built in parallel. Secondly, during the *probe phase*, the outer relation is piped bottom-up through all operators.

Figure 1 shows an example for a *pipeline segment*. R_i and I_i denote the inner input relations and the intermediate results, respectively. I_I denotes the outer input relation of the segment. Each input relation is either a base relation or the result of another pipeline segment. The R_i are all materialized on disk while I_I is to be read from disk or received directly from another process.

Figure 2 depicts the functional decomposition of the example into build phase and probe phase. B_i denotes the operation to build the hash table H_i and P_i denotes the operation to probe I_i against H_i.

Considering also the physical memory limits, Chen et al. introduce a decomposition of the right-deep trees into pipeline segments, which fit into main memory (Chen et al., 1992). Thus, I/O caused by swapping can be avoided. The segments are evaluated one at a time with maximal computing resources at their disposal. The processor scheduling is a grouping of processors which are assigned to single operators according to work load estimations. Shekita et al. extend this method to capture also bushy operator trees by decomposing bushy trees into right-deep pipeline segments, thus, combining the flexibility of bushy operator trees with pipelining execution (Shekita et al., 1993). Furthermore, not only join operators are considered but the more general notion of *blocking* and *nonblocking operators* is used: a pipeline segment is a sequence of non-blocking operators, which produce output on-the-fly—e.g. selection, projection without duplicate elimination, or the probe phase of either a hash join or a general index join. Only the last operator of the segment may be a blocking operator which has to collect all input before it produces any output—e.g. sort or aggregation operators.

Figure 2: Build phase and probe phase

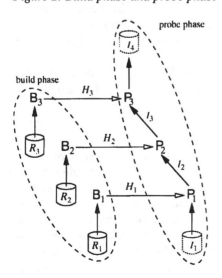

Though offering the high potential for performance improvements, the aforementioned techniques proof a pitfall as soon as the actual query execution does not match the assumptions the preceding optimization was based on. Dynamic processor scheduling helps overcome this drawback. In (Manegold et al., 1997), we presented *DTE*, a strategy that serves as a transparent interface to pipelining parallelism by dynamically assigning processors to operators and thereby achieving a near-optimal exploitation of CPU resources. DTE avoids the major problems conventional pipelining suffers from: *discretization error* and *startup/shutdown delay* (Ganguly et al., 1992; Srivastava and Elsesser, 1993; Wilschut and Apers, 1991; Wilschut et al., 1995).

While DTE solves most of the critical issues in CPU scheduling, the I/O processing is ignored and hidden in the assumption that all hash tables are built before-hand, as supposed in previous work. In general, the build phase is I/O-bound—i.e. building a hash table takes less time than reading the base relation from disk—while the probe phase is CPU-bound as no intermediate results are to be materialized on disk. Consequently, the execution cannot reach its optimal performance due to inefficient resource utilization: during the build phase the CPUs are idle, while during the probe phase the I/O system is idle.

To the authors' best knowledge—Hong is the only one addressing the integration of I/O processing. He proposes a scheduling algorithm that executes one CPU-bound and one I/O-bound task concurrently, to achieve a CPU-I/O-balanced workload in total (Hong, 1992). This in turn restricts the algorithm to scheduling of distinct data-independent tasks, only. Obviously, pipeline processing cannot benefit from this technique.

In this paper, we propose *floating probe*, a novel strategy to integrate both CPU scheduling and I/O processing on shared-everything platforms. We suppose that an optimizer has already generated a tree-shaped query plan and partitioned the plan in pipeline segments with the following characteristics: (1) Only the last operator of each segment might be a blocking operator, all other operators are non-blocking operators. The optimizer tuned the size of each segment that (2) all tables fit into main memory and (3) the probing then can be done without intermediate I/O (cf. (Chen et al., 1992; Schneider and DeWitt, 1990; Shekita et al., 1993)).

The key idea is to mesh build and probe phase as tightly as possibly, i.e. while conducting the probe for a group of operators, the hash tables of the successors can be loaded in the meantime. This procedure is subject to some constraints, e.g. during the very first build phase no probing can take place.

All segments are evaluated one after the other according to the producer/consumer data dependencies between them. We avoid parallel evaluation of data independent pipeline segments, as no performance improvements can be achieved that way (Shekita et al., 1993).

Floating probe establishes automatically balanced CPU and I/O workload throughout the whole execution, yielding not only shorter execution times in total but also lowering the memory requirements significantly.

Road-Map

The remainder of the paper is organized as follows. In the next section, we present the basic techniques for building the hash tables and discuss the two ways of parallelizing this step. Then, DTE, our strategy to implement the probe phase is introduced and discussed. We briefly point out the strength of DTE compared to conventional pipelining techniques in a representative selection of experiments. The next section concerns the problems occurring when both build and probe phase are combined. We present floating probe and show how I/O processing can be integrated with efficient CPU scheduling. The analysis of floating probe yields a near optimal upper bound. A simulation model and a comparative performance evaluation verifies the previously derived results. The work is concluded by a summary and a discussion of future work.

TABLE BUILDING PHASE

Shared-everything systems like SMPs provide uniform and parallel access to all attached disks. To exploit I/O parallelism we assume that each base relation is partitioned and fully declustered over all disks. Once, this is established, I/O parallelism utilizing the full I/O bandwidth can be used for every access to the base relations—even for exclusive access to a single relation. Furthermore, double buffering and asynchronous I/O allow an overlapping of CPU and I/O phases.

Building one single hash table in parallel

To build one single hash table in parallel,—i.e. using all disks and all CPUs—one thread per CPU, that reads tuples (one at a time) from a shared buffer pool, and inserts the tuple into the hash table, is started. Note, that CPU contention may occur if the number of threads exceeded the number of CPUs. Obviously, this strategy provides optimal load balancing.

The only problem occurring is to bridge the gap between the shared buffer pool and the disk I/O. As a simple solution to this problem, we extend one of the threads with some additional functionality: invoking asynchronous parallel I/O to read pages from disk. As the time to invoke the I/O of one page is by approximately three orders of magnitude smaller than the time to read a single page from disk, this additional task does not form a bottleneck.

In the reminder of this paper, we use $Build(R_i)$ to denote the parallel building of the hash table that belongs to the i-th join within the pipeline. This includes reading R_i from disk using parallel I/O.

Building multiple hash tables in parallel

With these preliminaries, two different methods for building the hash tables become feasible: building all hash tables simultaneously and execute $Build(R_1)$ through $Build(R_N)$ concurrently, or executing only one single $Build(R_i)$ at a time, i.e. executing $Build(R_1)$ through $Build(R_N)$ one after the other. Due to the full declustering of each base relation, both strategies can exploit the full I/O bandwidth. However, the first strategy would cause additional seek time as it has to cope with random disk access patterns when fragments of different relations—located on the same disk—are read concurrently. In contrast to this, the second strategy accesses larger homogeneous blocks and reduces the latency significantly. For this reason, we use the second strategy for our further considerations.

TUPLE PROBING PHASE

Our strategy to evaluate the probe phase of pipeline segments is *Data Threaded Execution (DTE)* (Manegold et al., 1997). In the reminder of this section, we first give a short overview of DTE and then we present a quantitative assessment of DTE.

The Model

The key idea of DTE is to dynamically assign the available processors to the data that is to be processed. We do this by gathering all operators of a pipeline segment into one stage and assigning all processors to this stage. This leads to optimal load balancing and efficient resource utilization without causing any additional overhead.

As it is not possible to perform two successive operators on the same input tuple in parallel, our approach is to switch from conventional operator parallelism to data parallelism. Data parallelism covers both, intra-operator (different tuples, same operator) and inter-operator (different tuples, different operators) parallelism.

To achieve this, DTE uses one thread per processor. Each thread is able to perform all operations within the active pipeline segment. The input tuples for the pipeline segment are provided in a global queue which can be accessed by all threads. Each thread takes one tuple at a time from the global input queue and guides it through all the operators of the pipeline segment by subsequently calling the procedures that implement the operators. A tuple does not leave the thread—and thus the processor—during its way through the pipeline segment, until it has been processed by the last operator or it failed to satisfy a selection or join predicate. As soon as one tuple has left a thread, the thread takes the next input tuple from the queue. In the case that one tuple finds more than one partner in a join, i.e. the operator produces more than one output tuple from one input tuple, the thread has to process all these tuples before it can proceed with the next input tuple from the queue. Figure 3 sketches the data threaded execution of a pipeline segment consisting of three joins on four processors.

There are no data dependencies between the threads. Thus, all threads start their processing simultaneously without any idle time, and none of them is idle until it finishes its work. In other words, there is no startup execution delay and there is no idle time due to synchronization among the processors. The only idle time that may occur is due to shutdown execution delay. As soon as a processor has finished its work and there are no more input tuples in the global queue, it is idle until the other processors have finished their work, too. This time is at most the time that one processor needs to process one tuple through the pipeline segment. In cases of extreme skew, the performance of DTE suffers from this shortcoming. We solved this problem by adding a simple but powerful redistribution mechanism to DTE yielding DTE/R (Manegold and Waas, 1998). As situations with extreme skew are not relevant in the context of this paper, we stick to the base version of DTE, for simplicity. The strategies presented in the remainder of this paper also apply to DTE/R.

DTE provides automatic and dynamic load balancing between the processors, as each thread can process the next input tuple as soon as it has finished the processing of the former tuple. Thus, all processors are working as long as there are input tuples in the queue, i.e. neither startup delay nor discretization error occur with DTE. DTE outperforms conventional pipelining strategies significantly (Manegold et al., 1997).

In particular, this kind of load balancing—and thus efficient resource utilization—does not depend on cardinalities. Therefore, the efficiency of DTE does not suffer from any errors when estimating cardinalities and selectivities at compile time. If such errors lead to a non-optimal query tree, DTE cannot compensate this error but still provides a stable execution in the sense of efficient resource utilization without overhead, i.e. the situation cannot exacerbate any further.

Quantitative Assessment

In order to assess DTE quantitatively and to compare it to conventional pipeline ex-

Figure 3: DTE

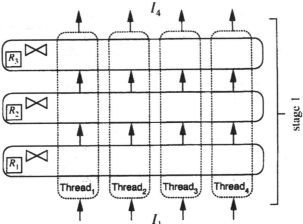

ecution *(PE)* as presented in the introduction of this chapter (for details see also (Manegold et al., 1997)), we implemented both strategies prototypically. Using this implementation, we ran several experiments on SGI Power Challenge and Onyx shared-memory machines with 4 processors each.

The queries investigated are marked by the parameters given in Table 1. For each configuration, we first generate the base relations according to the query specifications, then build the hash tables sequentially, and after that execute the strategy considered. To obtain stable results we take the median of 10 runs.

Wisconsin Benchmark.

The initial set of experiments deals with running two queries, namely joinAselB and joinCselAselB, of the Wisconsin Benchmark (Gray, 1993). We implemented the selection as semi join, thus, joinAselB and joinCselAselB consist of pipeline segments of length 2 and 3, respectively.

Figures 4 and 5 depict the relative execution times T_{PE}/T_{DTE} for joinAselB and joinCselAselB, respectively. PE performs substantially worse than DTE, mainly due to discretization error, as in both queries the first operator causes ten times as much work as the others. With DTE, each of the p processors used performs $(1/p)$-th of the total work. With PE, p-x processors ($x=1$ for joinAselB and $x=2$ for joinCselAselB) do $(10/(10+x))$-th of the total work, while x processors do $(1/(10+x))$-th each.

The Average Case.

The next series of experiments give an overall estimate for the average case. The base relation sizes were chosen randomly from our portfolio and one of the five distribution types was used to generate the attribute value distribution. For each query, all distributions were of the same type; the particular parameters are chosen as given in Table 1. All experiments were carried out on 4 processors.

In Figure 6, the response times for *round-robin* attribute value distribution are depicted—again, the values are scaled to the execution time of DTE. PE is limited by the number of processors and therefore only values for 2, 3 and 4 joins are available. The execution time of PE is up to 2.2 times longer than that of DTE.

Table 1: Query Parameters

name	description	value
n	number of joins	1 to 16
$\|R_i\|$	cardinality of base relations	5k to 200k
v	range of join attribute values	$1 \leq v \leq \|R_i\|$
δ	attribute value distribution of join attributes	round-robin, uniform, normal1 (mean=$\frac{v}{2}$, dev.=$\frac{v}{10}$), normal2 (mean=$\frac{v}{2}$, dev.=$\frac{v}{5}$), exponential (mean=$\frac{v}{2}$)
af_i	augmentation factor of join i	$af_i = \dfrac{\|I_{i+1}\|}{\|I_i\|}$

In Figures 7 through 10, the results for the remaining distributions—*uniform, normal1, normal2,* and *exponential*—are plotted. The savings are similar to the previous case.

Speedup and Scaleup.

Besides this overall performance comparison, we also ran experiments to measure the speedup and scaleup (DeWitt and Gray, 1992) of the different strategies. Figure 11 shows the speedup behavior of PE and DTE for a two-join-query with af_1=1 and af_2=1/3 (see Tab. 1). DTE provides near-linear speedup, whereas PE suffers from discretization error, obviously. Similarly, Figure 12 exemplary shows the scaleup behavior of PE and DTE for a two-join-query. We increased the weight of the pipeline segment with the number of processors by increasing af_2 appropriately while leaving af_1=1. DTE shows a negligible performance decrease of 1% when moving from one to two processors, but then, its scaleup is constant. PE shows a significantly worse scaleup behavior. Experiments with other kinds of queries show the same tendencies for both, speedup and scaleup.

The results obtained from the implementation of DTE are closed to our simulations

Figure 4: Wisconsin's joinAselB-query

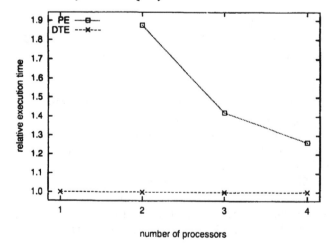

Figure 5: Wisconsin's joinCselB-query

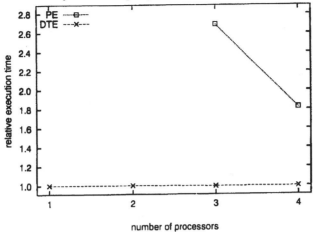

Figure 6: Average case (round-robin)

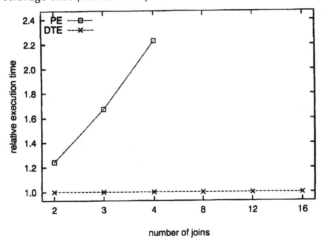

results presented in (Manegold et al., 1997) showing the adequacy of our simulator.

BUILDING AND PROBING

Before we discuss the different strategies of how to combine build phase and probe phase, we introduce further notation we use in the remainder of this chapter. $Build(R_i)$ (short B_i) denotes the building of the i-th hash table H_i (see earlier section in this chapter "Table Building Phase"). This includes reading R_i from disk. $Alloc(H_i)$ (A_i) denotes the allocation of memory for hash table H_i. Releasing the respective memory is denoted by $Free(H_i)$ (F_i). $Probe(I_i)$ (P_i) denotes the probing of intermediate result I_i through the i-th join within the pipeline using DTE. $Probe(I_i..I_j)$ ($P_{i..j}$) denotes the parallel probing of the joins i through j ($1 \le i \le j \le N$) using DTE. Thus, both $Probe(I_i)$ and $Probe(I_{i..j})$ represent the execution of the respective subset of operators of the whole pipeline ($Probe(I_1..I_N)$).

Figure 7: Average case (uniform)

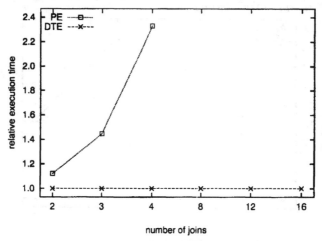

Figure 8: Average case (normal1)

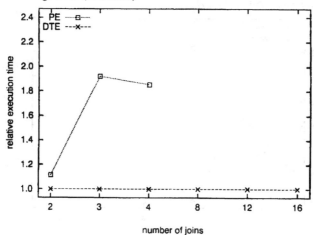

Table 2 gives further notation and some basic cost values taken from literature. In Figure 13, we present the cost functions for single operations we use in the remainder of this chapter.

Deferred Probe

A naive way to combine build and probe phase is to execute them one after the other: First, all hash tables are built, and after that, the probing is done (using DTE, in our case). We call this *deferred probe*.

The execution of the whole pipeline segment, i.e. build and probe phase, proceeds as follows: Alloc(H_1); Build(R_1); ...; Alloc(H_N); Build(R_N); Probe($I_1..I_N$); Free(H_1); ...; Free(H_N). For simplicity of presentation, we neglect the time consumed by Alloc(H_i) and Free(H_i). Assuming that CPU and I/O can overlap perfectly, the execution times of each single Build(R_i) as well as the execution time of Probe($I_1..I_N$) are given by the maximum

Figure 9: Average case (normal2)

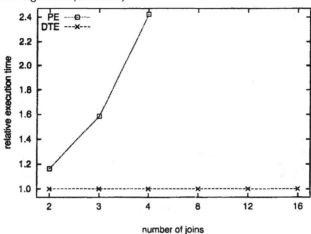

Figure 10: Average case (exponential)

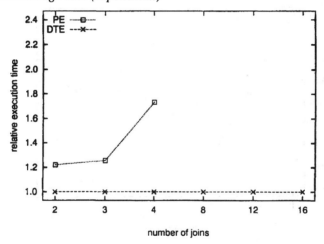

of the corresponding CPU and I/O times. Thus, the total execution time of the whole pipe-line segment is (cf. Fig. 13 and Tab. 2 for details):

$$T'_{defer} = T_{Build} + T_{Probe}$$
$$= \Sigma_{i=1}^{N} \max\{ O_s(R_i) , C_B(R_i) \} +$$
$$\max\{ O_r(I_1) + O_r(I_{N+1}) , C_{Px}(I_1 . I_N) \}.$$

Suppose that either both phases are I/O-bound

$$\forall i \in \{1,...,N\} : \qquad O_s(R_i) > C_B(R_i)$$
$$\wedge \qquad O_r(I_1) + O_r(I_{N+1}) > C_{PX}(I_1 . I_N)$$

or both phases are CPU-bound

$$\forall i \in \{1,...,N\} : \qquad O_s(R_i) < C_B(R_i)$$

Figure 11: Speedup

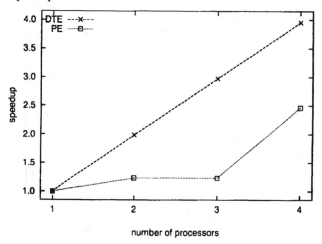

Figure 12: Scaleup

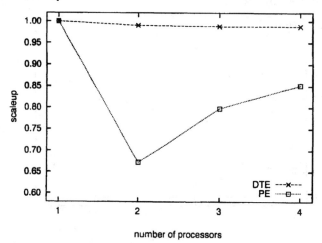

$$\wedge \qquad\qquad O_r(I_1) + O_r(I_{N+1}) < C_{Px}(I_1 .. I_N)$$

then deferred probe provides minimal execution time

$$T^{min}_{defer} = \max\{O_s(R_1 .. R_N) + O_r(I_{N+1}), C_B(R_1 .. R_N) + C_{Px}(I_1 .. I_N) \qquad\qquad \}.$$

However, in most environments the build phase is I/O-bound while the probe phase is CPU-bound—at least if the pipeline is long enough—, i.e.

$$\forall i \in \{1,...,N\}: \qquad O_s(R_i) > C_B(R_i)$$

$$\tag{*}$$

$$\wedge \qquad O_r(I_1) + O_r(I_{N+1}) < C_{Px}(I_1 .. I_N)$$

In this case, deferred probe has one shortcoming: Resources are not used as efficiently as theoretically possible. During the build phase, CPU capacities are left idle, while during

Table 2: Notation

name	description	value
p	number of CPUs	1 - 8
d	number of disks	1 - 8
T_M	time to access one tuple in memory	10.0 μs
T_B	time per tuple to build a hash table	5.5 μs
T_P	time to probe one tuple against a hash table	4.0 μs
T_G	time to generate one result tuple	30.0 μs
T_I	time to invoke I/O for one block	7.4 μs
T_W	time to setup I/O system	1.0 ms
T_S	average I/O seek time	1.2 ms
bw	I/O bandwidth per disk	3 MB/s
bs	size of one I/O block in bytes	8 kB
T_R	$= \dfrac{bs}{bw}$, I/O time to read one block	2.6 ms
ts_R	size of tuples of relation R in bytes	100-200 Bytes
$\|R\|$	size of relation R in tuples	10^3 - $2 \cdot 10^5$
$\|R\|$	$= \left\lceil \dfrac{\|R\| \times ts_R}{bs} \right\rceil$, size of R in blocks	13 - 4883
N	number of joins	4 - 16

Figure 13: Cost Functions

I/O time without disk arm contention (sequential I/O):

$$O_s(R_i) \quad = \quad T_S + \left\lceil \frac{|R_i|}{d} \right\rceil (T_W + T_R)$$

I/O time with disk arm contention (random I/O):

$$O_r(R_i) \quad = \quad \left\lceil \frac{|R_i|}{d} \right\rceil (T_S + T_W + T_R)$$

CPU time to initialize I/O and to access a relation in memory:

$$C_x(I_i) \quad = \quad \left\lceil \frac{|I_i|}{p} \right\rceil T_I + \left\lceil \frac{\|I_i\|}{p} \right\rceil T_M$$

CPU time to build a hash table (incl. initialization of I/O):

$$C_B(R_i) \quad = \quad \left\lceil \frac{|R_i|}{p} \right\rceil T_I + \left\lceil \frac{\|R_i\|}{p} \right\rceil T_B$$

CPU time to probe a join:

$$C_P(I_i) \quad = \quad \left\lceil \frac{\|I_i\|}{p} \right\rceil T_P + \left\lceil \frac{\|I_{i+1}\|}{p} \right\rceil T_G$$

CPU time to probe joins (incl. fetching the input, storing the output and initialization of I/Os):

$$C_{Px}(I_i..I_j) \quad = \quad C_x(I_i) + C_P(I_i..I_j) + C_x(I_{j+1})$$

convenient abbreviation ($\Phi \in \{O_s, O_r, C_x, C_B, C_P\}$):

$$\Phi(R_i..R_j) \quad = \quad \sum_{k=i}^{j} \Phi(R_k)$$

the probe phase, I/O capacities are not fully used. Thus, the execution time is not optimal:

$$T_{defer} = O_s(R_1..R_N) + C_{Px}(I_1..I_N) > (*) \, T^{min}_{defer}.$$

Figures 14 and 15 depict CPU and I/O load of deferred probe evaluating a pipeline segment with four joins.

Multi-user and multi-query environments may balance the utilization of CPU and I/O. But these environments suffer from the exhaustive use of memory of deferred probe. The memory for the hash tables is allocated—possibly long time—before the hash tables are used in the probe phase and all memory is released only after the whole pipeline is executed (cf. Fig. 16).

In multi-user or multi-query environments, not only execution time (T) and maximal memory usage (m) should be regarded, but also the *memory usage area* (M = amount of memory usage * time memory is occupied).

Floating Probe

To overcome the shortcomings of deferred probe, our approach is to let the build phase and the probe phase overlap. Opposed to deferred probe, this results in a single phase that integrates build and probe phase. Thus, resource utilization can be balanced by combining I/O-bound build and CPU-bound probe. We call our new strategy *floating probe*.

The point is, Probe(I_i) can be started as soon as Build(R_i) has finished, i.e. Probe(I_i) can be executed in parallel with Build(R_{i+1}). Thus, compared to deferred probe, some of the probe work is done before the build of the last hash table is finished. As building the hash tables is I/O-bound the elapsed time until all hash tables are build cannot be reduced. However, the probe work that has to be done after the last build is reduced and so is the overall execution time.

Two cases have to be distinguished first: Either Probe(I_1) is CPU-bound—e.g. I_1 already resides in memory, is received via a fast network, or even reading from disk is faster than performing the probing—or Probe(I_1) is I/O-bound, i.e. reading I_1 from disk is slower than performing the probing.

Probe(I_1) is CPU-bound.

In this case, floating probe proceeds as follows (cf. Fig. 17 for a sample schedule): At the beginning, the hash table H_1 of the first join is built (Build(R_1)). Thereafter, Probe(I_1) and Build(R_2) are started simultaneously and executed concurrently. As the output tuples produced by Probe(I_1) cannot yet be processed by Probe(I_2), they have to be buffered. To avoid intermediate I/O, this is done in memory. If Probe(I_1) ends before Build(R_2), H_1 is dropped. Otherwise, as soon as Build(R_2) has finished, Build(R_3) is started and the probe is extended, so that the remaining tuples of I_1 are piped through both probes (Probe($I_1..I_2$)). As before, the output of Probe($I_1..I_2$) is buffered in memory. If then Probe($I_1..I_2$) ends before Build(R_3), H_1 is dropped and the part of I_2 buffered in memory during Build(R_2) is processed through Probe(I_2). Otherwise, the probe is extended to Probe($I_1..I_3$), as soon as *Build*(R_3) is done. This proceeds until the last hash table H_N is built. After that, only probing is done until all tuples are processed: For each I_i that is partly buffered in memory Probe($I_i..I_N$) is executed. Figure 19 presents floating probe as pseudo code. The Procedures that are used here and with the pseudo codes of the following strategies are pre-

Figure 14: Sample CPU load (deferred probe)

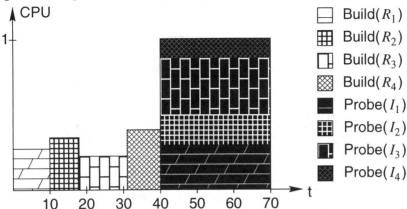

Figue 15: Sample I/O load (deferred probe)

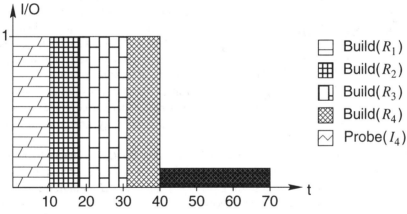

sented in Figure 18.

With floating probe, the pipeline segment is dynamically extended to the next join once its hash table is built. Thus, allocated memory is used as soon as possible. On the other hand, hash tables are dropped immediately after the respective probe is done. Thus, allocated memory is released as soon as it is no longer needed.

Figures 20 and 21 depict CPU and I/O load of floating probe evaluating a pipeline segment with four joins—I_1 is receive via the network and I_5 is written to disk—and Figure 22 shows the respective memory usage.

Probe(I_1) is I/O-bound.

Now, consider the case reading I_1 from disk is slower than performing the probe. As I_1 is also fully declustered across all disks, there is no sense in running Probe(I_1) and Build(R_2) in parallel due to disk access contention. We present two strategies, how to proceed in this case.

The first is to defer Probe(I_1) until enough, say g, hash tables are built, such that

Figure 16: Sample memory usage (deferred probe)

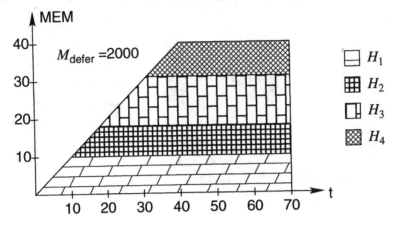

Figure 17: Sample schedule floating probe

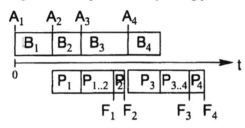

executing $\text{Build}(R_{g+1})$ and $\text{Probe}(I_1..I_g)$ concurrently is approximately CPU-I/O-balanced, or at least such that executing $\text{Probe}(I_1..I_g)$ is CPU-bound. Thus, running $\text{Probe}(I_1)$ I/O-bound is avoided. But on the other hand, the start of probing is deferred and $\text{Build}(R_2)$ through $\text{Build}(R_g)$ are run I/O-bound. As soon as $\text{Probe}(I_1..I_g)$ is started, execution continues as usual. We call this strategy *late probing* (cf. Fig. 23a).

The second strategy is to execute $\text{Probe}(I_1)$ right after $\text{Build}(R_1)$, materializing I_2 completely in memory, and to defer $\text{Build}(R_2)$ until $\text{Probe}(I_1)$ is done. As soon as $\text{Build}(R_2)$ has finished, processing resumes with starting $\text{Build}(R_3)$ and $\text{Probe}(I_2)$ simultaneously. Thus, $\text{Probe}(I_1)$ is run I/O-bound as well as $\text{Build}(R_2)$ thereafter. But on the other hand, probing is started as soon as possible. We call this strategy *early probing* (cf. Fig. 23b).

The case, that the result relation of the pipeline segment is not kept in memory, but rather written to disk, does not need any special treatment. $\text{Probe}(I_N)$ can only be processed after $\text{Build}(R_N)$ is done. Hence, there is no I/O interference.

The first advantage of floating probe is that the overall execution time is reduced as some of the probe work is done before $\text{Build}(R_N)$ has finished. In our example, deferred probe needs 70 units of time, whereas floating probe needs only 52 (cf. Figs. 14,15,20,21). There is a lower bound, as the execution time cannot be less than needed to do the total work without any overhead or synchronization. This bound is

$$T^{\min}_{\text{float}} = \max\{\ O_s(R_1..R_N) + O_s(I_1) + O_s(I_{N+1})\ ,\ C_B(R_1..R_N) + C_{Px}(I_1..I_N)\qquad\}$$
$$(*)$$
$$< O_s(R_1..R_N) + C_{Px}(I_1..I_N) = T_{\text{defer}}.$$

Obviously, if either building or probing dominates the overall execution costs, i.e. either $O_s(R_1..R_N) \gg C_{Px}(I_1..I_N)$ or $C_{Px}(I_1..I_N) \gg O_s(R_1..R_N)$, then floating probe cannot per-

Figure 18: Procedures

```
procedure Init() do   // initialization of global variables
    toBuild[1..N]   := {1, .., 1};   // part of Hᵢ that has to be built
    toProbe[1..N]   := {1, .., 1};   // part of Iᵢ that has to be probed
    allocated[1..N]  := no;          // memory for Hᵢ allocated ?
    next            := 1;            // next Hᵢ that has to be built
    first           := 1;            // first Iᵢ that has to be probed
    last            := 0;            // last Iᵢ that can be probed
    built           := 0;            // part of Hᵢ that has been built
    probed          := 0;            // part of Iᵢ that has been probed
od;


procedure BuildOnly(R_next) do
    if allocated[next] = no then Alloc(H_next); allocated[next] := yes; fi;
    Build(R_next);  toBuild[next] := 0;  next ++;  last ++;
od;


procedure ProbeOnly(I_first..I_last) do
    Probe(I_first..I_last);  probed := toProbe[first];
    foreach i ∈ {first, ..., last} do  toProbe[i] -= probed;  od;
    while toProbe[first] = 0 ∧ first ≤ N do  first ++;  Free(H_first);  od;
od;


procedure BuildAndProbe(R_next, I_first..I_last) do
    if allocated[next] = no then Alloc(H_next); allocated[next] := yes; fi;
    do built := Build(R_next) ‖ probed := Probe(I_first..I_last);
    until first of both ends;
    foreach i ∈ {first, ..., last} do  toProbe[i] -= probed;  od;
    while toProbe[first] = 0 ∧ first ≤ N do  first ++;  Free(H_first);  od;
    toBuild[next] -= built;
    if toBuild[next] = 0 then  next ++;  last ++;  fi;
od;
```

form much better than deferred probe. Further, the minimal execution time of floating probe cannot be less than half the execution time of deferred probe:

$$
\begin{aligned}
T^{min}_{float} &\overset{(')}{\geq} \max\{\, O_s(R_1..R_N),\quad C_{Px}(I_1..I_N)\,\} \\[4pt]
&\overset{(')}{\geq} \quad O_s(R_1..R_N) + C_{Px}(I_1..I_N)/2 = T_{defer}/2.
\end{aligned}
\tag{**}
$$

Here, equality holds, (') iff $O_s(I_1)=O_s(I_{N+1})=0 \wedge O_s(R_1..R_N)\geq C_B(R_1..R_N) + C_{Px}(I_1..I_N)$, and ('') iff $O_s(R_1..R_N) = C_{Px}(I_1..I_N)$.

The second advantage of floating probe is reduced memory consumption. If any probe finishes before $Build(R_N)$ is done, the corresponding hash table is released, and thus, the memory usage area M (cf. page 140) is smaller than that of deferred probe. In our example, the memory usage area of deferred probe amounts to 2000 units, whereas floating probe needs only 1219 units (cf. Figs. 16 & 22).

Figure 19: Floating probe (CPU-bound Probe(I_I))

```
begin
    Init();
    do
        if  next ≤ N  then
            if  first ≤ last  then
                BuildAndProbe(R_next, I_first..I_last);
            else  /* first > last */
                BuildOnly(R_next);
            fi;
        else  /* next > N */
            ProbeOnly(I_first..I_last);
        fi;
    until  first > N;
end.
```

Figure 20: Sample CPU load (floating probe)

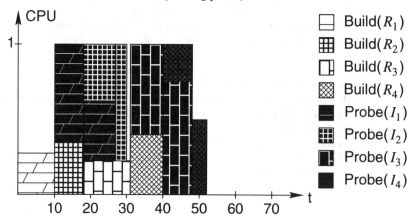

A drawback of floating probe is, that parts of intermediate results have to be material-ized in memory. This causes additional CPU costs and additional memory is needed. But the results of our simulation experiments show, that floating probe outperforms deferred probe, despite these overheads.

Neglecting these overheads—and most of the synchronization that arises due to data dependencies—for the moment, the execution time of floating probe is:

$$T_{\text{float}} = \max\{\ O_s(R_I)\ ,\ C_B(R_I)\ \} +$$
$$\max\{\ O_s(R_2..R_N) + O_s(I_I)\ ,\ C_B(R_2..R_N) + C_x(I_I) + C_P(I_I..I_{N-1})\ \} +$$
$$\max\{\ O_s(I_{N+1})\ ,\ C_P(I_N) + C_x(I_{N+1})\ \}$$
$$(*)$$
$$= O_s(R_I) +$$
$$\max\{\ O_s(R_2..R_N) + O_s(I_I)\ ,\ C_B(R_2..R_N) + C_x(I_I) + C_P(I_I..I_{N-1})\ \} +$$
$$\max\{\ O_s(I_{N+1})\ ,\ C_P(I_N) + C_x(I_{N+1})\ \}$$

Figure 21: Sample I/O load (floating probe)

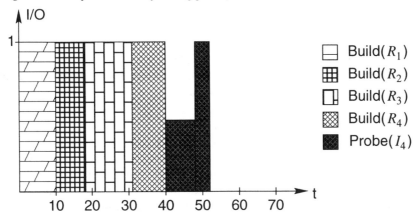

Figure 22: Sample memory usage (floating probe)

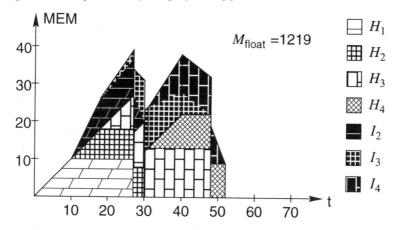

Figure 23: Floating probe (I/O-bound Probe (I$_I$))

```
Init();
do
     BuildOnly(R_next);
until  ProbeOnly(I_first..I_last) is I/O-bound;
```

a) Replacement for Init() in Fig. : *late probing*

```
Init();
BuildOnly(R_next);       // next = 1
ProbeOnly(I_first..I_last);  // first = last = 1
```

b) Replacement for Init() in Fig. : *early probing*

ANALYSIS

According to the presentation of floating probe in the previous section, it seems to be rather complicated to implement this strategy, as a lot of explicit scheduling overhead is necessary. In the following, we discuss a rather simple but effective method to avoid this scheduling overhead and describe our simulation model. Thereafter, we present the results of our experiments comparing deferred probe and floating probe.

Simulation Model

Although both phases are no longer executed one after the other, they are still in some sense independent of each other. The only dependency between the two phases is that a hash table has to be built before the respective intermediate result can be probed against it. Thus, our solution is to implement the build phase and the probe phase with separate threads. The only communication between build thread and probe thread is that the build thread has to inform the probe thread as soon as it has built a hash table. Using this information, the probe thread can decide, whether it can probe the current tuple through the next join or whether it has to materialize it as the next hash table is not yet built. Both threads are started concurrently. To guarantee that the probe thread only uses those CPU resources that are not used by the build thread, the probe thread is run with lower priority than the build thread. Using this implementation technique, scheduling is done by the operation system.

In order to compare floating probe to deferred probe, we designed and implemented an event driven simulator using the Sim++ package (Fishwick, 1995). The simulator is very detailed, i.e. it simulates each single page-I/O-operation as well as each single tuple-operation using the execution times from Table 2. According to the aforementioned strategy, the simulator assumes distinct build and probe threads, one of each per processor.

Experiments

We randomly generated pipeline segments of several classes. Each class is characterized by the length $N \in \{4,8,16\}$ of the pipeline segment and the location L of I_1 and I_{N+1}. $L(I_1) = \text{disk}$ means that I_1 is initially stored on disk and $L(I_1) = \text{net}$ means that I_1 is received via network. Analogously, $L(I_{N+1}) = \text{disk}$ means that I_{N+1} finally has to be stored on disk and $L(I_{N+1}) = \text{net}$ means that I_{N+1} is sent to the network. The location of I_{N+1} affects both strategies equally: If $L(I_{N+1}) = \text{disk}$, in both strategies I/O is needed during $\text{Probe}(I_N)$, i.e. after $\text{Build}(I_N)$ is done. If $L(I_{N+1}) = \text{net}$, however, no I/O is needed during $\text{Probe}(I_N)$ in either strategy. For this reason, we restrict our discussion here to the two cases that either $L(I_1) = L(I_{N+1}) = \text{disk}$, or $L(I_1) = L(I_{N+1}) = \text{net}$. In the second case, no I/O is needed to evaluate the probe phase. The results for the remaining two cases are similar to those presented.

We randomly generated 360 different segments for each class, with tuple sizes between 100 and 200 bytes and relation sizes between 10^3 and $2*10^5$ tuples. All segments fulfilled condition (*) on page 140.

For each segment $S_j^{L,N}$, we simulated the execution with both deferred probe and floating probe for different degrees of parallelism ($p \in \{1,2,4,8\}$, $d=p$). If I_1 and I_{N+1} were lo-

Figure 24: $\overline{T}_{f/d}(\mathtt{disk},N,p)$

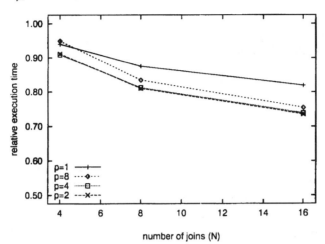

Figure 25: $\overline{T}_{f/d}(\mathtt{net},N,p)$

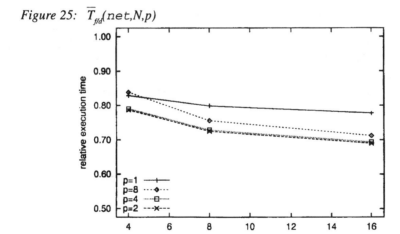

cated on disk, we simulated the execution for both variants of floating probe, early probing and late probing. The differences between both variants were not significant, thus, we present only those for late probing here. To compare the performance of deferred probe and floating probe, we calculated the relative execution time $T_{float}(S_j^{L,N},p) / T_{defer}(S_j^{L,N},p)$. Within each class—identified by L, N, and p—we calculated the average relative execution time over all the $n=360$ queries:

$$\overline{T}_{f/d}(L,N,p) = \frac{1}{n} \sum_{j=1}^{n} \frac{T_{float}(S_j^{L,N},p)}{T_{defer}(S_j^{L,N},p)}$$

Figures 24 and 25 show the average relative execution times with (L=disk) and without probe-I/O (L=net), respectively. Floating probe outperforms deferred probe in any case ($\overline{T}_{f/d}(L,N,p) < 1$). The improvement increases with the length of the pipeline segment, as then the contribution of Build(R_I) and Probe(I_N)—no improvement is possible during these operations due to data dependencies—to the total execution time becomes relatively small. Further, the results show that the performance gain of floating probe over deferred probe is bigger if no probe-I/O is needed. This is obvious, as without probe-I/O, more probe work can be done concurrently with the build.

Using floating probe instead of deferred probe saves up to 27% for L=disk and up to 31% of execution time for L=net. Remember, that at most 50% can be saved (cf. (**) on page 145). The average saving amounts to approximately 16% for L=disk and 24% for L=net.

In addition to the execution times, we also examined the memory usage of floating probe and deferred probe. During the simulation, we calculated the total memory usage $M(S_j^{L,N},p)$. Analogous to the average relative execution time, we calculated the average relative memory usage $M_{f/d}(L,N,p)$. Figures 26 and 27 show the results with (L=disk) and without probe-I/O (L=net), respectively. Again, floating probe performs better—i.e. needs less memory—than deferred probe. Here, the differences between L=disk and

Figure 26: $\overline{M}_{f/d}(disk,N,p)$

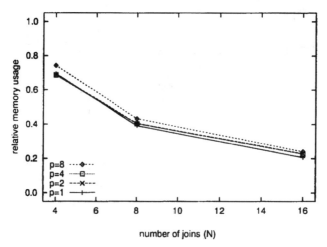

Figure 27: $\overline{M}_{fld}(\text{net},N,p)$

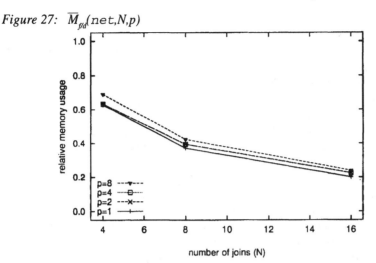

number of joins (N)

L=net are negligible. Floating probe saves up to 80% (55% on average) of memory allocation compared to deferred probe.

CONCLUSION

In this chapter we addressed the topic of efficient resource utilization to boost query execution in parallel database systems. We presented *floating probe*, a new technique to evaluate pipeline segments in shared-everything environments which overcomes severe drawbacks of former methods. Floating probe balances the CPU and I/O workload between the I/O-bound build phase and the CPU-bound probe phase of pipeline segments optimally with respect to the data dependencies between both phases. Furthermore, floating probe (1) provides shorter execution times and (2) consumes less memory than deferred probe. Floating probe achieves these improvements without explicit scheduling, thus, floating probe neither needs any a priori cost estimations nor does it cause any scheduling overhead.

These properties make floating probe an easy-to-control and transparent means of parallelism: only the size of the pipeline segment and the degree of parallelism have to be determined by the optimizer while the execution strategy then guarantees the best execution possible. Floating probe is a building block to comprehensive query execution in parallel databases.

In the future, we will focus on the investigation of other means to incorporate further optimization decisions into the execution technique and, therefore, liberating the optimizer from tasks like finding the appropriate length of a pipeline segment.

ACKNOWLEDGMENTS

We thank Johann K. Obermaier for his comments on a draft version of this paper.

REFERENCES

Chen, M.-S., Lo, M., Yu, P. S., and Young, H. C. (1992). Using Segmented Right-Deep Trees for the Execution of Pipelined Hash Joins. In *Proc. Int'l. Conf. on Very Large*

Data Bases, pages 15—26, Vancouver, BC, Canada.

DeWitt, D. J. and Gray, J. (1992). Parallel Database Systems: The Future of High Performance Database Systems. *Communications of the ACM*, 35(6):85—98.

Fishwick, P. A. (1995). *Simulation Model Design and Execution*. Prentice Hall, Englewood Cliffs, NJ, USA.

Ganguly, S., Hasan, W., and Krishnamurthy, R. (1992). Query Optimization for Parallel Execution. In *Proc. ACM SIGMOD Int'l. Conf.*, pages 9-18, San Diego, CA, USA.

Gray, J., editor (1993). *The Benchmark Handbook*. Morgan Kaufmann, San Mateo, CA, USA.

Hasan, W. and Motwani, R. (1994). Optimization Algorithms for Exploiting the Parallelism-Communication Tradeoff in Pipelining Parallelism. In *Proc. Int'l. Conf. on Very Large Data Bases*, pages 36—47, Santiago, Chile.

Hong, W. (1992). Exploiting Inter-Operation Parallelism in XPRS. In *Proc. ACM SIGMOD Int'l. Conf.*, pages 19—28, San Diego, CA, USA.

Manegold, S., Obermaier, J. K., and Waas, F. (1997). Load Balanced Query Evaluation in Shared-Everything Environments. In *Proc. European Conf. on Parallel Processing*, pages 1117-1124, Passau, Germany.

Manegold, S. and Waas, F. (1998). Thinking Big in a Small World — Efficient Query Execution on Small-scale SMPs. In *High Performance Computing Systems and Applications*. Kluwer Academic Publishers, Edmonton, AL, Canada.

Schneider, D. A. and DeWitt, D. J. (1990). Tradeoffs in Processing Complex Join Queries via Hashing in Multiprocessor Database Machines. In *Proc. Int'l. Conf. on Very Large Data Bases*, pages 469-480, Brisbane, Australia.

Shekita, E. J., Young, H. C., and Tan, K.-L. (1993). Multi-Join Optimization for Symmetric Multiprocessors. In *Proc. Int'l. Conf. on Very Large Data Bases*, pages 479-492, Dublin,Ireland.

Srivastava, J. and Elsesser, G. (1993). Optimizing Multi-Join Queries in Parallel Relational Databases.In *Proc. Int'l. Conf. on Parallel and Distr. Inf. Sys.*, pages 84-92, San Diego, CA, USA.

Wilschut, A. N. and Apers, P. M. G. (1991). Dataflow Query Execution in a Parallel Main-Memory Environment. In *Proc. Int'l. Conf. on Parallel and Distr. Inf. Sys.*, pages 68-77, Miami Beach, FL, USA.

Wilschut, A. N., Flokstra, J., and Apers, P. M. G. (1995). Parallel Evaluation of Multi-Join Queries.In *Proc. ACM SIGMOD Int'l. Conf.*, pages 115-126, San Jose, CA, USA.

CHAPTER 9

Rule Inheritance and Overriding in Active Object-Oriented Databases

Nauman Chaudhry, University of Michigan, USA
James Moyne, University of Michigan, USA
Elke Rundensteiner, Worcester Polytechnic Institute, USA

The concept of inheritance is among the most important features of object-oriented databases (OODBs). The different issues and trade-offs regarding inheritance have been studied for a number of years for passive OODBs. However, no general treatment of rule inheritance and overriding has been undertaken for active OODBs. Such treatment is conspicuously missing for rules that are defined over multiple classes, even though most active OODBs support the definition of such rules. In this chapter, we fill this gap by developing a formal model for rule inheritance and overriding in active OODBs. We identify important features required in an active OODB model, such as support for rule inheritance and rule overriding, and provision of the notion of syntactic compatibility. We then define a formal model for active rules by adapting the concept of multi-methods for use in defining inheritance and overriding of active rules. We extend the notion of syntactic compatibility to active rules and show how it is enforced in our formal model. The support for rule inheritance in our model is uniformly applicable to all active rules, including those rules that span across multiple classes. The work presented here thus makes the important contributions of identifying essential features missing in inheritance models of active OODB systems and of providing a formal model that incorporates these missing features.

INTRODUCTION

The concept of *inheritance* is one of the most important features of object-oriented (OO) systems. Though there are many varieties of inheritance models, inheritance fundamentally is a mechanism for sharing and incrementally modifying existing code to allow a child to inherit features (structure and behavior) from a parent (Taivalsaari, 1996). These features can then be *overridden* in the child thus facilitating evolutionary development of complex systems. In most models, inheritance is also viewed as a facility for conceptual modeling, where a child (called a subclass) specializes its parent (called a superclass)[1]. An instance of the subclass is then said to be *substitutable* for an instance of the superclass. However, since a subclass can override the features of the superclass, the substitutability of a subclass instance for a superclass instance will only be valid if the subclass and superclass are compatible in some sense. To guarantee this conceptual correspondence, various notions of compatibility between parents and children have been established (Wegner & Zdonik, 1988, Wegner, 1990, America, 1991). By requiring that the signature of inherited properties be compatible with the superclass signature, syntactic compatibility can ensure the type-safety of existing code as new subclasses are defined. If the object model supports multiple inheritance, additional constraints are required to ensure that inheritance of features from multiple parents does not lead to ambiguity among features in a subclass.

When a passive OODB model is extended to support active rules, inheritance and overriding models must be adapted to also work with such active OODBs. While many active OODB systems support some form of rule inheritance (e.g., Ode (Lieuwen, Gehani & Arlien, 1996), SAMOS (Geppert, et. al., 1995), Sentinel (Chakravarthy, et. al., 1994)) and rule overriding is provided by (at-least) one system (TriGS (Kappel, et. al., 1994)), no general model of rule inheritance in active OODB systems has been established to-date. Such treatment is conspicuously missing for rules that are defined over multiple classes, even though most active OODBs support the definition of such rules, including, e.g., SAMOS, Sentinel, TriGS.

In this chapter, we fill this gap by developing the first formal model for rule inheritance and overriding in active OODBs. We identify important inheritance features required in an active OODB model, such as the support for rule inheritance and rule overriding, and the provision of the notion of syntactic compatibility for rule overriding. We define a model of active rules by utilizing the concept of *multi-methods* and adapting it for use in defining inheritance and overriding of active rules. We extend the notion of syntactic compatibility to active rules and show how it is enforced in our formal model. We define precise constraints on our model that ensure unambiguity in rule inheritance. This support for rule inheritance is uniformly applicable to all active rules, even if the definition of these rules spans multiple classes. After the presentation of the formal model, we discuss some pragmatic issues regarding our model, including the issue of encapsulation in active OODBs. The work presented here makes the important contributions of identifying essential features missing in active OODB systems and then of providing a formal model that incorporates these missing features. The formal model developed is very general and can be used for extending various active OODB systems to provide support for the features of *rule inheritance* and *overriding* for both *class-specific* and *class-spanning* rules. These features can then be employed by application developers to develop active OODB applications that harness the full potential of OO technology.

The rest of the chapter is structured as follows. In the next section, we discuss the various dimensions of active rule models and identify the base active rule model that is extended later in this chapter. In the following section, we review inheritance and overriding in passive OO models, introduce an example to identify corresponding inheritance features needed in active OODBs and discuss the status of support of these features in existing active OODBs. We then outline our approach, based on the concept of multi-methods, to provide analogous support in active OODBs. After this, we present a well-known passive object data model (Abiteboul, Hull, & Vianu, 1995) that we use as a basis of our formal model for active rules. The formal OO model for active rules developed by us is then presented and is used to define inheritance, overriding, compatibility, and unambiguity of active rules in OODBs. This is followed by a discussion of certain pragmatic aspects of our model, related to encapsulation and its potential implementation to extend existing active OODBs. Conclusions are given at the end of the chapter.

Rule Modeling in Active OODBs

The development of various active OODB systems has been carried using a variety of approaches resulting in systems that differ with each other along a number of dimensions. A pre-requisite for developing a model for active rule inheritance is an adequate underlying active rule model. To arrive at such a model, we examine the various dimensions of active rules that are important for rule inheritance and overriding. We will then identify and discuss the choices that we have selected for the active rule model used as a basis for this research.

Dimensions of Active Rule Models

A comprehensive survey of various dimensions in providing active database functionality is given in Paton, et. al. (1993). These dimensions include knowledge model (what can be said about the active rules in the system), execution model (how a set of rules is treated at run-time), and rule management model (the facilities provided by the system for managing rules). For the purposes of rule inheritance and overriding, the knowledge and rule management models are of interest. The important dimensions and possible choices for these dimensions are shown in Table 1. In the table, the symbol $\subset$ denotes that the corresponding dimension can take more than one value, whereas $\in$ denotes that the corresponding dimension can take only one of the corresponding values.

These dimensions are described below:

Table 1. Dimensions of Active Rule Models

Dimension	Possible values
Rule representation	$\subset$ {Class-internal, Class-external}
Span of rule definition	$\subset$ {Class-specific, Class-spanning}
Operations on rules	$\subset$ {Activate, Deactivate}
Transition granularity	$\in$ {Collection, Instance}
Event source	$\subset$ {Method, Abstract, Transactional, Temporal}
Event type	$\subset$ {Primitive, Composite}
Event representation	$\subset$ {Part of rule, Independent of rule}
Condition specification mechanism	$\subset$ {Query language, Programming language}
Condition representation	$\subset$ {Part of rule, Independent of rule}
Action specification mechanism	$\subset$ {Query language, Programming language}
Action representation	$\subset$ {Part of rule, Independent of rule}
Underlying data model	$\in$ {Static, Dynamic}

- *Rule representation:* A rule model in which rules are defined within class definitions is said to provide class-internal rules, whereas if rules can be defined outside a class definition (as objects or by a special rule language) then the rule definition is termed class-external.
- *Span of rule definition:* A rule defined for a specific class (and its subclasses) is termed a class-specific rule, while a rule defined for more than one classes (and their subclasses) is termed class-spanning rule.
- *Operations on rules:* Certain rule models support activate and deactivate operations on rules. If rules in an active database system need to be activated, then a rule will be applicable to an instance only if it has been explicitly activated for that instance. Otherwise, the rule will not react to event occurrences for that instance and can never be fired for it. The deactivate operation causes a (previously) activated rule to be no longer considered for firing. These two operations thus provide a means of "switching-on" or "switching-off" rules at the instance level. Alternately, these operators can also be used to disable a rule for the whole class.
- *Transition granularity:* Instance level granularity means that events are raised in response to operations on single data items. For rules with collection-level granularity, events are associated with operations on a collection of objects (e.g., raising an event once for all the objects obtained as the result of a query).
  Important dimensions for the event part include:
- *Source of event:* This dimension dictates the sources that may provide events for active rules. Possibilities include: method events, i.e., events raised as a result of the invocation of methods of database objects; abstract events, i.e., special events that can be raised without calling a method; transactional events, i.e., events raised in response to transactional operations (e.g., transaction commit, transaction abort); temporal events, i.e., events raised at particular times or time intervals.
- *Type of event:* Many systems provide operators to define composite events in addition to primitive events. Composite events are defined by using composition operators with primitive or other composite events. Examples of composition operators include AND, OR, Sequence, etc.
- *Event representation mechanism*: Event part defined as an independent entity or as part of a rule.
- For the condition, as well as the action part, important dimensions include:
  Representation mechanism: Condition (or action) part defined as an independent entity or as part of a rule.
  Specification mechanism: Condition (or action) part restricted to using only a query language or allowed to use a programming language.
- *Underlying data model:* The underlying object-oriented data model can have dynamic or static typing.

Dimensions of the Chosen Base Active Rule Model

Various systems use different choices for the above dimensions resulting in divergent rule models. We now (informally) state choices in the rule model that we will formalize later. These choices are also shown in Table 2.

- *Rule representation:* Rules are defined externally to a class. This allows us to leave our base model unchanged[2].

Table 2. Dimensions of Our Base Active Rule Model

Dimension	Chosen values
Rule representation	{Class-external}
Span of rule definition	{Class-specific, Class-spanning}
Operations on rules	{Activate, Deactivate}
Transition granularity	{Instance}
Event source	{Method, Abstract, Transactional, Temporal}
Event type	{Primitive, Composite}
Event representation	{Independent of rule}
Condition specification mechanism	{Query language, Programming language}
Condition representation	{Independent of rule}
Action specification mechanism	{Query language, Programming language}
Action representation	{Independent of rule}
Underlying data model	{Static}

- *Span of rule definition:* Rule definitions may span one or more classes, i.e., both class-specific and class-spanning rules are allowed.
- *Operations on rules:* Activation and deactivation operations are allowed. To be applicable to certain objects, a rule has to be explicitly activated on these objects. Additional arguments may also be passed to the rule at the time of activation (as in Ode, SAMOS, Sentinel, among others).
- *Transition granularity:* Transition granularity is at the instance level. This choice is consistent with most active OODB systems in which the granularity is also at the instance level (e.g., Ode, SAMOS, REACH, NAOS).
- *Event source:* All event sources are allowed, such as method, transaction, temporal or abstract events.
- *Event composition:* Events may be composed using composition operators provided by the database system (the actual set of composition operators is not important for our model).
- *Event, condition and action representation:* Each of the event, condition and action parts can be defined independently of a rule. This allows maximum reuse of existing definitions of these rule parts. The basic results of our model though are independent of this choice of representation.
- *Condition and action specification mechanism:* Each of the condition and action parts can be defined using both programming and query languages. Our results are independent of this choice of specification mechanism.
- *Underlying data model:* The overriding constraints are defined considering a statically typed data model. This choice is consistent with most active OODB systems, since most of these are also based on a statically-typed object model (e.g., SAMOS, Sentinel, REACH, NAOS, Ode).

Background and Informal Problem Description

Since inheritance and overriding of properties has already been studied in passive OODBs (Zdonik & Maier, 1990), we first review relevant research in passive OODBs. We then introduce an example to motivate the need and define the scope of the problem of rule inheritance and overriding for active OODBs. This is followed by a review of current research in rule inheritance support in active OODBs.

Inheritance and Overriding in Passive Object Models

Inheritance is a mechanism for sharing and incrementally modifying existing code where a child inherits and possibly overrides properties (structure and behavior) from a parent (Taivalsaari, 1996). In most models, inheritance is also viewed as a facility for conceptual modeling, where a child (called a subclass) specializes its parent (called super-class). An instance of the subclass is then said to be *substitutable* for an instance of the superclass. To describe the conceptual relationship between a superclass and a subclass certain compatibility rules have been defined (Wegner & Zdonik, 1988, Wegner, 1990, America, 1991). The weakest level is *cancellation*, where a subclass can redefine or even remove a superclass property. The second level is *name compatibility*, where the subclass cannot remove any properties, but may redefine them (or add new ones). The next level is *signature compatibility*, in which a subclass has full syntactic/interface compatibility with the superclass. The strongest compatibility level is *behavioral compatibility*, where the subclass is fully behaviorally compatible with the superclass. We will refer to the first three levels as *syntactic compatibility* and focus on it in this chapter.

Even though there is no agreed upon OO data model, the various choices in defining such a model, and the impact of these choices on inheritance and subtyping in the resulting data model, are fairly well-understood (Zdonik & Maier, 1990). Decisions to have static/dynamic typing and to impose no/some constraints on the overriding of properties in the subclass are among these choices. Ideally one would like to combine static typing (to provide benefits of efficiency and type-safety) with minimum constraints on the specialization of properties in the subclass (to provide flexibility in introducing subclasses with specialized structure and/or behavior). It has been observed that if the OO system allows the definition of "mutators" (i.e., functions that can update the value of instances) on the classes, the three features of type-safety, substitutability and unrestricted specialization cannot co-exist (Zdonik & Maier, 1990). Since for almost all conceivable software systems mutators are needed, a decision has to be made about trade-offs among the desirable features. To provide unconstrained specialization, static typing may have to be given up (e.g., as done in Smalltalk, Goldberg & Robson, 1984). On the other hand, statically typed languages, with their emphasis on type-safety, impose fairly strict limits on property overriding in subclasses. Some form of syntactic compatibility, though, is provided in most OODB models. In particular, cancellation is rarely allowed and thus at least name compatibility is always provided.

To ensure that instances of subclasses are indeed substitutable in a type-safe manner, one needs to observe certain subtyping constraints that will ensure that the interface of the subclass conforms with the interface of the superclass. These constraints include (Kemper & Moerkotte, 1994):

- structure overriding in the subclass: invariance of attributes (for all attributes for which

mutators are defined),
- method overriding in the subclass: co-variance (i.e., the type can be more specific) in return types, contravariance (i.e., the type can be more general) in arguments (that are not used for method binding).

It can be easily shown that if the above rules are not observed, run-time errors can occur in a statically typed system[3] (Kemper & Moerkotte, 1994).

Motivating Example

We introduce an example to motivate the need and define the scope of the problem of rule inheritance and overriding. This example is derived from semiconductor manufacturing environment (Chaudhry, Moyne & Rundensteiner, 1998). We shall use this example to determine the features an OO rule model should support for rule inheritance and overriding. For our example, we assume that:

- In the specification of the active schema, the methods whose invocation raise events are identified.
- For a given rule there may be more than one (locally defined and inherited) *rule definition* and at run-time a specific rule definition is chosen for activation. This choice will be based on some notion of "closeness" between the *formal arguments* of the chosen rule definition and the *actual arguments* of the rule activation. For a given rule name r, we will denote the different definitions of the rule by r_1, r_2, etc.

Consider the (simplified) schema (depicted in Figure 1) for an active OODB application for control of semiconductor manufacturing. To fabricate a product, various processing steps are executed on a wafer. These steps are carried out in a certain sequence on different pieces of equipment. Monitoring and control of these processing steps and pieces of equipment is an important activity in semiconductor manufacturing environments. Active databases can be employed to support this activity. Certain control activities can be completely automated using active rules that modify various database objects, while other activities requiring human intervention can be facilitated by active rules that alert equipment operators. The schema shown contains a Step class hierarchy (modeling semiconductor manufacturing steps), an Equipment class hierarchy (to model the equipments on which processing steps are carried out), and an Operator class (modeling the person who operates an equipment).

Example 1: Consider that the following two rules are defined in the active OODB.

i) For the *class-specific* rule Pressure-Check, a definition Pressure-Check$_1$ specified at the Etch class:

Pressure-Check$_1$: Rule Pressure-Check@Etch (RIE rie)
Event: before execute
Condition: pressure > rie.pressure-limit
Action: abort-execute().

The Pressure-Check$_1$ definition states that when the rule is activated on an instance of class Etch, an instance of the class RIE is expected to be passed to the rule. At the invocation of the method execute the rule condition is checked by comparing the local attribute pressure and the attribute pressure-limit of the given RIE instance to check whether the

Figure 1: Example Schema of an Active OODB

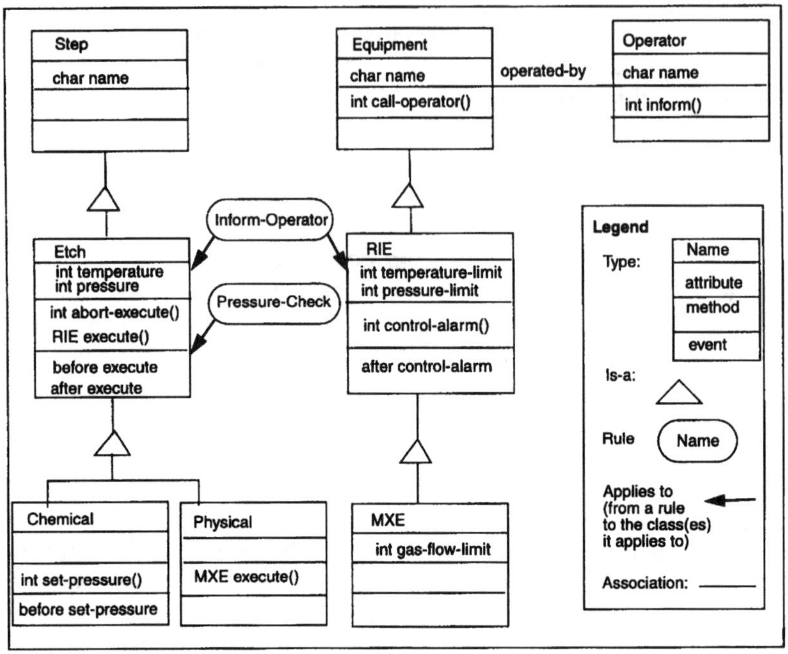

RIE instance is capable of providing the desired pressure. If the condition is true, then the execution of the step is aborted by the action of the rule.

ii) A definition Inform-Operator$_1$ of the *class-spanning* rule Inform-Operator.

Inform-Operator$_1$: Rule Inform-Operator (Etch etch, RIE rie)

Event: OR(after etch.execute, after rie.control-alarm)

Condition: etch.temperature > rie.temperature-limit

Action: rie.call-operator().

The rule definition Inform-Operator$_1$ can be activated on instances of the formal types Etch and RIE. After the method execute is invoked for the given instance of Etch or the method control-alarm is invoked for the given RIE instance, the rule condition is checked. If the condition is true, then the Operator of RIE is informed. ❑

Just as inheritance, overriding and reuse of superclass properties by subclasses is supported in the passive part of the schema, we would like to have analogous support for the active part of the schema. We will now highlight different issues to be considered for active rule inheritance by using the example code given in Figure 2 (in pseudo-C++ syntax).

1. *Rule Inheritance*: Rules defined for a superclass should be inherited by its subclasses.

Example 2: A definition of the Pressure-Check rule has been specified at the Etch class and should be inherited by its subclasses. It should be possible to activate the Pressure-Check rule on an instance of Chemical (as done in Line 09 in Figure 2). ❑

2. *Overriding of Rule Parts:* Just as passive properties can be overridden, overriding of rule definitions in the subclass should be allowed.

Example 3: For the class Chemical one could override the rule definition Pressure-

Figure 2: Example Code for an Application Based on the Schema of Figure 1

```
// pointers of type Etch
Line 01: Etch *etch, *chem, *phys;
Line 02: RIE *rie, *mxe;

// create an instance of Etch, etc.
Line 03: etch = new Etch;
Line 04: chem = new Chemical;
Line 05: phys = new Physical;
Line 06: rie = new RIE;
Line 07: mxe = new MXE;


Line XX: . . .


// activate rule Pressure-Check on instance chem
Line 09: chem->Pressure-Check(rie);

// invoke method execute
Line 10: chem->execute();


Line 11: phys->Pressure-Check(rie);
Line 12: phys->execute();


// activate rule Inform-Operator on the instances etch & mxe
Line 13: Inform-Operator(etch,mxe);


// activate rule Inform-Operator on the instances chem & mxe
Line 14: Inform-Operator(chem,mxe);
```

Check$_1$ by specifying another definition Pressure-Check$_2$ with a modified event part:
  Pressure-Check$_2$: Rule Pressure-Check@Chemical (RIE rie)
  Event: OR(before execute, before set-pressure).□

3. *Syntactic Constraints on Overriding:* In passive OODBs constraints on property overriding have been established to guarantee type safety. Similarly, there is a need to define constraints on rule overriding so that the rule definition in the subclass is syntactically compatible with the rule definition in the superclass.

  Example 4: Let's assume that in the class Physical, the rule Pressure-Check were overridden so that at activation time it is passed an instance of MXE instead of an RIE instance:

  Pressure-Check$_3$: Rule Pressure-Check@Physical (MXE mxe)
  Event: before execute
  Condition: pressure < mxe.gas-flow-limit * 20
  ...

  In Figure 2, the formal type of the variable phys is Etch (Line 01). For instances of the Etch class, a RIE instance is required when activating the rule Pressure-Check (definition Pressure-Check$_{1)}$. However, the actual type of phys is Physical (Line 05) and the overridden rule definition (Pressure-Check$_3$) for the class Physical expects an instance of the class MXE. The rule activation in Line 11 would thus cause an invalid assignment in the absence of dynamic type checking with a RIE instance passed where a MXE instance is expected. This will result in a run-time error when in the condition of Pressure-Check$_3$ the (non-existent) attribute gas-flow-limit is accessed for the RIE instance. ☐

4. *Unambiguity in Rule Inheritance:* The inheritance of active rules should be unambiguous. In the case of multiple inheritance, a subclass may inherit multiple definitions of a class-specific rule from two superclasses, resulting in ambiguity about which rule definition is applicable to the instances of the subclass. In the case of class-spanning rules, this ambiguity in inheritance of rule definitions can occur even for single inheritance.
    Example 5: Assume that rule Inform-Operator is overridden twice as follows:
    Inform-Operator$_2$: Rule Inform-Operator (Chemical chem, RIE rie)
    Event: OR(before chem.set-pressure, after rie.control-alarm)
    Condition: chem.temperature > rie.temperature-limit *1.2
    Action: rie.call-operator().
    Inform-Operator$_3$: Rule Inform-Operator (Etch etch, MXE mxe)
    Event: before etch.execute
    Condition: etch.temperature > mxe.temperature-limit * 1.5
    Action: mxe.call-operator().
The desired intent is that for instances of the class Chemical, the rule definition Inform-Operator$_2$ should be chosen, while for instances of MXE, rule definition Inform-Operator$_3$ should be applicable. Just as the run-time system in passive OODBs makes decisions about dynamic dispatch of methods, the applicability of active rules can be enforced at run-time. Thus based on the class of the *actual arguments* passed at the time of activation, one of the (three) definitions of Inform-Operator should be activated. In our example code, for the activation shown in Line 13 the definition Inform-Operator$_3$ is chosen (unambiguously) at activation time (since there is an exact match between the types of the formal and the actual arguments). The activation shown in Line 14 though results in an *ambiguous* situation:
    i) for Inform-Operator$_2$ there is an exact match for argument 1, while for argument 2 the actual argument is an instance of a subclass (MXE) of the class of the formal argument (RIE).
    ii) for Inform-Operator$_3$ again there is an exact match for one of the arguments (i.e., argument 2), while for argument 1 the actual argument (Chemical) is an instance of a subclass of the class of the formal argument (Etch). ☐
There is thus a need to constrain rule overriding so that it does not lead to ambiguity in rule applicability or alternately develop ways to disambiguate rule overridings.

Rule Inheritance in Current Active OODBs

Rule inheritance is provided by most active OODBs, although the exact mechanism for rule inheritance, and in particular rule overriding, is not widely discussed. To the best of our knowledge there has been no work on signature compatibility in active OODBs, and TriGS (Kappel, et. al., 1994) and NAOS (Collet, Coupaye & Svensen, 1994, Collet & Coupaye, 1996) are the only active OODB systems that discuss rule overriding. A key aim in TriGS is the seamless integration of active rules in an OO data model. Class-specific rules (local triggers in TriGS terminology) can be overridden. However, based on the underlying dynamically-typed object model, the rule specialization is not required to be signature compatible. Class-spanning rules (global triggers in TriGS terminology) apply to all objects that have methods corresponding to the event in the rule. Overriding of such rules though is not considered.

In NAOS (Collet, et. al., 1994, Collet & Coupaye, 1996), rules are defined as part of the schema and do not belong to a class. It is noted that providing rules as part of a class definition leads to schema update problems when modifying rules. User-defined event types are defined independently from a rule definition and belong to the schema, uniquely identified by their names. For rule overriding it is stated that the event for an overridden rule should be a sub-event type of the event of the original rule, though the meaning of subtyping for events is not presented. Similarly, there is no discussion of whether and how class-spanning rules may be overridden in NAOS.

In the SAMOS system, both class-specific and class-spanning rules are supported (Gatziu, Geppert & Dittrich, 1991, Geppert, et. al., 1995). Class-specific rules (class-internal rules in SAMOS terminology) can be encapsulated within the class and may not be visible to the user of the class. Events can be defined so that they have independent existence and can be reused in multiple rules. Class-spanning rules (class-external rules in SAMOS terminology) are identified with event definitions rather than class definitions. Rules are inherited by the subclasses. The semantics of inheritance for class-spanning rules and rule overriding though have not been discussed. The rule model for Sentinel (Chakravarthy, et. al., 1994) is fairly similar to the SAMOS rule model. In Chimera (Ceri, et. al., 1996, Meo, Psaila & Ceri, 1996) again a distinction is made between targeted rules (with events belonging to a single class, i.e., class-specific rules in our terminology) and un-targeted rules (class-spanning rules in our terminology). Issues related to rule overriding though are not discussed. In REACH (Buchmann, et. al., 1995, Zimmermann, et. al., 1996) rules are defined independently of class definitions and at the conceptual level are considered as n-ary relationships between classes involved in the ECA parts. However, by considering rule inheritance only in relation to events, but not to rules as a unit, rule overriding is not considered (Zimmermann, et. al., 1996). In Ode, rules are defined within the definition of a class and are inherited by subclasses (Lieuwen, et. al., 1996). Overriding of rules is not supported.

A recent work in rule inheritance and overriding in active OODBs, with particular reference to the Chimera active OODB (Ceri, et. al., 1996), is described in (Bertino, Guerrini & Merlo, 1997). The focus of this work is on, what we have termed, semantic compatibility for class-specific rules. Inheritance of class-spanning rules or issues of syntactic compatibility though are not investigated.

Rationale of Our Approach

As discussed in the previous section, current active OODB systems have overlooked the important aspect of inheritance and overriding of class-spanning rules. We now propose that the concept of multi-methods provides a natural building block on which a model for inheritance and overriding of class-spanning (as well as class-specific) active rules can be developed. In this section, we give a brief introduction to multi-methods. We then give an outline of our approach to building a formal object model for rule inheritance and overriding.

Multi-Methods

In most OO models, a method dispatch is based on the actual type of a single object - the receiver. The actual type of the rest of the arguments in the invocation is not used in this decision of which method to invoke in response to the message. This *single-dispatching* style works well for many kinds of messages. But for cases where the number of "interesting" arguments is more than one, single dispatching requires awkward work-arounds.

Example 6: Consider that the method displayOn(Shape s, Device d) displays the given Shape s on the given Device d, and that the particular implementation to be chosen depends on the actual types of both s and d. With single dispatching, the programmer has to decide which argument is more important and dispatch based on that. Then within the implementation of each of the singly-dispatched methods, dispatch based on the actual type of the other argument has to be hand-coded. ☐

Multi-methods provide a solution for such cases where single-dispatching poses a problem. In multi-methods, multiple arguments to a message can be used in method dispatch (Chambers, 1992). The programmer can define a number of methods with arguments that are more specific than the arguments of a more general method with the same name. Then depending upon the actual type of multiple arguments in an invocation, the method whose arguments most closely match those of the invocation is dispatched at run-time. However, an ambiguity may arise if there is no single method for which the match in argument is closer than all the other methods. Various techniques have been developed for carrying out (dynamic or static) type-checking of multi-methods to determine if the definition of multi-methods is ambiguous and to suggest or automatically carry out disambiguation (Agrawal, DeMichiel & Lindsay, 1991, Amiel & Dujardin, 1996). Note that singly-dispatched methods are a special case of multi-methods, i.e., multi-methods where the dispatch is based on only one argument (the receiver).

Outline of Approach

We now outline our approach of leveraging off multi-methods to develop a model for active rule inheritance and overriding. Consider three activations of rules on the schema illustrated in Figure 1 and reproduced below from the code fragment shown in Figure 2:

    // activate rule Pressure-Check on instance chem
    Line 09: chem->Pressure-Check(rie);

    // activate rule Inform-Operator on the instances etch & mxe
    Line 13: Inform-Operator(etch,mxe);

    // activate rule Inform-Operator on the instances chem & mxe
    Line 14: Inform-Operator(chem,mxe);

In Line 09, a class-specific rule is activated. This activation is very similar to a method dispatch and it is easy to see that the notions of inheritance, overriding and compatibility can be developed for such rules by extending the corresponding notion for methods. We observe however that the activations of the class-spanning rules, as shown in Line 13 and Line 14, correspond in some sense to the dispatch of a multi-method. Depending upon the actual type of multiple arguments in an activation, the rule whose arguments most closely match those of the activation should be activated at run-time. Just as singly-dispatched methods are a special case of multi-methods, we propose that class-specific rules be viewed as a special case of class-spanning rules.

The activation of rule Pressure-Check in Line 09 is then stated in our model as:

Line 09: Pressure-Check(chem, rie); // activate rule Pressure-Check on instance chem with activation dynamically carried out based on the actual type of only the first argument.

We thus state the key insight - *the concept of multi-methods can be adapted to define a model for rule inheritance and overriding*. In our model, rule definitions are specified with "links" to the event, condition and action parts, each of which is specified independently. Importantly, the span of rule definition for each rule in our model is specified via a designated set of classes. Inheritance of rules is then defined based on subclass relationships between this designated set of classes and other classes in the passive schema. With the above formulation, we are then able to define the notions of syntactic compatibility and unambiguity of inheritance for active rules.

A Base Passive Object Model

We now develop a formal model for rule inheritance in active OODBs. As our base model, we adapt the well-known object model presented in (Abiteboul, Hull & Vianu, 1995). This object model is presented in this section. In the next section, we will add appropriate constructs to this model to define active rule inheritance.

Informal Description of Base Object Model

We first informally describe the basic entities of our base object model. The formal definitions of these concepts follow in the next section.

- This data model includes values and objects (Definition 1). A value has a type. This type is recursively definable from atomic types and the set and tuple type constructors (Definition 2).
- An object has an identity and a state which is a value. An object belongs to a class. A value (and thus the corresponding object) can refer to other objects via their identities.
- A schema is specified by a user via a set of classes (modeling the application), the type of each of these classes (which can be defined in terms of the base classes and other user-defined classes by using the type constructors) and a subclass relationship for these classes (Definition 3).
- The data model includes definition of sub-typing relationships over a given set of classes (Definition 4).
- The user defined sub-class relationships have to respect these sub-typing relationships (Definition 5).
- The behavioral part of the schema is defined via a set of well-formed methods (Definition 6 and Definition 7).

Formal Object Model

Values and Object Identifiers

Assume the existence of a number of *atomic types* and their pair-wise disjoint corresponding domains: **integer, string, bool, float**. The set **dom** of atomic values is the (disjoint) union of these domains. The elements of **dom** are called *constants*.

Also assume an infinite set $\mathbf{obj} = \{o_1, o_2, \dots\}$ of object identifiers (OIDs), a set **class**

= $\{c_1, c_2, \ldots\}$ of class names, and a set **att** = $\{A_1, A_2, \ldots\}$ of attribute names. A special constant *nil* represents the undefined value.

Definition 1: Given a set O of OIDs, the family of values over O is defined so that

a) *nil*, each element of **dom**, and each element of O are values over O; and

b) if $v_1, \ldots, v_k$ are values over O, and $A_1, \ldots, A_n$ distinct attribute names, the tuple $[A_1: v_1, \ldots, A_n: v_n]$ and the set $\{v_1, \ldots, v_n\}$ are values over O.

The set of all values over O is denoted by **val**(O). An object is a pair (o, v) where o is an OID and v a value. ☐

Passive Types

All objects in a class have complex values of the same type. The type corresponding to each class is specified by the OODB schema.

Definition 2: Passive types are defined with respect to a given set C of class names. The family of types over C is defined so that:

a) **integer, string, bool, float** are types;

b) the class names in C are types;

c) if t is a type, then $\{t\}$ is a (set) type;

d) if $\tau_1, \ldots, \tau_n$ are types and $A_1, \ldots, A_n$ distinct attribute names, then $[A_1: \tau_1, \ldots, A_n: \tau_n]$ is a (tuple) type. ☐

We associate with each class c a type $\sigma(c)$, which dictates the type of objects in this class. In particular, for each object (o, v) in a class c, v must have the structure described by $\sigma(c)$.

The set of types over C together with the special class name **any** are denoted **types**(C). The virtual class **any** serves as the unique root of the ISA hierarchy. The class hierarchy has three components: 1) a set of classes, 2) the types associated with these classes, and 3) a specification of the ISA relationships between the classes.

Definition 3: A *class hierarchy* is a triple $(C, \sigma, \leq_S)$, where C is a finite set of class names, s a mapping from C to **types**(C), and $\leq_S$ a partial order on C. ☐

Definition 4: A subtyping relationship on **types**(C) is the smallest partial order $\leq_T$ over **types**(C) satisfying the following conditions[4]:

a) if $c_1 \leq_S c_2$, then $c_1 \leq_T c_2$;

b) if $\tau_i =_\tau \tau_i'$ for each $i \in [1, n]$ and $n \leq m$, then $[A_1: \tau_1, \ldots, A_n: \tau_n, \ldots, A_m: \tau_m] \leq_T [A_1: \tau_1', \ldots, A_n: \tau_n']$; and

c) for each τ, $\tau \leq_T$ **any** (i.e., **any** is the top of the hierarchy). ☐

Definition 5: A class hierarchy $(C, \sigma, \leq_S)$ is *well-formed* if for each pair c_1, c_2 of classes, $c_1 \leq_S c_2$ implies $\sigma(c_1) \leq_T \sigma(c_2)$. If $c_1 \leq_S c_2$ and $c_1 \neq c_2$, we say that $c_1 <_S c_2$. ☐

Adding Behavior

The final ingredient of the generic OODB model is *methods*. A method has three components:

a) a name,

b) a signature,

c) an implementation (or body).

The names and signatures of methods are specified at the schema level in our OODB model. We assume the existence of an infinite set **meth** of method names. Let $(C, \sigma, \leq_S)$ be a class hierarchy.

Definition 6: For method name m, a signature of m is an expression of the form m: c x τ_1 x ... x $\tau_{n-1} \rightarrow t_n$, where c is a class name in C and each τ_i is a type over C. The class c is termed the *receiver* of m. A set M of methods is *well formed* if it obeys the following two rules:

- Unambiguity: If c is a subclass of c' and c'' and there is a definition of m for c' and c'', then there is a definition of m for a subclass of c' and c'' that is either c itself, or a superclass of c.
- Co/contravariance: If m : c x $\tau_1{'}$ ... x$\tau_n \rightarrow \tau$ and m : c' x $\tau_1{'}$ x ... x $\tau_p{'} \rightarrow \tau'$ are two definitions, $c <_S c'$ and $n = p$, then for each i, $\tau_i{'} \leq_T \tau_i$ and $\tau \leq_T \tau'$ (i.e, contravariant in the formal arguments and covariant in the return type). $\square$

Schemas and Databases

Definition 7: A passive schema is a 4-tuple $S = (C, \sigma, \leq_S, M)$, where
- σ is a mapping from C to **types**(C) of tuple type only;
- $(C, \sigma, \leq_S)$ is a well formed class hierarchy; and
- M is a well-formed set of method signatures for $(C, \sigma, \leq_S)$. $\square$

Example 7: The set of classes C for the schema in Figure 1 is: {Step, Etch, Chemical, Physical, Equipment, RIE, MXE, Operator}. The definition of types of some of the classes and the specification of the subclass relationship is given below:

Step = [name: string]
Etch: super-class Step = [int: temperature, int: pressure],
Equipment = [name: string, operated-by: Operator].

The set of method signatures M is given by: {abort-execute: Etch $\rightarrow$ int, execute: Etch $\rightarrow$ RIE, execute: Physical $\rightarrow$ MXE, set-pressure: Chemical $\rightarrow$ int, call-operator: Equipment $\rightarrow$ int, control-alarm: RIE $\rightarrow$ int, inform: Operator $\rightarrow$ int}. The set is well-formed, with the two definitions of execute conforming to co/contravariance and unambiguity. Note that in the examples to follow, the return type of methods will be left unspecified to simplify the presentation. $\square$

Active Rules

We now define a formal model for active rules which will be used to define syntactic compatibility for rule inheritance and overriding. Active rules are specified with reference to a passive schema and include:
- a) a set of *event names* and the *types* for these events names;
- b) a set of *conditions*;
- c) a set of *actions*;
- d) a set of *rule names* and *a set of definitions* for each rule name.

Some Useful Definitions

Class Vectors: To simplify the presentation of our model, we will use $c^{-(n)}$ to represent a vector of classes $c_1, \ldots, c_n$.

Subclass Relation among Vectors: We will also use the notation $c^{-(n)} \leq_S b^{-(n)}$ to represent that the classes in the vectors $c^{-(n)}$ and $b^{-(n)}$ and stand in the relation $\leq_S$ point-wise, i.e., $c^{-(n)} \leq_S b^{-(n)} \equiv c_i \leq_S b_i$ for $i = 1, \ldots, n$.

Specificity of Vectors: If $c^{-(n)} \leq_S b^{-(n)}$ and for at-least one $i \in [1, n]$, $c_i \neq b_i$, we say that $c^{-(n)}$ is more specific than $b^{-(n)}$, denoted by $c^{-(n)} <_S {'}b^{-(n)}$.

Most Specific Vector: Given class vector $c^{-(n)}$ and a set $Vec^{(n)}$ of class vectors (all of the same size), $s^{-(n)} \in Vec^{(n)}$ is said to be most specific w.r.t. $c^{-(n)}$, if

$c^{-(n)} \leq_S s^{-(n)}$, and for all other $b^{-(n)} \in Vec^{(n)}$ if $c^{-(n)} \leq_S b^{-(n)}$ then $s^{-(n)} <_S b^{-(n)}$

Note that for an arbitrary set of class vectors, a most specific vector may not exist.

Events

Event types are defined using the primitive events and the composition operators provided by the system. Primitive events may include method events, transaction events, temporal events and abstract events. Of these, method events are related to the passive schema. Method events are identified by the schema designer by designating that an event be raised before/after the invocation of a particular method in the passive schema. Different composition operators are defined by various systems. Examples of composition operators include conjunction, disjunction, and sequence.

Assume the existence of a set E_m of method events of the form either *before m* or *after m* where $m \in M$; a set E_{temp} of temporal events; a set E_{abs} of abstract events; and a set E_{trans} of transaction events. We designate the set of primitive events by E_{prim}, i.e., $E_{prim} = E_m \cup E_{temp} \cup E_{abs} \cup E_{trans}$. We also assume a set $OP = \{op_1, op_2, \ldots, op_l\}$ of composition operators.

Definition 8: Event types are defined with respect to a given set of primitive events E_{prim} and operators belonging to the set OP, such that

i) each element of E_{prim} is an event type;

ii) $op(e_1, e_2, \ldots, e_q)$ is a (composite) event type if $e_1, e_2, \ldots, e_q$ are event types that can be legally composed using $op \in OP$.

The set of event types defined for a given set of primitive events E_{prim} and operators belonging to the set OP is denoted by **events**(E_{prim}, OP). ❑

Example 8: In the schema shown in Figure 1, four method events have been identified. Thus $E_m = \{$before execute: Etch, after execute: Etch, before set-pressure: Chemical, after control-alarm: RIE$\}$.

Using the composition operator OR, the composite event OR(after execute: Etch, after control-alarm: RIE) and the composite event OR(after control-alarm: RIE, before set-pressure: Chemical) have been defined in the rule definitions Inform-Operator$_1$ and Inform-Operator$_2$ respectively (in Examples 1 and 5). ❑

To simplify event definition, the return type of the primitive events will be left out in the future.

Conditions

The condition part of an active rule is a query over the database. Queries are specified by Boolean expressions in a query language and/or a programming language. The expression may range over attributes and methods of a set of classes (on which the condition is defined) and may include comparison operators, quantifiers and connectives provided by the query language. The interface of a condition will be included in the rule definition. This is modeled by a name, a signature (both of which are at the schema level) and a body (which is at the instance level). The signature of a condition contains the classes on which the condition is specified (i.e., the classes whose attributes and methods are used in the condition body) and the parameters that may be passed to the condition at evaluation time.

Definition 9: For each condition named *cond*, there is a signature of *cond* which is an expression of the form $cond$: c_1 x . . . x c_k x τ_1 x . . . x τ_{p-1} →**bool**, where c_1, . . ., c_k are class names in C and $\tau_k \in \sigma(C)$, for $k = 1, . . ., p$ - 1. The set of condition names for a given active schema is denoted by M_C. ❒

Example 9: The body of the condition for rule definition Pressure-Check$_1$ (Example 1) is pressure > rie.pressure-limit. The condition is defined on the class Etch and it uses an instance of RIE in its evaluation. Its name and signature are given: cond$_1$: Etch x RIE → **bool**. The name and signature of the condition for rule definition Inform-Operator$_1$ (Example 1) is given by: cond$_2$: Etch x RIE → **bool.** ❒

Since the return type of all conditions is **bool**, we will leave it unspecified in examples in the future.

Actions

Actions in our model are methods defined in the given passive schema S.

Definition 10: For each action named *action*, there is a signature of *action* $\in M$. The set of action names for a given active schema is denoted by the set M_A. ❒

Example 10: The signature of the action of rule definition Pressure-Check$_1$ (again leaving the return type unspecified) is abort-execute: Etch. ❒

Rules

Rule types are defined using a rule constructor with respect to a given set R of rule names, a given passive schema S, the set $E \subset$ **events**(E_{prim}, OP) of events, the set M_C of condition names, and the set M_A of action names. We will denote the various definitions for a rule name r by r_1, r_2, etc.

Definition 11: For each rule $r \in R$, a type definition (or simply definition) r_i of r is given by a *rule type* which has the following form:

r_i = <name: r, class$_1$: c_1, . . ., class$_n$: c_n, event: e, condition: f_c, action: f_a, par$_1$: τ_1, . . ., par$_p$: τ_p>

where $c_i \in C$, for $i = 1, . . ., n$; $e \in E, f_c \in M_C, f_a \in M_A, \tau_k \in \sigma(C)$, for $k = 1, . . ., p$, and for each method event in (the primitive or composite) e, the receiver c_m of the method appears in $c_1, . . ., c_n$. ❒

Here e, f_a, and f_c specify the event, condition and action of the rule respectively. c_1 to c_n represent the classes to which the rule applies. An instance of each of these classes will be passed to the rule at activation time. The par$_k$ represents any other parameters passed to the rule. The restriction on the method events, stated in Definition 11, ensures that only those method events that are raised by methods of the classes to which the rule applies can effect the rule firing.

Example 11: The type of the two rule definitions introduced in Example 1 is as follows:

Pressure-Check$_1$ = <name: Pressure-Check, class$_1$: Etch, event: before execute: Etch, condition: cond$_1$: Etch x RIE, action: abort-execute: Etch, par$_1$: RIE>.

Inform-Operator$_1$ = <name: Inform-Operator, class$_1$: Etch, class$_2$: RIE, event: OR(after execute: Etch, after control-alarm: RIE), condition: cond$_2$: Etch x RIE, action: call-operator: RIE>. ❒

Definition 12: The term **class-vector**(r_i) represents the classes to which the definition r_i applies, i.e., **class-vector**(r_i) = $c^{-(n)}$. ❒

Example 12: The class vector of the definition Inform-Operator$_1$ is: **class-**

vector(Inform-Operator$_1$) = <Etch, RIE>, while the class vector of the definition Pressure-Check$_1$ of rule Pressure-Check is given by: **class-vector**(Pressure-Check$_1$) = <Etch>. ❑

Rule Inheritance

We first consider the case of rule inheritance in the absence of overriding. A rule r defined on a given class-vector is inherited by all the class vectors that are more specific than this vector.

Definition 13: A rule definition r_j, with | **class-vector**(r_j) | = l is applicable to and hence can be activated for instances of all class vectors $a^{(l)}$ belonging to $C´ C´ \dots ´ C$ (l-times), such that $a^{(l)} <_S$ **class-vector**(r_j). The set of all such class vectors '$a^{(l)}$ is denoted by **Inherits**(r_j). ❑

Example 13: The definition Inform-Operator$_1$ of rule Inform-Operator is defined on the class vector: <Etch, RIE>. This rule is inherited by the class vectors defined by: <Etch, MXE>, <Chemical, RIE>, <Chemical, MXE>, <Physical, RIE>, <Physical, MXE>. This means that this rule definition applies to and can be activated on instances of any of these class vectors. ❑

Rule Overriding

A rule definition can be overridden by specifying another rule definition with the same name but a different type. Some or even all of the event, condition and action attributes may be modified in this overridden rule. The scope of the overridden rule definition is specified via a different class-vector which represents the classes for which the overridden rule definition is applicable.

Definition 14: Given rule definitions r'_j = <name: r, class$_1$: c'_1, ..., class$_n$: c'_n, event: e', condition: f_c, action: f_a, par$_1$: τ'_1, ..., par$_p$: τ'_p> and r_j = <name: r, class$_1$: c_1, ..., class$_n$: c_n, event: e, condition: f_c, action: f_a, par$_1$: τ_1, ..., par$_p$: τ_p>, if $c'^{(n)} <_S c^{(n)}$ then r'_j overrides r_j. ❑

Example 14: Consider the two definitions Pressure-Check$_1$ and Pressure-Check$_2$ of rule Pressure-Check (Example 1 and Example 3 respectively). These are given in our formal model as:

Pressure-Check$_1$ = <name: Pressure-Check, class$_1$: Etch, event: before execute: Etch, condition: cond$_1$: Etch x RIE, action: abort-execute: Etch, par$_1$: RIE>.

Pressure-Check$_2$ = <name: Pressure-Check, class$_1$: Chemical, event: OR(before execute: Etch, before set-pressure), condition: cond$_1$: Etch x RIE, action: abort-execute: Etch, par$_1$: RIE>.

Here Pressure-Check$_2$ overrides Pressure-Check$_1$ for the class Chemical. The scope of the rule definition labeled Pressure-Check$_2$ is specified with the class-vector <Chemical> and <Chemical> $<_S$ <Etch>. The event is overridden by a composite event, while the condition and action parts are left unchanged[5]. ❑

Ensuring Compatibility

When the definition of a rule is overridden by specifying another definition, we need to ensure compatibility of the new definition with the existing definitions of the rule. To achieve this, we require that each rule must have a *most-generic* definition and any definition that overrides the most-generic definition must be *compatible* with this most-generic definition. Similarly, if certain definitions already override a most-generic definitions, then any new definition must be mutually-compatible with all these existing definition. This notion is made precise below.

Definition 15: For each rule $r \in R$, a particular rule type definition r_i must be identified as most-generic. The corresponding class-vector is termed **generic-class-vector**(r). ☐

Example 15: For the rule Pressure-Check, we specify that the rule definition Pressure-Check$_1$ is most-generic. Thus **generic-class-vector**(Pressure-Check) = <Etch>. For the rule Inform-Operator, we specify that the rule definition Inform-Operator$_1$ is most-generic. Thus **generic-class-vector**(Inform-Operator) = <Etch, RIE>. ☐

Obviously, for overriding to make sense, the class vector of the more specific rule definition should itself be more specific than the class vector of the most-generic definition.

Definition 16: For each rule name $r \in R$, the *rule overridings* of r is a set of rule definitions (denoted by **Overriding**(r)) of the following form:

<name: r, class$_1$: c'_1, . . ., class$_n$: c'_n, event: e', condition: f'_c, action: f'_a, par$_1$: τ_1, . . ., par$_p$: τ_p> where $c'_i \in C$, for $i = 1, . . ., n$, $\tau'_k \in \sigma(C)$, for $k = 1, . . ., p$; $e' \in E, f'_c \in M_C, f'_a \in M_A$ and $c'^{-(n)} \leq_S$ **generic-class-vector**(r). π

Example 16: The rule overridings for Inform-Operator are the definitions Inform-Operator$_1$, Inform-Operator$_2$ and Inform-Operator$_3$ with the **class-vectors** <Etch, RIE>, <Chemical, RIE> and <Etch, MXE> respectively. Note that the most-generic definition of $r \in$ **Overriding**(r). ☐

Name Compatibility

For passive object models, name compatibility requires that a subclass may redefine a superclass property (or add new properties), but it may not remove any superclass properties. The analogous concept in the case of rules is that if a rule r is applicable to (and hence can be activated on) instances of a class c, and $c' <_S c$ then r should also be applicable to instances of c'.

Proposition 1: Consider a rule r defined with a certain class-vector $c^{-(n)}$ that includes a class c. Then Definition 13 specifies that this rule can be activated on the class-vector '$c'^{(n)}$ in which c is replaced by any subclass of c (since $c^{-(n)}$ is more specific to $c^{-(n)}$, and hence by Definition 13 it is included in **Inherits**(r)). Name compatibility is thus ensured by our model. ☐

Signature Compatibility

Signature compatibility for passive object models implies full compatibility of the interface of a class with the interface of its superclass. In the application code, a rule definition is chosen for activation on certain objects and the required parameters are passed to this rule definition. Thus for each rule definition, the interface consists of the formal types of the classes on which the rule definition can be activated and the types of the parameters that can be passed to the rule definition. By adapting the definition of compatibility for multi-methods (Castagna, 1995), we can see that signature compatibility requires that in all overridings of a rule r the class vector should become more specific (i.e., covariant) and the parameter overriding can only be made less specific (i.e., contravariant).

Definition 17: Two type definitions of r, r'_j = <name: r, class$_1$: c'_1, . . ., class$_n$: c'_n, event: e', condition: f'_c, action: f'_a, par$_1$: τ'_1, . . ., par$_p$: τ'_p> and r_j = <name: r, class$_1$: c_1, . . ., class$_n$: c_n, event: e, condition: f_c, action: f_a, par$_1$: τ_1, . . ., par$_p$: τ_p> are said to be *signature compatible* if $c^{-(n)} <_S c^{-(n)}$, then also for each i, $\tau_i \leq_T \tau'_i$. The *rule overridings* of a rule r exhibit signature compatibility if each of them is mutually signature compatible. ❐

Example 17: For the rule Pressure-Check consider the three definitions Pressure-Check$_1$, Pressure-Check$_2$, and Pressure-Check$_3$ in Examples 1, 3 and 4 respectively. Here:

class-vector(Pressure-Check$_1$) = <Etch> and activation of Pressure-Check$_1$ expects an instance of RIE as its parameter,

class-vector(Pressure-Check$_2$) = <Chemical> and activation of Pressure-Check$_2$ expects an instance of RIE as its parameter,

class-vector(Pressure-Check$_3$) = <Physical> and activation of Pressure-Check$_3$ expects an instance of MXE as its parameter.

Now class-vector(Pressure-Check$_2$) $<_S$ class-vector(Pressure-Check$_1$) and RIE $\leq_T$ RIE, therefore Pressure-Check$_1$ and Pressure-Check$_2$ are signature compatible. However, class-vector(Pressure-Check$_3$) $<_S$ class-vector(Pressure-Check$_1$), but RIE $\leq_T$ MXE does not hold true. The rule overridings of Pressure-Check are thus not signature compatible, since the parameter overriding is not contravariant. Note that if Pressure-Check$_1$ and Pressure-Check$_2$ were the only definitions of rule Pressure-Check then the rule overridings of Pressure-Check would be signature compatible. ❐

Unambiguity of Rule Inheritance

Unambiguity in rule inheritance requires that for a given rule r and a given class vector there should be a unique definition of r that is applicable to this class vector. This can be enforced by requiring that a set of rule overridings be well-formed as defined below.

Definition 18: A set of rule overridings of r is well-formed if for each $a^{-(n)} \in$ **Inherits**(r), there exists a $c^{-(n)} \in$ **Overridings**(r) which is most-specific w.r.t. $a^{-(n)}$. ❐

Example 18: Consider the set of overridings Inform-Operator$_1$, Inform-Operator$_2$, Inform-Operator$_3$ specified for the rule Inform-Operator. Observe that a most specific class-vector <Etch, MXE> exists w.r.t. the class vector <Physical, MXE>. However, for the class vector <Chemical, MXE> no such class vector exists (since <Chemical, MXE> $<_S$ <Etch, MXE> and <Chemical, MXE> $<_S$ <Chemical, RIE> and neither <Etch, MXE> $<_S$ <Chemical, RIE> or <Chemical, RIE> $<_S$ <Etch, MXE>). This set of overridings thus does not meet our condition of being well-formed. If now another definition of Inform-Operator is specified with the class-vector <Chemical, MXE>, the set of overridings of Inform-Operator becomes well-formed. ❐

DISCUSSION

Our basic rule model, though formal, is similar to the informal model described for the SAMOS system in (Gatziu, et. al. 1991, Geppert, et. al., 1995). In SAMOS events, conditions and actions can be defined independently of rules. Both class-specific and class-spanning rules are supported and are inherited by the subclasses. As mentioned earlier, the semantics of inheritance for class-spanning rules and rule overriding though have not been discussed for SAMOS. In addition, the concepts of name and signature compatibility have not been investigated in SAMOS or any other active OODB system that we are cognizant of.

It should be noted here that it has been argued elsewhere that class-spanning rules violate the notion of encapsulation and hence do not match well with the OO paradigm (Kemper, et. al., 1994). However, the utility of class-spanning rules is obvious and these rules are provided by almost all active OODBs[6]. In fact, this provision of class-spanning rules (which is analogous to multi-methods) need not completely violate encapsulation. The key concept for encapsulation of rules is lexically restricted scope of access to a class. This can be achieved via constructs similar to the "friend" construct of C++, which gives access to private properties of a class to a function defined outside this class (Stroustrup, 1991).

For active rules specified using the model presented in the chapter, checking for ambiguous rule definition and resolving such ambiguities becomes an important task. Type checking of multi-methods can be carried out statically using polynomial-time algorithms presented in, e.g., Chambers & Leavens (1995). The same basic algorithm would be applicable for our rule model. Similarly ambiguity in rule definition can be solved in a manner similar to the corresponding solution in the area of multi-methods. Different mechanisms for the definition of most specific methods are discussed in Amiel & Dujardin (1996). These include, for example, establishing precedence based on argument order, precedence based on inheritance order, or explicitly asking the user to specify the precedence. The first two mechanisms are examples of implicit disambiguation, where there is an automatic resolution of ambiguity without requiring programmer input. Requiring programmers to solve ambiguity is called explicit disambiguation. It has been argued in Amiel & Dujardin (1996) that implicit disambiguation generally hides programmer errors that are the cause of ambiguity in the first place. The authors thus argue for explicit disambiguation. In case of rule inheritance, we feel that a similar argument suggests that rule disambiguation should also be carried out explicitly. This will ensure that the rule programmer is aware of the interaction among inherited rules and can make use of this fact when disambiguating the rules.

CONCLUSIONS

Inheritance, though a key feature of OO systems, has been surprisingly under-explored in active OODBs. This has resulted in active OODB systems lacking the important features of overriding of class-spanning rules and notions of syntactic compatibility. In this chapter, we have presented a formal model which covers the overlooked aspects of inheritance and overriding of class-spanning rules and also lays down a formal foundation of the concept of syntactic compatibility for rule overriding. This model has been developed by adapting the concept of multi-methods and can be used in the implementation of active OODB systems to provide the presented functionality.

For future work, we note that the focus of the active rule inheritance model introduced in this chapter has been on defining the notion of syntactic compatibility for rule inheritance and overriding. For this model to be implemented in an active OODB system and hence be available for use to application developers, there is a complementary need to provide language support for rule inheritance. Extensions can be carried out to rule definition languages to provide reuse of rule specifications by supporting the definition of a more specific rule in terms of an existing rule that is being overridden. Compilers for such extended rule languages can provide type checking to ensure syntactic compatibility, thus providing complete support for the formal model defined in the chapter.

Lack of support for inheritance and overriding is not the only feature for which support for active capabilities lags the corresponding support for passive capabilities. There has been little or no research for providing support for active schema evolution. The area of schema evolution has been researched in the context of passive OODB systems (Zicari, 1992, Ra & Rundensteiner, 1995). There is a need for developing a corresponding framework to support schema evolution in active databases. Rule-base, and in particular event-base, modification has been studied in Geppert, Gatziu & Dittrich (1995). The emphasis is on carrying out the evolution of composite events while taking into account the events that have already taken place before the evolution. However, a general framework, encompassing operators for active schema modification and notions of consistency for active and passive schema is missing. We feel that a framework for schema evolution in active OODB systems can be developed using the formal model for active rules presented in this chapter.

ENDNOTES

[1] Since the meaning of and relation between certain object-oriented terms (e.g., subclass, subtyping) varies in different object models, note that in our chosen object model a subclass relationship between two classes implies the existence of subtype relationship between the types of these classes. This appears to be the common approach in OODBs, although certain OO programming languages (e.g., Cecil in Chambers (1992)) decouple subclass relationship (mechanism for code inheritance) and subtype relationship (mechanism for interface inheritance).

[2] In type-theoretic terms, we have an overloading-based object model as opposed to a record-based object model (Castagna, 1995). However, as noted in Castagna (1995), ignoring implementation issues, these two ways of grouping methods are essentially equivalent at the formal level, and hence this choice does not restrict the formal power of our model.

[3] To handle cases where these rules appear too strict, techniques have been developed which allow some type unsafe statements with conditions and exception handling code around them (Amiel, et. al., 1996). Alternately the user may be encouraged to follow the constraints without the system enforcing them completely (e.g., C++ (Stroustrup, 1991)).

[4] To ensure type safety, the legal subtyping relationships defined here are different from the one presented in (Abiteboul, et. al., 1994), and correspond to the GOM model defined in (Kemper & Moerkotte, 1994).

[5] With a suitable rule definition language one should be able to define a more specific rule in terms of the existing rule that is being overridden. Similarly, it is possible to give short names to the events and use these names in the rule definition. This issue though is orthogonal to our formal model.

[6] It may be noted here that SQL3 includes multi-methods (Melton, 1996). A requirement that rules do not span classes thus seems undue if the semantics of the application require such functionality.

REFERENCES

Abiteboul, S., Hull, R. & Vianu, V. (1995). *Foundations of Databases.* Reading, MA: Addison-Wesley.

Agrawal, R., DeMichiel, L. & Lindsay, B. (1991). Static Type Checking in Multi-Methods. *Proc. of 6th Annual Conference on Object-oriented Programming, Systems, Lan-*

guages and Applications, 113-128.

America, P. (1991). In M. Lenzerini, D. Nardi, & M. Simi (Eds.), *Inheritance Hierarchies in Knowledge Representation and Programming Languages*. New York: John Wiley & Sons.

Amiel, E. et. al. (1996). Type-safe Relaxing of Schema Consistency Rules for Flexible Modelling in OODBMS. *The VLDB Journal*, 5 (2), 133-150.

Amiel, E. & Dujardin, E. (1996). Supporting Explicit Disambiguation of Multi-Methods. *Proc. of 10th European Conference on Object-Oriented Programming*, 167-188.

Bertino, E., Guerrini, G. & Merlo, I. (1997). Trigger Inheritance and Overriding in Active Object Database Systems. *Proc. of the 5th International Conference on Deductive and Object-Oriented Database*, 193-210.

Buchmann, A. et. al. (1995). Building an Integrated Active OODBMS: Requirements, Architecture, and Design Decisions. *Proc. of 11th IEEE International Conference on Data Engineering*, 117-128.

Castagna, G. (1995). Covariance and Contravariance: Conflict without a Cause. *ACM Transactions on Programming Languages and Systems*, 17 (3), 431-447.

Ceri, S. et. al. (1996). In J. Widom & S. Ceri (Eds.). *Active Database Systems: Triggers and Rules for Advanced Database Processing*. San Francisco, CA: Morgan Kaufmann.

Chakravarthy, S. et. al. (1994). *ECA Rule Integration into an OODBMS: Architecture and Implementation* (Report No. UF-CIS-TR-94-023). Dept. of Computer & Information Science, University of Florida, Gainesville, Florida.

Chambers, C. (1992). Object-Oriented Multi-Methods in Cecil. *Proc. of 6th European Conference on Object-Oriented Programming*, 33-56.

Chambers, C. & Leavens, G. (1995). Typechecking and Modules for Multi-Methods. *ACM Transactions on Programming Languages and Systems*, 17 (6), 805-843.

Chaudhry, N., Moyne, J. & Rundensteiner, E. (1998). Active Controller: Utilizing Active Databases for Implementing Multi-Step Control of Semiconductor Manufacturing. *IEEE Transactions on Components, Packaging and Manufacturing Technology, Part C: Manufacturing Technology*, to appear.

Collet, C., Coupaye, T. & Svensen, T. (1994). NAOS - Efficient and Modular Reactive Capabilities in an Object-Oriented Database System. *Proc. of 20th International Conference on Very Large Databases*, 132-143.

Collet, C. & Coupaye, T. (1996). Composite Events in NAOS. *Proc. of 7th International Conference on Database and Expert Systems Applications*, 244-253.

Gatziu, S., Geppert, A. & Dittrich, K. (1991). Integrating Active Concepts into an Object-Oriented Database System. *Proc. of 3rd International Workshop on Database Programming Languages*, 399-415.

Geppert, A., Gatziu, S. & Dittrich, K. (1995). *Rulebase Evolution in Active Object-Oriented Database Systems: Adapting the Past to Future Needs* (Report No. 95.13). Computer Science Department, University of Zurich, Switzerland.

Geppert, A. et. al. (1995). *Architecture and Implementation of the Active Object-Oriented Database Management System SAMOS* (Report No. 95.29). Computer Science Department, University of Zurich, Switzerland.

Goldberg, A. & Robson, D. (1984). *Smalltalk-80: the Interactive Programming Environment*. Reading, MA: Addison-Wesley.

Kappel, G. et. al. (1994). TriGS - Making a Passive Object-Oriented Database System Active. *Journal of Object-Oriented Programming*, 7 (4), 40-63.

Kemper, A. et. al. (1994). Autonomous Objects: A Natural Model for Complex Applications. *Journal of Intelligent Information Systems*, 3 (2), 133-150.

Kemper, A. & Moerkotte, G. (1994). *Object-Oriented Database Management: Applications in Engineering and Computer Science*. Englewood Cliffs, NJ: Prentice Hall.

Lieuwen, D., Gehani, N. & Arlien, R. (1996). The Ode Active Database: Trigger Semantics and Implementation. *Proc. of the 12th International Conference on Data Engineering*, 412-420.

Melton, J. (1996). SQL-3 Update. *Proc. of the 12th International Conference on Data Engineering*, 666-672.

Meo, R., Psaila, G. & Ceri, S. (1996). Composite Events in Chimera. *Proc. of 5th International Conference on Extending Database Technology*, 56-76.

Paton, N. et. al. (1993). Dimensions Of Active Behaviour. *Proc. of the 1st International Workshop on Rules in Database Systems*, 40-57.

Ra, Y-G. & Rundensteiner, E. (1995). A Transparent Object-Oriented Schema Change Approach Using View Evolution. *Proc. of 11th IEEE International Conference on Data Engineering*, 165-172.

Stroustrup, B. (1991). *The C++ Programming Language*. (2nd ed.). Reading, MA: Addison-Wesley.

Taivalsaari, A. (1996). On the Notion of Inheritance. *ACM Computing Surveys*, 28 (3), 438-479.

Wegner, P. (1990). Concepts and Paradigms of Object-oriented Programming. *ACM OOPS Messenger*, 1 (1), 7-87.

Wegner, P. & Zdonik, S. (1988). Inheritance as an Incremental Modification Mechanism or What Like Is and Isn't Like. *Proc. of the 2nd European Conference on Object-Oriented Programming*, 55-77.

Zdonik, S. & Maier, D. (Eds.) (1990). *Readings in Object-Oriented Databases*. San Francisco, CA: Morgan Kaufmann.

Zicari, R. (1992). In F. Bancilhon, C. Delobel & P. Kanellakis (Eds.), *Building an Object-Oriented Database System, The Story of O2*. San Francisco, CA: Morgan Kaufmann.

Zimmermann, J. et. al. (1996). Design, Implementation and Management of Rules in an Active Database System. *Proc. of 7th International Conference on Database and Expert Systems Applications*, 422-435.

CHAPTER 10

Unbundling Active Database Systems

Arne Koschel, Forschungszentrum Informatik, Germany
Stella Gatziu, University of Zurich, Switzerland
Günter von Bültzingsloewen, Swiss Bank Corporation
Hans Fritschi, University of Zurich, Switzerland

New application areas or new technical innovations expect from database management systems more and more new functionality. However, adding functions to the DBMS as an integral part of them tends to create monoliths that are difficult to design, implement, validate, maintain and adapt. Such monoliths can be avoided if one configures DBMS according to the actually needed functionality. In order to identify the basic functional components for the configuration the current monoliths should be broken up into smaller units, or in other words they should be "unbundled". In this chapter we apply unbundling to active database systems. This results in a new form of active mechanisms where active functionality is no longer an integral part of the DBMS functionality. It allows the use of active capabilities with any arbitrary DBMS and in broader contexts such as today's heterogeneous and distributed information systems. Furthermore, it allows the adaptation of the active functionality to the application profile. Such aspects are crucial for a wide use of active functionality in real (database or not) applications. Furthermore, this paper gives a discussion with problems and questions arising from the unbundling process. Eventually we show, how unbundling is exploited in two current projects, namely FRAMBOISE and C^2offein, which represent examples for architectures, that result from two different unbundling steps.

INTRODUCTION

Active functionality, as it is offered today by active database management systems (active DBMS), is the ability to react not only after an explicit request from the application or the user, but also when a specific situation of interest has occurred in the DBS or its environment. The basic notion of active DBMS are Event/Condition/Action-Rules (ECA-Rules), meaning WHEN a certain event occurs and IF a given condition holds THEN a certain action is executed.

In order to offer active functionality, new components (so-called activity components) implementing tasks like (ECA) rule management and (ECA) rule execution are required in addition to the known components of a DBMS.

Today, activity components are developed for a particular DBMS. By implementing the activity components as an integral part of a DBMS, active functionality is rather tightly coupled to the DBMS behind it. Thus, the active DBMS becomes part of large monolithic pieces of software. Such software is difficult to implement, validate, maintain and adapt. Even where active DBMS have a layered system architecture, with the activity components residing "on top" of a conventional DBMS, the active functionality remains tightly interconnected and as such bound to the particular target DBMS.

In either architectural approach, a substantial effort is required to adopt active functionality for various DBMS. It is close to impossible to develop activity mechanisms that can be ported from one DBMS to the other. Today, a few commercial DBMS offer restricted active mechanisms while the more expressive ones are only found in research prototypes.

Moreover, active functionality tightly coupled to a concrete environment (a particular DBMS environment) hampers its adaptation to changes in the information technology scene. Just consider the present change of information systems in environments with several (existing and newly developed) heterogeneous and distributed information sources. Active mechanisms, e.g., complex situation monitoring or cooperation and coordination should take into account heterogeneity and distribution.

A further weakness of the tight coupling of active and conventional database mechanisms is that active functionality is not usable on its own, i.e., without the "added" DBMS features. However, active functionality is also needed in applications which require either no database functionality at all or just some like persistence. Thus, active functionality should be offered not only as part of the functionality of a DBMS, but also as a separate service which can be combined with other services like a persistence service. In this way, users could develop "lean" solutions without much overhead due to unneeded components.

As a solution we investigate the provision of active database mechanisms as an individual service. In other words, we unbundle active functionality from the DBMS. Thus, we follow a general direction that database research is currently about to take, namely to provide individual database management services that can be used and combined in a variety of ways and in a variety of environments (Adler 1996, Blakeley 1996, Geppert, Dittrich et al.. 1997, Database Working Group 1996, Vaskevitch 1995). Note, components for database construction have been developed earlier (Carrey, Witt 1987, Batory 1996), however, not with respect to active functionality, heterogeneity, and distribution. The unbundling process starts with a domain analysis of active DBMS-style active functionality. The main task is the identification of components and the cooperation between them. This leads to several (architectural) configurations.

The motivation and the advantages of unbundling active functionality have been presented in (Gatziu, Koschel et al.. 1997). In this paper we investigate in much more detail the unbundling process and its impact on the design and implementation of concrete systems. The major contributions of this paper are:

- The proposal of several architectures arising from unbundling. These architectures are suitable for different needs ranging from activity services as enhancement of passive DBMS to activity services for heterogeneous, distributed environments. It is the developer's task to choose an adequate configuration taking into account possible trade offs.

- The discussion on problems arising from unbundling, and
- The demonstration how unbundling is applied in two current projects. Thus, we illustrate how various configuration of services are concretely used.

The rest of this paper is organized as follows: In the next section we discuss the rationale for unbundling the active DBMS and briefly describe the process to do so. This works major results, the architectures arising from unbundling the active DBMS, are presented in the following section, followed by a discussion on problems from unbundling. Two systems developed by us are briefly presented as unbundling examples in the next section. A conclusion finishes the paper.

UNBUNDLING THE ACTIVE DBMS

Unbundling is the activity to break up monolithic software systems into smaller units with a fair degree of autonomy. Each unit provides a specific service of the software system, which should not only be useful in combination with the further functionality of the system but also separate from it. In contrast to monolithic systems, the communication and the cooperation between the units is not hidden within the system but can clearly be identified from outside.

Considering database management systems as a form of traditionally large and monolithic software systems, it makes sense to build them from a number of cooperating components, and perhaps hope to provide these components for other application areas as well. A still relatively new DBMS part, with increasing importance for supervision, coordination, and cooperation in today's more and more heterogeneous and distributed IS, is active functionality as known from active DBMS, which we assume the reader to be familiar with (see also (ACT-NET Consortium 1996, Paton, Diaz et al. 1994, Widom, Ceri 1996, Fraternali, Tanca 1995)).

Unbundling active functionality from an active DBMS means first to separate the active part from the active DBMS and then eventually to break up this active part into units which provide specific services like detection of events, definition, management, and execution of ECA-rules.

Advantages from Unbundling Active DBMS

Unbundling active functionality from a concrete DBMS offers a number of new opportunities which are critical for a wide use of active functionality in real (database or not) applications:

Use of active capabilities with arbitrary DBMS. Today, active mechanisms are always tightly coupled to a specific DBMS. Typically, active functionality is rather restricted and provided only by few DBMS. There are many applications with active behavior where a DBMS is used, which fulfills almost all application requirements (e.g., performance, programming environment), but offers no or only a restricted active functionality. With independently usable activity components, passive DBMS can more easily be enhanced by activity. This eases the implementation of active mechanisms and should contribute to wider utilization.

Use of active capabilities in broader contexts separate from a DBMS. A range of applications like workflow management, environmental monitoring, etc. require active functionality. However, they do not necessarily require the whole spectrum of database functionality but only parts like persistence or query facilities. However, tight integration of active and database mechanisms in one system forces users to accept both, the entire database functionality and the active functionality.

Instead, a separation of active and conventional database mechanisms would allow the use of active capabilities without any overhead due to unneeded components. This fits well into an environment of combinable services (like CORBA (Object Management Group 1995, Orfali, Harkey et al. 1996) or OLE/DCOM (Orfali, Harkey et al. 1996)). It is natural to add to this infrastructure higher-level services for active functionality. Applications could then combine active functionality with other services.

Use of active functionality in heterogeneous environments. Today's database applications often refer to several (existing and newly developed) heterogeneous and distributed information sources. The need for active functionality in heterogeneous, distributed environments is obvious in the area of data warehousing (Widom 1995) and has also been reported, e.g, in (Pissinou, Vanapipat 1996, Su, Lam et al. 1995, Bültzingsloewen, Koschel et al. 1996).

The impact of heterogeneity on active DBMS is primarily the richer set of information resources that must be monitored. This means that relevant information may not only reside in a database system but also in files, on web pages, etc. Furthermore, checking complex situations like an environmental pollution, a business opportunity, or an emerging traffic congestion usually requires more complex computations than supported by database conditions. Typically, some specific analysis tools have to be invoked. Thus, such analysis and processing tools may become important resources as well (Bültzingsloewen, Koschel et al. 1996, 1997). Hence, the means of the interaction between a service offering active functionality and the heterogeneous environment (e.g., the information sources) becomes much more diverse.

Tailoring active functionality to the application profile. In the more general environment sketched above active functionality plays more roles than what has been used in active DBMS. Supporting advanced active functionality to fulfill the requirements of every application area is not a solution, because there are many cases where the system is overloaded with functionality which is not necessarily needed. Active mechanisms should be tailorable to the application profile. Consequently, collecting all active functionality that could conceivably be used by some application into one system is not the answer. Instead, the unbundling of active mechanisms from the DBMS should be continued into the unbundling of these capabilities themselves. E.g., active functionality could be split into separate functions like composite event detection or rule execution. These functions can be selected individually and configured and interconnected independently. (See (Koschel 1997) for a classification of different usage examples for different active functionality for environmental information systems.)

The Unbundling Process

The unbundling process consists of two major steps (a) the domain analysis where we identify the functionality covered in terms of the services provided and (b) the description of the unbundled system, based on an architectural model, in the form of a specific architecture (Geppert, Dittrich 1997).

In case of unbundling active functionality the domain analysis consists of a review of existing work. This is feasible because after around 10 years of research in active DBMS the basic concepts and functionalities for active behavior and especially the semantics behind them are well-understood and established in these systems (Dayal 1995). This has recently lead to a consensus on those base concepts, which spawned several comprehensive overviews on the concepts and dimensions of active functionality in active DBMS (Fraternali, Tanca 1995, Paton, Diaz et al. 1994, ACT-NET Consortium 1996, Widom, Certi 1996).

In order to describe the architecture of an unbundled system we adopt a rather general architectural model from (Garlan, Shaw, Shaw, DeLine et al. 1995). Our architectural model consists of components, connectors (between components) and a policy restricting the ways how components and connectors can be arranged/interacted. An architecture of a particular unbundled system is then defined by a number of (more or less) autonomous processing components, so-called services (or agents), which cooperate with each other. The regulations which govern the cooperative behavior of the components are captured by connectors among a set of components.

UNBUNDLED SERVICES TO SUPPORT ACTIVE FUNCTIONALITY

In this chapter we discuss the several steps of the unbundling process of active functionality. We start with the monolithic active DBMS. In a first step, we separate active capabilities from the active DBMS to become usable on their own. The second step unbundles these capabilities by themselves, that means, they become separately usable components for (partial) active functionality. This could consist of separate components for e.g. event detection, rule execution etc. As the third (optional) step we extend the separated active capabilities for better support of heterogeneity and distribution in nowaday's (information) systems.

Given the separately usable components an adaptation of active functionality to a given application profile is possible by choosing the right set of components with the right set of abilities. This implies the idea of a configurable set of components. It needs an individual analysis of the needed application-dependent active functionality, e.g., by identification and classification of several scenarios with respect to needed active functionality.

Figure 1   The Monolithic Active DBMS

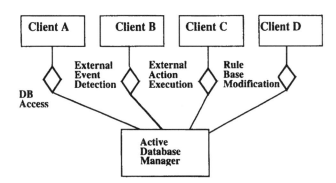

Monolithic Active DBMS

In a monolithic active database environment, the only autonomous components are a number of clients and the active database manager, shown in Figure 1. (Note: Architectures consisting of components and connectors can be described by means of ER-style diagrams, denoting components as rectangular boxes and connectors as diamond-shaped relationships.)

Four different connectors regulate the interaction among these components:

- **Database Access.** This connector allows clients to establish a session with the database manager, to start and end transactions, and to access or modify data items (e.g. relations, objects) within the database. Thereby, the database manager synchronizes concurrent client accesses. In case of a passive DBMS this is the only connector.
- **Rule Base Modification.** Clients may modify the rule base e.g., adding/removing rules.
- **External Event Detection and External Action Execution.** To trigger a rule, clients (e.g., the system clock or an application program) may raise events, so-called external or abstract events, indicating some specific occurrence of interest. Furthermore, a rule may trigger an action which is to be executed by some client. The protocols enforced by the external action execution connector depend on the rule execution model.

Step 1: Separating the Activity Service

A first unbundling step in Figure 2 is the separation of the active mechanisms from the DBMS. This enables the use of active functionality in different environments, e.g., with various existing commercial database systems. From a software engineering perspective, active capabilities have to be developed only once and can be re-used in different contexts.

Active functionality offered by an activity service includes rule management and rule execution. Both are related to passive database functionality. Rule management can exploit database services to store the rule base persistently. Rule execution requires the ability to detect events, to evaluate conditions, and to execute actions. The passive database manager is involved in rule execution as an important event source, to evaluate conditions that refer to database states, and execute actions modifying the database. Three new connectors regulate this interaction between the passive database manager and the activity service:

- **Database Event Detection.** This connector determines what kind of events the database manager produces and what kind of events the activity service subscribes to. Database events are raised in the context of some database access; thereby, an access may raise several events (e.g., a set-oriented insert raises several tuple insert events) and one event may depend on several accesses (e.g. the net effect of all updates during a transaction). Depending on event semantics and coupling mode the database event detection connector enforces that the activity service performs certain steps before the database manager may proceed with processing the access raising a certain event. E.g., a rule of the form
ON BEFORE UPDATE OF REL_A IF Condition DO Action [Immediate]
enforces the condition to be checked and (if the condition holds) the action to be

executed before the update is performed. The database event detection connector is also invoked in the context of a rule base modification.

- **Condition Evaluation and Database Action Execution.** To evaluate conditions and to execute database actions that refer to database states, the activity service and the passive database manager have to cooperate. The activity service determines when evaluation of the database condition must be initiated and when an action has to be executed according to the rule execution model. Furthermore, it propagates information attached to an event occurrence. The database manager is responsible for the actual condition evaluation and action execution. These two connectors require database access capabilities as provided by the database access connector. Moreover, they require a transaction service allowing database accesses to be performed as part or subtransaction of a transaction performed on behalf of some client (at least if all coupling modes are to be supported).

  If the database manager requires that access commands are statically compiled before they are executed (as opposed to dynamic invocation), the corresponding compilation is also performed via the condition evaluation or database action execution connector during a rule base modification.

  Furthermore, the activity service may also make direct use of the database access connector in order to store and manage rules persistently (not shown in the figure).

Step 2: Offering an Event and a Rule Service

In a second unbundling step we split the activity service into an event service and a rule service. This allows the flexible configuration of active functionality for specific application profiles. Active mechanisms are decomposed into two components which can be selected individually and configured and interconnected independently. For example, for different applications event detection (supported by the event service) may require different types of primitive and composite events, different event consumption modes, or different durations over which events are kept as a history. Rule execution (supported by the rule service) may demand different application specific execution guidelines. Furthermore, the event detection and rule execution can now be used each on their own, independently from

Figure 2   Step 1: Separating the Active Functionality from the Active DBMS

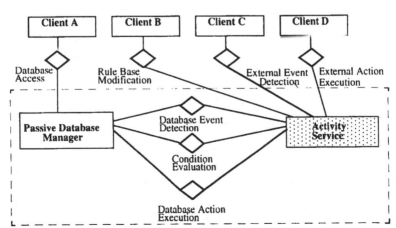

Figure 3   Step 2: Offering an Event and a Rule Service

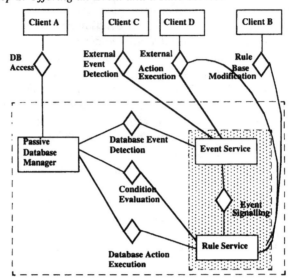

the complete active functionality. For example, we can provide separate event monitoring and production rule facilities.

The corresponding architecture is depicted in Figure 3. Two components responsible for the two new services, Event and Rule Service, and a new connector, the Event Signalling, are introduced:

- Event Service The Event Service records events, maintains a (persistent) event history consisting of all event occurrences and detects composite events. It is informed about the occurrence of primitive events via the event detection connectors, and it provides event information to condition evaluation and action execution using the appropriate connectors.

- Rule Service The Rule Service is responsible for the maintenance of the rule base and implements the rule execution cycle.

- Event Signalling is a connector between Event Service and Rule Service. The Rule Service subscribes to events which may trigger a rule. Events are signalled as soon as they are recorded in the event history.

Furthermore, the Event and the Rule Service may also make direct use of the DB Access connector in order to store rules persistently, to search the rule base, and to retrieve rules (not shown in the figure).

Step 3: Supporting Heterogeneous Environments

To provide active functionality in a distributed, heterogeneous environment, we have to generalize the activity service. Thereby, active functionality is detached from the context of one particular database system. Our goal, however, is to use whenever possible the uniform active functionality as before, in particular, to keep a well-defined semantics.

Up to now, the information resources which interact with the activity service (or in the second step with the event and the rule service) are the passive database manager and clients acting as event sources or executing actions. In order to support a heterogeneous set of information resources, we have to generalize this interaction. Heterogeneity of information resources directly impacts the connectors for event detection, condition evaluation and action execution which link these resources to the activity service.

There are two basic architectural options to support heterogeneity. Specific connectors can be provided for each individual resource, or, heterogeneity could be hidden by more general connectors. It is desirable to keep the activity service as independent as possible from the set of information resources required by a particular application, therefore, we favor the second option. The basic idea is to generalize connectors into more abstract contractors hiding a set of heterogeneous components. This idea can be directly applied to the architecture we have derived so far in step 2. In particular, abstract connectors for event detection, condition evaluation and action execution are required.

Let us consider event detection. The existing connectors External Event Detection and Database Event Detection both subscribe to primitive events. Therefore, we obtain the abstract connector for the Primitive Event Detection, shown in Figure 4. This connector hides the fact that several different event sources exist. Thus, the Event Service now has to issue event subscriptions only to this one connector. The connector can decide (by means of an internal component Primitive Event Mediator), which event source actually needs to be addressed, and issue the corresponding subscription. Thus, heterogeneity of event sources is hidden to the subscriber.

In exactly the same way, we can hide heterogeneity in the case of condition evaluation and action execution. This leads to the architecture of Figure 5 which illustrates the unbundling in a heterogeneous environment.

In general, arbitrary information resources including different kinds of databases, processing tools and communication services can be involved in event detection, condition evaluation and action execution by means of mediators. Of course, the problems arising from this kind of heterogeneity have to be addressed by the corresponding connectors. In fact, knowledge model and execution model may have to be modified in comparison to a monolithic active DBMS, e.g., to support heterogeneous event types or non-transactional information resources. Regarding the implementation, the connectors have to exploit the

Figure 4   The new Connector Primitive Event Mediator

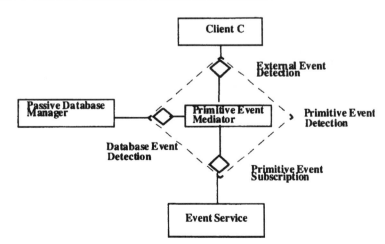

specific functionality of the resources. For example, some resources may be sufficiently active to signal event occurrences on their own, while other sources may need to be polled in order to detect events.

DISCUSSION ON UNBUNDLING

With the unbundling steps presented above we defined several architectures for active functionality, resulting eventually in an architecture providing active functionality for (possibly distributed) heterogeneous information systems. However, there are also several questions arising from the unbundling process. The most prominent ones are: Can active DBMS-style ECA functionality "survive" the whole unbundling process, giving the full semantics as in traditional active DBMS? Does an active DBMS correspond to a passive DBMS plus an (unbundled) activity service? In this section we sketch several examplary problems areas. An in-depth discussion of problems arising from unbundling or even solutions for them goes far beyond this paper.

Questions on Architectures Arising From Unbundling

Even when looking only at the architecture from step 1, we see that active DBMS-functionality will in the general case only partially be providable, simply because the active part can only be layered on top of the existing passive DBMS. This means, each active DBMS-style functionality which requires deep access to the underlying systems may not be supported. This holds for coupling modes, concurrency control for rule execution, the state of the system during condition checking and so on. All this can be supported only if the underlying systems provide interfaces for them. For example, coupling modes, which rely directly on transactions, can be supported only if there is an interface to directly influence the processing of a transaction. However, this does not hold for several existing passive DBMS.

Questions on Heterogeneity and Distribution of Information Sources

Having an increasing flexibility together with increasing heterogeneity of (event) information sources, we also have even more problems than those from above. As mentioned above, we can only sketch some of the problems here. (A more general discussion on ECA rule processing in distributed environments is currently under preparation by us). Some questions and issues regarding heterogeneity and distribution of sources are:

- Primitive events (modeling, detection, and semantics): In case of supporting only database (event) sources, primitive event types can be easily restricted to the very general types from (ACT-NET Consortium 1996) (time events, method events, transaction events, and external events). However, in case of (several) heterogeneous sources, a more expressive modeling of event types should be provided, to give clearer understandable ECA rules. This means, the monitored entities of a certain event source should be explicit describable, e.g., monitor inserts on all tables in a relational DBMS event source.

  Event sources often support mechanisms which can be used for the implementation of event detection, like trigger mechanisms, or different kinds of polling, like a query interface or log-files which can be examined etc. An event detection component should be able to make use of such source specific support. (See a classification of event

Figure 5   Step 3: Supporting Heterogeneous Environments

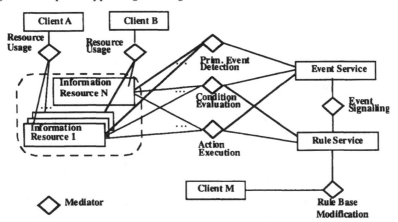

sources and source specific monitoring techniques with further references in (Bültzingsloewen, Koschel et al. 1997)).

Semantics regarding the passing of events during ECA rule processing, like event granularity (e.g. set or instance-oriented), may also depend on source specific support. For example, is the source able to signal sets of events, like all tuples influenced by a database insert? Also the event binding, that means, the information which is passed with the event itself (like the attribute values of an inserted database row), is source specific.

- Context and state during condition evaluation and action execution. Since we have no central database anymore, we have to decide which context we can rely on during rule processing. Beside the information given with event binding, other sources may be queried or, e.g., processing tools may be invoked. Take, e.g., an attribute value from the event has to be compared with a value from another source. What is then the accessible (queryable) information context during condition/action processing for this event? Only the source from which the event arose? All information sources in the system? So which information is "visible" to the condition/action part of the ECA rule?

Moreover, since we have several concurrently operational information sources, the question is, what is the state of their information during a query in a condition/action? Is it, e.g., the actual information state or the information state during the time the event occurred? At least in larger systems it is almost (from a practical view) impossible to collect the overall state of all possible sources. Some of them may not even provide an interface to do so. Whatever information context is eventually introduced for condition/action processing, this heavily influences the expression power of the rule language. The chosen information state furthermore influences the ECA rule processing semantics.

- Transactions. As mentioned before for different DBMS, there is often a lack of transaction support in information sources. This increases with the heterogeneity of sources. Therefore, for global (component spanning) transactions, often only modified transaction properties and not ACID properties will be possible. This means that a modified transaction semantic could be a transition from one consistent state to another consistent state, but not necessarily a return to the same state in case of a transaction rollback.

Of course, lack of transactions can also be taken for given, supporting non-transactional sources just by not introducing transactions during rule processing at all (giving no rollback feature). This is still sufficient for many applications, which need, e.g., complex situation monitoring and notification.

- The rule base. What is the rule base for an unbundled system with heterogeneous sources? Is it a global one or a set of local rule bases? What is the structure of the rule base? Are rules separated into parts, e.g., specifying events at the event sources, conditions at the rule execution engine, and actions at another point?

- Distribution. Even more questions arise with distribution. An event occurs at a certain point in time. Hence, what is this point in a distributed system without global time? Especially for event ordering in composite event detection this plays a major role. How should one deal with unpredictable response times or partial failures of distributed components? Maybe there is some support by the underlying communication infrastructure (e.g., a middleware layer like CORBA). However, we have still to check the execution semantics with respect to active DBMS-style execution semantics.

Questions on Quality of Service

While the two preceeding paragraphs mostly described issues which may result in modified functionality of an unbundled activity service with respect to active DBMS functionality, there may also be other problems regarding the Quality of the Service (QoS). However, such problems are in general known in distributed and concurrent systems. A major issue is here to look for appropriate solutions and to transfer them into the area described here. We list a few questions:

- Performance and Scalability. Layered approaches are known to raise performance problems (Widom, Ceri 1996) as compared to monolithic solutions, because of additional protocol overhead etc. This holds at least for non-concurrent unbundled systems.

  Here distribution of the unbundled services may help, giving the possibility to scale the number of services (e.g. several event histories, several rule processing units etc.). However, there may be more coordination overhead between instances of a service. This could outweigh the performance advantages possible through scaling.

- Reliability. As sketched above, care should be taken to deal with service or node failures in order to provide a reliable unbundled system.

- Security. In monolithic active DBMS one can mostly rely on security features of the underlying DBMS, e.g. a user management. What is security in unbundled systems?

FIRST EXPERIENCES WITH USING UNBUNDLING IN CONCRETE PROJECTS

Unbundling refers to the process of breaking up monoliths into smaller units. The construction of a system by putting together these units is called rebundling in (Geppert, Dittrich 1997). It is defined as the cost-effective construction of a system by assembling preexisting reusable and compatible components in a systematic way. In order to show the usefulness of our unbundling steps, we give here two examples for unbundled and again rebundled systems, FRAMBOISE as an example for unbundling step 2 and the C^2offein approach, which is based on unbundling step 3.

The FRAMBOISE Project

FRAMBOISE (Fritschi, Gatziu et al. 1997) is a construction system which is used to build software that allows the definition and execution of ECA rules in the context of traditional DBMSs. The software constructed by means of FRAMBOISE is called an ECA-System (ECAS). FRAMBOISE provides specification mechanisms, implemented components realizing specific ADBMS tasks (e.g., event definition or rule execution), facilities for selecting the respective components and tools to build specially tailored ECASs. ECASs can be constructed for DBMSs with either an object-oriented or a relational data model.

A specific ECAS is built by the so-called ADBMS-implementor (ADBI) according to the following procedure: First the ADBI outlines the system requirements and specifies the functionality of the ECAS to be built by means of the functional specification language of FRAMBOISE. In particular, the ADBI specifies the knowledge and rule execution model of the prospective system, observing the so-called construction constraints which ensure that these models are consistent and coincide with features of the underlying DBMS. The functional specification language provides constructs to describe which dimensions of active behavior should be realized in an ECAS (e.g., which event sources are provided). Furthermore, it allows the declaration of characteristics of the underlying DBMS like its data model. Using the respective specification, the ECA generator of FRAMBOISE chooses the specific components from the component repository and subsequently generates a generic ECAS. The component repository incorporates the components themselves (i.e. the component library) as well as metadata containing further information about the components such as the construction constraints. A generic ECAS incorporates no software components to interact with the respective DBMS, but it must be enhanced with DBMS-specific adapters in order to become operational. The adapters are supplied by the ADBI. The integration tools of FRAMBOISE support the ADBI in the provision of the adapters and assemble them and the generic ECAS to the operational system.

Operational ECAS may be provided in a form that allows their further incorporation in additional software systems like applications or specific DBMS middleware. Thus, they are supplied, as interface definitions and linkable binary files. Instead, it is possible to build ECAS as "ready-to-run" software systems e.g., in order to process triggers asynchronously similar to the approach presented in (Hanson, Koshla 1997). In order to assist application programmers with the use of the ECAS, FRAMBOISE provides additional tools like rule browser, rule compiler or a rule analyzer.

Generative and specification-driven approaches like FRAMBOISE are typically application-area specific. They adopt a standard system structure (a reference architecture or generic architecture) and standard component interfaces. Accordingly, the architecture of all ECAS is consistent with the reference architecture depicted in Figure 6.

This reference architecture is actually an outcome of the unbundling procedure, performed as one of the first steps in the FRAMBOISE project. The architectural model of step 2 presented in this paper was used as a conceptual grid in order to design the various elements of the FRAMBOISE component library. The latter has subsequently been implemented as an object-oriented framework whose structure is derived from the reference architecture of an ECA-System. It basically incorporates the DBMS-independent components, necessary to build the various generic ECASs. In order to realize an operational ECAS, the DBMS-specific adapters to be supplied by the ADBI are provided as specific framework enhancements.

The event service introduced in step 2. is performed by the cooperation of the event history component, the complex event detector and the event manager. The connectors for database and external event detection depicted in Figure 3, are realized by means of the database event detector and the environment event detectors. The event manager acts as a mediator between the different event detectors, the log facility, the event history and the rule manager. Thus, it incorporates also functionality of the event signalling connector of Figure 3. This connector is actually provided as a part of the event manager by separate software components (i.e., classes). According to the composition of the respective ECAS, these classes may execute simple calls of the signal event method of the assigned rule manager. On the other hand they may implement rather complex interprocess communication facilities if the rule manager runs in a process of its own.

The rule manager component of FRAMBOISE provides in cooperation with the rule execution monitor the rule service. It maintains the rule base and controls the triggering of rules upon notification of an event occurrence. The actual rule execution process is handled by the rule execution monitor by creating temporary rule execution objects, which contain all the information needed for condition evaluation and action execution. Subsequently the rule execution monitor guides condition evaluation and action execution according to the respective rule execution strategy and delegates the particular operation to specific condition or action adapters. These adapters are specialized for the interaction with specific DBMSs as well as for the operating system/application environment. Analogous to the event signalling connector classes these adapter classes subsume the database execution and condition evaluation connectors of Figure 3 and may encapsulate operations of various complexity.

The C²offein System

An example for unbundling step 3 is the C²offein system (see also (Koschel ,

Figure 6   The Reference Architecture of an ECA System

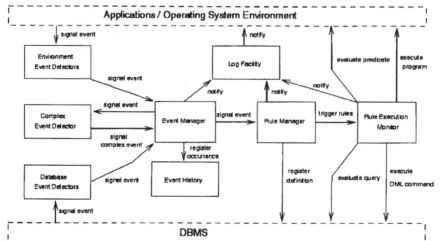

Lockemann 1998, Koschel, Kramer et al. 1997, Bültzingsloewen, Koschel et al. 1997)), currently under development. With C2offein we propose a configurable service set or toolbox for active DBMS-style active functionality especially for CORBA-based, distributed, heterogeneous system environments. The rationale is to construct a service set of individually compilable and flexibly combinable – also separately usable – services. These services shall provide different kinds of active functionality to address a large spectrum of different applications. The services range from pure event detection up to active DBMS-style E,C,A rule processing e.g., for complex distributed situation monitoring. Thus, C^{2}offein is tailorable (configurable) to the application profile.

System Architecture with respect to unbundling steps and unbundling problems

The C^{2}offein system enables E,C,A rule based detection, processing, and report of events and complex situations providing separately usable components for active functionality in CORBA-based systems with heterogeneous and distributed information sources. It is thus an example for a fully unbundled (up to step 3) E,C,A rule processing systems for heterogeneous, distributed environments. Note, we write E,C,A, because C^{2}offein's services are separately usable, also its rule parts, event, conditions, actions are separated, with CORBA IDL descriptions for all parts, forming together ECA rules. The rules may be distributed among several independent rule bases. The C^{2}offein system architecture consists of the components proposed in the third unbundling step (shown in Figure 7). We relate (due to space limits only some of) them to unbundling:

- Wrappers for event detection in principal arbitrary heterogeneous sources. Sources are encapsulated by means of CORBA wrappers. To address heterogeneity, several types of wrappers for different categories of event sources are provided. They utilize source category specific support for event signalling like database triggers or polling mechanisms based on source support for queries, log files etc. Also source specifics for different event granularities, event signalling times and event are utilized.
  By providing a CORBA IDL based extensible event type model, heterogeneous event types are supported. Also generic wrappers for arbitrary CORBA method calls and CORBA exceptions are provided.
  C^{2}offein thus extends active DBMS capabilities into these directions, but also imposes limitations resulting from this. An example is the missing of most transaction capabilities due to uncooperative sources.
- Event Storage and Complex Event Detection. The event storage collects events from different event sources, works as mediator to map them to a uniform event structure, and passes events to the next component.
  The complex event detection component uses a special rulebase to check occurring events for being part of a complex event. For correct temporal ordering of distributed complex events, an artificial global time based on (Schwiderski 1996) is planned as a system option.
- Rule Processing Unit. Rule processing uses an expert system shell supporting classical production rules. C^{2}offein's E,C,A rules are mapped to a set of such production rules. Rule processing is initiated is by corresponding event facts generated by the event storage. Rules are processed in decoupled, either immediate or deferred, mode.
- Information Source Access and Action Execution. In C^{2}offein conditions may include accesses to external sources. Corresponding condition parts are defined using the re-

Figure 7   The Architecture of C²offein

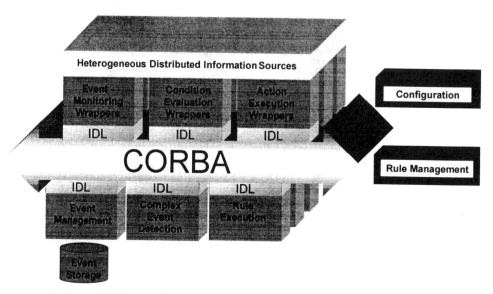

sults from CORBA method calls, e.g., dynamic or parameterized SQL queries. The state during the accesses is actual. (Simple) mediators are used for uniform access to heterogeneous information sources. Actions execution is realized with CORBA method calls, too, e.g., integrated sending of e-mails or database operations.

- Configurability. A configuration component manages information about the current component interconnections. It offers a shell interface for composing system configurations, e.g., the current location of a component, actual components of the system, etc. Additionally, the configuration component allows to choose among different protocols necessary for different configurations, e.g., a/synchronous communication between components, with or without the OMG event service. Replication of components is possible. Beside this configurability, dynamic parametrization of event types (utilizing, e.g., dynamic trigger generation) is contributed.

CONCLUSION

Despite their recent progress, active DBMS have rarely become an ingredient of applications. One major reason is the monolithic nature of existing active DBMS. Active functionality should be offered as a separate facility which could be combined with further facilities, e.g., certain DBMS functions, only to the needed extent. In other words, active functionality should be usable as just one component among others, but should still rely on the consensus-based functionalities and semantics as contained in active DBMS. As such it should support heterogeneous and distributed information systems.

To address these problems, we have discussed in this paper initial ideas towards a new form of active mechanisms where the active functionality is not an integral part of the DBMS functionality like in current approaches. Unbundling is the activity to break up traditionally monolithic software systems into smaller units. We apply the unbundling process to active database systems. Resulting from this, we present several possible architectures.

There are several questions arising from unbundling and many problems must be solved. The most important one may be whether active DBMS-style ECA functionality can "survive" the whole unbundling process, giving the full semantics as in traditional active DBMS. Is an active DBMS the same as a passive DBMS plus a service offering active functionality? We think that in the general case this is not possible, at least not without modifications, since unbundling essentially means to give up the "closed world" assumption which traditionally underlies a DBMS.

Furthermore, much more experience is needed with the concrete investigation of the development of services offering active functionality outside the DBMS.

ACKNOWLEDGMENTS

The work described here has been supported by the ACTNET-Network. We gratefully acknowledge Klaus Dittrich's and Peter C. Lockemann's comments on earlier versions of the paper.

LITERATURE

Adler, Richard M. (1995). Emerging Standards for Component Software. *IEEE Computer,* March.

Batory, D.S. (1996). GENESIS: A Project to Develop an Extensible Database Management System. In *Proc. of the 1996 Workshop in Object-Oriented Database Systems.*

Blakeley, J. (1996). Data access for the masses through ole db. *Proc. of the Intl. Conf. of the ACM SIGMOD.*

Carrey, D.J. & DeWitt, M.J. (1987). An Overview of the EXODUS Project. In *IEEE Database Engineering,* 10:2.

Dayal, U. (1995). Ten years of activity in active database systems: What have we accomplished? *Proc. of th Intl. Workshop in Active and Real-Time Database Systems.*

Fraternali, P. & L. Tanca (1995). A Structured Approach for the Definition of the Semantics of Active Databases. *ACM TODS: Transactions on Database Systems*, 20(4):414–471, December.

Fritschi, H., S. Gatziu, & K. Dittrich (1997). *FRAMBOISE – an Approach to construct Active Database Mechanisms.* Technical Report ifi-97.04, Institut für Informatik, Universität Zürich.

Garlan, D. & M. Shaw. *An introduction to software architecture. volume 1 of Advances in Software Engineering and Knowledge Engineering.* World Scientific Publishing Company.

Gatziu, Stella, Arne Koschel, Günter von Bültzingsloewen, Hans Fritschi (1997). Unbundling Active Functionality. Technical Report 97.11, Department of Computer Science, University of Zurich, Zurich, Swiss, August. App. in SIGMOD Record, March, 1998.

Geppert, A. & K.R. Dittrich (1997). *A new construction paradigm for persistent systems?* Technical Report Technical Report 97.08, Department of Computer Science, University of Zurich, July.

Hanson, E.N. & S. Koshla (1997). An Introduction to the TriggerMan Asynchronous Trigger Processor. In A. Geppert and M. Berndtsson, editors, *Proc. Rules in Database Systems,* Third International Workshop, RIDS'97, Skovde, Sweden, number 985 in Lecture Notes in Computer Science, pages 51–67, Berlin, Germany, June 1997. ACT-

NET, Springer.

Koschel, Arne (1997). *CORBA-based Active Functionality – E,C,A Rules, Application Classification, Configurability –*. FZI-Bericht 3/97, Forschungszentrum Informatik (FZI), Karlsruhe, March.

Koschel, Arne (1997). CORBA-basierte aktive Regelverarbeitung und Klassifikation aktiver Funktionalität für Einsatzmöglichkeiten in Umweltinformationssystemen. In 4. Tagung Wissensbasierte Systeme, XPS-97. Workshop-Proc.: Wissensbasierte Systeme in Umweltanwendungen, Bad Honnef, Germany, March 1997. http://iaias4.iai.fzk.de/XPS-97/Forum/t3/topic.html.

Koschel A. & P.C. Lockemann (1998). Distributed Events in Active Database Systems - Letting the Genie out of the Bottle. *Journal of Data and Knowledge Engineering* (DKE). Special Issue on Vol. 25.

Koschel, Arne, Ralf Kramer, Günter von Bültzingsloewen, Thomas Bleibel, Petra Krumlinde, Sonja Schmuck, Christian Weinand (1997). Configurable Active Functionality for CORBA. In ECOOP'97 Workshop – CORBA: Implementation, Use and Evaluation, Jyväskulä, Finnland, June 1997. URL: http://sirac.inrialpes.fr/~bellissa/wecoop97.

Object Management Group (1995). *CORBAservices: Common Object Services Specification*. OMG Document 95-3-31, Object Management Group, Inc. (OMG), March 1995. revised edition.

Object Management Group (1995). *The Common Object Request Broker: Architecture and Specification,* Version 2.0. OMG Document, Object Management Group, Inc. (OMG), July 1995.

Report of Database Working Group (1996). *Database systems - breaking out of the box,* June.

Orfali, R., D. Harkey, & J. Edwards (1996). *The Essential Distributed Objects Survival Guide.* John Wiley & Sons, Inc., New York, USA.

Paton, N.W., O. Diaz, M.H. Williams, J. Campin, A. Dinn, & A. Jaime (1994). Dimensions of Active Behaviour. *Proc. 1st Intl. Workshop on Rules in Database Systems.* Springer,.

Pissinou, N. & K. Vanapipat (1996). Active Database Rules in Distributed Database Systems. International *Journal of Computer Systems*, 11(1):35–44.

Schwiderski, S. (1996). Monitoring the Behaviour of Distributed Systems. PhD thesis, Selwyn College, University of Cambridge, University of Cambridge, Computer Lab, Cambridge, United Kingdom.

Shaw, M.,R. DeLine, D.V. Klein, T.L. Ross, D.M. Young, & G. Zelesnik (1995). volume 21 of *IEEE Transactions on Software Engineering* (TSE), Apr.

Su,S.Y.W. , H. Lam, J. Arroyo-Figueroa, T. Yu, Z. Yang (1995). An Extensible Knowledge Base Management System for Supporting Rule-based Interoperability among Heterogeneous Systems. In *Conference on Information and Knowledge Management,* CIKM'95, Baltimore, MD, U.S.A, November.

The ACT-NET Consortium (1996). The Active Database Management System Manifesto: A Rulebase of ADBMS Features. *ACM SIGMOD Record,* 25(3), September.

Vaskevitch, D. (1995). Very large databases how large? how different? *Proc. 21th Intl. Conf. on Very Large Data Bases* (VLDB), Sept.

von Bültzingsloewen, Günter ,Arne Koschel, & Ralf Kramer (1996). Active Information Delivery in a CORBA-based Distributed Information System. In Karl Aberer and Abdelsalam Helal, editors, *Proc. 1st IFCIS International Conf. on Cooperative IS,* pages 218–227, Brussels, Belgium, June , IFCIS, IEEE CS Press, Los Alamitos, California.

von Bültzingsloewen, Günter , Arne Koschel, & Ralf Kramer (1997). Poster on Accept Heterogeneity: An Event Monitoring Service for CORBA-based Heterogeneous Information Systems. In *Proc. 2nd IFCIS Conference on Cooperative Information Systems*, South Carolina, USA, June.

Widom, J., S. Ceri, editors (1996). *Active Database Systems: Triggers and Rules for Advanced Database Processing*. The Morgan Kaufman Series in Data Management Systems. Morgan Kaufmann Publishers, Inc., San Francisco, California, U.S.A, 1996.

Widom, Jennifer (1995). Research Problems in Data warehousing. In *Proceedings of 4th Int. Conference of Information and Knowledge Management* (CIKM'95), November.

CHAPTER 11

A Stratum Based Approach to Access Degenerate Temporal Relations

Mario A. Nascimento
Empresa Brasileira de Pesquisa Agropecuaria, Brazil

We present an approach which yields efficient access to degenerate temporal relations, i.e., temporal relations where valid time behaves as transaction time. The approach is built on a stratum between the application and the DBMS and transforms a temporal relation into two temporal relations. Access to the data is accomplished through two standard B+-trees (other indices are optional). Such B+-trees have trivially specialized node split policies, yielding a high node utilization ratio. In some existing DBMSs, e.g., Oracle's, such specialization is obtained at the expense of setting a single parameter when creating the indices. We compare the proposed approach, which we name 2S, to the Monotonic B+-tree (Elmasri et al, 1992). For intersection queries, in all but one of the several investigated scenarios, 2S provided at least comparable query processing time. On the other hand, it was always faster when processing inclusion queries. Our simulations also showed that the 2S approach always yielded a much smaller structure. The main contribution we present though, lies in the fact that the 2S approach does not require novel access structures but well-known B+-trees, available in virtually every DBMS on the market. We also present examples of how SQL queries can be written to explore the proposed approach.

INTRODUCTION

In the context of temporal databases, the transaction time of a tuple is the time when it were/is current in the database and may be retrieved. Orthogonal to transaction time is valid time. The valid time of a tuple is the time when it was/is/will be valid in the modeled world (Jensen et al, 1994). In this paper we are particularly interested in a special type of temporal relation, namely, degenerate temporal relations. In a degenerate temporal relation the valid time of any given tuple is equal to its transaction time (Jensen and Snodgrass, 1994). That is, tuples become (and end) being current as soon as they become (and end) being valid.

Once a tuple in such a temporal relation is updated the newer version (immediately) replaces the older one, but the older is only logically, instead of physically, deleted. For simplicity, throughout this chapter we refer to the temporal attribute of such degenerate temporal relation as transaction time. Note though, that this is irrelevant as both transaction and valid timestamps are identical. We denote the transaction time of a data record R^k, by the time interval $T_t^k = [T_s^k, T_e^k]$. Initially, the current version of R^k has its transaction start time (T_s^k) set to the timestamp of the transaction that wrote the data and the transaction end time (T_e^k) is left open. When the current version is updated, the open transaction end time is set to a constant T_e^k accordingly. An open transaction end time is usually denoted by setting $T_e^k = NOW$. (NOW denotes the current instant in time - for a thorough discussion on the semantics of NOW refer to (Clifford et al, 1996)).

We assume that all timestamps are positive integers. However, we do not assume an actual transaction timestamp. Instead, we assume that several data items may have the same transaction start time (or end time). That is, the transaction time has a coarser granularity than the actual transaction timestamp of the DBMS. Example of domains with such characteristic are:

- Telephone calls accounting, where a tuple could have the format: <user_number, called_number, start_time, end_time> and
- Stock market quotes, where a simple schema may be similar to: <stock_name, price, start_time, end_time>.

In both of those domains it seems reasonable to assume it is not possible to perform a retroactive nor a predictive update. Even if updates were performed in error they must not be physically deleted, as that would imply "losing" the past, based on which some decisions may have been taken. Hence, within both domains, the valid time dimension follows a transaction time behavior. In addition, we may have several phone calls starting (or ending at the same point in time). Likewise several stock prices variations may be recorded at the same time.

We therefore address the problem of indexing degenerate temporal relations. Although more than 1,000 papers have been published in the area of temporal databases (Tsotras and Kumar, 1996), relatively few have addressed temporal access structures (Salzberg and Tsotras, 1994). Almost all access structures proposed in those papers do have their merits, but lack one quite desirable property: *feasibility*. They all require modifications to the underlying DBMSs. A notable exception is the recent work by Goh et al (1996) which also uses B+-trees. Goh's approach, unlike ours, aims mainly at valid time relations, and as such do not take advantage of the transaction time's behavior. On this chapter, we aim at providing the basics for a stratum, to be positioned between the applications and the DBMS, which can provide efficient access to temporal relations. Briefly put, a stratum can be understood as an intermediate layer through which application's requests must pass before being actually processed by the DBMS. Likewise, answers provided by the DBMS pass through the stratum before being delivered back to the requesting application. The use of strata to provide temporal facilities for non-temporal DBMS has been investigated in (Vassilakis et al, 1996) and (Korp et al, 1997). The exact type of stratum to be used, from those described by those authors, is still a matter of future research. Our concern in this research is to investigate whether the idea of using such stratum based approach is viable.

The approach we propose re-uses the B+-tree structure (refer to (Elmasri and Navathe, 1994, Chapter 5) for an introduction) in an approach we name 2S (short for Two-Stage). It is important to notice that, by re-using well-known B+-trees, we also inherit all previous research on it, such as concurrency control and recoverability (Johnson and Shasha, 1993). Not much has been done regarding those issues in most of the previously proposed temporal access structures. As we shall discuss in the following section, 2S yields an structure whose size is linear on the number of updates and which has logarithmic update and (exact match) search time. For intersection queries (also called range queries), 2S's performance depends on how large the largest indexed lifespan is. The smaller it is the more efficient 2S is. We believe that in many application domains, including the two discussed above, the modeled objects have a relatively short lifespan. For inclusion queries, however, such dependency does not exist.

The rest of the chapter is organized as follows. Next section presents the main contribution of the chapter, the 2S approach. We show that using standard B+-trees, with trivially specialized split policies, we may ensure a high node utilization ratio (close to 100%). Comments on how to actually achieve this in an existing DBMS are also provided. The procedures needed to process intersection and inclusion queries are presented, as well as their "translation" into SQL. We then compare the performance of the proposed approach against that of the Monotonic B+-tree (Elmasri et al, 1992), which, despite its high storage requirement, is regarded as efficient in terms of query processing. A summary of our findings and directions for future research close the chapter.

THE 2S APPROACH

Our approach has two stages, both functioning possibly concurrently. The idea is to be able to handle both open and closed ranges. In the Current Stage (CS) ranges which are open are indexed, by their transaction start time (T_s^k), under the Current B+-tree (CT); in the Historical Stage (HS) all ranges that have been closed are transformed into points, and are indexed under the Historical B+-tree (HT).

Let us now briefly explain the rationale behind each stage. Initially, i.e., until the first transaction time range is closed, HS does not function. CS is responsible for managing, through CT, all incoming transaction start times. When one or more records are closed, they are deleted from CT and moved onto HT. Note that all such records will have the same transaction end time but not necessarily the same transaction start time. Before they are inserted into HT though, these (closed) ranges are transformed, through a mapping function, into a point. This transformation is such that it will maintain the incoming points in a convenient order. This order will guarantee that any other range which is closed and

Figure 1. Illustration of CS (CT) and HS (HT).

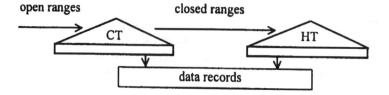

input into HT will not precede, with respect to this mapped value, any other range already input into HT. Thus, if the underlying B+-tree uses a node split policy that instead of splitting nodes by "half" simply overflows to a newly created node, we may achieve a usage ratio close to 100%. Similar reasoning may be applied to CS. The overall idea is illustrated on Figure 1. We detail Stages CS and HS next.

Stage CS

Stage CS is responsible for maintaining all ranges which are open. As such, it functions since the first update occurs, and needs to index only the transaction start time of the records. Recall that all open ranges have the same transaction end time, namely T_e = NOW. A simple B+-tree suffices to handle the ranges in CS. It is important to note that the transaction start time grows monotonically. Thus, we can modify a little bit the standard B+-tree node split policy in order to achieve a much better space usage. We explain this modification next. Assume a standard B+-tree of order n, i.e., a node holds n pointers and (n -1) indexed data values. Once a value is to be inserted into a full node, a new node is created and the set of indexed values of the full node plus the new value is divided evenly among those two nodes. Such splits may propagate upwards causing similar node splits in internal nodes of the tree. Such policy yield, in average, 69% node utilization ratio (Yao, 1978), i.e., almost a third of the slots in each node is not used.

As noted above, the transaction start time, which is the data value being indexed, grows monotonically, i.e., any new data value being indexed is always greater than all other ones already indexed. Using the standard node split policy is a bad idea in such a case. Once a node is split it will never receive any value again, because all new incoming values are certainly greater than the last value indexed, which is, by construction, always the rightmost one on the rightmost leaf node. Therefore the standard split node policy yields an average node utilization ratio of 50% when indexing monotonically growing data values. Note that such behavior also happens in the internal nodes, and therefore the ratio of 50% is valid to all nodes in general, internal and leaves.

To address this severe shortcoming we propose the use of a trivial node split policy, which we call "lazy". In the lazy node split policy, the full node, which is receiving the incoming value, remains full and a new node is created to host the incoming value. This leads to a much better node utilization. In fact, all nodes but the rightmost are full, which yields an asymptotic node utilization of 100%. Expanding this argument to the case when internal nodes are split, we reach similar conclusion, i.e., in all levels of the tree all but the rightmost node will be 100% full. We must make clear though that we do not claim such lazy policy to be novel. In fact, it has been also proposed for the Monotonic B+-tree (Elmasri et al 1992).

However, it is noteworthy pointing out that this strategy, unlike all others, need not be actually implemented from scratch. For instance, Oracle's DBMS provides a directive PCTFREE be used (optionally) when a CREATE INDEX command is issued. In fact, "PCTFREE is the percentage of usage to leave free for updates and insertions within each of the index's data block" (Oracle, 1992). Thus, if we assume an index is created for CT on the transaction start time using the option PCTFREE 0, then we may assume the lazy split policy explained above is actually being realized. Therefore the modified node split policy discussed above is indeed feasible to achieve. Furthermore, the very nature of transaction start time (i.e., increasing monotonically) does facilitate maintaining the aimed high fill factor in CT.

Unlike insertion, deletion of indexed values can occur in any order. This may yield some "holes" in tree nodes (internal and leaves), and eventually lead some nodes to underflow. Fortunately, the traditional strategy employed by B+-trees (merge-at-half) serves to handle well such cases. Alternatively, the "free-at-empty" policy (Johnson and Shasha, 1993) could be used as well. The important point is that, given that most nodes will be fully utilized, the average node utilization ratio should remain well above Yao's expected 69%.

Figure 2 illustrates the reasoning above. Assume the node shown in Figure 2(a) after inserting values, 7, 8, 10 and 12. Attempting to insert values 13, 15 and 16, under the B+-tree's standard split policy results in the nodes shown in Figure 2(b). Note that the left node (containing values 7, 8 and 10) will remain half empty forever. If, on the other hand, the lazy split policy discussed above is used, the insertions would yield the nodes shown in Figure 2(c). It is clear that the nodes are much better utilized in the latter case.

Finally note that, overall, CT is simpler to implement than a standard B+-tree (should one decide to implement it from scratch). Searching CT is also straightforward (details are given later in the chapter).

Stage HS

This is probably the main stage, as it will maintain all closed versions within HT and it is reasonable to expect that, soon after startup, the closed temporal ranges will outnumber the open ones.

First let us discuss how HS works. Suppose that at a given time t, some number of versions are closed. HS then receives from CS a set of ranges which also possesses an interesting property: all the incoming ranges have the same transaction end time, and such transaction end time is (1) greater than all other transaction end times already indexed under HT, and (2) smaller than all other transaction end times that will possibly appear in the future. Thus, in a sense, HT holds several groups of ranges (grouped by transaction end time) and we use this to our advantage. If we are able to maintain a relative order among those groups, then we can guarantee that the index, will grow only to the right, in an "append only" manner. This is important as we can make better use of space.

The chief question we need to answer is how to index the closed ranges, in order to keep the grouping mentioned above. Unlike in the CS, we now have two values (T_s and T_c) for each record. We propose to do this using an approach similar to the one used in (Nascimento and Dunham, 1998) to index valid time, which is to use a function which maps ranges to points. The function originally used in that paper preserved the original lexicographical order of the ranges, i.e., the ranges were ordered by transaction start time

Figure 2. Different split policies for B+-tree nodes

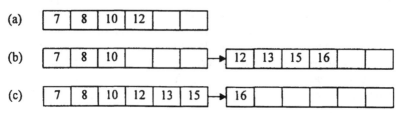

and secondarily by transaction end time. We modify the mapping function such that the ranges are primarily ordered by transaction end time and secondarily by transaction start time, i.e., a backwards lexicographical order. Such order reflects the desired grouping on the leaf nodes of the indexing tree. Formally, we define the mapping function in question as follows:

$$\phi(T) = \phi([T_s, T_e]) = T_e \times 10^\alpha + T_s$$

where a is the maximum number of digits needed to represent any time value. Any transaction time range $T = [T_s, T_e]$ can thus be indexed using the value provided by $\phi(T)$ into HT. Obtaining the original range from $\phi(T)$ is straightforward: $T_s = \phi(T) \bmod 10^a$ and $T_e = \lfloor \phi(T)/10^a \rfloor$.

When a closed range is inserted into HT (which is a B+-tree) it must be first mapped into a point via the function $\phi(.)$ above. We could use a standard B+-tree insertion (and node split) procedure, but given the order imposed by the mapping above we can achieve a much better space utilization by using the very same approach used for CT, provided we can do some pre-processing in main memory. At any given point in time there may be a number of open ranges being closed with the same transaction end time, but not necessarily same transaction start time. Let us assume this number to be not very large, i.e., it is much smaller than the total number of indexed closed ranges. If we sort those ranges based on their transaction start time, then we can input them, in sorted order, into HT using the very same approach described for CT. Again, this strategy can be actually realized as explained earlier, that is, by simply setting the PCTFREE 0 option when a CREATE INDEX command is issued (assuming Oracle to be the underlying DBMS).

For a better idea of how both CT and HT cooperate consider the data set shown in the left of Figure 3. Assume that at time 0, 2 and 3 the first versions of A1, B1, ..., F1 are input into the database. Suppose that at time 5 and 6 new versions of B1 and F1 are input, and at time 5 C1 is deleted. This implies that B1, C1 and F1 are not current any longer and therefore must be closed. The new versions B2 and F2, must also be input into CT. Figure 3 shows the resulting trees (internal nodes and details of the leaf nodes are omitted for simplicity).

Note that, due to the very nature of transaction time databases, data is not ever deleted, thus deletions never occur in HT. Therefore, unlike CT, HT is guaranteed to have a

Figure 3. CT and HT indexing a sample data set at time 6.

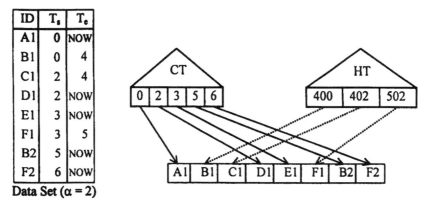

node utilization ratio very close to 100%.

Let us assume that some extra metadata is available about the indexed closed ranges, indexed under HT.

Namely, consider that we know an upper bound for the length of the indexed closed ranges, and let us call it Δ, that is:

$$\Delta = \max_k \{T^k_e - T^k_s\}.$$

The Δ value of the indexed ranges can be easily maintained in some sort of dictionary by the DBMS. For example, every time a range is closed, its length is checked against the current Δ which is then updated (if needed). Recall that transaction time databases do not allow correction nor deletion of data. Hence, Δ is dynamic and always correct. The need for knowing Δ becomes clearer in the next section.

QUERY PROCESSING USING 2S

Framework

In order to better understand the ideas that follow let us first present how one can use standard SQL to modify a temporal table into a "2S-ready" one. In what follows we use the SQL*Plus syntax from Oracle (Oracle, 1992). Wherever arithmetic expressions are shown, it is for the sole purpose of presentation. In reality all such expressions would be substituted by constant values, e.g., using embedded SQL, before the actual SQL code is passed onto the DBMS. Some of the following SQL code is adapted from (Nascimento and Dunham, 1998).

Assume a database with a temporal table named empid, containing data about employees, the department they are allocated to, and the time during which this information stored is/was valid, defined as follows:

```
CREATE TABLE empdep (
  empid NUMBER NOT NULL,
  dep CHAR(5),
  ts NUMBER NOT NULL,
  te NUMBER,
  PRIMARY KEY (empid)
);
```

Note that te may be NULL, meaning that the tuple is valid until NOW. The first task is to decompose the given table into two, one for each of the above described stages. This can be done as follows:

```
CREATE CLUSTER empid_cl (empid NUMBER);
CREATE INDEX empid_cl_ind ON CLUSTER empid_cl;

CREATE TABLE empdep_cs (
  empid NUMBER NOT NULL,
  dep CHAR(5)
```

```
  ts NUMBER NOT NULL
) CLUSTER empid_cl (empid);
CREATE INDEX empdep_ct_ind ON empdep_cs (ts) PCTFREE 0;

CREATE TABLE empdep_hs (
  empid NUMBER NOT NULL,
  dep CHAR(5)
  ts NUMBER NOT NULL,
  te NUMBER NOT NULL,
  tets NUMBER NOT NULL
) CLUSTER empid_cl (empid);
CREATE INDEX empdep_ht_ind ON empdep_hs (tets) PCTFREE 0;
CREATE INDEX empdep_te_ind ON empdep_hs (te);
CREATE INDEX empdep_ts_ind ON empdep_hs (ts);
```

Note that the previous primary key on empid no longer exists as there will be several versions of the same empid on the database. Nonetheless the cluster empid_cl (and its index empid_cl_ind) serves the purpose of such an index as the various versions of the same empid will be physically closed (and indexed) on disk. Also, in relation empdep_hs both ts and te (and naturally tets = ϕ(ts, te)) must be not NULL as all tuples in such a relation have already been closed. Finally, the indices empdep_te_ind and empdep_ts_ind are not mandatory, i.e., the 2S approach does not require them, but they may be useful for queries based only on the edges of the ranges.

Now both relations empdep_cs and empdep_hs need be populated. This can be accomplished with a series of INSERT commands. A tuple from the original relation empdep is input into empdep_cs or empdep_hs depending on the value of its attribute te, i.e., whether the tuple is open (te = NULL) or not. Given a value for α, the following SQL code could be used (note that a could be read from some sort of metadata relation at execution time):

```
INSERT INTO empdep_cs
  SELECT empid, dept, ts
  FROM empdep
  WHERE te = NULL;

INSERT INTO empdep_hs
  SELECT empid, dep, ts, te, te x 10^α + ts
  FROM empdep
  WHERE te NOT NULL;
```

At this point the original relation empdep may be "dropped". From now on tuples are initially input into empdep_cs and remain there until they are closed, when they are moved onto empdep_hs. Let us illustrate how closing a tuple works. For instance, suppose that employee 001 has been with department A since time 2, and at time 12 he/she is assigned to department B. This means that at time 2 the following INSERT was issued:

INSERT INTO empdep_cs (001, "A", 2, NULL);

When that particular tuple is versioned at time 12 the following set of instructions are executed:

INSERT INTO empdep_hs
   SELECT empid, dep, ts, 12, 12 x 10^{α}+ts
   FROM empdep
   WHERE empid = 001

UPDATE empdep_cs
   SET ts = 12, dep= "B"
   WHERE empid = 001;

Processing Intersection Queries

An intersection query is one which, given a range $Q = [Q_s, Q_e]$, it returns all ranges intersecting with Q.

We assume that NOW is greater than any other currently indexed time point. As such, to find all open ranges in CT that intersect with Q, one needs to search from the initial indexed value (possibly 0) until Q_e, as obviously any range starting after Q_e cannot intersect with Q and all open ranges starting before Q_e do intersect with Q as it is assumed that all open ranges are valid until NOW (which is farthest in the future than any Q_e).

Using the knowledge about Δ, we need only to search HT through the ranges from the groups with transaction end times equal to $Q_s, Q_s + 1, ..., Q_e, Q_e + 1, ..., Q_e + \Delta$. That is, the range farther in the past that can intersect with Q is $[Q_s - \Delta, Q_s]$ and the one farther in the future is $[Q_e, Q_e + \Delta]$. Therefore, we must search the leaves in HT from value $\phi([Q_s - \Delta, Q_s])$ up to value $\phi([Q_e, Q_e + \Delta])$. Note that all time values are assumed to be positive integers, hence we also assume $NOW > Q_e \geq Q_s \geq 0$. Furthermore, if $Q_s - \Delta < 0$ we should use 0 instead. We must remark that should Δ not be known, searching HT would imply searching all of its leaves, which is not acceptable.

Let us illustrate the algorithm above through an example (for simplicity we do not consider open-ranges). Consider the ranges: A:[1, 2], B:[0, 3], C:[2, 4], D:[3, 5], E:[4, 7], where X:[s, e] denotes that X is current during time interval [s, e]. Let the query range be $Q = [2, 3]$. If we cannot make use of Δ one must search through all the index. However, if we know that in this case we have $\Delta = 3$, it is obvious that no range ending before $Q_s = 2$ or after $Q_e = 6$ will intersect Q. Thus it suffices to search from the indexed point 20 (mapped range [0, 2]) until the indexed point 63 (mapped range [3, 6]). Using the mapping ϕ defined above, the time intervals for A, B, C, D and E would be mapped respectively to 21, 30, 42, 53 and 74. Therefore searching HT would retrieve A, B, C and D, which is indeed the right answer.

Notice that we might read indexed points which correspond to ranges that will not belong to the query's answer. For example, if the Δ value associated to the ranges above were 5 instead of 3, we would have to search from the indexed point 20 (mapped range [0,2]) until the indexed point 83 (mapped range [3,8]). This would make us read the indexing point 74 (mapped range [4, 7]) which does not belong to the answer (i.e., it obviously does not intersect with [2,3]). However, not all types of queries depend on Δ.

Next section investigates one such type of query.

To illustrate the discussion above, consider the "2S-ready" version of the empdep relation above. Suppose the query of interest is the following one:

Find all employees in table empdep with time ranges that intersect with range Q = [Qs, Qe].

An "equivalent" 2S-based SQL could be:

SELECT empid
FROM empdep_cs
WHERE ts $\leq$ Qe
UNION
SELECT empid
FROM empdep_hs
WHERE tets BETWEEN (Qs-Δ) x 10^a+Qs AND Qe x 10^α + (Qe+Δ)
        AND te$\geq$ Qs

Suppose that values 15 and 3 where obtained, from the metadata relations, for D and a respectively. If Q = [65, 87] we would have the following query passed onto the actual DBMS.

SELECT empid
FROM empdep_cs
WHERE ts $\leq$ 87
UNION
SELECT empid
FROM empdep_hs
WHERE tets BETWEEN 50065 AND 87102
        AND te $\geq$ 65

Processing Inclusion Queries

Inclusion queries take as argument a range Q = [Q_s, Q_e] and return all ranges which are strictly contained within Q. First note that CT need not be searched at all. CT indexes only open ranges, i.e., all with T_e = NOW, and as we assume NOW > Q_e, no range in CT can be included within Q. Searching HT is also straightforward. No range starting before Qs can be included in Q, similarly no range ending after Q_e can be included in Q either. We therefore must search HT's leaves from range [Q_s, $\bar{Q}_s$] (i.e., mapped value $\phi(Q_{s, Qs})$) to range [Q_e, $_{Qe}$] (i.e., mapped value $\phi(Q_e, Q_e)$).

Again, assuming the above, "2S-ready", table empdep, the query:

Find all employees in table empdep with time ranges that are included within range Q = [Qs, Qe].

could be "translated" in SQL as follows:

SELECT*   *

FROM empdep_hs
WHERE tets BETWEEN Qs x 10^a + Qs AND Qe x 10^α + Qe
    AND te $\leq$ Qe

It is important to notice that there are two remarkable differences between algorithms 2S-Intersection and 2S-Inclusion. Unlike the former, the latter processes only one B+-tree (HT) and does not depend on Δ.

PERFORMANCE ANALYSIS

In this section we investigate the performance of the proposed 2S approach. Using the Monotonic B+-tree (MBT) (Elmasri et al, 1992) as a reference, we investigate 2S's storage requirements and query processing time. To accomplish that, we use intersection and inclusion queries discussed above. We chose the MBT because, despite its inefficient use of storage, it is indeed efficient (actually asymptotically optimal (Salzberg and Tsotras, 1994)) for query processing and yet it is quite simple to simulate. It is important to stress though, that none of the previously proposed structures are actually available in existing DBMSs, as such, the 2S approach has really no competitor. Nevertheless, for the sake of completeness we compare 2S to the MBT.

The basic idea behind the MBT is that both the transaction start and end time are indexed, and the tuple ids are maintained in an incremental manner throughout the index. That is, they appear in the bucket associate the time point when they were inserted, deleted and in the leading entry of all leaves between those two time values. Refer to the original paper by Elmasri ct al (1992) for further information regarding the MBT.

For simplicity, we use the number of leaf blocks used at leaf node level (the leaves themselves and the incremental buckets in MBT's case) and the number of leaf blocks read during query processing as the indicators for the structures' size and query processing time. We have used 8 and for 4 bytes for the sizes of a pointer to a record (or set thereof) and the size of the data type representing a time value. It is important to recall that the size (in bytes) of the data type indexed under HT is twice as big as those under CT and the MBT (due to the mapping used). This was taken into account when we performed the simulations that follow. Finally, as described earlier, we assume that CT is compact, i.e., its usage ratio approaches 100%. We believe this is not a strong assumption for two reasons: as lifespans are short, CT's update ratio is high and the nodes first created tend to be fully deleted relatively fast; also, CT is expected to be quickly outsized by HT, which will thus dominate query performance.

We investigate how the sizes of the structures behave as a function of six variables: B, N, Δ, T_{max}, P_o and L_q; meaning respectively: size of the disk block (in bytes); number of ranges indexed, average lifespan length, time value of NOW, ratio open/closed ranges, and average length of query ranges. We have used the values shown in Table 1. We vary the parameters one at a time, while keeping the others fixed at the default values. All values for the generated ranges and queries used a uniform distribution.

Space Requirements

As discussed earlier we compute only the number of leaf nodes disregarding the internal nodes. In the case of the MBT we must also compute the number of disk blocks used for the incremental buckets as it is an integral part of the overall structure. It is obvi-

Table 1. Parameters used in the performance analysis.

Notation	Values (default in **bold**)
B	1,024; 2,048; 4,096 and **8,192**
N	5,000; 10,000; **50,000** and 100,000
D	250, 500; **1,000** and 2,500
T_{max}	5,000; **10,000**; 20,000 and 50,000
P_0	0%, **25%**, 50% and 75%
L_q	250, 500; **1,000** and 2,500

ous that varying L_q does not affect the index sizes and therefore we disregard this parameter in the simulations presented in this section.

Varying B — It is natural to observe that, given a fixed number of indexing values, the smaller the leaf nodes, the more nodes are needed to store such values. However, in the MBT each leaf node maintains several incremental buckets. It then follows that the smaller the leaves, the more incremental buckets will exist. Thus, enlarging the nodes, benefits the MBT much more than 2S. This is reflected in Figure 4(a). The MBT was, in average, 205% larger than 2S. We should point out that the reason we chose the default value of B equal to 8 Kbytes was exactly to try to diminish the effect of MBT's incremental buckets and therefore favor it.

Varying N — The results, depicted in Figure 4(b), show that the MBT's size grows slightly faster with N than 2S's and also that it was, in average, 189% larger than the 2S. Unlike the 2S approach, the MBT may replicate pointers to tuples. In 2S every record will contribute with at a single entry being added into CT or HT.

Varying Δ — While D is an important factor for 2S's query performance this is not the case in terms of storage (Figure 5(a)). On the other hand, the MBT, which used about 150% more storage space than 2S, is sensitive to D as a greater lifespan yields more replication in its incremental buckets.

Varying T_{max} — The MBT is affected by the length of the total time frame being modeled, while 2S is totally insensitive to it, as evidenced in Figure 5(b). Once again, this is due to MBT's incremental buckets. This is a quite important feature of 2S, as in a temporal database, NOW and thus the range [0, NOW], is always growing. The MBT required from 122% up to nearly 260% more space than the 2S.

Figure 4.

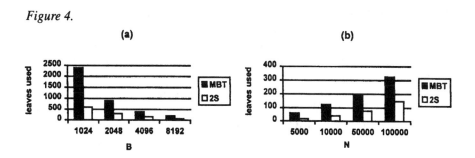

Figure 5.

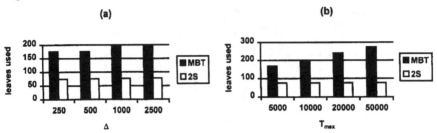

Figure 6.

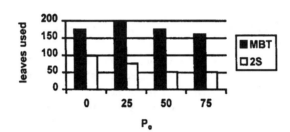

Varying P_o — We can see in Figure 6 that with the increase of P_o, both structures decrease in size, however, the MBT's size decrease much slower, again due to its incremental buckets. As far as 2S is concerned, by keeping N constant and augmenting the ratio P_o, we are in effect exchanging a larger data type (the mapped ranges) by a smaller data type (the transaction start times), hence the faster size decrease in 2S. In fact, with P_o set to zero the MBT is about 75% larger whereas when P_o is set to 75% it is about 215% larger than the 2S.

Query Processing Time

We assume that query processing time is mainly driven by the number of I/Os performed, as one I/O is several orders of magnitude slower than a CPU instruction. We do not compute the number of I/Os due to the retrieval of the actual data records, but only the I/Os needed to obtain the pointers which are used to retrieve them. We vary the same parameters used in the previous section with the addition of L_q. Unlike before, it is expected that query processing time depends on the length of the queried range. We analyze the results obtained, when processing each type of query, next.

Varying B — Figures 7(a) and (b) reveal a fairly natural result, already explained earlier. Both 2S and MBT gain by using larger disk blocks. The larger the block the smaller the relative advantage of 2S. When processing inclusion queries we noted that the relative advantage of 2S remains nearly constant (averaging 50%), whereas it diminishes with B for intersection queries (ranging between 30% and 12%).

Varying N — Figures 8(a) and (b) show us that both structures are equally affected by the increase in N, independently of the query type. While processing inclusion queries 2S was about 30% faster than the MBT, the relative advantage remained constant throughout our experiments. This was also the case for inclusion queries, with the relative gain being

Figure 7.

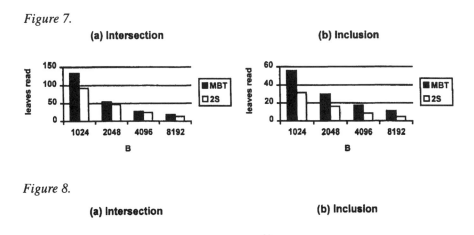

Figure 8.

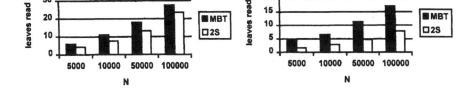

about 57%.

Varying Δ — We can see in Figure 9(a) that, for some types of query, a large Δ may be 2S's biggest shortcoming. As the largest indexed lifespan gets larger, the performance for intersection queries becomes proportionally slower. This happens because under 2S the search has to scan the index for ranges starting as far as Δ time points before the actual query start time until the query end time, whereas the MBT must scan only from the query start time until the query end time. As we keep all other parameters fixed, the MBT shows that it is not much sensitive to the Δ factor, unlike 2S. In our experiments 2S ranged from being more than 50% faster to being 39% slower in the case Δ was up to 25% as big as T_{max}. Even though we believe that a temporal database is of more value when managing highly dynamic data, and therefore relatively short lifespans, it is important to reveal that a large Δ may hurt 2S's performance considerably. On the other hand, it is also worthwhile to note that for some other types of queries, the inclusion query in particular, Δ does not play a role. In fact, for all values of Δ, 2S was about 57% faster than the MBT.

Varying T_{max} — For this case in particular (Figure 10(a) and (b)) both access structure delivered virtually the same relative performance. This is important given that in a temporal database T_{max} is ever increasing. Even though one may think that MBT's processing should degenerate as its size did, that is not the case. Increasing T_{max} does increase the number of indexed points, and therefore the number of leaf nodes, However, as N and Δ remain fixed, each incremental bucket becomes smaller, hence can be read faster. 2S required an average of 23% and 55% less time to process intersection and inclusion queries respectively.

Varying P_o — When no open ranges exist all of 2S's effort is spent on HT, which indexes a larger data type and, in the case of intersection queries, is subject to the Δ constraint. As more open ranges are considered, more of 2S's effort is devoted to CT which is

Figure 9.

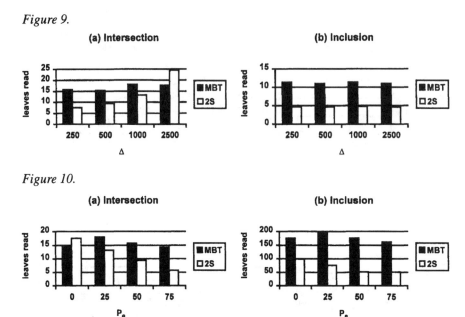

Figure 10.

smaller and, in a sense, easier/faster to process. Figure 11(a) shows that 2S may be 16% slower when no open ranges are considered and as much as 60% faster when the majority of ranges are open. When processing inclusion queries we can see (Figure 11(b)) that the MBT also does not gain from a larger P_o, unlike 2S, which was between 43% and 70% faster.

Varying L_q — Even though both structures must perform a larger index scan as the query length gets larger, Figures 12(a) and (b) show that the MBT suffers more. For 2S a larger scan implies in proportionally more leaves being read. For the MBT however, not only more leaves are read but also the incremental buckets associated to them, hence the faster degeneration in MBT's performance. When processing intersection queries, the MBT and 2S delivered the same performance for small queries and about 40% slower for the larger ones. In the case of inclusion queries 2S's relative advantage decreases from 70% to about 47% when the queries get larger.

SUMMARY AND FUTURE RESEARCH

This chapter presented 2S, an approach based on two B+-trees which can be used to index degenerate temporal relations. We have shown that, exploring the characteristics of the temporal relation, we may achieve close to 100% node utilization. One of 2S's great appeals is that it is straightforward to implement using facilities of existing DBMSs, unlike all other existing proposals to index temporal ranges. We have also presented how some temporal tables and queries can be transformed to take advantage of 2S.

Even though there is no real competitor to 2S, i.e., there is no available access structures for temporal ranges in existing DBMSs, we compared it to the Monotonic B+-tree (MBT). We reached three main conclusions:

- 2S always yields an structure smaller than the MBT, regardless of the underlying scenario.

Figure 11.

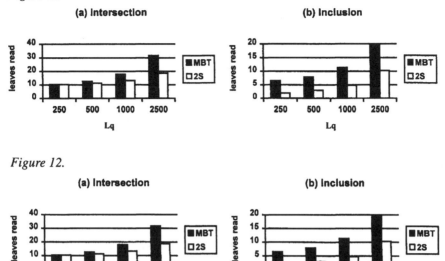

(a) Intersection

(b) Inclusion

Figure 12.

(a) Intersection

(b) Inclusion

- 2S delivered a performance at least comparable to MBT's. For several scenarios (and for inclusion queries in particular), 2S is bound to provide a much better query processing time.
- A notable exception for the previous observation is the case of intersection queries where the maximum lifespan length is relatively large.

Future research will focus on overcoming or minimizing the effect that a single large lifespan (yielding a large Δ) can have in the overall index performance. Our preliminary studies have indicated two simple but yet promising ways of pursuing this issue. One is to use several HTs for different ranges of lifespan sizes. For instance, one HT for short ranges, and one for medium and large ranges. Assuming large ranges are relatively infrequent, the HT indexing short ranges would dominate the performance. In addition, such HTs could be updated and searched in parallel. Another approach is to break larger ranges into smaller ranges in order to guarantee a smaller Δ at the expense of larger storage. The cost of this trade-off is yet to be explored.

Finally, the development of a set of benchmarking temporal data is a (non-trivial) necessity in the area of temporal databases.

ACKNOWLEDGMENTS

An earlier version of this chapter appeared in the International Workshop on Application and Issues on Database Technology, held in Berlin, Germany, in July/1998. Richard Snodgrass' insightful comments helped improve the presentation of this chapter considerably. Comments on this work, by Margaret H. Dunham, Michael H. Böhlen and Christian S. Jensen, are also gratefully acknowledged. The author was partially supported by a research grant from the Brazilian National Council of Research (CNPq, Process 300208/

97-9) and is also with the Institute of Computing of the State University of Campinas (mario@dcc.unicamp.br). Oracle is a trademark of Oracle Corp.

REFERENCES

Clifford, J. et al. (1997). On the semantics of "NOW" in databases. *ACM Transactions on Database Systems*, 22(2):171-214.

Elmasri, R. et al. (1992). Partitioning of Time Index for optical disks. *Proceedings of the 8th Intl. Conf. on Data Engineering*, pages 574-583, Phoenix, USA.

Elmasri, R. and Navathe, S. (1994). *Fundamentals of Database Systems*. Benjamin/ Cummings, Redwood City, USA, 2nd edition.

Goh, C. H. et al. (1996). Indexing temporal data using existing B+-trees. *Data and Knowledge Engineering*, 18:147-165.

Jensen, C. et al. (1994). A consensus glossary of temporal database concepts. *ACM SIGMOD Record*, 23(1):52-64.

Jensen, C. S. and Snodgrass, R. (1994). Temporal specialization and generalization. *IEEE Transactions on Knowledge and Data Engineering*, 6(2):954-974.

Johnson, T. and Shasha, D. (1993). The performance of current data structure algorithms. *ACM Transactions on Database Systems*, 18(1):51-101.

Nascimento, M. A. and Dunham, M. H. (1998). Indexing valid time databases via B+-trees - the MAP21 approach. To appear in *IEEE Transactions on Knowledge and Data Engineering*. (Also available as TimeCenter's Technical Report TR-26 - http:// www.cs.auc.dk/research/DBS/tdb/TimeCenterPublications/TR-26.ps.gz).

Oracle (1992). *SQL*Plus User's Guide and Reference, Vol. 3.2*. Oracle Corp.

Salzberg, B. and Tsotras, V. (1994). A comparison of access methods for time evolving data. . To appear in *ACM Computing Surveys*. (Also available as TimeCenter's Technical Report TR-18 - http://www.cs.auc. dk/research/DBS/tdb/TimeCenterPublications/ TR-18.ps.gz).

Torp, K. et al. (1998). Supporting temporal data management applications via stratum approaches. *Proceedings of the II Intl. Database Engineering and Applications Symposium*. Cardiff, U.K. (Also available as TimeCenter's Technical Report TR-05 - http://www.cs.auc.dk/research/DBS/tdb/TimeCenter Publications/TR-05.ps.gz

Tsotras, V. and Kumar, A. (1996). Temporal database bibliography update. *ACM SIGMOD Record*, 25(1):41-51.

Vassilakis, et al. (1996). A comparative study of temporal DBMS architectures. *Proceedings of the 7th Intl. Workshop on Databases and Expert Systems Applications*, pages 153-164. Zurich, Switzerland.

Yao, A. (1978). 2-3 trees. *Acta Informatica*, 2(9):159-170.

CHAPTER 12

Three-Dimensional Spatial Match Representation and Retrieval for Iconic Image Databases

Jae-Woo Chang, Chonbuk National University, South Korea
Yeon-Jung Kim, Chonbuk National University, South Korea

In multimedia information retrieval applications, content-based image retrieval is essential for retrieving relevant multimedia documents. The purpose of our chapter is to provide both effective representation and efficient retrieval of images when a pixel-level original image is automatically or manually transformed into its iconic image containing meaningful graphic descriptions, called icon objects. For this, we first propose new spatial match representation schemes to describe three-dimensional spatial relationships between icon objects accurately by using precise direction codes or positional operators. In order to accelerate image searching, we also design an efficient retrieval method using a signature file organization. Finally, we compare the proposed representation schemes in terms of retrieval effectiveness.

INTRODUCTION

Recently, much attention has been paid to Multimedia Information Retrieval(MIR) because we have had so many applications that should be supported by handling multimedia data, such as text, image, video, audio, and animation. The applications include digital libraries, advertisements, medical information, remote sensing and astronomy, cartography, digital newspapers, and architectural design. So far, text attributes in multimedia documents have mainly been used for supporting queries by content. The approach using text content(e.g., captions and keywords) has a couple of problems. First, the original keywords do not allow for unanticipated searching. The other problem is that the caption is not adequate to describe the layout, sketch, and shape of the image. Therefore, in order to support MIR applications effectively, content-based image retrieval is essential because it plays an important role in retrieving relevant multimedia documents.

Given a pixel-level original image, various image processing and understanding techniques are used to identify domain objects and their positions in the image. Though this task is computàtionally expensive and difficult, it is performed only at the time of image insertion into the database. Moreover, this task may be carried out in a semi-automated way or in an automated way, depending on the domain and complexity of the images. An iconic image is obtained by associating each domain object of the original image with a meaningful graphic description, called an icon object. Thus, an iconic image representation can provide users with a high level of image abstraction. The iconic image representation has some advantages. First, the use of iconic images avoids the need for repeated image understanding tasks. Processing an original image for interactive responses to high level user queries is inefficient because the number of images tends to be large in most MIR applications. Secondly, the iconic image representation is useful in a distributed database environment where an original image is stored only at a central node and its iconic image is stored at each local node. Finally, the representation of original images into iconic images enables users to achieve domain independence and to deal with a group of icon objects in a systematic way.

In the chapter, we assume that all images at the pixel level are analyzed prior to storage so that icon objects can be extracted from their content and stored into the database together with the original images. The icon objects are used to search the image database and to determine whether an image satisfies query selection criteria. Ultimately, the effectiveness of MIR systems depends on the type and correctness of image content representation, the type of queries allowed, and the efficiency of search techniques designed. The purpose of our chapter is to provide both effective representation and efficient retrieval of images when a pixel-level original image is automatically or manually transformed into its iconic image including icon objects. For this, we propose new three-dimensional spatial match representation schemes to support the content-based image retrieval in an effective way. The proposed representation schemes can describe three-dimensional spatial relationships between icon objects accurately by precise direction codes or positional operators. In order to accelerate image searching, we also design an efficient retrieval method using a signature file organization.

The remainder of this chapter is organized as follows. A review of related work done in the area of iconic image databases is introduced in "Related Work." The proposed three-dimensional spatial match representation schemes are described in "New Three-Dimensional Representation Schemes." A new efficient retrieval method to accelerate image searching is presented in "A New Efficient Retrieval Method." "Performance Evaluation" provides a comparison of the proposed representation schemes in terms of retrieval effectiveness. Finally, "Conclusions and Future Work" concludes the paper with some issues for future research.

RELATED WORK

There have been many proposals for spatial match representation and retrieval in order to search symbolic images efficiently, satisfying certain spatial relationships (Chang, 1987, Lee, 1990, Chang, 1991, Chang, 1994). In particular, there have been two previous efforts on spatial match representation schemes using signature file techniques, namely the 2D (Dimensional)-string scheme(Lee, 1990) and the 9DLT(Direction Lower Triangular) scheme (Chang, 1994).

The 2D-string scheme

Chang, Shi and Yan (Chang, 1987) first proposed a 2D string to represent symbolic images. The 2D string makes use of a symbolic projection to represent a symbolic image by preserving some spatial knowledge of objects embedded in an original image. Here, a symbol in the symbolic image corresponds to an object in its original image. In addition, they defined three types (type-0, type-1, and type-2) of 2D sequence pattern matching. For type-0 matching, an arbitrary number of symbols, rows, and columns can be deleted from a symbolic image and can be merged together in order to make it the same as a pattern. Type-1 matching is the same as type-0, except that adjacent rows or columns of a symbolic image cannot be merged. Type-2 matching does not permit any rows and columns to be deleted from a symbolic image.

Lee and Shan (Lee, 1990) proposed a 2D-string representation scheme to express some types of spatial relationships of symbolic images. In this scheme, they generated four kinds of two-level signature files by associating each symbolic image with a record signature and by relating some images with a block signature. These signatures are retrieved by either specifying a symbol or specifying a type-i match for i=0, 1, or 2. In addition, they adopted a superimposed coding technique to use the spatial relationships among symbols in a symbolic image as well as to filter quickly for any of the four types of queries. For convenience of signature generation, they defined a spatial string to

Figure 1 : Example symbolic image

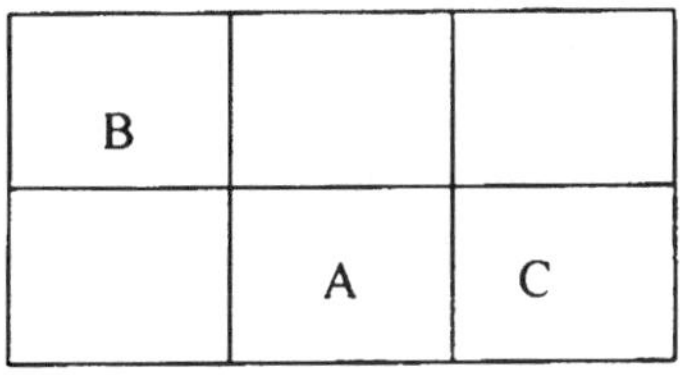

represent the pairwise spatial relationships embedded in a 2D string. A type-i 1D spatial character V^{AB} is a character describing the spatial relationship between A and B symbols in the 1D string as follows:

(type-0) $V^{AB} = $ "0" if $r(A)=r(B)$
  $V^{AB} = $ "0" and "1" if $r(A)<r(B)$
  $V^{AB} = $ "0" and "2" if $r(A)>r(B)$

(type-1) $V^{AB} = $ "0" if $r(A)=r(B)$
  $V^{AB} = $ "1" if $r(A)<r(B)$
  $V^{AB} = $ "2" if $r(A)>r(B)$

(type-2) $V^{AB} = $ "0" $+ str(r(A)-r(B))$ if $r(A)=r(B)$
  $V^{AB} = $ "1" $+ str(r(B)-r(A))$ if $r(A)<r(B)$
  $V^{AB} = $ "2" $+ str(r(A)-r(B))$ if $r(A)>r(B)$

Here $r(X)$ is the rank of symbol X, "+" denotes the string concatenating operator, and $str(X)$ is a transformation function from integer to string; for example, $str(3)=$ "3". A type-i 2D spatial string for symbols A and B when i=0, 1, and 2, S^{AB}_i, is a string formed by concatenating A, B, and type-i spatial characters V^{AB}_x and V^{AB}_y, where V^{AB}_x is a spatial character along the X-axis and V^{AB}_x is a spatial character along the Y-axis. Therefore, S^{AB}_i is written as $A+B+ V^{AB}_x+V^{AB}_y$. S_i is a set of S^{AB}_i for all pairs of symbols A and B in an symbolic image. For example, when a symbolic projection is given as shown in Figure 1, a set of type-0, type-1, and type-2 representation strings for the example can be obtained as follows:

type-0 : (A,B,2,1), (A,B,2,0), (A,B,0,1), (A,B,0,0), (A,C,1,0), (A,C,0,0), (B,C,1,2),
   (B,C,1,0), (B,C,0,2), (B,C,0,0)

type-1: (A,B,2,1), (A,C,1,0), (B,C,1,2)

type-2: (A,B,2,1,1,1), (A,C,1,1,0,0), (B,C,1,2,2,1)

The 9DLT scheme

Chang (Chang,1991) proposed 9DLT direction codes to describe the type-1 spatial relationship embedded in a 2D string. Therefore, nine integers(i.e., 1, 2, 3, 4, 5, 6, 7, 8, and 0) are used to represent pairwise spatial relationships embedded in a 2D string. Figure 2 shows the nine direction codes, where R indicates the reference symbol, 1 stands for "north of R," 2 stands for "northwest of R," and 0 stands for "at the same location as R," and so on.

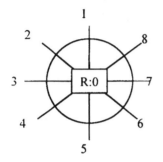

Figure 2 : 9DLT direction codes

Chang and Jiang (Chang, 1994) proposed a 9DLT representation scheme to express three types of spatial strings so that they can fully support the description of type-0, type-1, and type-2 pairwise spatial relationships embedded in a 2D string. They also designed a quick-filter based signature file organization as a filter for spatial match retrieval of images. The 9DLT scheme describes a spatial representation between A and B symbols as follows.

(type-0) $ST^{AB}_0 = (A,B, D'_{AB})$

$D'_{AB} = 0$	if $D_{AB} = 0$
$D'_{AB} = 0$ and 1	if $D_{AB} = 1$
$D'_{AB} = 0$ and 3	if $D_{AB} = 3$
$D'_{AB} = 0$ and 5	if $D_{AB} = 5$
$D'_{AB} = 0$ and 7	if $D_{AB} = 7$
$D'_{AB} = 0,1,2$ and 3	if $D_{AB} = 2$
$D'_{AB} = 0,3,4$ and 5	if $D_{AB} = 4$
$D'_{AB} = 0,5,6$ and 7	if $D_{AB} = 6$
$D'_{AB} = 0,1,7$ and 8	if $D_{AB} = 8$

(type-1) $ST^{AB}_1 = (A,B, D_{AB})$

(type-2) $ST^{AB}_2 = (A,B, D_{AB}, SC^{AB}_X, SC^{AB}_Y)$

$SC^{AB}_X = 1$	if $|r_X(A) - r_X(B)| \leq 1$
$SC^{AB}_X = 0$	if $|r_X(A) - r_X(B)| > 1$
$SC^{AB}_Y = 0$	if $|r_Y(A) - r_Y(B)| \leq 1$
$SC^{AB}_Y = 1$	if $|r_Y(A) - r_Y(B)| < 1$

Here, S^{AB}_i represents the type-i spatial strings for A and B symbols, and (A, B, D_{AB}) denotes the 9DLT representation of symbols A and B. SC^{AB}_X and SC^{AB}_Y represent the spatial codes for symbols A and B in the X-axis and the Y-axis, respectively. Expression $|t|$ denotes the absolute value of t; for example, $|-2|=2$. For example, when we have the same symbolic projection as that in Figure 1, a set of type-0, type-1, and type-2 representation strings can be obtained as follows:

type-0: (A,B,0), (A,B,1), (A,B,2), (A,B,3), (A,C,0), (A,C,7), (B,C,0), (B,C,5), (B,C,6),

(B,C,7)
type-1: (A,B,2), (A,C,7), (B,C,6)
type-2: (A,B,2,0,0), (A,C,7,0,0), (B,C,6,1,0)

NEW THREE-DIMENTIONAL REPRESENTAION SCHEMES

For image indexing, a large number of known image processing and understanding techniques (Faloutsos, 1994) can first be used to identify some domain objects and their relationships in an original image. Next, we can easily obtain an iconic image by associating a meaningful icon object with each domain object in the original image. By using some spatial match representations, we can finally obtain spatial strings from spatial relation-

Figure 3: The architecture of a spatial match retrieval system

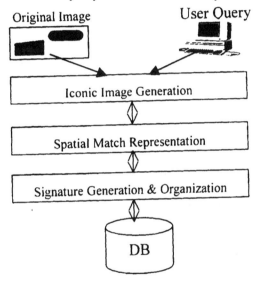

ships between icon objects. For image retrieval, a user query can first be transformed into an iconic image in the same way as that used in the image indexing. Next, we can represent the query iconic image as spatial strings by using some spatial match representations. Then, we can generate a query signature from the spatial strings and can get some potential matches by comparing the query signature with all of the signatures in the signature file. By excluding some false matches from the potential ones, we can finally retrieve some iconic images to satisfy the user query. The architecture of a spatial match retrieval system is shown in Figure 3.

For spatial match representations, there have been two main representation schemes to search image results efficiently, satisfying certain spatial relationships (Chang, 1987, Chang, 1991). However, both representation schemes have a critical problem in that they can represent spatial relationships between icon objects for only the two-dimensional (2D) images. As a result, they are not suitable to expressing spatial relationships between objects for handling three-dimensional (3D) images. In order to support 3D content-based image retrieval, we propose new three-dimensional representation scheme for iconic image indexing and querying, such as 27DLT, basic, and detail ones.

27DLT representation scheme

To describe the spatial relationship between icon objects for 3D images, we first propose 27DLT direction codes which extends the 9DLT codes for handing relationship embedded in a 3D images. Therefore, twenty-seven integers from -8 to 18 are used to represent pairwise spatial relationships embedded in a 3D string. Figure 4 shows the twenty-seven direction codes, where R indicates the reference icon object. The codes from 1(North) to 8 (Northeast) denote directions in a counterclockwise order on the same plane as R and 0 stands for "at the same location on the same plane as R". The codes from -1 to -8 denote the same directions as those of 1 to 8 except that they are described on the inner plane of R. The integer 0 stands for "at the same location as R on the inner plane". Similarly, the codes from 11 to 18 denote the same directions as those of 1 to 8 on the outer plane of R. The integer 10 stands for "at the same location as R on the outer plane".

Thus, an exact-match direction character, RE_{AB} is a character describing the 3D spatial relationship between objects A and B when the projects of A and B are represented as a point in a 3D space, respectively. The exact-match direction character is written as the following:

$RE_{AB} = 1$ if B is north of A in the same plane
$RE_{AB} = 2$ if B is northwest of A in the same plane
$RE_{AB} = 3$ if B is west of A in the same plane
$RE_{AB} = 4$ if B is southwest of A in the same plane
$RE_{AB} = 5$ if B is south of A in the same plane
$RE_{AB} = 6$ if B is southeast of A in the same plane
$RE_{AB} = 7$ if B is east of A in the same plane

Figure 4 : 27DLT direction codes

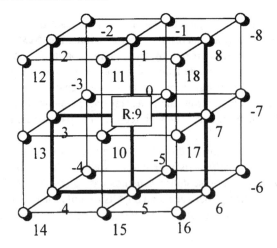

$RE_{AB} = 8$ if B is northeast of A in the same plane
$RE_{AB} = 9$ if B is at the same location as A in the same plane
$RE_{AB} = -1$ if B is north of A in the inner plane
$RE_{AB} = -2$ if B is northwest of A in the inner plane
$RE_{AB} = -3$ if B is west of A in the inner plane
$RE_{AB} = -4$ if B is southwest of A in the inner plane
$RE_{AB} = -5$ if B is south of A in the inner plane
$RE_{AB} = -6$ if B is southeast of A in the inner plane
$RE_{AB} = -7$ if B is east of A in the inner plane
$RE_{AB} = -8$ if B is northeast of A in the inner plane
$RE_{AB} = 0$ if B is at the same location as A in the inner plane
$RE_{AB} = 11$ if B is north of A in the outer plane
$RE_{AB} = 12$ if B is northwest of A in the outer plane
$RE_{AB} = 13$ if B is west of A in the outer plane
$RE_{AB} = 14$ if B is southwest of A in the outer plane
$RE_{AB} = 15$ if B is south of A in the outer plane
$RE_{AB} = 16$ if B is southeast of A in the outer plane
$RE_{AB} = 17$ if B is east of A in the outer plane
$RE_{AB} = 18$ if B is northeast of A in the outer plane
$RE_{AB} = 10$ if B is at the same location as A in the outer plane

In addition, an approximate-match direction character, RA_{AB} is a character describing the 3D spatial relationship between objects A and B when the projects of A and B are represented as a point in a 3D space, respectively. The approximate-match direction character is written as the following:

$RA_{AB} = 9$ if $RE_{AB} = 9$
$RA_{AB} = 1$ and 9   if $RE_{AB} = 1$
$RA_{AB} = 3$ and 9   if $RE_{AB} = 3$
$RA_{AB} = 5$ and 9   if $RE_{AB} = 5$
$RA_{AB} = 7$ and 9   if $RE_{AB} = 7$
$RA_{AB} = 1, 2, 3$ and 9   if $RE_{AB} = 2$
$RA_{AB} = 3, 4, 5$ and 9   if $RE_{AB} = 4$
$RA_{AB} = 5, 6, 7$ and 9   if $RE_{AB} = 6$
$RA_{AB} = 1, 7, 8$ and 9   if $RE_{AB} = 8$
$RA_{AB} = 0$ if $RE_{AB} = 0$
$RA_{AB} = -1$ and 0   if $RE_{AB} = -1$
$RA_{AB} = -3$ and 0   if $RE_{AB} = -3$
$RA_{AB} = -5$ and 0   if $RE_{AB} = -5$
$RA_{AB} = -7$ and 0   if $RE_{AB} = -7$
$RA_{AB} = -1, -2, -3$ and 0   if $RE_{AB} = -2$
$RA_{AB} = -3, -4, -5$ and 0   if $RE_{AB} = -4$
$RA_{AB} = -5, -6, -7$ and 0   if $RE_{AB} = -6$
$RA_{AB} = -1, -7, -8$ and 0   if $RE_{AB} = -8$
$RA_{AB} = 10$ if $RE_{AB} = 10$
$RA_{AB} = 10$ and 11   if $RE_{AB} = 11$

RA_{AB} = 10 and 13   if RE_{AB} = 13
RA_{AB} = 10 and 15   if RE_{AB} = 15
RA_{AB} = 10 and 17   if RE_{AB} = 17
RA_{AB} = 10, 11, 12 and 13   if RE_{AB} = 12
RA_{AB} = 10, 13, 14 and 14   if RE_{AB} = 14
RA_{AB} = 10, 15, 16 and 17   if RE_{AB} = 16
RA_{AB} = 10, 11, 17 and 18   if RE_{AB} = 18

Based on the 27DLT direction codes, we propose a 27DLT representation scheme to express both exact-match and approximate-match of spatial strings so that we can support the full description of pairwise spatial relationships embedded in a 3D string. An approximate-match spatial string of objects A and B, STA^{AB}, and an exact-match spatial string, STE^{AB}, are expressed as follows:

- approximate-match string
  $$STA^{AB} = (A,B,RA_{AB})$$
- exact-match string
  $$STE^{AB} = (A,B,RE_{AB})$$

Basic representation scheme

A generic scene S of an original image is defined as a set of icon objects O in its iconic image. Therefore, an iconic description of the scene is a set of spatial relationships between pairs of icon objects. The spatial relationship(SR) is expressed as $SR_i = {}_pO_p q$, where p and q are the projections over the i-axis (i.e., i = X, Y, or Z) of A and B objects, respectively, and O_p is a positional operator, which relates the intervals originated by the projections of p and q on the i-axis. For this, we propose nine positional operators which can express basic ones among all of the possible relationships between a pair of intervals. The proposed nine operators are sufficient to handle such images that their objects rarely have an adjacency with the other objects. These images are widely used in many application areas dealing with real photos like human face images. For the i-axis, projections of p and q are referred to as $p = [x_{p1}, x_{p2}]$ and $q = [x_{q1}, x_{q2}]$, respectively, where $x_{p1} < x_{p2}$ and $x_{q1} < x_{q2}$. Here "d" indicates the threshold value of the distance between two objects. The naïve value of d can be determined as the average length of reference intervals, and the optimal value can be determined by a large number of experiments.

(a) p far-away-after (>>) q   iff $x_{p1} \geq x_{q2} + d$
(b) p strictly-after (>+) q   iff $x_{q2} < x_{p1} < x_{q2} + d$
(c) p after (>) q   iff $x_{q1} < x_{p1} \leq x_{q2}$ and $x_{q2} < x_{p2}$
(d) p includes (><) q   iff $x_{p1} \leq x_{q1}$ and $x_{q2} < x_{p2}$ or $x_{p1} < x_{q1}$ and $x_{q2} \leq x_{p2}$
(e) p spatial-coincidence (=) q   iff $x_{p1} = x_{q1}$ and $x_{p2} = x_{q2}$
(f) p is-included-by (<>) q   iff $x_{q1} \pounds x_{p1}$ and $x_{p2} < x_{q2}$ or $x_{q1} < x_{p1}$ and $x_{p2} \leq x_{q2}$
(g) p before (<) q   iff $x_{q1} \pounds x_{p2} < x_{q2}$ and $x_{p1} < x_{q1}$
(h) p strictly-before (<+) q   iff $x_{p2} < x_{q1} < x_{p2} + d$
(i) p far-away-before (<<) q   iff $x_{q1} \approx x_{p2}$

The visual sketch of the meanings of positional operators used for our basic representation scheme is given in Figure 5. For convenience of signature generation, we also define a spatial string to represent the pairwise spatial relationships between objects in a two-

Figure 5 : Positional operators of our basic representation scheme

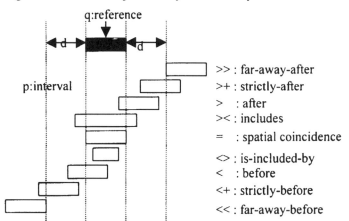

q:reference

p:interval

>> : far-away-after
>+ : strictly-after
> : after
>< : includes
= : spatial coincidence
<> : is-included-by
< : before
<+ : strictly-before
<< : far-away-before

dimensional image. For this, we express two types of spatial strings so that they can fully support the description of all the spatial relationships embedded in a 2D string (Lee, 1990). Thus, the type-0, 1, and 2 spatial relationships encoded by a 2D string can be transformed into exact-match and approximate-match spatial strings for our basic representation scheme. An exact-match i-axis spatial character, BE^{AB}_i, is a character describing the spatial relationship between A and B objects when the projections of A and B in terms of the i-axis are referred to as $p = [x_{p1}, x_{p2}]$, and $q = [x_{q1}, x_{q2}]$ respectively, where $x_{p1} < x_{p2}$ and $x_{q1} < x_{q2}$. This character is used to support the exact match of user queries holding certain spatial relationships. The exact-match spatial character is written as the following:

$$BE^{AB}_i = 0 \quad \text{if } p >> q$$
$$BE^{AB}_i = 1 \quad \text{if } p >+ q$$
$$BE^{AB}_i = 2 \quad \text{if } p > q$$
$$BE^{AB}_i = 3 \quad \text{if } p >< q$$
$$BE^{AB}_i = 4 \quad \text{if } p = q$$
$$BE^{AB}_i = 5 \quad \text{if } p <> q$$
$$BE^{AB}_i = 6 \quad \text{if } p < q$$
$$BE^{AB}_i = 7 \quad \text{if } p <+ q$$
$$BE^{AB}_i = 8 \quad \text{if } p << q$$

An approximate-match i-axis spatial character, BA^{AB}_i, is a character describing the spatial relationship between objects A and B, being used to support the approximate match of user queries. To determine if a positional operator holds a approximate-match relationship with another operator, we classify nine positional operators into five groups, i.e., after group(>>,>+,>),is-included group(<>),same group(=),include group(><), and before group(<,<+,<<). A procedure to determine approximate-match relationships among operators are as follows:

1. Determine intra-group approximate-match relationships among the three operators

for the after group as well as for the before group, respectively.

2. Establish no approximate-match relationship between two operators, one coming from the after group and the other coming from the before group. This is because there is no approximate-match relationship between the two groups.

3. Similarly, establish no approximate-match relationship between two operators, one coming from the is-included group and the other from the include group.

4. Finally, establish approximate-match relationships between the same group and the include group, as well as between the same group and the is-included group.

According to this procedure, the approximate-match character is written as the following:

$BA^{AB}_i = 0$ and 1   if $p \gg q$
$BA^{AB}_i = 0,1$ and 2   if $p >+ q$
$BA^{AB}_i = 1$ and 2   if $p > q$
$BA^{AB}_i = 3$ and 4   if $p >< q$
$BA^{AB}_i = 3,4$ and 5   if $p = q$
$BA^{AB}_i = 5$ and 6   if $p <> q$
$BA^{AB}_i = 6$ and 7   if $p < q$
$BA^{AB}_i = 6,7$ and 8   if $p <+ q$
$BA^{AB}_i = 7$ and 8   if $p \ll q$

Therefore, an exact-match spatial string of objects A and B, SBE^{AB}, is a string formed by concatenating A, B, and exact-match spatial characters BE^{AB}_x, BE^{AB}_y, and BE^{AB}_z, where BE^{AB}_x, BE^{AB}_y, and BE^{AB}_z are the spatial character along the X-axis, the Y-axis, and Z-axis, respectively. Similarly, an approximate-match spatial string of objects A and B, SBA^{AB}, is a string formed by concatenating A, B, and approximate-match spatial characters BA^{AB}_x, BA^{AB}_y, and BA^{AB}_z. Thus, the exact-match and the approximate-match spatial strings of objects A and B are expressed as follows:

- exact-match string
    $SBE^{AB} = (A,B, BE^{AB}_x, BE^{AB}_y,$ and $BE^{AB}_z)$
- approximate match string
    $SBA^{AB} = (A,B, BA^{AB}_x, BA^{AB}_y,$ and $BA^{AB}_z)$

Detailed representation scheme

For new positional operators, we can extend some operators used for the specification of temporal relationships between time intervals in interval logic (Halpern, 1991, Bimbo, 1993). We propose new fifteen positional operators to express all of the possible relationships between a pair of intervals. For each i-axis (i.e., $i = X$, Y, or Z), the projections of p and q are referred to as $p = [x_{p1}, x_{p2}]$, and $q = [x_{q1}, x_{q2}]$, respectively, where $x_{p1} < x_{p2}$ and $x_{q1} < x_{q2}$. Here "d" indicates the threshold value of distance between two objects.

(a) p far-away-after ($\gg$) q   iff $x_{p1} \approx x_{q2} + d$
(b) p strictly-after ($>+$) q   iff $x_{q2} < x_{p1} < x_{q2} + d$
(c) p after with right adjacency ($>=$) q   iff $x_{q2} = x_{p1}$
(d) p after ($>$) q   iff $x_{q1} < x_{p1} < x_{q2}$ and $x_{q2} < x_{p2}$
(e) p is-included-by with left adjacency ($>-$) q   iff $x_{q1} < x_{p1}$ and $x_{p2} = x_{q2}$

(f) p includes with right adjacency (>|) q iff $x_{q1} = x_{p1}$ and $x_{q2} < x_{p2}$

(g) p includes (><) q iff $x_{p1} < x_{q1}$ and $x_{q2} < x_{p2}$

(h) p spatial-coincidence (=) q iff $x_{p1} = x_{q1}$ and $x_{p2} = x_{q2}$

(i) p is-included-by (<>) q iff $x_{q1} < x_{p1}$ and $x_{p2} < x_{q2}$

(j) p includes with left adjacency (<|) q iff $x_{q1} > x_{p1}$ and $x_{q2} = x_{p2}$

(k) p is-included-by with right adjacency (<-) q iff $x_{q1} = x_{p1}$ and $x_{p2} < x_{q2}$

(l) p before (<) q iff $x_{q1} < x_{p2} < x_{q2}$ and $x_{p1} < x_{q1}$

(m) p before with left adjacency (<=) q iff $x_{p2} = x_{q1}$

(n) p strictly-before (<+) q iff $x_{p2} < x_{q1} < x_{p2} + d$

(o) p far-away-before (<<) q iff $x_{q1} \approx x_{p2} + d$

The visual sketch of positional operators used for our detailed representation scheme are given in Figure 6. For the convenience of signature generation, we also define a spatial string to represent the pairwise spatial relationships between objects in a two-dimensional image. For this, we express two types of spatial strings so that they can support both the exact and the approximate match. First, an exact-match i-axis spatial character, $DE^{AB}{}_i$, is a character describing a spatial relationship between objects A and B when the projections of A and B in terms of the i-axis are referred to as $p = [x_{p1}, x_{p2}]$, and $q = [x_{q1}, x_{q2}]$, respectively, where $x_{p1} < x_{p2}$ and $x_{q1} < x_{q2}$. The exact-match spatial character is written as the following:

$DE^{AB}{}_i = 0$ if p >> q

$DE^{AB}{}_i = 1$ if p >+ q

$DE^{AB}{}_i = 2$ if p >= q

$DE^{AB}{}_i = 3$ if p > q

$DE^{AB}{}_i = 4$ if p >- q

$DE^{AB}{}_i = 5$ if p >| q

$DE^{AB}{}_i = 6$ if p >< q

$DE^{AB}{}_i = 7$ if p = q

$DE^{AB}{}_i = 8$ if p <> q

$DE^{AB}{}_i = 9$ if p <| q

$DE^{AB}{}_i = 10$ if p <- q

$DE^{AB}{}_i = 11$ if p < q

$DE^{AB}{}_i = 12$ if p <= q

$DE^{AB}{}_i = 13$ if p <+ q

$DE^{AB}{}_i = 14$ if p << q

An approximate-match i-axis spatial character, $DA^{AB}{}_i$, is a character describing a spatial relationship between A and B objects so that it can be used to support the approximate match of user queries. To determine if a positional operator holds an approximate-match relationship with another operator, we classify the fifteen positional operators into five groups, i.e., after group (>>,>+,>=,>),is-included group (>-,<>,<-), same group(=), include group (>|,><,<|), and before group(<,<=,<+,<<). A procedure to determine approximate-match relationships among operators are as follows:

1. Determine intra-group approximate-match relationships among all operators for each group.

Figure 6: Positional operators of our detailed representation scheme

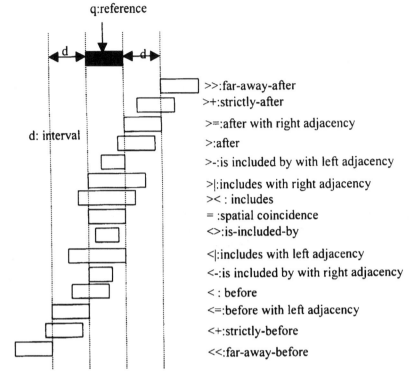

2. Establish no approximate-match relationship between two operators, one belonging to the after group and the other belonging to the before group. This is because there is no approximate-match relationship between the two groups.
3. Similarly, establish no approximate-match relationship between two operators, one belonging to the is-included group and the other belonging to the include group.
4. Determine approximate-match relationships between the after group and the is-included group, as well as between the after group and the include group. For this, establish an approximate-match relationship between two operators, one coming from the after group and the other from the is-included group. Also, establish an approximate-match relationship between two operators, one from the after group and the other from the include group.
5. Similarly, determine approximate-match relationships between the before group and the is-included group, as well as between the before group and the include group. For this, establish an approximate-match relationship between two operators, one coming from the before group and the other from the is-included group. Also, establish a relationship between two operators, one from the before group and the other from the include group.
6. Finally, determine approximate-match relationships between the same group and the is-included group, as well as between the same group and the include group. For this, establish the approximate-match relationships of the same operator with all of the operators in the include group, as well as with all of the operators in the is-included

group.

According to the above procedure, the approximate-match spatial character is written as the following:

$DA^{AB}_i = 0$ and 1	if p $>>$ q
$DA^{AB}_i = 0,1$ and 2	if p $>+$ q
$DA^{AB}_i = 1,2$ and 3	if p $>=$ q
$DA^{AB}_i = 2,3,4$ and 5	if p $>$ q
$DA^{AB}_i = 3,4,7$ and 8	if p $>-$ q
$DA^{AB}_i = 3,5,6$ and 7	if p $>\!\mid$ q
$DA^{AB}_i = 5,6$ and 9	if p $><$ q
$DA^{AB}_i = 4,5,7,9$ and 10	if p $=$ q
$DA^{AB}_i = 4,8$ and 10	if p $<>$ q
$DA^{AB}_i = 6,7,9$ and 11	if p $<\!\mid$ q
$DA^{AB}_i = 7,8,10$ and 11	if p $<-$ q
$DA^{AB}_i = 9,10,11$ and 12	if p $<$ q
$DA^{AB}_i = 11,12$ and 13	if p $<=$ q
$DA^{AB}_i = 12,13$ and 14	if p $<+$ q
$DA^{AB}_i = 13$ and 14	if p $<<$ q

Therefore, an exact-match spatial string of objects A and B, SDE^{AB}, is a string formed by concatenating A, B, and exact-match spatial characters DE^{AB}_x, DE^{AB}_y, and DE^{AB}_z, where DE^{AB}_x, DE^{AB}_y, and DE^{AB}_z are the spatial characters along the X-axis, the Y-axis, and the Z-axis, respectively. Similarly, an approximate-match spatial string of objects A and B, SDA^{AB}, is a string formed by concatenating A, B, and exact-match spatial characters DA^{AB}_x, DA^{AB}_y, and DA^{AB}_z. Thus, the exact-match and the approximate-match strings of objects A and B are expressed as follows:

- exact-match string
  $SDE^{AB} = (A,B, DE^{AB}_x, DE^{AB}_y, and\ DE^{AB}_z)$
- approximate-match string
  $SDA^{AB} = (A,B, DA^{AB}_x, DA^{AB}_y, and\ DA^{AB}_z)$

Example

We assume that we have an iconic image consisting of A, B, and C icon objects as shown in Figure 7. Spatial relationship strings for our 27DLT representation scheme can be obtained as follows:
- exact-match representation
  (A,B,17)
- approximate-match representation
  (A,B,10),(A,B,17)

Also, when we have the same iconic image as that in Figure 7, spatial relationship strings for our basic representation scheme can be obtained as follows:
- exact-match representation
  (A,B,1,5,7)
- approximate-match representation
  (A,B,0,5,6),(A,B,0,5,7),(A,B,0,5,8),(A,B,0,6,6),(A,B,0,6,7),(A,B,0,6,8),(A,B,1,5,6),(A,B,1,5,7),

Figure 7: An Example iconic image

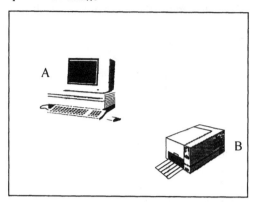

(A,B,1,5,8),
(A,B,1,6,6),(A,B,1,6,7),(A,B,1,6,8),(A,B,2,5,6),(A,B,2,5,7),(A,B,2,5,8),(A,B,2,6,6),(A,B,2,6,7),(A,B,2,6,8)
Finally, when we have the same iconic image as that in Figure 7, spatial relationship strings for our detailed representation scheme can be obtained as follows:

- exact-match representation
    (A,B,1,10,13)
- approximate-match representation
    (A,B,0,7,12),(A,B,0,7,13),(A,B,0,7,14),(A,B,0,8,12),(A,B,0,8,13),(A,B,0,8,14),(A,B,0,10,12),
    (A,B,0,10,13),(A,B,0,10,14),(A,B,0,11,12),(A,B,0,11,13),(A,B,0,11,14),(A,B,1,7,12),
    (A,B,1,7,13),(A,B,1,7,14),(A,B,1,8,12),(A,B,1,8,13),(A,B,1,8,14),(A,B,1,10,12),(A,B,1,10,13),
    (A,B,1,10,14),(A,B,1,11,12),(A,B,1,11,13),(A,B,1,11,14),(A,B,2,7,12),(A,B,2,7,13),(A,B,2,7,14),
    (A,B,2,8,12),(A,B,2,8,13),(A,B,2,8,14),(A,B,2,10,12),(A,B,2,10,13),(A,B,2,10,14),(A,B,2,11,12),
    (A,B,2,11,13),(A,B,2,11,14)

A NEW EFFICIENT RETRIEVAL METHOD

In order to support fast searching of spatial strings for iconic images, it is necessary to construct an efficient retrieval method using a signature file technique because of its main advantages: fast retrieval time and low storage overhead(Faloutsos, 1984). When an iconic image consists of both icon objects and a set of spatial strings among them, we first create an object signature for each object in the iconic image and superimpose all of the signatures by using a superimposed coding technique. Then, we create an approximate-match signature by superimposing all of the signatures, each of which is made from each approximate-match spatial string for the iconic image. In the same way, we also construct an exact-match signature for the iconic image. Superimposing signatures leads to reducing the disk space to be accessed dramatically. We finally construct an image signature by concatenating the object, the approximate-match, and the exact-match signatures by using a disjoint coding technique.

Therefore, we can offer a way to answer a variety of user queries effectively since an image signature is composed of three parts of signatures. For example, if a user query needs some image results, including icon objects A and B, we can access only a portion of object signatures, thus dramatically reducing the query processing time. Similarly, if a user query requires all relevant images satisfying a certain relationship approximately, we can access only a portion of approximate-match signatures to answer the query. In order to accelerate the search for these signatures, we design an efficient retrieval method based on a signature file technique (Kim, 1994).

Signature generation

With a set of exact-match spatial relationship strings (ESRs) corresponding to a given iconic image, we can generate a set of approximate-match spatial relationship strings (ASRs) as well as an object list (OL). Given the OL, a set of ASRs, and a set of ESRs, we can also generate three kinds of signatures, i.e., the object, the approximate-match, and the exact-match signatures for the iconic image. Then, an image signature for the iconic image is constructed by concatenating these three signatures into one signature. The algorithm to generate an image signature is illustrated below.

[Algorithm 1] Generation of image signature

Input: a set of ESRs for an iconic image, each being (A,B,R^{AB}) or $(A,B,P^{AB}_X,P^{AB}_Y,P^{AB}_Z)$

Output: image signature, IS

Variables:

S_{obj}, S_{app}, S_{exa} : object, approximate-match, and exact-match signature for an iconic image, respectively

so_k : object signature for the k-th object of the OL

sa_i, se_i : approximate-match and exact-match signature for the i-th ESR, respectively

s^j_i : approximate-match signature for the j-th ASR of the i-th ESR

Begin:
```
S_obj = 0; S_app = 0; S_exa = 0;
Compute the OL from a set of ESRs;
while(each k-th object of the OL for some k) {
    Create so_k from the k-th object of the OL; S_obj = S_obj V so_I;
} /* while loop for k */
while(each i-th ESR for some i) {
    Create se_i from the i-th ESR; S_exa = S_exa V se_i;
    Determine a set of ASRs from the i-th ESR; sa_i = 0;
    while(each j-th ASR for some j) {
        Create s^j_i from the j-th APR; sa_i = sa_i V s^j_i;
    } /* while loop for j */
    S_app = S_app V sa_i;
} /* while loop for i */
RS = S_obj || S_app || S_exa;
```
End:

Insertion and Retrieval

When a set of signatures for an iconic image is generated using Algorithm 1, we can store the object signature and the approximate-match signature into an object signature file and an approximate-match one, respectively. We also store the superimposing one of both general and distance-considered signatures into an exact-match signature file. Therefore, the insertion of an image signature can be easily handled because it only needs to append its three parts of signatures to those three signature files.

When a user query is given, it can be transformed into a query signature using Algorithm 1. Depending on whether the query belongs to an approximate-match or an exact-match type, we can decide in what sequence three signature files should be accessed so that we may achieve good retrieval performance. After accessing the corresponding signature files, we can obtain some qualifying signatures to satisfy the relationship strings in the query. Finally, we can find iconic image results by examining whether the iconic images corresponding to the qualifying signatures actually satisfy the query. If necessary, we can retrieve some pixel-level original images given by the iconic image results. Both the insertion and retrieval algorithms are omitted because of their simplicity.

Example

We assume that we have four iconic images consisting of icon objects A and B as shown in Figure 8. A set of approximate-match and exact-match spatial relationship strings in our basic representation can be obtained as follows:

- exact-match representation
  (Image-1)   (A,B,1,5,7)
  (Image-2)   (A,B,2,5,6)
  (Image-3)   (A,B,0,5,7)
  (Image-4)   (A,B,1,5,8)

- approximate-match representation
(Image-1)   (A,B,0,5,6), (A,B,0,5,7), (A,B,0,5,8), (A,B,0,6,6), (A,B,0,6,7), (A,B,0,6,8),
            (A,B,1,5,6), (A,B,1,5,7), (A,B,1,5,8), (A,B,1,6,6), (A,B,1,6,7), (A,B,1,6,8),
            (A,B,2,5,6), (A,B,2,5,7), (A,B,2,5,8), (A,B,2,6,6), (A,B,2,6,7), (A,B,2,6,8)
(Image-2)   (A,B,1,5,6), (A,B,1,5,7), (A,B,1,6,6), (A,B,1,6,7), (A,B,2,5,6),
            (A,B,2,5,7),(A,B,2,6,6), (A,B,2,6,7)
(Image-3)   (A,B,0,5,6), (A,B,0,5,7), (A,B,0,5,8), (A,B,0,6,6), (A,B,0,6,7), (A,B,0,6,8),

Figure 8: Four iconic images as example

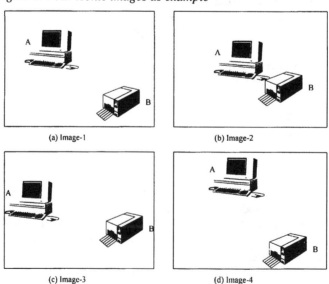

(a) Image-1   (b) Image-2

(c) Image-3   (d) Image-4

(A,B,1,5,6), (A,B,1,5,7), (A,B,1,5,8), (A,B,1,6,6), (A,B,1,6,7), (A,B,1,6,8)

(Image-4)   (A,B,0, 5,7) (A,B,0,5,8) (A,B,0,6,7) (A,B,0,6,8) (A,B,1,5,7) (A,B,1,5,8) (A,B,1,6,7) (A,B,1,6,8) (A,B,2,5,7) (A,B,2,5,8) (A,B,2,6,7) (A,B,2,6,8)

To create the signature of the four iconic images, we assume that the object signature has 6 bits in length, the approximate-match signature has 18 bits, and the exact-match signature has 12 bits. In addition, we assume that three hashing functions are used to generate these signatures, such as h_{obj}, h_{app}, and h_{exa}. Table 1, Table 2, and Table 3 list the object, the approximate-match, and the exact-match signatures, respectively. Based on them, we can generate the signatures of the four images as shown in Table 4.

Figure 10 illustrates a signature file structure after we insert the four image signatures shown in Table 4. Here the SRS file is the one storing a set of approximate-match, and exact-match spatial relationship strings(SRS) for all of the iconic images. For example, suppose that we have a query to find such an iconic image as Image-Q in Figure 9. To answer this query, we first generate a set of SRS for Image-Q in our basic representation as follows:

- exact-match representation(A,B,1,5,6)
- approximate-match representation
  (A,B,0,5,6),(A,B,0,5,7),(A,B,0,6,6),(A,B,0,6,7),(A,B,1,5,6),(A,B,1,5,7),(A,B,1,6,6),(A,B,1,6,7), (A,B,2,5,6),(A,B,2,5,7),(A,B,2,6,6),(A,B,2,6,7)

Next, we create the object, the approximate-match and the exact-match signature of Image-Q by using Table 1, Table 2, and Table 3 as follows:

$IS^Q_{obj} = 011011$

$IS^Q_{app} = 011011\ 011011\ 011011$

$IS^Q_{exa} = 000010\ 000010$

Finally, if we require some exact-match answers, we can compare IS^Q_{exa} with the four signatures in the exact-match signature file. This leads to one qualifying

Figure 9: Image-Q: A query iconic image

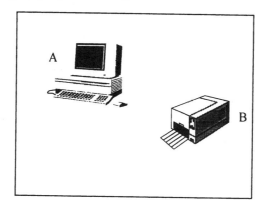

Table 2 : Approximate-match signature

ASR	Approximate-match signature
(A,B,0,5,6)	000000 000000 000001
(A,B,0,5,7)	000000 000000 000010
(A,B,0,5,8)	000000 000000 000100
(A,B,0,6,6)	000000 000000 001000
(A,B,0,6,7)	000000 000000 010000
(A,B,0,6,8)	000000 000000 100000
(A,B,1,5,6)	000000 000001 000000
(A,B,1,5,7)	000000 000010 000000
(A,B,1,5,8)	000000 000100 000000
(A,B,1,6,6)	000000 001000 000000
(A,B,1,6,7)	000000 010000 000000
(A,B,1,6,8)	000000 100000 000000
(A,B,2,5,6)	000001 000000 000000
(A,B,2,5,7)	000010 000000 000000
(A,B,2,5,8)	000100 000000 000000
(A,B,2,6,6)	001000 000000 000000
(A,B,2,6,7)	010000 000000 000000
(A,B,2,6,8)	100000 000000 000000

Table 1: Object signature

Object	Object signature
A	001001
B	010010

Table 3 : Exact-match signature

ESR	Exact-match signature
(A,B,0,5,7)	000001 000001
(A,B,1,5,6)	000010 000010
(A,B,1,5,7)	000100 000100
(A,B,1,5,8)	001000 001000
(A,B,2,5,6)	010000 010000

Table 4 : Image signatures for the four example iconic images

Image	IS_{obj}	IS_{app}	IS_{cxa}
Image-1	011011	111111 111111 111111	000100 000100
Image-2	011011	011011 011011 000000	010000 010000
Image-3	011011	000000 111111 111111	000001 000001
Image-4	011011	110110 110110 110110	001000 001000

signature because the fourth signature in the exact-match signature file satisfies the bit pattern of IS^Q_{cxa}. Therefore, we obtain one qualifying iconic image, i.e., Image-4 because the SRS of image-4 actually contain the query's SSR. Finally, if we require some approximate-match answers, we can search for only the four signatures of the approximate-match signature file. We obtain two qualifying signatures, i.e., the third and the fourth of the approximate-match signature file, because they contain the bit pattern of IS^Q_{app}. Thus, we can access the ARS of iconic images corresponding to the qualifying signatures so that we can find out some false drops. As an approximate-match answer, we finally obtain two qualifying iconic images, i.e., Image-3 and Image-4, because both the SRS of Image-1 and those of Image-2 both include the SRS of Image-Q.

Figure 10: A new signature file organization

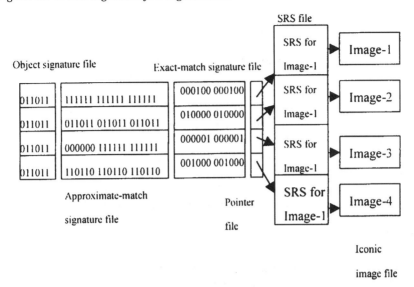

PERFORMANCE EVALUATION

We assume that a pixel-level original image should be automatically or manually transformed into its iconic image including only icon objects, prior to storage into the database. This is because the purpose of our paper is to provide effective representation and fast searching of images after their icon objects are extracted by image analysis preprocessing. We also assume that an iconic image consists of icon objects, each having its icon name, its size, and its position.

For our experiment, we generate the following iconic databases(Gudivado, 1994):

- Icon objects have 25 different types.
- An iconic image consists of two to ten icon objects.
- The total number of iconic images used for our experiment is 5,000.
- A query iconic image contains two to three icon objects.
- The number of queries for the experiment is 200.

In order to evaluate retrieval effectiveness(Salton, 1989), we make use of recall and precision measures. Let IRT be the number of iconic images retrieved by a given query, IRL be the number of iconic images relevant to the query, and IRR be the number of relevant iconic images retrieved. The relevant images can be determined by computing the similarity between two iconic images, based on both their spatial relationship and on their icon size. The recall and precision measures are computed as the following:

Re*call*= IRR/IRL

Pre*cision*= IRR/IRT

When a variety of queries are executed two hundred times, Table 5 shows the retrieval effectiveness of the proposed spatial match representation schemes, in terms of precision and recall measures. For the approximate match, our detailed representation scheme, improves the retrieval effectiveness considerably. Compared to our basic and 27DLT schemes. the representation scheme improves retrieval precision by 0.09-0.18, while its recall value is kept higher than those of our other schemes. For the exact match, it is also shown that our basic and detailed representation schemes hold about 0.2 higher precision value than our 27DLT one. This is because our detailed representation scheme reserves all of the possible spatial relationships for an iconic image.

In order to evaluate the retrieval efficiency, we make use of the probability of false drops(Chang, 1994, Kim, 1994). Let N be the number of iconic images (i.e., the number of signatures), Ms be the number of qualifying signatures, and Mf be the number of false drops. The false drop probability, Fd, can be computed as the following:

$$Fd=Mf/N-(ms-Mf)$$

Table 6 shows the retrieval efficiency of retrieval method for our spatial match representation schemes, in terms of Fd. The retrieval efficiency for our basic and detailed representation schemes is slightly decreased, compared to that for our 27DLT one. Namely, Fd is increased by up to 0.015 in the exact match, and by up to 0.01 in the approximate match. Moreover, Table 6 shows the storage overhead(SO) of our retrieval schemes. i.e., a ratio of signature file size to real data size. It is shown from the results that our basic and detailed schemes require three and twelve times higher, storage overhead, respectively, in the approximate match than our 27DLT one, while they require almost the same in the exact match.

CONCLUSIONS AND FUTURE WORK

Recently, much attention has been paid to Multimedia Information Retrieval(MIR) because there are so many applications which require multimedia data. In order to support MIR in an effective way, content-based image retrieval is essential for retrieving relevant multimedia documents. The purpose of our chapter is to provide effective representation and efficient retrieval of images after a pixel-level original image is transformed into its iconic image. For this, we proposed our three-dimensional spatial match representation schemes so as to support content-based image retrieval in an effective way. Our representation schemes accurately described spatial relationships between icon objects because they could make use of precise direction codes or positional operators.

In order to compare among our three-dimensional representation schemes on retrieval

Table 5 : Retrieval effectiveness of spatial match representation schemes

Retrieval effectiveness	Our 27DLT Scheme		Our Basic Scheme		Our Detailed Scheme	
	App.	Exa.	App.	Exa.	App.	Exa.
Precision	0.198	0.242	0.103	0.422	0.282	0.486
Recall	0.309	0.264	0.626	0.493	0.650	0.397

Table 6 : Fd and SO of our retrieval method for spatial match representation scheme

Efficiency measures	Our 27DLT Scheme		Our Basic Scheme		Our Detailed Scheme	
	App.	Exa.	App.	Exa.	App.	Exa.
Fd	0.026	0.023	0.037	0.038	0.038	0.034
SO(Mbyte)	0.944	0.282	3.146	0.297	12.024	0.297

effectiveness, we evaluated the performances of our schemes, in terms of both precision and recall measures. We showed from our experiment that our basic and detailed representation schemes improved retrieval precision by about 0.09-0.18 in the approximate match, compared with our 27DLT scheme. We also showed that our detailed scheme outperformed our 27DLT one by 0.2 on the precision, while their recall values were kept almost the same. However, our detailed scheme required considerably larger signature storage in the approximate match, compared to our 27DLT scheme. For further work, our representation schemes should be applied to real application areas using iconic images, proving the efficiency of our schemes in these areas.

REFERENCES

Chang, S.K., Shi, Q.Y., and Yan, C.W.,(1987). Iconic Indexing by 2d strings. *IEEE Transactions on Pattern Recognition and Machine Intelligence*, 9(3):413-428.

Lee, S.Y., and Shan, M.K., (1990). Access methods of image databases. *International Journal of Pattern Recognition and Artificial Intelligence*, 4(1):27-44.

Chang, C.C.,(1991). Spatial match retrieval of symbolic pictures. *Information Science and Engineering*, pages 142-145.

Chang, C.C. and Jiang, J.H.,(1994). A fast spatial match retrieval using a superimposed coding technique. In *Proceeding Of the International Symposium on Advanced database Technologies and Their Integration*, pages 71-78, Nara, Japan.

Faloutsos, C., et al.(1994). Efficient and effective querying by image content. *Journal of Intelligent Information Systems*, 3:231-262.

Halpern, J., Shoham, Y., (1991). A propositional model logic of time intervals. *Journal of Association Computing Machinery*, 38:935-962.

Bimbo, A.D., Campanai, M., Nesi, P,(1993). A three-dimensional iconic environment for image database querying. *IEEE Transactions on Software Engineering*, 19(10):997-1010.

Faloutsos, C., Christodoulakis, S.,(1984). Signature files : An access methods for documents and its analytical performance evaluation. *ACM Transactions on Database Systems*, 2(4):267-288.

Kim, J.K. and Chang, ,J.W.,(1994). A two-dimensional dynamic signature file methods. In *proceeding of the International Symposium on Advanced database Technologies and Their Integration*, pages 63-0, Nara, Japan.

Gudivado, V.N.,(1994). Tessa – an image testbed for evaluating 2d spatial similarity algorithms. *ACM SIGIR Forum*, pages 17-36, Fall.

Salton, G.,(1989). *Automatic Text Processing*. Addison-Wesley.

CHAPTER 13

WebCDS - A Java Based Catalogue System for European Environment Data

Wassili Kazakos, Forschungszentrum Informatik, Germany
Ralf Kramer, Forschungszentrum Informatik, Germany
Ralf Nikolai, Forschungszentrum Informatik, Germany
Claudia Rolker, Forschungszentrum Informatik, Germany
Sigfus Bjarnason, European Environment Agency, Denmark
Stefan Jensen, Ministry of Environment, Lower Saxony, Germany

The Catalogue of Data Sources (CDS) of the European Environment Agency is an environmental meta-information system to direct the user toward information about the state of the environment in Europe. The CDS comprises metadata (data about data sources of European interest), addresses, and a multilingual thesaurus.

To provide global access to the CDS data via the Web, WebCDS has been developed. Major requirements were multilingual search and result forms, multilingual search by use of the multilingual thesaurus, independence of platforms, DBMS, and Web servers, user friendliness, and easy extensibility.

The Web application incorporates Java (at the server site), JDBC, RMI, servlets, and HTML. Servlets are utilized in order to overcome the problems of the classical HTML/CGI approach, e.g. servlets allow the communication of a client with an initialized service. We combined Java and HTML in WebCDS in order to gain nearly all advantages of Java without requiring Java capable Web browsers.

INTRODUCTION

Motivation

In 1995 the European Environment Agency (EEA) was launched by the European Union (EU) with a mandate to orchestrate, cross-check and put to strategic use information of relevance to the protection and improvement of Europe's environment and to ensure that the public is properly informed about the state of the environment (http://

www.eea.eu.int/). For the development of a versatile tool that directs the user toward information about the state of the environment in Europe the European Topic Centre on Catalogue of Data Sources and Thesauri (ETC/CDS) was founded by the EEA. The Ministry of Environment of Lower Saxony, Germany, was appointed as the Leading Organization. To fulfil its task the ETC/CDS developed an environmental catalogue system, the Catalogue of Data Sources (CDS) and - to cope with the variety of European languages - the General European Multilingual Environmental Thesaurus (GEMET).

Public access to environmental information is an important right and an essential support to environmental policy making. Therefore, the primary goal of the CDS is to direct the users—the importance of the general public was strengthened recently through the Aarhus Convention signed by European Environment Ministry—towards environmental information relevant on a European scale. To ensure the broad dissemination of information on the state of the environment to the general public, new telematics technology such as the Web play a key role.

Whereas the CDS is an on-going project, the meta-data collection has just started. Already in this early stage a tool is required that allows access to the CDS data via the Web: WebCDS. The importance attached to this tool will of course increase simultaneously with the increase of the volume of the available meta-data. The requirements identified for WebCDS include multilingual search and result forms, multilingual search by use of the multilingual thesaurus, portability by independence of platforms (operating system, database management system (DBMS), and Web server), user friendliness, extensibility, and performance. An approach considering these requirements as well as up-to-date Web technology and design methods are presented in this chapter.

Outline

The remainder of this chapter is organized as follows. In the section CORNER STONES, the corner stones are introduced. The section REQUIREMENTS AND APPROACH focuses on the requirements for WebCDS. In section RELATED WORK we briefly review related work. In section ARCHITECTURE details of the software architecture are presented. Section CONCLUSIONS concludes the chapter with a brief summary and an outlook on current and future work.

CORNER STONES

In this section we provide the background necessary to understand catalogues and catalogue systems and thesauri as an important means to search for information in catalogues. Furthermore, we introduce the Catalogue of Data Sources (CDS) as the starting point for WebCDS. We assume that the reader is familiar with standard Web techniques such as HTML, HTTP, and CGI (for an overview, we refer to, e.g. Kramer (1997)).

The Web provides transparent access to distributed documents. It follows a strict client-/server architecture. The stateless HyperText Transfer Protocol (HTTP) is used for the communication between the client (browser) and the Web server. The most common format to present information on the Web is the HyperText Markup Language (HTML), a standardized language for creating formatted hypertext documents, which can even include executable content.

These documents are addressed by using Uniform Resource Locators (URLs). Additionally to such documents, i.e., static HTML pages, Web servers can as well provide transparent access to other information sources such as DBMSs. For this purpose the Web server communicates with application programs via the standardized Common Gateway Interface (CGI) (McCool, 1994).

CGI

The oldest and probably most widely used approach to access databases from the Web is based on the Common Gateway Interface (CGI) (Rowe, 1996). CGI is a standard that allows Web servers to access arbitrary external applications, so-called CGI scripts. CGI is supported by all Web servers.

A CGI script is executed at the server site. It is started by the Web server upon client request. The CGI script receives the parameters supplied by the user and hidden variables, generates HTML pages dynamically (e.g., on the basis of data retrieved from a database by the CGI script), and delivers them to the Web server. The Web server then transfers the generated HTML pages to the Web client.

CGI scripts can be implemented in any programming language. However, to ensure portability of the application at the server site, widely supported technologies should be used. One possibility to achieve this is to implement CGI scripts in Java as suggested for WebCDS (Kramer et al., 1996). To overcome some of the deficiencies of the CGI approach (e.g., connect/disconnect to/from the database for each database access), numerous CGI tools are available.

Catalogues

In order to react upon complex environmental problems, it is necessary to have information of various application fields at hand which, in most cases, will be located at different sites. Only if the respective information is sufficiently available is it possible to find complex interrelations, to effectively survey environmental laws, but also to mutually use available information. Both the recollection of data that already has been collected and keeping data without any further use because of missing knowledge about the data can be avoided.

The answer to a certain question requires learning *which* information is available, *where* the information is managed, *how* this information can be obtained, and *how* to interpret the information correctly. The information that is necessary to obtain above mentioned information is called *meta-information*. This information can be compared to the information of classical index cards in library catalogues, which describe books but are not the books themselves (Crossley, 1996). Due to the present explosion of the volume of data, it becomes even more important for the user to rely on information about existing data in order to find what he or she needs. Equivalent to the library catalogues which contain index cards, meta-information systems or *catalogue systems* are the more general electronic form.

Thesauri

Thesauri are a proven means to provide a uniform and consistent vocabulary for indexing and retrieval of information bearing objects (IBOs (Smith, 1997), such as catalogue entries and addresses) and to supply users with a certain vocabulary for the retrieval of IBOs in such systems. A *thesaurus* is a set of terms selected from a natural language representing the vocabulary of a certain field; it is used for the indexing, saving, and retrieval of IBOs (Wersig, 1985).

Thesaurus terms can be classified by *descriptors* and *non-descriptors*. Descriptors are terms used directly for the indexing and retrieval of objects. Non-descriptors are not used for indexing; they are supplementary entry points for the user, providing a wider range of terms for the retrieval of objects. Information about descriptors, e.g., an explanation of the meaning of a term, can be stored in scope notes. The terms in a thesaurus are related to each other through diverse relationships (DIN 1463/1987, 1987) such as hierarchical relationship, equivalence relationship, and associative relationship.

A *multilingual thesaurus* is a regular thesaurus, with an equivalent term for every descriptor (possibly for non-descriptors as well) in each of the languages covered (DIN 1463, Teil 2, 1993). The advantage of multilingual thesauri is that users do not have to be familiar with a particular language. They can use several languages for the retrieval from an information system, even though terms of just one language were used for indexing. Therefore multilingual thesauri are the basis for multilingual access to IBOs.

CDS

In Europe environmental metadata are stored and managed at different levels, e.g., regional metadata are managed by the environmental ministries of the states, national metadata are managed by federal environment agencies, and metadata of European-wide interest are managed by the EEA. For the latter case, the Catalogue of Data Sources (CDS) was developed.

The CDS is an environmental catalogue system to direct the user towards information about the state of the environment in Europe. It comprises metadata (data about data sources of European interest), addresses, and a multilingual thesaurus, the General European Multilingual Environmental Thesaurus GEMET (CNR, Rome, Umweltbundesamt, Berlin, 1997). The CDS is designed for the collection, management, and dissemination of detailed descriptions of information resources. Currently for the collection and maintenance of metadata mainly a MS Windows based application (WinCDS) is used. WebCDS as presented in this paper is the retrieval tool which allows global access via the Web.

CDS records are classified into several classes (documents, datasets, ...), indexed by subject by using GEMET. The records can be flexibly linked (parent/children relationship) in order to interconnect resources. The CDS will be the complete inventory of official EIONET resources and the starting point for a uniform access to EIONET data.

The data model for the metadata itself is split into three levels:

- The *core level* contains core attributes for European and EEA requirements. Attributes included in the core level are recommended to be used in all national CDS for compatibility reasons. These attributes are the basis for interoperability between environmental catalogues. The attributes are an exact representation of the Global Environment Locator System (GELOS) element set.
- *Level 1* attributes contain core level attributes and additional attributes needed by the EEA.
- *Level 2* attributes contain core level attributes and additional attributes which are defined by national authorities for national CDSs.

The CDS is a focal point for interoperability among environmental data catalogues (Kramer et al., 1997b), because data from national catalogues is used to fill parts of the

CDS. For compatibility with other international metadata standards and with other environmental meta-information systems, the CDS data model draws upon existing international standards like the Global Information Locator Service (GILS).

Java

Java (Gosling et al., 1996) is an object-oriented programming language that has been designed especially to be used on networks of heterogeneous computers (platform independence). Java can be used both stand-alone and in conjunction with the Web. Small Java programs, so-called Applets, are transferred as byte code from a Web server to a browser using HTTP. These Applets are executed by a virtual machine that runs in the browser. Just-in-time compilers improve the performance. The execution model ensures a fairly good degree of security even for Applets that are downloaded across the Internet.

Programs written in Java allow for more elaborate interaction with database systems, basically because they allow to overcome the limitations of the stateless HTT protocol. Hence, the combination of Java and databases is of great importance. Among the various approaches, the most important one is Java Database Connectivity (JDBC) (Hamilton and Cattell, 1996), the open standard for accessing relational database systems using Java. JDBC is an API for database access that is supported by several vendors.

Servlets

In the past there have been different approaches to solve the drawbacks of a CGI-based access to applications through the Web. In most approaches a server-site API is defined, like NSAPI (Netscape, 1996). The advantage of such approaches is usually fairly good performance: it is possible to store states, the re-initialisation overhead for every CGI call can be reduced. In case of a Java-based CGI program, a restart of the virtual machine on every call would be required.

With the first alpha release of the Java Web Server, formerly known as Jeeves, Sun introduced the Java servlet API with the goal to overcome the drawbacks of the CGI approach and to present a Java-based solution (JavaSoft, 1997b). The Servlet API has the potential to become the standard for server-site Java applications, not only because it is developed by Sun, the developer of Java. Many Web server developers have announced, or already implemented the Java servlet API (VPRO, 1997). The most important of them is the W3-Consortium with the Web server Jigsaw (W3C, 1997). Additionally, Sun offers the Java Servlet Development Kit which contains all the pieces necessary for implementing Servlets on other Web servers (JavaSoft, 1997c).

Servlets are Java objects that correspond to a given interface and that extend the functionality of the Web server. They are similar to Applets, inasmuch as they can be downloaded through the net from other servers, but they have no GUI since they are executed on the server site, and the administrator has the possibility to give a servlet full access rights to the local resources.

It is not our intention to describe the Java servlet API in detail and to show the differences to other API approaches, but there are two points in favour of using servlets:
- Portability. Not only the applications written in Java are plattform independent, but also the Web server itself.
- Standard. The Java servlet API is likely to become the de facto-standard for server-site Java applications. Many developers of Web servers announced to support the new API. Hence, we talk about a Web server independent API.

Remote Method Invocation (RMI)

A remote object is an object whose methods can be invoked from objects executed under the control of a different virtual machine. Correspondingly, a remote interface defines the methods of a remote object, and a remote method invocation (RMI) is the action of invoking a remote object. It has the same syntax as the invocation of methods of local objects, i.e., objects of the same virtual machine (JavaSoft, 1997d). The RMI object model was designed following the object model of Java. Nevertheless, the two object models have some differences:

- Clients interact always with the remote interface and never with implementing classes of that interface.
- Non-remote objects are passed by value and remote objects are passed by reference.
- New Exceptions are defined for the remote method invocation.

A reference to the remote object is needed before a remote method can be invoked. A client has two possibilities to get such a reference: Either another method returns the reference, or the object uses the RMI name service. Every remote server object can get registered via the method bind() or rebind() at the RMI name service. Afterward the clients can localize the remote object via the lookup()-method of the name service. The return value is a stub object of the remote server object, which the client object interacts with.

Design Method

This section provides a brief overview about the design methods used for the WebCDS. The main base on which the design relies are so-called design patterns, elements of reusable object-oriented software as described in Gamma et al. (1995). To specify what exactly design patterns are, Gamma uses the definition of the architect Christopher Alexander: "Each pattern describes a problem which occurs over and over again in our environment, and then describes the core of the solution to that problem, in such a way that you can use this solution a million times over, without ever doing it the same way twice" (Gamma et al., 1995).

To make the reuse of design information possible, design patterns are described in a consistent format. This way software designers can easier use and re-use this patterns for

Figure 1: Using the facade pattern

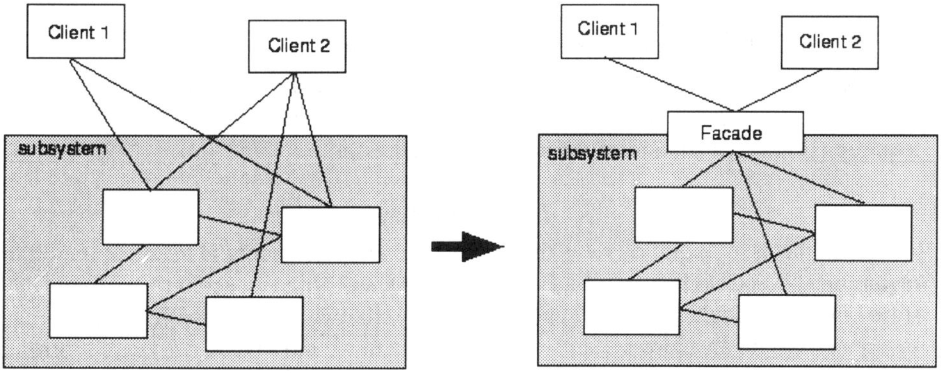

the particular application. Through the design of the WebCDS, three main design patterns have been used: the facade, the strategy, and the abstract factory.

Facade

The intention of a facade is to provide a unified interface to a set of interfaces in a subsystem. We can talk about a higher level interface that makes the subsystem easier to use. Figure 1 shows the main structure of the facade pattern.

This design pattern can be used if you want to provide a simple interface to a complex system, there are many dependencies between clients and the implementation classes of an abstraction, and you want to decouple the subsystem from the clients, or if you want to layer your subsystems. A facade can be used to define an entry point to each subsystem.

The strategy pattern defines a family of algorithms, encapsulates each one, and makes them interchangeable. The pattern can be used if:

- many related classes differ only in their behaviour;
- you need different variants of an algorithm;
- the algorithm uses data that clients should not know about;
- a class defines multiple conditional statements in its operations. Instead of many conditionals move related conditional branches into their own strategy class.

Abstract Factory

The intention of an abstract factory is to provide an interface for creating families of related or dependent objects without specifying their concrete classes. The use of the abstract factory pattern is suggested if:

- a system should be independent of how its products are created, composed and represented;
- a system should be configured with one of multiple families of products;
- a family of related product objects is designed to be used together, and you need to enforce this constraint;
- you want to provide a class library of products, and you want to reveal just interface, not their implementations.

One possible scenario for an abstract factory is the configuration of a system on start-up with one of many possible alternatives. At runtime only one concrete factory is used.

REQUIREMENTS AND APPROACH

The requirements for WebCDS can be grouped into five categories: functionality, multilinguality, portability, extensibility, and of course performance. We describe these requirements in turn and indicate how they are addressed.

Functionality

From the user's point of view, the basic retrieval functionality is the most important requirement WebCDS has to fulfil. For this purpose, and with respect to the different data stored in the catalogue, the catalogue system supports two different search types: a data source search and an address search. For both of them we introduced two search forms: a simple search form and an expert search form. This gives an experienced user the opportunity to refine the search and to add more constraints to the request.

Independent of the selected search form, the user should have the possibility to use terms from a thesaurus which the data sources and addresses are indexed with for the retrieval. For this purpose a search type independent thesaurus search module assists the user in selecting the proper terms. Currently, this HTML-based search module can be reached from every search form. It supports a multilingual thesaurus descriptor search with the possibility of translation and refinement of the terms retrieved. A Java-based general thesaurus module is currently under development.

Multilingual Aspects

The CDS is an European catalogue that will be used all over Europe. Hence, support for multilinguality was one of the major requirements. In contrast to other settings such as local area networks, the Internet is a challenge for multilingual applications because of its global character. Usually, English is used to support access to local data for foreign people. However, this approach is insufficient, if - as in the case of WebCDS - the user should have the opportunity to search data as well in his native language, and especially if the data itself is multilingual as well.

Multilingual GUI

The problem of a multilingual user interface covers two major aspects: First, the search forms and the result pages should be displayed in the language the user has chosen. This implies that all visible fields should be language sensitive. For this purpose we use the resource bundle functionality as suggested by the internationalisation specification for Java (JavaSoft, 1997a). The abstract class ResourceBundle gives us the possibility to build locale sensitive resources. The resource bundle approach gives us the possibility to switch between the different languages, with the special advantage of an easy extensibility of the catalogue system.

The second aspect, which cannot be solved by this approach, is the problem to represent multilingual data. In an ideal case, all data retrieved from the catalogue should be represented also in the language of the user interface. Because this is not possible without translating all data in all languages supported, we decided to support multilingual representations as far as possible. Attributes with restricted sets of values can be translated in all supported languages. In doing so, most information retrieved is represented in the native language of the user.

Multilingual Retrieval

The CDS supports the indexing of data sources and addresses with terms from one or more multilingual thesauri, as described in Section THESAURI. Usually, a new data source will be indexed with terms from one or maximal two languages. This results in two more aspects which should be considered by the catalogue system:

- Users searching for proper thesaurus descriptors and data sources indexed with these descriptors, do not need to know in which languages the data were indexed. Not only should this be transparent to the user, but he or she should also find all indexed data sources, independent of the language selected.

- The thesaurus descriptors associated with a data source or address should be displayed in the native language of the user and not in the language that was initially used for indexing.

Portability

Due to the fact that the WebCDS server will be installed on different plattforms all over Europe one of the basic requirements was to achieve portability. The independence of the operating system was achieved using Java to implement WebCDS. For performance reasons and limited browser support for JDK 1.1, we preferred an HTML-based client instead of a more flexible Java-based one.

Another design aspect was the independence of the Web server. Currently the only real Web server independent standard for accessing applications through the Web is CGI. But CGI has too many severe drawbacks to be the only access method supported. We needed a hybrid approach which overcomes the problems of CGI whenever possible, but still supports it in cases where the Web server does not support other access methods.

Last but not least different installations of the catalogue system may need different underlying DBMS. Most installations of the WebCDS will use Oracle, but while designing the catalogue system we also considered that future installation may want to use other DBMS. The only assumption we could make was that it should be a relational DBMS, which supports the SQL-2 standard.

Extensibility

The catalogue system is a fairly dynamic system. A system like the WebCDS should be adaptable to user demands quite easily. Moreover we had also some additional requirements which should be considered during the first design and implementation phase: altering the schema of the database and even replacing the DBMS itself should be possible; furthermore future releases should be able to support several thesauri simultaneously. In future, WebCDS will be extended to support more languages.

Performance

The choice of Java for the server-site application has many advantages with respect to portability, multilinguality, and distributed computing. As Java is interpreted Java applications are slower than compiled applications. To solve potential performance problems, just-in-time compilers have been introduced, which compile the byte code on the fly, so that the execution is speed up. Java compilers that generate native code have been suggested as well.

In case of accessing a database from the Word Wide Web, two other bottlenecks are even more run-time consuming. Both cannot be influenced by the choice of the programming language - the first is the Web access itself, and the other the database access. The first factor can only be influenced by the amount of data transmitted through the net, which is more or less application- or even query-dependent, and in so far fixed.

The biggest performance optimization can be reached by optimizing the database queries and the overall database access mechanisms. Whenever possible, a user query should result in exactly one database query. The reuse of results should be encouraged. The result set should be cached, so that the user can navigate through them without the need of new database queries, and it should be possible for other users to re-use the results. The optimization of database queries can result in an important performance improvement. We cannot rely on the optimization capabilities of the underlying DBMS, because they change from DBMS to DBMS and there is no single best optimization of a specific application (or query).

RELATED WORK

In this section, we place our work in the context of three approaches that we think are the most closely related ones.

WWW-UDK

The UDK (Umweltdatenkatalog, Environmental Data Catalogue) has been developed and is maintained by a group of several German states, Austria, and Lichtenstein (Schütz and Lessing, 1993; Günther et al., 1996). Its goal is to allow an integrated handling of all environmentally related meta-information allowing a coherent search for heterogeneous, distributed base data. A thesaurus was also developed allowing the consistent indexing of all data items in the database (Batschi, 1994; Lippke and Wagner GmbH, 1995).

Originally, the UDK was used from an application program that mainly runs on PCs. Due to both the decentralized nature and the lack of a connecting network the update cycles for the decentralized updates of different UDK-installations are fairly cumbersome.

Since 1995, online database access to UDK data via Web is available. WWW-UDK (Kramer et al., 1997a) provides a multilingual user interface, which is currently available in English and German on the Internet. However, the thesaurus is available in German only. WWW-UDK links its environmental meta-information to several other information systems like a GIS-viewer and to a legislation information system. WWW-UDK is realized by the use of classical Web technology (Web browsers, HTTP, CGI scripts) and C programs with embedded SQL statements for access and integration of database sources. The approach is service-based, providing several more or less small (independent) services. Nevertheless it is not a simple task to maintain the C programs which comprise several different versions (customized for the different states, running against Oracle and Informix database). A further limitation is that each of the database accesses (required for the dynamic construction of HTML pages) has to perform its own connection to and disconnection from the database via standard CGI.

Search Engines

Web search engines are tools used for the set-up of Web search services (e.g., Alta Vista, Lycos, Infoseek, Magellan, and Yahoo). For this purpose they establish metadata that is being automatically updated continuously by navigating through the Internet. The majority of Web search engines establishes a full text index of the documents. Some, such as Harvest Gatherer (see http://harvest.transarc.com/), furthermore try to make an extract from a technical report such as author, title, abstract or to parse the HTML meta tag which can be followed by arbitrary (metadata) attribute/value pair.

Web search services make several 10 million documents available to probably some 100 million potential users (as of the beginning of 1997). Web search services are an indispensable help when searching for information in the Internet. However, the search engines that are presently used have certain limitations (see also Koch et al., (1996) including the indexing of static HTML documents only (no databases or GIS).

In general, the effort for automated metadata collection or the generating of a full-text index (as done by crawlers, spiders, ...) is much lower, but the quality is worse than the one of metadata collected manually for a catalogue system such as the CDS. Whereas customized thesauri can be used together with some search services, multilingual access is not supported.

Airbase

Airbase is a relational database containing meta-information on air quality monitoring networks and stations, raw air quality data for a selection of stations and a number of components (Sluyter et al., 1997). It is accessible on the Web at http://www.etcaq.rivm.nl/airbase/index.html.

We take the Airbase Web application here as one example of a navigational Web-based metadata information system. The Airbase Web-Application uses metadata to find raw air quality data. Metadata for air quality data are country, network, station and measurement parameter. The user has to give a value for each of these metadata before he may start the search for raw data. As the four types of metadata are not independent from each other (i.e., not all measurement parameters are measured at each station), the user is lead through a sequence of HTML-forms each of which provides one criterion. Depending on the already defined values for the previous criteria, the values that make sense for the next criterion are computed and presented to the user for selection. Using these context-sensitive criteria, the user never produces a combination of attribute values that yields an empty result. On the other hand, several database queries are necessary to get to the raw data, as all of these context-sensitive criteria require a database query. Hence, it is a fairly time-consuming process to achieve results.

The Airbase Web application offers a monolingual user interface (English) while WebCDS is a multilingual application. Moreover, these two differ in their data access strategie. WebCDS users have to fill in all criteria at once and immediately get the metadata result. Users of the Airbase Web application follow a long track and fill in several context-sensitive criteria. At the end, they get the raw data.

ARCHITECTURE

Access Though the WWW

The first problem which has to be solved while designing a Web application is the way the access via the Web is handled. As explained in Section REQUIREMENTS AND APPROACH, we need a hybrid approach to target all requirements of operating system independence and performance. The result is a Web access as shown in Figure 2. By introducing an additional layer between the server and clients, we decouple WebCDS completely from the Web server. In doing so, we are able to access WebCDS via servlets and, if needed, via CGI.

WebCDS was implemented as an RMI server. We chose RMI instead of middleware solutions, such as CORBA, for several reasons. The clients and the server are written entirely in Java, we did not have the need for an intermediate object model and the RMI technology is distributed with the JDK and therefore free of charge. In addition, we avoid the installation and administration of an object request broker (ORB) at every location at which WebCDS is installed. Last but not least, we did not encounter any performance drawbacks.

The central part of the server is the dispatch manager. It implements the RMI inter-face, and decides what to do with the incoming requests. Depending on the request type it dispatches the incoming parameters to the corresponding subsystems. The two indepen-dent subsystems are the ones for the database access and for the HTML-Generation.

Database Access

The subsystem for the database access takes care of the functionality needed for the data retrieval. To hide the complexity of the subsystem from the clients we introduced a DB facade (see also section Facade).

Figure 3 shows the main parts of the subsystem which interact as follows:
*   The DB facade receives the parameters needed for a query.
*   If the result of the query is already cached, it is returned to the client, i.e., to the

Figure 2: *General structure of WebCDS*

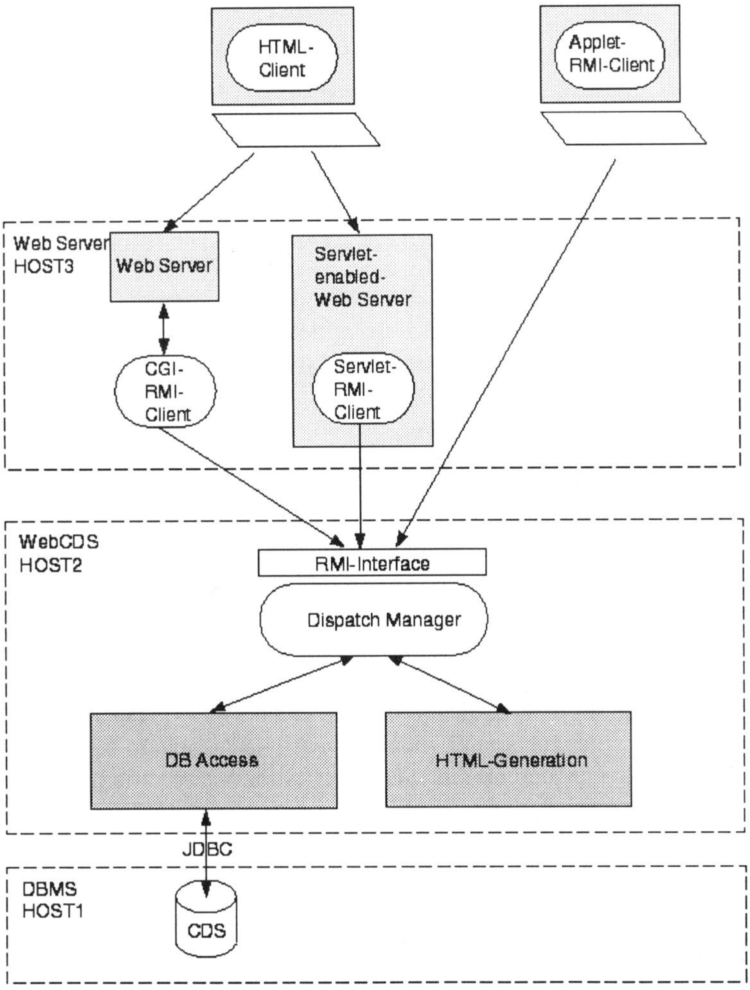

Figure 3: Subsystem for the database access

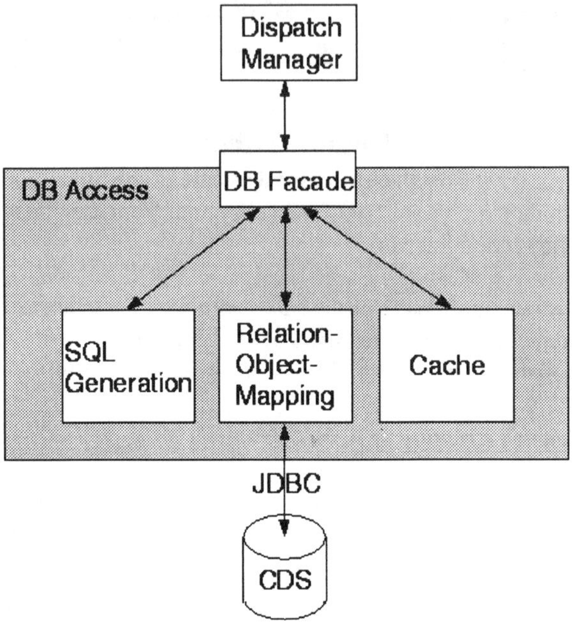

dispatch manager.

- If the result is not cached, the subsystem for the SQL-generation builds a valid SQL statement depending on the type of the request and the value of the parameters.
- The query is transferred via JDBC to the database. The result is mapped to a Java object, so that it can be cached and returned to the caller. For this mapping, we use the ResultVector class developed in a parallel project at FZI, which overcomes some limitations of the standard Java ResultSet class.

The cache is implemented as a Hashtable, which overloads the get() and put() methods to reduce the maximum count of stored objects to a predefined number. This meets our performance requirements for the current version. In future releases, we could easily change the caching mechanisms if needed.

The major part of the database access subsystem takes the subsystem for the generation of the SQL statements. Every type of a query is build in its own class via a createStatement()-method. This corresponds to the strategy pattern as introduced in (Gamma et al., 1995).

To avoid the problems of incompatible SQL dialects of different underlying DBMS, we introduced a kind of strategy factory. On initialization time of the catalogue system, the server decides which set of strategies to use and creates the corresponding strategy objects. This way the catalogue system should be easily adaptable to other DBMS. As an extra effect we could now optimise the SQL-queries for one specific DBMS, and do not have to rely on the optimizer of the DBMS.

User Interface

In the current release of WebCDS, we implemented an HTML-based user interface. Both the search forms and the result pages are generated dynamically on demand. The dynamic parts are the language specific fields and, of course, the database results which are represented in a unique way. The only static HTML page, is the starting page with the language selection.

Figure 4 shows the main structure of the subsystem for the HTML generation. On demand the HTML director decides which kind of HTML page to build, informs the correlating class, and passes it to the language specific values. These are taken from the language resource bundle. In case of a result page the object containing the database result is also needed. All classes implement a create() method in which the instructions for generating the HTML pages are stored. This cycle allows us on demand an easy extension with new classes or an alteration of the existing classes.

Subsystems Integration

The connecting element of the subsystems of the WebCDS server is the dispatch manager. It implements the RMI interface, receives the request from the clients, maps the requests to an internal representation, and dispatches the result to the two subsystems depending on the request type. Currently, only HTML pages are returned from WebCDS. Especially the subsystem for the database access is designed for a future re-use by Java-based clients.

CONCLUSIONS

In this chapter, we presented WebCDS, a catalogue system for European environmental data that takes advantage of most recent Java technology at the server site. We presented the requirements with respect to functionality, multi-linguality, portability, extensibility, flexibility, and performance. Main features of the software architecture developed are support for both the common gateway interface CGI and the Servlet approach at the server-site. The three main components of the architecture are Web access, database access and user interface generation. Design patterns were used throughout the designed process of these components. Since May 1997, several versions of WebCDS have been made available (start at the URL http://www2.mu.niedersachsen.de/system/cds/).

Figure 4: Subsystem for generating HTML pages

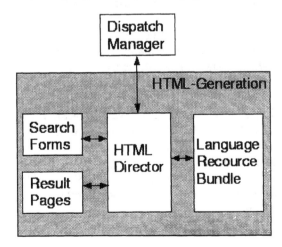

Our current work focuses on incremental improvements based on user feedback and extensions of the functionality. A general Thesaurus module that can be used both stand alone and in conjunction with the EEA CDS and other catalogue systems is designed and implemented as a Java Applet. Based on previous experience, we address the distributed data maintenance of a central catalogue as well by employing Java Applets. Future work will furthermore address the issues of interoperability between the CDS and other catalogue systems (Kramer et al., 1997b) by in-depth analysis and concentration on emerging international standards and related systems.

ACKNOWLEDGMENTS

Prof. Dr. P.C. Lockemann's comments on an earlier version of this chapter and the comments from two of the reviewers are gratefully acknowledged.

REFERENCES

Batschi, W.-D. (1994). Environmental Thesaurus and Classification of the Umweltbundesamt (Federal Environmental Agency), Berlin. In Stancikova, P. and Dahlberg, I., editors, *Environmental Knowledge Organization and Information Management*, pages 57-62. INDEKS Verlag, Frankfurt/Main.

CNR, Rome, Umweltbundesamt, Berlin (1997). Gemet - general european multilingual environment thesaurus. Technical report, European Environment Agency. Version 1.0.

Crossley, D. (1996). Wais through the web - discovering environmental information. http://www.ncsa.uiuc.edu/SDG/IT94/Proceedings/Searching/crossley/paper.ps.

DIN 1463, Teil 2 (1993). DIN 1463: Erstellung und Weiterentwicklung von Thesauri, Teil 2: Mehrsprachige Thesauri.

DIN 1463/1987 (1987). Richtlinien für die Erstellung und Weiterentwicklung von Thesauri. Technical report, Deutsche Industrienorm.

Dr. Lippke und Dr. Wagner GmbH (1995). *Das Thesaurusmodul im UDK*.

Gamma, E., Helm, R., Johnson, R., and Vlissides, J. (1995). *Design Patterns*. Addisson Wesley.

Gosling, J., Joy, B., and Steele, G. (1996). *The Java Language Specification*. Addison-Wesley.

Günther, O., Lessing, H., and Swoboda, W. (1996). UDK: A European Environmental Data Catalogue. In *Third International Conference/Workshop Integrating GIS and Environmental Modeling*, Santa Fe, New Mexico, USA. http://ncgia.ucsb.edu/conf/SANTA_FE_CD-ROM/sf_papers/guenther_oliver/my_paper.html.

Hamilton, G. and Cattell, R. (1996). JDBC: A Java SQL API. Technical report, Sun Microsystems Inc., 2550 Garcia Avenue, Mountain View, CA 94043, U.S.A. URL: ftp://splash.javasoft.com/pub/jdbc.ps.

JavaSoft (1997a). intlspec.doc1.html. http://www.javasoft.com:80/products/jdk/1.1/intl/html/intlspec.doc1.html.

JavaSoft (1997b). Java server documentation. http://jserv.javasoft.com/products/java-server/documentation/index.html.

JavaSoft (1997c). Java servlets. http://java.sun.com/products/java-server/servlets/index.html.

JavaSoft (1997d). Rmi documentation. http://java.sun.com/products/jdk/1.1/docs/guide/rmi/index.html.

Koch, T., Ardö, A., Brümmer, A., and Lundberg, S. (1996). The building and maintenance of robot based internet search services: A review of current indexing and data collection methods. Technical report, Lund University Library, NetLab, Box 3, S-221 00 Lund, Sweden. http://www.ub2.lu.se/desire/radar/reports/D3.11/tot.html.

Kramer, R. (1997). Databases on the Web: Technologies for Federation Architectures and Case Studies. In Peckman, J., editor, *Proc. ACM SIGMOD International Conference on Management of Data*, volume 26(2), pages 503-506. ACM.

Kramer, R., Nikolai, R., Koschel, A., Rolker, C., Lockemann, P., Keitel, A., Legat, R., and Zirm, K. (1997a). WWW-UDK: A Web-based Environmental Metainformation System. *ACM SIGMOD Record*, 26(1):http://www.cs.umd.edu/areas/db/record/issues/9703/index.html.

Kramer, R., Nikolai, R., and Rolker, C. (1996). World Wide Web Access to CDS: Software Design and Demonstration of First Prototype. In *Proc. 3rd Workshop on Catalogue of Data Sources (CDS) and Thesaurus*, pages 81-91, Copenhagen, Denmark. European Environment Agency, ETC/CDS.

Kramer, R., Nikolai, R., Rolker, C., Bjarnason, S., and Jensen, S. (1997b). Interoperability Issues of the European Catalogue of Data Sources (CDS). In *Proceedings of the 2nd IEEE Metadata Conference*.

http://computer.org/conferen/proceed/meta97/papers/rkramer/rkramer.html.

McCool, R. (1994). Common gateway interface overview. Technical report, National Center for Supercomputiong Applications (NCSA), http://hoohoo.ncsa.uiuc.edu/cgi/overview.html.

Netscape (1996). The netscape server api. http://live.netscape.com/newsref/std/server_api.html.

Rowe, J. (1996). *Building Internet Database Servers with CGI*. New Riders Publishing.

Schütz, T. and Lessing, H. (1993). Metainformation von Umwelt-Datenobjekten (UDK Niedersachsen). In Jäschke, A., Kämpke, T., Page, B., and Radermacher, F. J., editors, *Informatik für den Umweltschutz, Proceedings 7. Symposium GI-FA 4.6*, pages 19-28, Berlin Heidelberg. Springer.

Sluyter, R., Mol, W., and Potma, C. (1997). Airbase - background information. http://www.etcaq.rivm.nl/airbase/background.html.

Smith, T. R. (1997). Meta-information in digital libraries. *Journal On Digital Library, Special Issue on Metadata for Digital Libraries*, 1(2):105-107.

VPRO (1997). James homepage. http://james.vpro.nl/.

W3C (1997). Jigsaw overview. http://www.w3.org/pub/WWW/Jigsaw/.

Wersig, G. (1985). *Thesaurus-Leitfaden*. K.G.Saur Verlag KG, München.

CHAPTER 14

Mining Library Catalogues: Best-Match Retrieval Based on Exact-Match Interfaces

J.E. Wolff, University of Bonn, Germany
J. Kalinski, University of Bonn, Germany

The MYVIEW system aims at gathering bibliographic information from heterogeneous distributed Internet repositories like electronic journals and traditional libraries. It maintains a personalized warehouse for bibliographic data in a unified scheme which is locally available for browsing, ad-hoc queries, rearrangements, and analysis. Users should be able to specify their interests in a simple and comfortable way. Building on experiences gained by the information retrieval community, we propose employing sets of weighted terms and best-match retrieval for this purpose. However, many on-line library catalogues provide only a Boolean interface (exact-match retrieval). We have therefore to tackle the problem of mapping a set of weighted terms to an appropriate collection of Boolean queries, considering the restrictions of local warehouse resources and generated net load. In this chapter the mapping problem and optimal solutions are defined in exact terms. We develop two heuristic algorithms for the weighted and unweighted case and discuss some important implementation aspects.

INTRODUCTION

The design and analysis of query languages is at the heart of database research. Expressiveness of database query languages and the relationships between expressiveness and computational complexity are intensively studied by database theorists (Abiteboul et al., 1995), where mostly the logical data model is assumed. On the application side, SQL has been established as a standard for relational databases. In recent years the maintenance of different kinds of objects has increasingly become the focus of the database community. The growing importance of text (digital libraries) and multimedia documents requires a combination of logical/relational query languages with alternative paradigms.

While the handling of information which is distributed across heterogeneous databases has been analyzed in depth (Computing Surveys, 1990), the World Wide Web as a "distributed system" is somewhat different. It consists of a large number of distributed, autonomous information repositories without any global underlying schema, where each information server supports a different query language. Approaches like WebSQL (Lakshmanan and Subramanian, 1996), W3QS (Konopnicki and Shmueli, 1995) and WebLog (Mendelzon et al., 1997) try to query the web analogously to relational/logical databases and accordingly adapt SQL and logical rules, respectively.

In contrast to these approaches, our own work in the context of the MYVIEW[1] system—a database for bibliographic data which is locally available for browsing, ad-hoc queries, rearrangements and analysis - aims at a different direction. The extraction of bibliographic information from Internet sources for loading it into the local database is supported in a user-friendly and simple way, namely by specifying a set of terms defining the individual information need. We thus do not propose another new language for directly querying the web. This approach naturally raises the problem of mapping the intended meaning of a term set on the restricted query capabilities of existing repository interfaces.

Many libraries provide Internet access to their catalogues via a Boolean retrieval interface. A Boolean query describes the relevant documents by a Boolean combination of keywords. Documents about information retrieval or databases can thus be selected by

$$(\textit{information} \lor \textit{retrieval}) \land \textit{database},$$

It is generally accepted that similarity-based (best-match) retrieval is superior to Boolean (exact-match) retrieval. In this case qualifying documents are returned as a list ordered by the degree to what extent a document fits a query. When queries are expressed by a sequence of keywords like

information retrieval database,

the order can, in the most simple case, be given by the number of keywords which occur in a document (known as coordination level match). A survey of more sophisticated ranking schemes can be found in (Harman, 1992).

Although in MYVIEW the user's information need is described by a set of keywords and phrases (which clearly calls for best-match retrieval), traditional libraries usually support only exact-match queries. We will therefore discuss how an information need can be translated into a set of exact-match queries taking into account the limited storage capacity of the local database.

The motivation for personalized bibliographic information systems is given in the next section which also introduces the concepts of information needs and Boolean queries as well as their formal representations. For reasons of space, we sketch only the major features of MYVIEW. The third section presents the unweighted specification of information needs and develops a heuristic algorithm. Furthermore an optimization of the algorithm is given. In the fourth section we describe the general case, where information needs are expressed by weighted terms and present an adapted algorithm. Since the algorithms rely on the use of hit counts of all potential queries, the efficient computation of these result sizes is considered in the fifth section. Some important implementation aspects are presented in section six, followed by an empirical evaluation. Finally, related work is presented and a conclusion is given.

SPECIFYING THE INFORMATION NEED

The MYVIEW System

The quantity of data available on the World Wide Web is continuously increasing. Ironically, this same flood of information that threatens to drown the individual information need also carries with it opportunities for successful working by satisfying personal demands. The key is not to dam the flood, but to filter and manage the flow.

Electronic information must be extracted, sorted and displayed according to user-defined criteria. This also holds for the particular domain of libraries as information repositories. The recent developments in multimedia technology and the growth of the World Wide Web will have profound influence on libraries of the future. Many research projects in the USA (Digital Library Initiative[2]), UK (eLib Project[3]), Germany (Medoc[4]) and other countries have invested in digital library development. Nevertheless, whatever digital libraries will look like and whatever information they will provide in the end, the general problem for the user remains the same: how to query distributed repositories of knowledge efficiently and effectively with regard to their personal information needs.

The vision behind MYVIEW is the realization of a personalized bibliographic database, tailored for its user's information needs with efficient query evaluation and customized result presentation, with ad hoc analysis and sophisticated ranking techniques (e.g. weighted search terms, or selections based on publishing date, for example) and with the integration of both traditional as well as digital documents.

To support these functionalities, a personalized collection of bibliographic data about "documents" is needed. MYVIEW gathers this information from multiple heterogeneous distributed information sources containing bibliographic data such as digital libraries, traditional library catalogues, pure text archives (e.g. FTP Server) and free style WWW pages (e.g. catalogues of publishing houses or electronic journals). We will subsequently call these servers *(bibliographic) data repositories* and the information they provide *(bibliographic) data records* (e.g. title, author, publisher, year).

After gathering bibliographic data the records are transformed into a uniform scheme and stored in a personal database. In the database community this approach has recently become popular as *data warehousing* (Widom, 1995), (Hull and Zhou, 1996). Efficient data retrieval and query post processing on the local warehouse can be realized. The interested reader can find more information about MYVIEW in (Wolff and Kalinski, 1997).

Term Sets vs. Queries

The personalized collection of bibliographic data records provided by MYVIEW is the result of the individual user's specification. Thus the description of the possibly complex information need is of essential significance. Since the local warehouse resources are limited, it seems useful to associate the description of the information need to a thematically restricted work, e.g. a scientific project or an industrial study. Relevant information servers are queried based on the specification, and result sets are stored in the local warehouse.

As the formulation of the specification itself should be user-friendly and simple, we suggest the use of sets of weighted terms. Each term can be a keyword or a keyword phrase. Information needs are typically characterized by some general as well as more specific terms. The weights express the relative importance of the different terms. This design decision was chosen in contrast to a complex query language to avoid the following drawbacks, but see (Chang et al., 1996) for a different approach:

- Learning just another query formalism to express the complex specifications.
- Uncertainty in formulating the vague information need, particularly at the beginning of the work.

Thus, the use of a complex query language not only seems to be problematic but even unsuitable for the specification of a user's information need. In the following we will assume that a set of weighted terms has been given by the user. What remains is to find "good" queries to fill the warehouse accordingly.

Basic Concepts and Notation

We intend to find documents that are relevant with respect to a specific information need and that are distributed on a multitude of Internet servers. Bibliographic data records about relevant documents will be transferred into the local warehouse. When dealing with this problem, two crucial restrictions have to be taken into account:

1. In general, bibliographic data repositories support only exact-match queries.

    If all the repositories supported the same best-match query evaluation, the term set would be submitted as one single query to each of them and their results would be merged (Callan et al., 1995). However, this is the exception. When dealing with traditional libraries, we have to cope with exact-match query processing. The conjunction of the entire information need will yield hardly any records at all, since the probability of getting a hit decreases, the more terms are gathered in a conjunction.

2. The resources, i.e., the storage capacity N of the local warehouse and the acceptable transmission costs, are limited.

    The result of the disjunction of all query terms will contain all available data records, but most certainly exceed any such restriction.

Intuitively speaking, an information need has to be translated into an "appropriate" set of exact-match retrievals which permit the collection of N "best" records. In what follows, we will present optimization criteria which aim at expressing "appropriateness" and "goodness" in formal terms.

An information need is given through a topical circumscription. It is modeled by a set $I = \{t_1,\ldots,t_n\}$ of terms together with a weight function w on I such that $w(t) > 0$ for all terms $t \in I$. There are no logical connectives like $\wedge$ or $\vee$ between these terms.

In general, data repositories will only be capable of evaluating Boolean queries like a b or $b \vee (a \wedge c)$.

Furthermore we prefer to denote a conjunction of terms $t_1 \vee \ldots \vee t_k$ by the set $\{t_1,\ldots,t_k\}$. Every subset $T \subseteq I$ can now be interpreted as a conjunctive query q. We are looking for a set $Q = \{T_1,\ldots,T_m\}$ of conjunctive queries T_i which most adequately expresses a user's information need. The set $\{T_1,\ldots,T_m\}$, where T_i is the set representation of conjunctive query q_i, is interpreted as the query $q_1 \vee \ldots \vee q_m$ (disjunctive normal form).

We consider a fixed data repository R. For a conjunctive query T let $docs_R(T)$ denote the *result set* of T, i.e., the data records qualifying for query T. Let $docs\_count_R(T)$ denote the *hit count*, i.e., the number of records in repository R exactly matching T. The cardinality of set X is denoted by $|X|$ or $card(X)$, its power set by $\wp(X)$. We have $docs\_count_R(T) = |docs_R(T)|$.

Both $docs_R()$ and $docs\_count_R()$ correspond to *concrete* functions offered by the interface of many document repositories.[5] As the Boolean query *true* (represented by $T = \varnothing$ in our framework) is usually not supported by data repositories, we will subsequently always confine our attention to non-empty queries.

UNWEIGHTED INFORMATION NEEDS

Basic Idea

Let us introduce our approach by assuming that information needs are simple sets of *unweighted* terms. This restriction will be lifted in the following section.

Example 1 *For illustration consider the information need I_1 = {animal, brain, cancer}.[6] The Hasse diagram in Figure 1 depicts the power set lattice for I_1.*

As mentioned above, every subset of I_1 can be interpreted as a conjunctive query. Thus the following query sets (amongst others) are possible alternatives for expressing I_1:

- Q_1 = { {b}, {a,b}, {b,c} }
- Q_2 = { {c} }
- Q_3 = { {b}, {a,c} }

We aim at maximizing the number of highly relevant data records that are transferred into the warehouse. A record will be regarded as more relevant than another if it has more terms in common with the information need (known as coordination level match). We thus have a virtual best-match ranking of all data records. An information need has to be translated into a set of exact-match retrievals which permit the collection of the N best matches.

Consider the above example. Query set Q_1 would be a bad choice. Query {b} initiates a transmission of *all* data records concerning the brain topic. Therefore, queries {a,b} as well as {b,c} are wasted efforts. They cannot yield any additional records. Considering query sets Q_2 and Q_3, both will cause the two {a,b,c} records to be transferred. But Q_3 also gets *all* {a,b}, {a,c} and {b,c} records, while Q_2 will miss some of them, namely all {a,b} records.

Figure 1: The lattice of conjunctive queries with accompanying hit counts

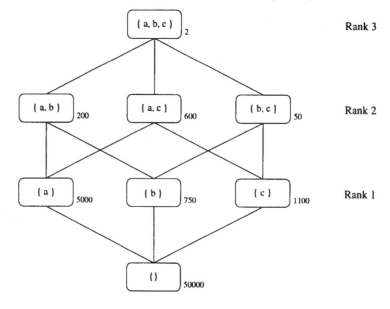

Formalization

In order to formulate our goal more precisely, some formal prerequisites are necessary. The following property mirrors the fact that the data repository implements Boolean retrieval.

Property 1 *For conjunctive queries T and T' the following holds:*

$$\text{docs}_R(\,T\,) \cap \text{docs}_R(\,T'\,) = \text{docs}_R(\,T \cup T'\,)$$

This property implies a useful anti-monotonicity result.

Lemma 2 *If $T \subseteq T'$, then $\text{docs}_R(\,T\,) \supseteq \text{docs}_R(\,T'\,)$.*

Different translations of the information need I will be compared on the basis of their result sets. For this purpose, a query set Q will be characterized by its distribution $D_R(\,Q\,)$ $= (d_1,\dots,d_n)$. It represents the fact that in all of the data records selected by Q there are d_i records which have exactly i terms in common with I.

The formal definition of $D_R(\,Q\,)$ needs some explanation. Consider rank i. The number of documents which have *at least* i terms in common with I is obtained by taking into account every conjunctive query T' with $|\,T'\,| = i$. However note that by Lemma 2 the query set Q may as well select any of these records by containing just a subset of T'. Since for each rank we are interested in the number of documents which have *exactly* i terms in common with I, documents of higher ranks must finally be subtracted (principle of inclusion and exclusion).

Definition 3 *Let $I = \{t_1,\dots,t_n\}$ be an information need, $Q \subseteq \wp(\,I\,)$ a query set and R a data repository. The distribution of Q wrt R is the tuple $D_R(\,Q\,) = (d_1,\dots,d_n)$ where*

$$d_i = \text{card}\left(\bigcup_{\substack{T' \supseteq T \in Q \\ \text{card}(T')=i}} \text{docs}_R(T') - \bigcup_{\substack{T' \supseteq T \in Q \\ \text{card}(T')>i}} \text{docs}_R(T') \right)$$

for $1 \le i \le n$.

Definition 4 *Let I and R as above. Let $Q \subseteq \wp(\,I\,)$ and $Q' \subseteq \wp(\,I\,)$ be query sets with distributions $D_R(\,Q\,) = (d_1,\dots,d_n)$ and $D_R(\,Q'\,) = (d'_1,\dots,d'_n)$, respectively. Query set Q is better than Q', if and only if there is some k such that*

$$d_k > d'_k \quad \text{and} \quad d_i = d'_i \quad \text{for } k < i \le n \text{ (reverse lexicographic order).}$$

Consider the data repository R_1 as illustrated in Figure 1. Every query T is labeled with the value of $\text{docs\_count}_{R1}(\,T\,)$. For example, there are 1,100 documents about cancer, two of them mentioning the animal and brain topic as well. The query sets induce the following distributions (a detailed derivation of these figures is presented below):

$$D_{R1}(\,Q_1\,) = (502, 246, 2),\ D_{R1}(\,Q_2\,) = (452, 646, 2)\ \text{and}$$
$$D_{R1}(\,Q_3\,) = (502, 844, 2).$$

As can be seen Q_3 is the best of these query sets.

We already mentioned that without any resource restrictions the disjunction of all terms of I, i.e., $Q^{opt} = \{\{t_1\},...,\{t_n\}\}$ will be the best translation for I. It consists of the most general queries possible, asking for all records that contain at least one of the terms of I. Its distribution $D_R(Q^{opt}) = (d^{opt}_1,...,d^{opt}_n)$ represents the fact that there are d^{opt}_i records in the repository that have exactly i terms in common with I. Our Example 1 yields $D_{R1}(Q^{opt})$ = (5156, 844, 2).

Proposition 5 *Let I and R as above. Then no query set* $Q \subseteq \wp(I)$ *is better than* Q^{opt}.

Because of resource restrictions we cannot execute the optimal query set. Therefore our goal is to find a query set which is as close as possible to Q^{opt}.

Goal 1 *Given information need* $I = \{t_1,...,t_n\}$ *and resource restriction N, find a query set* $Q \subseteq \wp(I)$ *with distribution* $D_R(Q) = (d_1,...,d_n)$ *such that*
1) $T \not\subset T'$ for all queries $T \neq T'$ in Q,
2) $\Sigma d_i \leq N$, and
3) there is no better query set satisfying conditions (1) and (2).

Condition (1) says that Q should not contain unnecessary queries and condition (2) is the resource restriction.

Example 2 *For repository* R_1 *and resource restriction N = 200 the best query set according to Goal 1 is* $\{\{a,b\}\}$ *with distribution* (0,198,2).

Algorithm *BestLoadUnweighted*

The N best data records could be obtained by a naive top-down traversal of the power set lattice $\wp(I)$. First collect $docs_R(T)$ with $T = I$, then $docs_R(T')$ for every $|T'| = n - 1$, and so on, until the resource limit N has been reached. However note that, as long as the resource limit is not exceeded, every data record of the highest rank n will also be transferred by every query of rank $n - 1$, and so on. In the worst case $2^n - 1$ queries will be submitted to repository R and each of the best records will be transferred $2^n - 1$ times. For larger n, this is hardly acceptable.

We thus propose a top-down procedure which takes into account the subsumption condition (1) of Goal 1. The basic idea of algorithm *BestLoadUnweighted* (see Figure 2) is to initially submit hit counts for every $T \subseteq I$ and to collect potential queries T with $docs\_count_R(T) \neq 0$ together with their hit counts in a pool P (line (1)). After all hit counts have been obtained, the power set lattice is traversed from top to bottom (line (4)) and a set of query candidates Q maintained (lines (8) and (9)).

After a query $T \in P$ is selected, line (6) determines the resources that have been reserved for supersets of T. By the removal of these queries from Q, their resources may be consumed by T. Whenever the resource limit permits the collection of all documents of T (line (7)), T is added to Q. In order to reduce multiple record transmissions, every superset $T' \supset T$ is removed from Q (line (8)). Notice that for the removal to be allowed, *all* of $docs_R(T)$ must fit into the warehouse.

Figure 2: Algorithm BestloadUnweighted

  (1) compute the collection of all hit counts
       $P = \{ (T,c) \mid T \subseteq I, c = \text{docs\_count}_R(T) > 0 \}$
  (2) $Q = \varnothing$
  (3) $L = 0$
  (4) **for** $(k = n; k \geq 1; k = k - 1)$ **do**
  (5)   **for all** $(T,c) \in P$ with $\mid T \mid = k$ (randomly chosen) **do**
  (6) $c_{\text{old}} = \sum_{\substack{(T', c') \in P \text{ with} \\ T' \supset T \text{ and } T' \in Q}} c'$
  (7)   **if** $L + c - c_{\text{old}} \leq N$
  (8) $Q = Q - \{ T' \mid T' \in Q, T' \supset T \}$
  (9) $Q = Q \cup \{T\}$
  (10) $L = L + c - c_{\text{old}}$

It is not hard to see that finding a query set which approaches N as closely as possible includes the Knapsack problem (Horowitz and Sahni, 1978), (Garey and Johnson, 1979). Algorithm *BestLoadUnweighted* therefore randomly chooses single elements of P (line (5)). Other Knapsack algorithms can be used instead. As another simplification the computation of c_{old} in line (6) and its subtraction in line (10) yields an upper bound for resources consumed by Q, because the result sets of different queries need not be disjoint. This impreciseness will be discussed in the next section.

Proposition 6 *Let Q be a query set determined by algorithm* BestLoadUnweighted. *Then Q satisfies conditions (1) and (2) of Goal 1.*

Algorithm *BestLoadUnweighted* constitutes the basis for the considerations in the rest of the paper.

Computation of Qualification Counts

The Algorithm *BestLoadUnweighted* in the previous section uses the hit counts to determine the resources reserved for supersets of a selected query. Since different queries may have overlapping result sets, this computation can only be an estimation of the real set cardinalities. Although the algorithm satisfies conditions (1) and (2) of Goal 1 it can be improved by using a different form of document counting. Let $\text{qual\_count}_R(T)$ denote the *qualification count,* i.e., the number of documents which embody only the terms of the query T and do not contain any other terms of the information need I.

For illustration consider Figure 3 which depicts the data repository R_1 of Example 1 (see Figure 1) together with the cardinalities of all subsets of I_1. Set A contains all documents about the topic animal, B all documents about brain and so on.

Consider, for instance, the computation of $\text{qual\_count}_{R1}(\{b\})$, i.e., we are only interested in the number of documents which *solely* have the topic brain in common with I_1 and nothing more. Then we have to subtract those documents from $\text{docs}_{R1}(\{b\})$ which also mention animal (the set $\{a,b\}$) or cancer (the set $\{b,c\}$) or both (the set $\{a,b,c\}$). Note that by Lemma 2 only documents of rank 2 have to be considered for subtraction (documents of higher ranks are included in these sets). But as both $\{a,b\}$ and $\{b,c\}$ are subsets of

Figure 3: Illustration of data record distribution and corresponding set cardinalities for Example 1

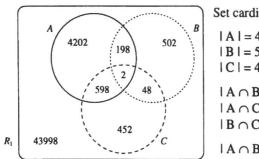

Set cardinalities:

$|A| = 4202 + 198 + 598 + 2 = 5000$
$|B| = 502 + 198 + 48 + 2 = 750$
$|C| = 452 + 598 + 48 + 2 = 1100$

$|A \cap B| = 198 + 2 = 200$
$|A \cap C| = 598 + 2 = 600$
$|B \cap C| = 48 + 2 = 50$

$|A \cap B \cap C| = 2$

$\{a,b,c\}$ the two documents are subtracted twice and a correction term has finally to be added (principle of inclusion and exclusion). By using the hit counts we get

$$\text{qual\_count}_{R_1}(\{b\}) = \underset{\{b\}}{750} - \underset{\{a,b\}}{200} - \underset{\{b,c\}}{50} + \underset{\{a,b,c\}}{2} = 502$$

This idea of deriving the qualification counts from the given hit counts is now formalized.

Definition 7 *Let I, T and R as above. The* qualification count *of T wrt R is the number*

$$\text{qual\_count}_R(T) = \text{card} \left(\text{docs}_R(T) - \underset{t' \in I\text{-}T}{U} \text{docs}_R(\{t'\}) \right)$$

Lemma 8 *For I, T and R as above we have*

$$\text{docs}_R(T) - \underset{t' \in I\text{-}T}{U} \text{docs}_R(\{t'\}) = \text{docs}_R(T) - \underset{T' \supset T}{U} \text{docs}_R(T')$$

Proposition 9 *Let I, T and R as above. The hit count and qualification count are related as follows:*

$$\text{docs\_count}_R(T) = \underset{T' \supseteq T}{\Sigma} \text{qual\_count}_R(T')$$

This proposition can be directly incorporated in an algorithm for computing the qualification counts (see Figure 4). We assume that the pool P of potential queries is given as above (for efficient computation of P see below) and make use of the fact that

$$\text{qual\_count}_R(T) = \text{docs\_count}_R(T) - \underset{T' \supsetneq T}{\Sigma} \text{qual\_count}_R(T')$$

Algorithm *QualificationCount* traverses the power set lattice $\wp(I)$ in a top-down manner, i.e., the subsets are inspected by decreasing set cardinality (lines (3) - (4)). The smaller the sets the more general they are, and thus the more specific queries they subsume (see Lemma 2). In line (5) this superset condition for queries already collected in QC (with higher ranks) is checked and the corresponding values are subtracted. QC finally collects all non-empty queries $T \subseteq I$ together with their qualification counts.

Algorithm *BestLoadUnweighted* can be improved by using qualification counts derived from the given hit counts. As mentioned above the use of c for calculating c_{old} and L yields an upper bound for resources consumed by Q. By using the qualification counts qc instead this inaccuracy can be avoided at the expense of computing QC in advance.

The revised version of *BestLoadUnweighted* is shown in Figure 5.

Computation of Query Set Distributions

In Definition 3 the distribution of a query set Q is defined by using the result sets $docs_R(T)$ of queries $T \in Q$. Since we have no representation of document sets efficiently supporting set operations like union, the definition cannot be directly transformed in an algorithm for efficient computation of distribution values d_i. However, the results of the previous section can be used to carry this out.

Algorithm *QualificationCount* was presented for computing the set QC. Given these qualification counts, the d_k of the distribution of a query set Q can easily be computed by adding the values of

1. all queries in Q with rank k and
2. all supersets with rank k of queries in Q

Figure 4: Algorithm QualificationCount

(1) compute the collection of all hit counts
$$P = \{\ (T,c)\ \mid\ T \subseteq I,\ c = docs\_count_R(T) > 0\}$$
(2) $QC = \{(I, docs\_count_R(I\ ))\}$
(3) **for** $(k = n - 1; k \geq 1; k = k - 1)$ **do**
(4) **for all** $(T,c) \in P$ with $|T| = k$ **do**
(5) $\quad qc\ =\ c\ -\ \displaystyle\sum_{\substack{(T',\,qc')\,\in\,QC \\ \text{with } T' \supset T}} qc'$
(6) $\quad QC = QC \cup \{(T,qc)\}$

Figure 5: Algorithm BestLoadUnweighted *revised*

(1) compute the collection of all hit counts P
and all qualification counts QC
(2) $Q = \varnothing$
(3) $L = 0$
(4) **for** $(k = n;\ k \geq 1;\ k = k - 1)$ **do**
(5) **for all** $(T,qc) \in QC$ with $|T| = k$ (randomly chosen) **do**
(6) **if** $L + qc \leq N$
(7) $\quad Q = Q - \{\ T'\ \mid\ T' \in Q, T' \supset T\ \}$
(8) $\quad Q = Q \cup \{T\}$
(9) $\quad L = L + qc$

as shown in algorithm *CalcDistribution* (see Figure 6).

For illustration, let us consider query set $Q_3 = \{\ \{b\}, \{a,c\}\ \}$ from Example 1. For $k = 1$ we can always look up the values in QC directly. Thus $d_1 = 502$. For $k = 2$ we have to add the value of $\{a,c\} \in Q_3$ and the values of $\{a,b\}$ and $\{b,c\}$. The two last queries are supersets of $\{b\} \in Q_3$:

$$d_2 = 598 + 198 + 48 = 844.$$

Finally, the value of d_3 can be looked up in QC again without any further additions. Thus the query set Q_3 induces the distribution $D_R(Q_3) = (502, 844, 2)$.

WEIGHTED INFORMATION NEEDS

Basic Concepts

We now return to the general case, where information needs are expressed by weighted terms.[8] An information need is thus modeled by a set I of terms in combination with a weight function w on I.

Example 3 *For illustration consider the term set I_1 with weight function w_1 defined as follows:*

$$w_1(\ animal\ ) = 2,\ \ w_1(\ brain\ ) = 4\ \ and\ \ w_1(\ cancer\ ) = 8.$$

In the unweighted case the relevance of a document was measured by the number of search terms it contains. Instead of simply counting the number of terms, we will now have to take the term weights into account.

Consider two documents d_1 and d_2. Let us assume that they have *exactly* the terms of T_1 and T_2, respectively, in common with I. Then d_1 will be more relevant than d_2, if

$$\sum_{t \in T_1} w(t)\ \ >\ \ \sum_{t \in T_2} w(t)$$

This once again permits the definition of a ranking of documents.

Definition 10 *Let I be an information need with weight function w and $T \subseteq I$ a query. The* query weight *is given by*

Figure 6: Algorithm CalcDistribution

    (1)   compute the collection of all hit counts P
           and all qualification counts QC
    (2)   **for** $(k = 1;\ k \leq n;\ k = k + 1)$ **do**
    (3) $d_k\ \ =\ \ \displaystyle\sum_{\substack{(T',\ qc') \in QC\ \text{with} \\ |T'| = k\ \text{and}\ T' \supseteq T \in Q}} qc'$

$$w(T) := \sum_{t \in T} w(t)$$

The different possible ranks are now given by the different possible weights:

$$W = \{ \sum_{t \in T} w(t) \mid T \subseteq I, T \neq 0 \}$$

If $W = \{r_1, \ldots, r_m\}$, then there are m different possible ranks for documents.

Example 4 *For I_1 with w_1 there are seven possible query weights, namely*
$w_1(\{a\}) = 2 \ < \ w_1(\{b\}) = 4 \ < \ w_1(\{a,b\}) = 6 \ <$
$w_1(\{c\}) = 8 \ < \ w_1(\{a,c\}) = 10 \ < \ w_1(\{b,c\}) = 12 \ <$
$w_1(\{a,b,c\}) = 14.$
A document in which only c occurs will thus be more relevant than a document with a and b.

Definition 11 *Let R, I, w and W be as above and $Q \subseteq \wp(I)$ a query set. If $W = \{r_1, \ldots, r_m\}$ with $r_1 < \ldots < r_m$, then the distribution of Q wrt R and w is the tuple $D_{R,w}(Q) = (d_1, \ldots, d_m)$ where*

$$d_i = \mathrm{card} \ (\bigcup_{\substack{T' \supseteq T \in Q \\ w(T') = w_i}} docs_R(\{T'\}) \ - \ \bigcup_{\substack{T' \supseteq T \in Q \\ w(T') > w_i}} docs_R(T') \ )$$

for $1 \leq i \leq m$.

Definition 4, Proposition 5 and Goal 1 can now be adapted for weighted information needs using $D_{R,w}(Q)$. Notice that if all the terms are assigned equal weight, say w_0, one obtains

$$W = \{ kw_0 \mid 1 \leq k \leq n \}$$

such that there are n possible ranks, and that the approach collapses to the unweighted case.

Example 5 *For repository R_1, weight function w_1 and resource restriction $N = 200$ the best query set according to Goal 1 properly adapted is $\{ \{b,c\} \}$ with distribution $(0,0,0,0,0,48,2)$. Query set $\{ \{a,b\} \}$ has a worse distribution namely $(0,0,198,0,0,0,2)$.*

Algorithm *BestLoad*
The idea of algorithm *BestLoadUnweighted* is to visit queries which select highly ranked documents first, and then descend with respect to the ranks. When information needs are unweighted term sets, ranks correspond to the cardinalities of queries. Visiting query nodes of the power set lattice in decreasing rank ordering could thus be reduced to a top-down traversal of the lattice.

This will no longer be true, when information needs consist of weighted terms. Query T may have smaller cardinality than query T', but still select more relevant documents, when $w(T) > w(T')$ (see Example 4).

Visiting queries in decreasing rank now requires making the ranking explicit in the algorithm. We thus iterate through the pool QC, ordered by decreasing rank (line (5) of Figure 7). Note that if the weight function is constant ($w(t) = w_0$ for all $t \in I$), the algorithm once again realizes a top-down traversal of the power set lattice.

COMPUTATION OF HIT COUNTS

In order to compute all hit counts in line (1) of the two *BestLoad* algorithms, it is not actually necessary to submit count queries $\text{docs\_count}_R(T)$ for each of the $2^n - 1$ non-empty subsets of $T \subseteq I$.

Corollary 12 *If* $\text{docs}_R(T) = \varnothing$*, then* $\text{docs}_R(T') = \varnothing$ *for every* $T' \supseteq T$*.*

This corollary can be incorporated in a bottom-up computation of hit counts for potential queries P as follows (see Figure 8 which is to replace line (1) of Figure 2 and Figure 7).

In algorithm *HitCount* all queries T with non-empty hit count and cardinality $k - 1$ are gathered in C. When inspecting rank k in the next iteration (lines (8) - (15)), new query candidates are generated from this pool. A query T' with $|T'| = k$ can only have a non-zero hit count, when all its subsets of cardinality $k - 1$ are in C (line (9)). Only for these T' hit counts will be submitted to R (line (12)).[9]

We expect that information needs can be rather large such that only a few terms will actually co-occur in data records and the bottom-up computation of hit counts will then significantly prunes the power set lattice.

IMPLEMENTATION ASPECTS

The pseudo-code algorithms presented above rely on efficient operations on set collections. Sets of queries Q and of query candidates C and C' are all collections of sets of terms. We will now briefly describe which data structures efficiently support the needed operations.

For $I = \{t_1, \ldots, t_n\}$ let every subset $T \subseteq I$ be represented by a bit vector denoted by

Figure 7: Algoritm BestLoad

(1)	compute the collection of all hit counts P and all qualification counts QC
(2)	sort QC by decreasing $w(T)$
(3)	$Q = \varnothing$
(4)	$L = 0$
(5)	**for all** $(T, qc) \in QC$ (decreasing $w(T)$) **do**
(6)	**if** $L + qc \leq N$
(7)	$Q = Q - \{T' \mid T' \in Q, T' \supset T\}$
(8)	$Q = Q \cup \{T\}$
(9)	$L = L + qc$

Figure 8: Algorithm HitCount

(1) $P = \varnothing$
(2) $C = \varnothing$
(3)   **for all** $t \in I$ **do**
(4) $c = \text{docs\_count}_R(t)$
(5)   **if** $c \neq 0$
(6) $P = P \cup \{(\{t\}, c)\}$
(7) $C = C \cup \{\{t\}\}$
(8)   **for** $(k = 2; k \leq n; k = k + 1)$ **do**
(9) $C' = \{ T' \mid T' \subseteq I,\ |T'| = k,\ C \text{ contains}$
                    $\text{all } k \text{ subsets } T \subset T' \text{ with } |T| = k - 1 \}$
(10) $C = \varnothing$
(11)   **for all** $T' \in C'$ **do**
(12) $c' = \text{docs\_count}_R(T')$
(13)   **if** $c' \neq 0$
(14) $P = P \cup \{(T', c')\}$
(15) $C = C \cup \{T'\}$

rep$(T) := (b_1 \ldots b_n) = \boldsymbol{b}$. In this vector bit $b_i = 1$, if and only if $t_i \in T$. Subset checking, set union and intersection can then be reduced to bitwise operations.

A collection of queries like Q is represented by the trie of bit vectors rep(T) for all $T \in Q$. Remember that a trie is a digital search tree where at every inner node branching is determined by the single bits of the vectors: At the first level we branch to the left, if $b_1 = 0$ (FALSE), and to the right, if $b_1 = 1$ (TRUE); at the second level we branch according to b_2 and so on. The complete bit vectors are stored in the external nodes. For more details the reader may consult a text book about data structures (e.g. (Sedgewick, 1989)), where he or she can also find optimized variations like Patricia tries.

Example 6 *The trie for the query set* $\{ \{a,h\}, \{b,d\}, \{b,e\}, \{d,e\}, \{d,h\} \}$ *is depicted in Figure 9.*

Tries offer efficient support for bit vector search and prefix search:

- Searching a bit vector $\boldsymbol{b} = (b_1 \ldots b_m)$ amounts to descending the trie, thereby branching according to the bits of $\boldsymbol{b}$.
- Following the branches according to $\boldsymbol{b}$ we might end up in an inner node K. Then the subtrie rooted in K contains all bit vectors $c = (c_1 \ldots c_n)$ with $n \geq m$ which have $\boldsymbol{b}$ as a prefix (i.e., $b_i = c_i$ for $1 \leq i \leq m$).

In our application we sometimes iterate sequentially through all members of a given trie. For such cases it would be useful to additionally maintain the external nodes in a doubly-linked list.

Example 7 *Considering the trie of Figure 9 prefix search for* (01) *yields the bit vectors* (01001000) *and* (01010000). *This prefix iteration can be interpreted as a search for all sets of the trie which do not contain a but do contain b. It therefore yields the sets* $\{b,e\}$ *and* $\{b,d\}$.

Figure 9: The trie for Example 6

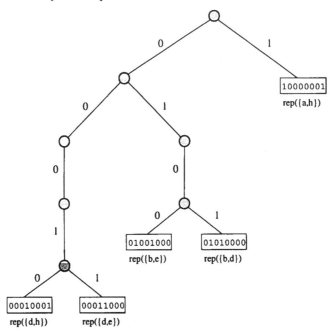

A critical step in algorithm *HitCount* (see Figure 8) is the generation of the set C' of query candidates. The solution to this problem is based on an observation which we will first illustrate by means of an example.

Example 8 *Let us assume that the trie of Figure 9 represents the set C of all queries with exactly two query terms and non-zero hit count. Furthermore assume that for $k = 3$ we have $\{b,d,e\} \in C'$. By definition C must contain every $T' \subset \{b,d,e\}$ with $|T'| = 2$, especially the sets $\{b,d\}$ and $\{d,e\}$ where the last or the first term respectively is missing.*

In general, if $\{t_1,\dots,t_k\} \in C'$, then both $\{t_1,\dots,t_{k-1}\}$ and $\{t_2,\dots,t_k\}$ must be in C. This necessary condition can be used in reverse direction for generating possible members of C' from C: We have to search for two sets like $\{t_1,\dots,t_{k-1}\}$ and $\{t_2,\dots,t_k\}$. Their union is a possible member of C'. It is a member of C', if all the other subsets with cardinality $k - 1$ are in C as well.

When term sets are represented by bit vectors, the preceding observation reads as follows.

Observation 13 *If $T' \in C'$ with $|T'| = k$, then there must be two sets T_1 and T_2 in C such that the following holds:*

1. *rep(T_1) and rep(T_2) each have exactly $k - 1$ TRUE bits.*
2. *rep(T_1) is identical to rep(T') from the first bit up to the $(k - 1)$th TRUE bit, with trailing 0s.*
3. *rep(T_2) is identical to rep(T') from the second TRUE bit up to the last bit, with leading 0s.*

Note that rep(T') = rep(T_1) $\vee$ rep(T_2). It can be shown that the collection of all such pairs T_1 and T_2 can be generated by means of trie operations (Wolff and Kalinski, 1997). It then remains to be tested whether all the other subsets of the new set are in C.

EMPIRICAL EVALUATION

The empirical evaluation analyzes the feasibility of the *BestLoad* algorithms. We will in particular consider how many hit counts must be submitted under realistic circumstances and to what extent algorithm *HitCount* achieves an optimization.

Our tests are based on library data records (taken from (Balownew et al., 1997)) in combination with 5 artificial information needs which we have obtained by grouping thematically related librarians' queries. The information needs consist of 11, 13, 15, 15, and 18 terms. The largest queries that can be constructed as their subsets having non-empty result sets are comprised of 5, 6, 6, 7, and 6 terms.

Let us first analyze to what extent algorithm *HitCount* saves hit count submissions. Column A of Table 1 contains the minimal number of submissions that have to be made under a bottom-up construction of pool P. In Column B we find the number of submissions made by algorithm *HitCount*.

Column C shows the minimum number of count requests that have to be sent to the repository for one-term and two-term queries only. The crucial point is that, on the basis of *all* one-term queries and at least *one* two-term query, the hit counts for the larger queries can be estimated and thus be computed by the MYVIEW system. To see how this can be done, let S denote the size of the data repository, and let c_1 and c_2 denote the hit counts of two one-term queries T_1 and T_2 generated from a given information need. The relative hit counts c_1/S and c_2/S represent the probability that an arbitrarily chosen data record qualifies for T_1 and T_2, respectively. Let c_{12} denote the two-term query $T_{12} = T_1 \cup T_2$. The relative hit count c_{12}/S represents the probability that a data record qualifies for T_{12}. If we make the simplistic assumption that term occurrences are independent (as it is often made, but debatable, of course), then

$$c_{12}/S = c_1/S \cdot c_2/S$$

which implies $S = c_1 \cdot c_2/c_{12}$ as an estimation for S.

What is needed to estimate S is at least *one* two-term query. In our test, however, we computed for every information need this estimation for *each* term pair and used the average S_{avg} of these estimations for further calculations. For every query $\{t_1,...,t_k\}$ with more

Table 1: Hit count submissions

Information need	A	B	C
1	1,023	94	≥ 12
2	5.382	333	≥ 14
3	16,383	489	≥ 16
4	16,383	585	≥ 16
5	31,179	302	≥ 19

than two terms ($k > 2$) the independency assumption yields

$$c_{1...k}/S = c_1/S \cdot ... \cdot c_k/S$$

As the values for $c_1,...,c_k$ are already known, $c_{1...k}$ can be estimated using S_{avg} for S. These estimated values replace the exact hit count values in algorithm *HitCount*.

For every information need let $Q_{i,\text{Exact}}$ denote the set of all queries on rank i that have non-empty result sets and $Q_{i,\text{Est.}}$ the set of all queries on rank i that have an estimated non-zero hit count. Table 2 shows for every information need and for every rank i, how many queries are in $Q_{i,\text{Exact}}$ and $Q_{i,\text{Est}}$. The most significant measure is the cardinality of the intersection $Q_{i,\cap} := Q_{i,\text{Exact}} \cap Q_{i,\text{Est.}}$, because it reveals the correctness of the *BestLoad* algorithms when working with estimated values. Each last column contains this number of queries with an estimated non-zero hit count that in fact have a non-empty result set.

The tests are encouraging in so far as they demonstrate that algorithm *HitCount* is a significant improvement on the basic algorithm (Table 1). Our interpretation of the results depicted in Table 2 is that in cases where algorithm *HitCount* requires too many count submissions, estimated values are an adequate basis for the *BestLoad* algorithms.

RELATED WORK

In (Chang et al., 1996) a translation problem is studied which is in some way similar to ours. While we are discussing the gap between information needs as term sets and Boolean queries, the cited paper concentrates on exact-match queries in "rich" Boolean lan-

Table 2: Exact vs. estimated hit counts

Information need 1

Rank	$|Q_{i,\text{Exact}}|$	$|Q_{i,\text{Est.}}|$	$|Q_{i,\cap}|$
3	35	50	31
4	13	18	10
5	2	0	0

Information need 2

Rank	$|Q_{i,\text{Exact}}|$	$|Q_{i,\text{Est.}}|$	$|Q_{i,\cap}|$
3	107	125	93
4	104	115	88
5	46	57	36
6	7	10	2

Information need 3

Rank	$|Q_{i,\text{Exact}}|$	$|Q_{i,\text{Est.}}|$	$|Q_{i,\cap}|$
3	169	191	140
4	160	136	107
5	58	24	22
6	7	0	0

Information need 4

Rank	$|Q_{i,\text{Exact}}|$	$|Q_{i,\text{Est.}}|$	$|Q_{i,\cap}|$
3	187	193	147
4	185	107	72
5	87	8	5
6	22	0	0
7	3	0	0

Information need 5

Rank	$|Q_{i,\text{Exact}}|$	$|Q_{i,\text{Est.}}|$	$|Q_{i,\cap}|$
3	119	142	82
4	64	49	30
5	12	0	0
6	1	0	0

guages. Besides the logical connectives (AND, OR, NOT), library systems sometimes provide extensions like proximity operators, for example. Even mappings from one Boolean dialect into another are becoming non-trivial under these circumstances.

Voorhees (Voorhees, 1995) examines how to merge ranked retrieval results from multiple independent repositories with different ranking schemes into a single result set. In our terms the so-called collection fusion problem can be stated as follows: Given an information need, data repositories $R_1,...,R_r$ and a resource restriction N, how many documents should be transferred from each R_i in order to maximize the total number of relevant documents received?

Blair describes an approach where a set of weighted query terms entered by the user is automatically converted into a set of conjunctive Boolean queries (Blair, 1984). The use of weights is to reflect how successful the user believes them to be in the search as index terms. So conjunctive queries containing few search terms are preferred to those containing many, because the more terms that are included, the lower is the probability of getting a result. Therefore queries are considered in ascending cardinality, and when their hit count does not exceed a given threshold, they are accepted. Using our terminology, Blair performs a bottom-up traversal of the power set lattice. As can be seen, his use of weights is significantly different from ours. We do not expect that the user estimates the suitability of a term for searching, but that he describes the relevance of the terms among one another.

In Wolff and Kalinski (1997) we discuss a different algorithm (*FastLoad*) for the unweighted approach. Its purpose is to avoid the two disadvantages of the *BestLoad* algorithms. In the worst case the number of queries in Q is exponential in n, and a term t may be completely ignored in Q. *FastLoad* instead reduces the number of queries to n and tries to construct a query set whose storage costs are uniformly distributed among the terms of I.

A system which aims at integrating distributed Internet resources and uses word-frequency information is *GlOSS* (Gravano et al., 1993). It focuses on the identification of relevant text databases for a given query and uses the word frequencies to estimate the result sizes of the query. This estimation is comparable to the one we used in our empirical evaluation. The hard problem of modeling a user's information need is not tackled in *GlOSS*.

The Harvest system (Bowman et al., 1994), (Hardy et al., 1996) is an integrated set of customizable tools for gathering information from diverse Internet repositories and their subsequent effective use. The architecture enables the construction of topic-specific content indexes, but the definition of a personalized view is not directly supported. Furthermore some types of information repositories cannot be handled, such as e.g. traditional library catalogues.

CONCLUSION AND FUTURE WORK

In the context of our MYVIEW system, we assume that all document repositories support a Boolean query language. Boolean query interfaces are in fact the workhorse of many commercial and high-performance applications like on-line library catalogues. At the same time we assume that the transparent user interface permits the specification of the user's information need by a set of keywords. We analyze how best-match information needs can be expressed by means of Boolean queries.

The idea of the approach which we have presented is to maximize the number of highly relevant data records that are transferred into the warehouse with resource restriction N. To avoid redundant record transmissions, hit counts are submitted to construct an appropriate query set. An optimization for the computation of hit counts is also given.

Depending on the use of term weights, different relevance measures are used (unweighted case: coordination level match, weighted case: highest weight) which are incorporated in the corresponding algorithms. The realization of the required set operations is efficiently supported by bit vector encoding and the use of tries.

In this chapter, optimal translations of information needs into Boolean queries are defined and two solutions for the weighted and unweighted case are presented. The practical usage strongly depends on the number of terms and actual retrieval costs. A detailed consideration of these aspects is beyond the scope of the present study. We have established a general framework for finding "good" queries.

ENDNOTES

[1] The MYVIEW project is a joint research proposal of Prof. A.B. Cremers and Prof. R. Manthey.

[2] http://dli.grainger.uiuc.edu/national.htm

[3] http://www.ukoln.ac.uk/services/elib/

[4] http://medoc.informatik.tu-muenchen.de/

[5] Consider, for instance, the Z39.50 protocol (NISO, 1995) which is widely used by libraries and catalogue centers for supporting information retrieval services. Although many functionalities are defined in this standard, only a few are actually provided by every Z39.50 server, typically linking query terms by Boolean operators and counting the result size of a query.

[6] The single terms will subsequently be abbreviated by their initial letters.

[7] To simplify matters we compute the hit counts for all $T \subseteq I$ in advance instead of separately ranking by rank during the top-down traversal. This results in some wasted computation, but since an improvement of this step will be presented later in this paper, this has no significance at this point.

[8] Remember that we are considering data repositories implementing Boolean retrieval, so Property 1 and Lemma 2 still hold.

[9] Let us mention that this idea has also been used in the mining of association rules (Agrawal et al., 1993). Line (8) can be strengthed as follows:

(8') **for** ($k=2$; $k \leq n$ and $k \leq |C|$; $k=k+1$) **do**

REFERENCES

ACM Computing Surveys (1990). *ACM Computing Surveys,* Special Issue on Heterogeneous Databases, Vol. 22, No. 3.

Abiteboul, S., Hull, R., and Vianu, V. (1995). *Foundations of Databases.* Addison-Wesley.

Agrawal, R., Imielinski, T., and Swami, A. (1993). Mining association rules between sets of items in large databases. In *Proc. of the 1993 ACM SIGMOD Int. Conference on Management of Data*, pages 207-216.

Balownew, O., Bode, T., Cremers, A. B., Kalinski, J., Wolff, J. E., Rottmann, H. (1997). A Library Application on Top of an RDBMS: Performance Aspects. In *Proc. of the 8th Int. Conference and Workshop on Database and Expert Systems Applications*, pages 488-497.

Blair, D. C. (1984). The data-document distinction in information retrieval. *Communications of the ACM*, 27(4):369-374.

Bowman, C. M., Danzig, P. B., Hardy, D. R., Manber, U., Schwartz, M. F., and Wessels, D. P. (1994). Harvest: A Scalable, Customizable Discovery and Access System. Technical Report CU-CS-732-94, University of Colorado - Boulder.

Callan, J. P., Lu, Z., and Croft, B. W. (1995). Searching distributed collections with inference networks. In *Proc. of the 18th Int. ACM SIGIR Conf. on Research and Development in Information Retrieval*, pages 21-28.

Chang, K. C.-C., García-Molina, H., and Paepcke, A. (1996). Boolean query mapping across heterogeneous information sources. *IEEE Transactions on Knowledge and Data Engineering*, 8(4):515-521.

Garey, M. R. and Johnson, D. S. (1990). *Computers and Intractability - A Guide to the Theory of NP-Completeness*. W.H. Freeman and Company.

Gravano, L., García-Molina, H., and Tomasic, A. (1993). The efficacy of GlOSS for the text database discovery problem. Technical Report STAN-CS-TN-93-2, Stanford University.

Hardy, D. R., Schwartz, M. F., and Wessels, D. (1996). *Harvest User's Manual*. University of Colorado. Version 1.4 patchlevel 2.

Harman, D. (1992). Ranking algorithms. In Frakes, W. B. and Baeza-Yates, R., editors, *Information Retrieval - Data Structures & Algorithms*, chapter 14, pages 363-392. Prentice Hall, Englewood Cliffs, New Jersey.

Horowitz, E. and Sahni, S. (1978). *Fundamentals of Computer Algorithms*. Computer Science Press.

Hull, R. and Zhou, G. (1996). A framework for supporting data integration using the materialized and virtual approaches. In *Proc. of the 1996 ACM SIGMOD Int. Conference on Management of Data*, pages 481-492.

Konopnicki, D. and Shmueli, O. (1995). W3QS: A Query System for the World-Wide Web. In *Proc. of the 21th Int. Conference on Very Large Data Bases (VLDB)*, pages 54-64.

Lakshmanan, L. and Subramanian, I. (1996). A Declarative Language for Querying and Restructuring the World-Wide-Web. In *Proc. of the 6th Int. Workshop on Research Issues in Data Engineering, RIDE'96*. In conjunction with ICDE'96.

Mendelzon, A., Mihaila, G., and Milo, T. (1997). Querying the World Wide Web. *Int. Journal on Digital Libraries*, 1(1):54-67.

National Information Standards Organization (1995). Information Retrieval (Z39.50): Application Service Definition and Protocol Specification. NISO Press.

Sedgewick, R. (1989). *Algorithms*. Addison-Wesley, 2nd edition.

Voorhees, E. M. (1995). Siemens TREC-4 Report: Further Experiments with Database Merging. In *Proc. of the 1995 Text Retrieval Conference (TREC4)*.

Widom, J. (1995). Research problems in data warehousing. In *Proc. of the 4th International Conference on Information and Knowledge Management*.

Wolff, J. and Kalinski, J. (1997). The MYVIEW System: Tackling the Interface Problem. Technical Report IAI-TR-97-5, Institute of Computer Science III, University of Bonn, Roemerstr. 164, D-53117 Bonn, Germany.

About the Authors

Sena (Nural) Arpinar is a Ph. D. candidate at the Computer Engineering Department of the Middle East Technical University. Currently she is working on advanced agent architectures for electronic commerce. She can be reached at nural@srdc.metu.edu.tr.

Nauman Chaudhry received his B.Sc. (E.E.) degree from The University of Engineering and Technology, Lahore, Pakistan, in 1991, and his M.S.E. degree in Computer Science & Engineering from The University of Michigan, Ann Arbor, in 1994. He is currently a Ph.D. candidate at the Software Systems Research Laboratory at The University of Michigan. His doctoral research has been focussed on extending database technology for manufacturing and control applications. His research interests include object-oriented and active databases, data models for imprecise data, work-flow and manufacturing process automation.

Ahmet Cosar was born in Turkey, in 1965. He recieved his B.S. in Computer Engineering from the Computer Engineering Department in METU, Ankara, M.S. in Computer and Informatics from Bilkent University, Ankara, and PhD degree from the University of Minnesota in 1996. His research interests are Databases, Query Processing and Optimization, Wide Area Networking, and Parallel Processing.

Asuman Dogac is a professor and the director of Software Research & Development Center at the Computer Engineering Department at the Middle East Technical University, Ankara, Turkey. Her current research interests includes electronic commerce, workflow systems and distributed object computing. She can be reached at asuman@srdc.metu.edu.tr.

Ilker Durusoy is a Ph. D. candidate at the Computer Engineering Department of the Middle East Technical University. Currently he is working on an electronic market architecture. He can be reached at ilker@srdc.metu.edu.tr.

Farshad Fotouhi received his B.S. in 1981 and M.S. in 1982, both from Western Michigan University and Ph.D. in computer science from Michigan State University in 1988. His research interests include, database management systems: Multimedia/Hypermedia information systems and Data Warehousing. Dr. Fotouhi has published over 50 technical papers in related database journals and conferences. He has also given seminars on topics such as Object-Oriented databases, Object-Oriented Analysis and Design, and Distributed Databases to local industries as well as professional organizations. Dr. Fotouhi is currently a member of the Editorial Board of the Journal of Database Management and a member of ACM and IEEE Computer Society.

Hans Fritschi received his Diploma (Masters) in Economics with specialization in Computer Science from the University of Zurich in 1994. He is PhD student and research assistant in the Database Technology Research Group at the University of Zurich. There he is involved in the FRAMBOISE research project. His research interests include object-oriented and active database management systems as well as database construction.

Stella Gatziu received her Bachelor degree in Mathematics from the University in Athens in 1985 and her diploma (Masters) in Mathematics with a specialization in Computer Science from the University of Zurich in 1989. In 1994 she received her Ph.D. in Computer Science from the University of Zurich. Since 1995 Stella is a senior research associate in the Database Technology Research Group at the University of Zurich. Stella is also an external lecturer for databases at the Lichtenstein School of

Engineering and at the Luzern School of Engineering. Her current research interests include object-oriented and active database systems, workflow management systems and data warehousing.

Andreas Geppert received a diploma in Computer Science from the University of Karlsruhe in 1989 and a PhD in Computer Science from the University of Zurich in 1994. From 1994 to 1998, he has been a senior research associate at the Department of Computer Science at the University of Zurich. Currently, he is on leave from the University of Zurich and is a Visiting Scientist at IBM Almaden Research Center. His current research interests comprise object-oriented and active database systems, workflow management, as well as workflow system and database management system construction.

Jürgen Kalinski is teaching computer science at the University of Bonn, Germany. In his diploma thesis (1986, University of Dortmund, Germany) he implemented a universal relation interface on top of the relational DBMS Ingres. From 1988 to 1990 he worked for a consulting group. His doctoral thesis (1994, Bonn) studies autoepistemic reasoning from a logic programming perspective. His current research topics include information retrieval, database systems and the combination of both areas.

Wassili Kazakos studied computer science (Dipl. Inform.) at the University of Karlsruhe and is Microsoft Certified Professional for Windows NT Workstation. Since August 1997, he has been working as a research assistant in the database research group (DBS) at FZI, Karlsruhe. His experience covers Catalogue Systems, WWW-database access and Java-based software development. His main research interests are Environmental Information Systems, distributed systems, knowledge discovery in databases and the Web, and component oriented software development.

Pinar Koksal is a Ph. D. candidate at the Computer Engineering Department of the Middle East Technical University. Currently she is working on component-based adaptable workflow systems for electronic commerce. She can be reached at pinar@srdc.metu.edu.tr.

Markus Kradolfer is a research associate at the Department of Computer Science at the University of Zurich. He received his diploma in Computer Science and Business Administration from the University of Zurich in 1994. His current research interests include workflow schema evolution, and reuse of workflow specifications. Recently, he started working for ACE-Flow, a research project aiming at market-based, inter-organizational workflow management.

Arne Koschel studied computer science (Dipl. Inform.) at the Technical University of Braunschweig, Germany from 1988 till 1993. Since April 1994 he works as a scientific staff member in the database research group (DBS) at the Forschungszentrum Informatik (FZI), Karlsruhe, Germany. Beside his studies he worked as a developer for companies and public institutes. He has special knowledge in database systems in general, covering theoretical background as well as many practical experiences with several relational and also object-oriented database systems. Other knowledges include data modelling, object-orientation, information systems and software development. The latter one on several system platforms, using a variety of programming languages. Arne Koschel has a variety of publications and presentations in national and international conferences and workshops. His main research interests cover the area of distributed, heterogeneous information systems, especially combining Object Management Group's (OMG) Common Object Request Broker Architecture (CORBA) and World-Wide Web (WWW) technology (CGI, Java) in a federation architecture. For such CORBA-based information systems his focus is in the development and application of configurable Event-Condition-Action (ECA) rule based active mechanisms as well as in wrapper technologies for monitoring event sources. The main application area he is currently involved in is Environmental Information Systems (EIS). Recently he also worked as an software architect for a large CORBA-based financial data integration system He can be reached at: koschel@fzi.de; http://www.fzi.de/koschel.html

Ralf Kramer is head of the database research group at FZI, Karlsruhe, Germany. He holds a Diploma degree (Dipl.-Wi.-Ing., 1988) from the Faculty of Economics and a Ph.D. (Dr. rer. nat., 1992) from the Faculty of informatics both at the University of Karlsruhe, Germany. His experience covers parallel database systems, advanced querying tchniques based on fuzzy set theory, making databases available on the Internet and on intranets using the tools and techniques of the World-Wide Web, developing federation architecture for dataintensive, distributed applications based on the Common Object Request Broker Architecture (CORBA), the World-Wide Web (WWW), and Java, metainformation systems and metadata management, universal database design for storage and warehouse systems, and process modelling techniques for scientific information systems. His main research interests are databases in distributed, heterogeneous information systems, both from a technical and from an application's point of view and metainformation systems.

Stefan Manegold received his M.Sc. in computer science from the Technical University Clausthal, Germany, in 1994. Since 1997, he has been working as a database researcher at the Centrum voor Wiskunde en Informatica (CWI), Amsterdam, The Netherlands. His research interests include distributed and parallel database systems, query processing, and cost models.

James Moyne received his B.S.E.E. and B.S.E. - Math, M.S.E.E. and Ph.D. degrees from The University of Michigan in 1983, 1984 and 1990 respectively. His dissertation title is System Design for Automation in Semiconductor Manufacturing. Since 1992 he has been employed as an Assistant Research Scientist in the Department of Electrical Engineering and Computer Science at The University of Michigan – Ann Arbor. His research interests and publication topics include discrete manufacturing (run-to-run process and inter-process) control, sensor bus device and network modeling, database design and implementation, and network modeling, protocol development and standardization. He also authored a number of communications standards for the semiconductor industry. Additionally, he has a background in local area networks, solid-state circuits, and mathematics, and has a patent on a generic cell controller design which is currently being used in discrete process control in the semiconductor manufacturing industry.

Peter Muth received the diploma degree (Dipl.-Inform.) and the doctoral degree (Dr.-Ing.) both in computer science from the University of Darmstadt, Germany, in 1989 and 1994, respectively. Dr. Muth is an Assistant Professor in the Department of Computer Science of the University of the Saarland at Saarbruecken, Germany. Until 1994 he was leading a department in the Integrated Publication and Information Systems Institute (IPSI) of the National Research Center for Information Technology (GMD) in Darmstadt. Dr. Muth's research interests include parallel and distributed information systems, mutlimedia information systems and workflow management.

Mario A. Nascimento obtained his Ph.D. from Southern Methodist University in 1996. His B.S. degree on Applied Mathematics and M.S. degree on Electrical Engineering were both earned at the State University of Campinas, in 1987 and 1990, respectively. Since 1989 he has been a researcher with the Brazilian Agency for Agricultural Research and, starting in the Fall of 1997, he has also been a part-time professor at the State University of Campinas. His main research interests are databases in general and access structures in particular. Thus far he has published over 20 conference papers and 4 journal papers. Further information can be found at http://www.dcc.unicamp.br/~mario.

Ralf Nikolai studied computer science at the University of Karlsruhe from 1988 until 1995. He has worked as a research assistant in the database research group at FZI, Karlsruhe, since June 1995. His main research interests are Environmental Information Systems, metadata management, interoperable and distributed systems, fuzzy databases, and thesauri.

Don Ragan received his B.S. degree in Physics from New Mexico State University, Las Cruces, New Mexico, and his M.A. and Ph.D. degrees in Physics from Washington University, St. Louis, Missouri. He is currently professor and director of information systems in the department of radiation oncology at the Wayne State University School of Medicine. He is member of the Sigma Pi Sigma Honorary Physics Society, a fellow of the Center for the Biology of Natural Systems and a fellow of the American College of Medical Physics. Dr. Ragan has pioneered the development of computer systems in radiation oncology. His recent projects include the development of MS Windows based record and verify system; development of a CT simulation system that includes the development of a Conformal Field Projector (CFP) to carry the treatment design to patient marking; and the development of a Web based oncology patient record for the Karmanos Cancer Institute.

Wenny Rahayu has been a lecturer in Computer Science at La Trobe University, Australia, since

1994. She holds a Master's degree in Information Technology from Swinburne University of Technology. Currently, she is completing a Ph.D. in Computer Science at La Trobe University. Her research interests are mainly in the area of Object-Relational Databases, particularly the transformation methodology from an object-oriented conceptual model to relational database implementation. She has published one book and numerous research papers.

Claudia Rolker studied computer science (Dipl. Inform.) at the Technical University of Karlsruhe, Germany from October 1990 till March 1996. Since April 1996, she has been working as a scientific staff member in the database research group (DBS) at the Forschungszentrum Informatik (FZI), Karlsruhe, Germany. Her main research interests are in the area of distributed information systems. This includes Environmental Information Systems (EIS), metadata management, expert systems, scientific information systems, fuzzy databases, and WWW related technologies.

Elke Angelika Rundensteiner is currently Associate professor of the Department of Computer Science at the Worcester Polytechnic Institute, after having been a faculty member in the Department of Electrical Engineering and Computer Science at the University of Michigan for several years. She has received a BS degree (Vordiplom) from the Johann Wolfgang Goethe University, Frankfurt, West Germany, an M.S. degree from Florida State University, and a Ph.D. degree from the University of California, Irvine. Dr. Rundensteiner has been active in the database research community since over 10 years. Her current research interests include object-oriented databases, data warehousing, database and software evolution, multi-media databases, distributed and web database applications, GIS, and information visualization. She has more than 100 publications in these areas. Her research has been funded by government agencies including NSF, ARPA, NASA, CRA, DOT; and by industry including IBM, AT&T, Informix and GE. She is regularly on Program Committees of the key conferences in the database field such as IEEE ICDE, ACM SIGMOD, VLDB, as well as others. Dr. Rundensteiner has received numerous honors and awards, including a Fulbright Scholarship, an NSF Young Investigator Award, and an Intel Young Investigator Engineering Award, and an IBM Partnership Award.

David Taniar is a computing lecturer at Monash University, Australia. Prior to taking up this appointment in 1997, he had taught computing at Swinburne University of Technology, Australia, since 1991. He has also held a number of technical positions in industry, where he worked as a programmer. David Taniar earned his PhD in Computer Science from Victoria University of Technology, Australia. His PhD thesis is entitled "Query Optimization for Parallel Object-Oriented Database Systems". His research interests are in the Database and Object-Orientation areas with particular attention focused on parallel database processing, object-oriented queries and optimization, object-relational databases, multimedia databases, and object modelling. He has published three books and numerous research papers.

Nesime Tatbul is a Ph.D. student at the Computer Engineering Department of the Middle East Technical University. Currently she is working on multi-party, multi attribute agent negotiation. She can be reached at tatbul@srdc.metu.edu.tr.

Rahul Tikekar obtained his Bachelor of Engineering degree in computer science from Bangalore University in India, and his M.S. and Ph.D. degrees in computer science from Wayne State University in Detroit. He is currently manager of information systems at the Thesaurus Linguae Graecae project at the University of California, Irvine. Before taking this position he worked at the Wayne State University School of Medicine and at the Augustana College in Sioux Falls, South Dakota. His current research interests include large database systems, multi-lingual databases and Internet-based database development.

Dimitrios Tombros is a research associate at the Department of Computer Science at the University of Zurich. He received a diploma in Computer Science and Business Administration from the University of Zurich in 1991 and a M.Sc. in Computer Science from Stanford University in 1994. His current research interests include workflow management, software system composition, and event-based software architectures.

Aphrodite Tsalgatidou holds a B.Sc. in Chemistry from the University of Athens in Greece and a M.Sc.

and Ph.D. in Computation from the University of Manchester (UMIST), UK. She has worked as a software engineer at the Hellenic Telecommunications Organization and as a director of the Office Automation Department of Elvil S.A. Currently, she is an assistant professor at the Department of Informatics of the University of Athens in Greece. She has participated in or managed research projects in the areas of rule-based development of information systems, object-oriented development, development of formal requirements specifications using Petri Nets, office automation, telepublishing, multimedia and hypermedia application development, mainly funded by the European Commission. Her research interests include requirements engineering, conceptual modeling, methodologies for information systems development, business process modeling and re-engineering, workflow management and electronic commerce (http://www.di.uoa.gr/~afrodite).

Günter von Bültzingsloewen works for Swiss Bank Corporation (SBC) in Basel where he is engaged in strategic platform projects and in particular leading the development of the new data architecture and shared data services. Before joining SBC in 1996, he was 11 years with the Computer Science Research Center at the University of Karlsruhe, leading the database research group since 1991. During this time, he worked in various database research areas including parallel DBMS, object-oriented DBMS, active DBMS, database support for engineering applications, and information system integration using distributed object technology. Günter von Bültzingsloewen holds a Masters Degree in Computer Science from the University of Wisconsin, and Diploma and Ph.D. degrees from the University of Karlsruhe.

Florian Waas received his M.Sc. in computer science from Passau University, Germany, in 1995. Since 1997, he has been working as a database researcher at CWI, Amsterdam, The Netherlands. His research interests include query optimization and processing in distributed and parallel database systems.

Gerhard Weikum received the diploma degree (Dipl.-Inform.) and the doctoral degree (Dr.-Ing.) both in computer science from the University of Darmstadt, Germany, in 1982 and 1986, respectively. Dr. Weikum is a Full Professor in the Department of Computer Science of the University of the Saarland at Saarbruecken, Germany, where he is leading a research group on database systems. His former affiliations include MCC at Austin, Texas, and ETH Zuerich in Switzerland. During his sabbatical in 1997, he was a visiting Senior Researcher in the database research group of Microsoft. Dr. Weikum's research interests include parallel and distributed information systems, transaction processing and workflow management, and database optimization and performance evaluation. Dr. Weikum serves on the editorial boards of ACM Transactions on Database Systems, The VLDB Journal, and the Distributed and Parallel Databases Journal. He has served on numerous program committees of international conferences, and he was the program committee co-chair of the 4th International Conference on Parallel and Distributed Information Systems. Dr. Weikum has recently been elected onto the board of trustees of the VLDB Endowment.

Jeanine Weissenfels received the diploma degree (Dipl.-Inform.) in computer science from the University of the Saarland, Germany, in 1994. She is a research assistant in the Department of Computer Science of the University of the Saarland at Saarbruecken, where she is working in the database research group. Her research interests include distributed systems and workflow management.

Jens E. Wolff is a teaching and research associate of computer science at the University of Bonn, Germany. He received the diploma (M.S. degree) in computer science from the University of Kaiserslautern, Germany in 1993. He has been at the University of Bonn since 1994 as a Ph.D. student of Prof. A.B. Cremers. His areas of interest include database systems, information retrieval, and data mining.

Index

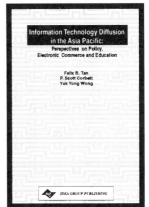

Journal of
Database Management

An official publication of the Information Resources Management Association

Editor-in-Charge:
Shirley Becker
Florida Institute of Technology

ISSN 1063-8016 • Annual subscription fee per
volume (four issues) Individual $85; Institutional $175

MISSION

The *Journal of Database Management* (JDM) is a refereed, international publication featuring the latest research findings dealing with all aspects of database technology management. It strives to provide comprehensive coverage of the managerial and organizational issues of database technology by providing access to leading articles on tools, techniques, and methodologies for applying database technologies in organizations.

COVERAGE

JDM covers topics with a major emphasis on database technology management. Some of the topics covered include:

- ◆ Database Administration
- ◆ Strategic Data Management
- ◆ Database Warehousing
- ◆ Data Quality Control
- ◆ Object-Oriented Databases
- ◆ Database Security

- ◆ Emerging Technologies
- ◆ Success Factors for Database
- ◆ Requirements Analysis
- ◆ Data Modeling
- ◆ DB and Human Factors
- ◆ Database Networking

For more information about this publication, check the JDM
website at http://www.idea-group.com/jdm.htm

IDEA GROUP PUBLISHING

Publisher in information science, education, technology and management
1331 E. Chocolate Avenue • Hershey, PA 17033-1117 USA
Tel: 717/533-8845 • Fax: 717/533-8661
http://www.idea-group.com